LEONORA CARRINGTON

Surrealism, Alchemy and Art

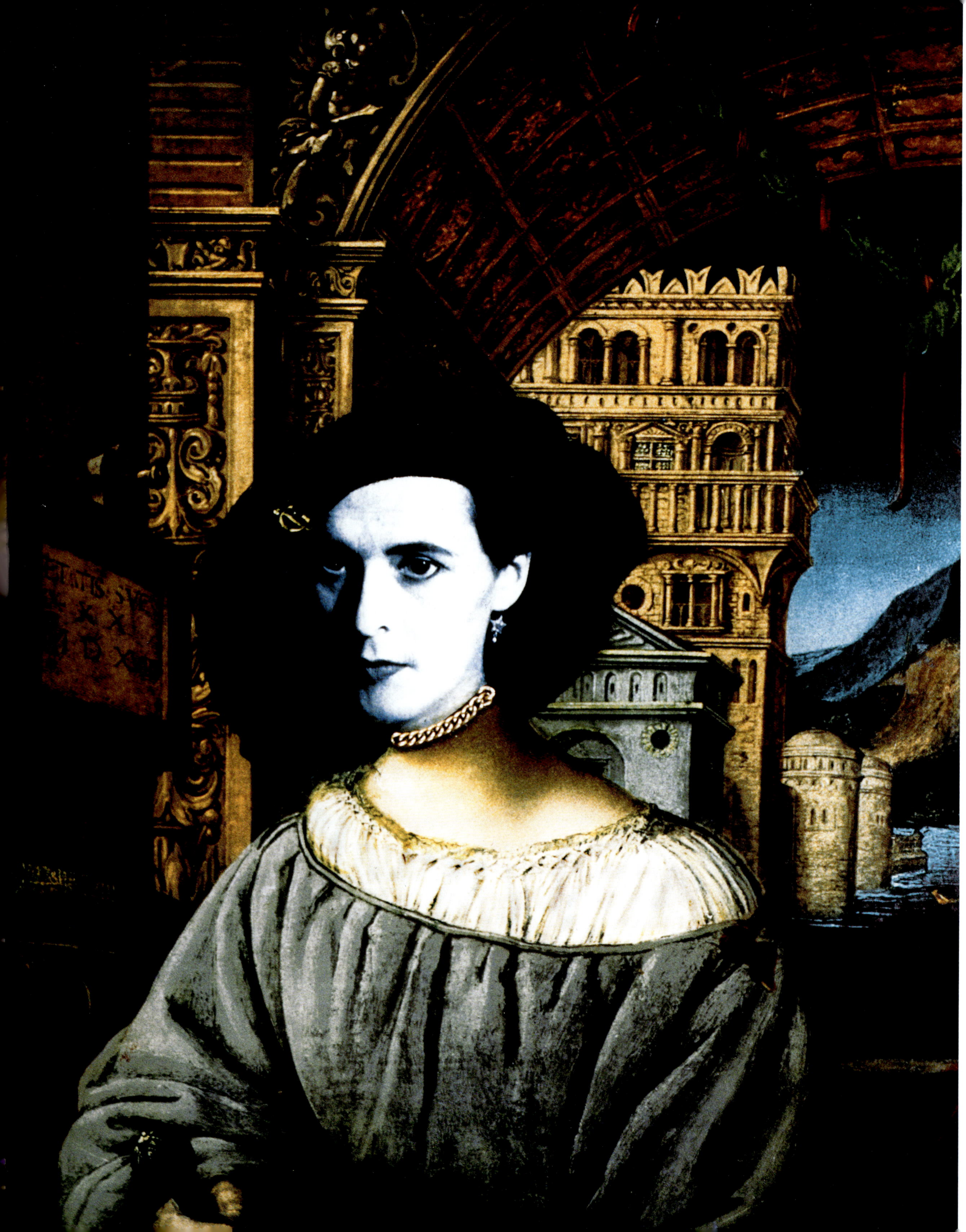

Susan L. Aberth

LEONORA CARRINGTON

Surrealism, Alchemy and Art

Lund Humphries

This paperback edition first published in 2010 by

Lund Humphries
Second Home Spitalfields
68-80 Hanbury Street
London
E1 5JL
UK

Reprinted in 2012, 2015, 2018, 2020, 2021, 2022 and 2025

www.lundhumphries.com

British Library Cataloguing-in-Publication Data
A catalogue record for this book is available from the British Library

Library of Congress Control Number 2009941693
ISBN 978-1-84822-056-0

Designed by Chrissie Charlton & Company
Printed in Bosnia and Herzegovina

Front cover: **Darvault** (see p.76)
Back cover: ***AB EO QUOD*** (see p.92)

MIX
Paper | Supporting responsible forestry
FSC® C118234

This book would not have been possible without the generous assistance of Leonora Carrington, who provided many transparencies and photographs, not to mention countless hours of her time. Special thanks go to Pablo Weisz Carrington, Mia Kim, Joanne Soja, Miguel Escobedo, Edward J. Sullivan, Amy Sillman and the numerous other individuals who made this book possible. I dedicate this book to my parents, Alice and Bill Aberth, with great respect and love.
Susan Aberth, 2004

The publishers would also like to thank Helen Escobedo, Jorge Pinto, Nina Zambrano, Alejandra Reygadas de Yturbe, Mariana Pérez Amor, Luis Carlos Emerich, Laura Pacheco, Pepita Morillo and Jorge Garza Aguilar.

1
Photo Kati Horna
Leonora Carrington collage, April 6th 1987
Kati Horna Foundation

CONTENTS

Introduction	The Magical Art of Painting	7
Chapter 1	The Reluctant Débutante	11
Chapter 2	Ernst, Surrealism and the *femme sorcière*	25
Chapter 3	Heaven and Hell: Wartime Experiences	37
Chapter 4	The Alchemical Kitchen: Domestic Space as Sacred Space	57
Chapter 5	Esoteric Interests	97
Notes		142
Jezzamathatics or Introduction to the Wonderful Process of Painting by Leonora Carrington		149
Bibliography		151
Index		158

2
The Lovers
1987
Oil on canvas
76 x 103 cm / 30 x $40\frac{1}{2}$ in
Private collection

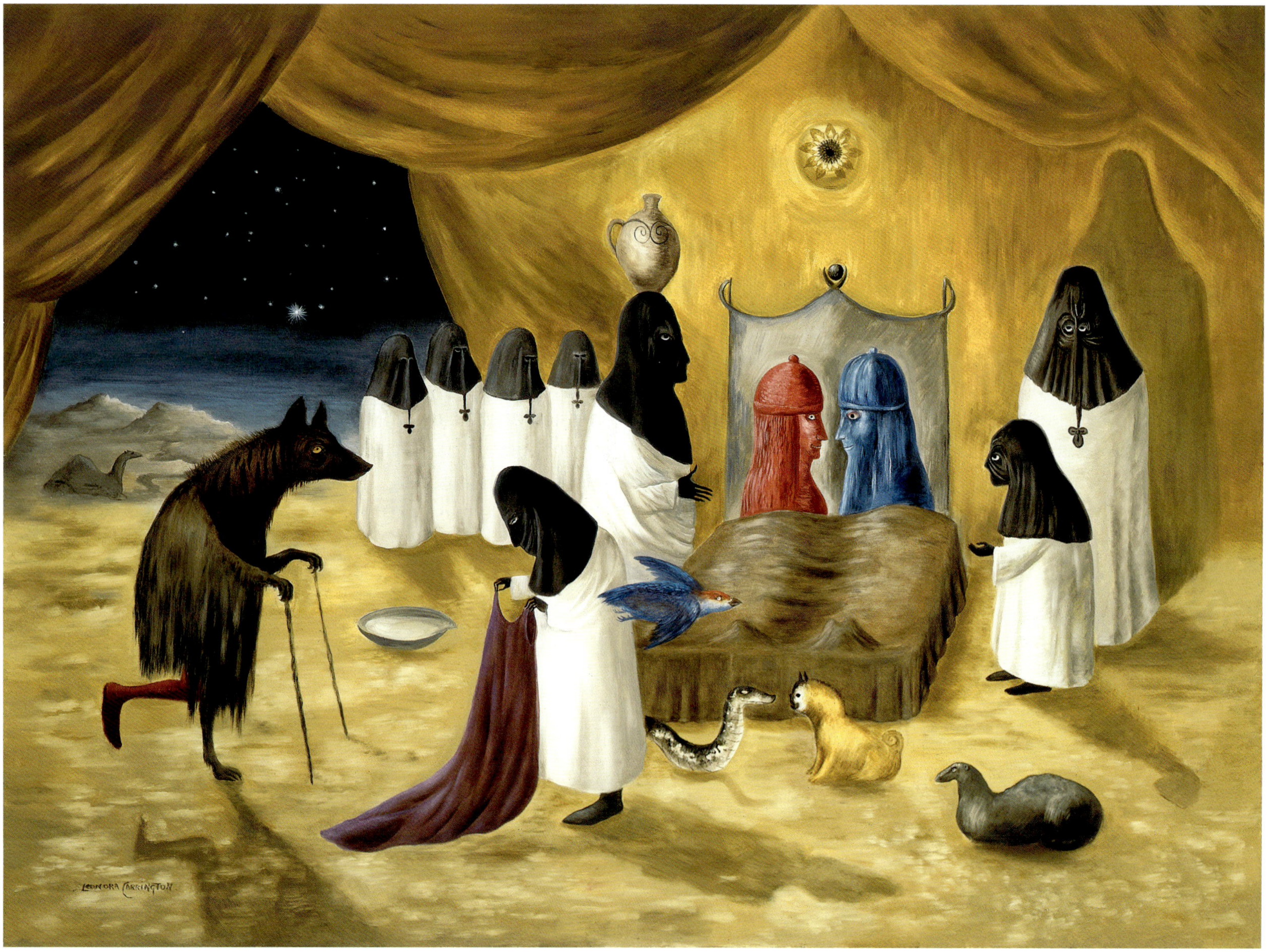

INTRODUCTION THE MAGICAL ART OF PAINTING

The British-born artist and writer Leonora Carrington has always been known and savoured, like a beautifully prepared gourmet dish, by those conversant with Surrealism. For many decades now she has delighted, perplexed and haunted a select and appreciative audience who revel in her visual conundrums, verbal play and subtle ritual evocations. In Mexico, Europe, the United States, Japan and elsewhere her work has been exhibited, published and performed with great delectation by and for those fortunate enough to be familiar with her complex and prolific œuvre. Although it is difficult to share a rare and singular treasure, the time has come for Carrington's work to cast a wider sphere of influence and to garner greater recognition. Like the alchemical processes of distillation and transmutation that abound in her work, she continues to shift across boundaries and to elude easy classification. Furthermore, Carrington's life can be viewed as cinematic in its scope and dramatic intensity, driven by an uncompromising dedication to the free expression of her personal vision. It is this dynamic combination of life and work, I believe, that makes her strikingly contemporary and ripe for further investigation and analysis. That she is British but has long lived in Mexico and the United States, has written and been published extensively in French, English and Spanish,[1] and that the iconography she uses is influenced by the magical beliefs and practices of diverse cultures and time periods, has proclaimed her a global artist long before such a concept became popular. Perhaps we are ready now to gauge her with a fresh eye, one less filtered through French Surrealism, and to make her work more accessible to a new generation who need an introduction to her works.

Indebted to Surrealism, yet possessed of a unique personal vision, Carrington has the ability to construct alternate worlds, both fantastical and believable. It is this perpetual tension between the real and the imagined that lends her work it's compelling nature and is an idiom she shares with other Surrealists. Lifting the veil of ordinary sight, she permits us a momentary glimpse into another dimension where traditional spatial relationships have collapsed and where strange entities are often frozen in gestures evocative of both ritual and dialogue. Like a true magician, Carrington has chosen not to reveal certain aspects of her production in order to preserve a more enigmatic and enduring meaning. Playful and cryptic, at times displaying a deliriously vibrant use of colour, her art has long resisted interpretation. Leonora Carrington is a consummate mythmaker – she has always spun tales – in her artwork, in her writings, and in recounting her life. Myths are not static, they expand and contract in unexpected ways and she understands that if they are to remain potent they must be constructed with equal parts of omission and inclusion. Therefore, she mixes meticulous detail with nebulous space, pairs semi-narrative arrangements with single iconic elements, and creates a prevailing atmosphere of inscrutable mystery.

Leonora Carrington's meeting and subsequent relationship with the already famous Surrealist Max Ernst, in 1936 at the age of 19, drastically altered her life and the development of her work. Although she was painting and drawing extensively before she met Ernst, he gave her the support and impetus to express herself creatively, and provided her entrée into the Parisian Surrealist circle. It is true that he helped to liberate her vast potential by teaching her his painting techniques (such as *frottage*), encouraging the type of experimentation practised by the Surrealists (such as automatism and *cadavres exquis*) and reinforcing her interest in alchemy and fairy tales with his own enthusiasms for these subjects. It is also true that Carrington, more than any other Surrealist, went on to explore a wide range of esoteric themes, incorporating imagery and ideas from a vast repertoire of historical periods, cultures and types of mystical practices.

The Surrealists themselves treated Carrington with a mixture of respect and reverence that, although at times was problematic, certainly set the stage for future mythologies surrounding her life and work. From the very beginning of her first contact with the Surrealists in Paris in 1937 she was given unparalleled opportunities to exhibit her paintings, publish her stories and to participate in the movement's activities. Ernst may have introduced her to the Surrealist circle, but she made a strong impression on her own and was treated no differently after her liaison with him ended in 1940. The movement's founder and leader, André Breton, was particularly captivated by this young woman's beauty and originality, and she appeared to him to be a spectacular embodiment of his cherished belief in the inspirational role of the *femme enfant*, the girl-child Muse. That Carrington was opposed to the relegation of women artists to the role of Muse is a profound understatement and although she could not control being labelled a *femme enfant* by her entranced male Surrealist admirers, there is no doubt that developing as an artist was her primary focus. In response to the stress of the Second World War and to Ernst's repeated internment in concentration camps, Carrington suffered a brief but terrible mental breakdown during 1940–41. This gave her notoriety and a certain cachet within Surrealist circles as well, especially after the publication of *Down Below*,[2] Carrington's highly original account of her experience in a mental asylum in Spain. Breton and others had long been interested in the revolutionary possibilities inherent in hysteria, madness and other heightened mental states, and Carrington was now perceived as an ambassador back from the 'other side' – a seer, the *femme sorcière* who had returned from the underworld armed with visionary powers.

Carrington has long been considered part of the artistic heritage of Mexico. In addition to being an integral part of the émigré Surrealist circle in Mexico City from 1943 on, she has also actively participated in the intellectual and cultural life of that country for over 50 years. She has had close friendships with leading Mexican writers, artists and actors, her work has been acquired by Mexican collectors, and from 1950 on, the Mexican press has paid her attention and great respect. It was the presence of Mexico's hybrid Catholicism, which freely mixed Spanish and indigenous Mexican iconographies and forms, that freed her to reconcile the official religion of her childhood with not only her Celtic ancestry but also with her consuming interests in other religious traditions. Nevertheless she has eschewed promoting any one national identity and her politics have tended toward the universal, such as women's rights, rather than the particular. In fact, Carrington has spent a lifetime portraying aspects of feminine intellectual and spiritual authority and has always been passionately committed to feminism. It is unsurprising then that her work has appealed to those interested in women's autonomy, even outside the narrow purview of the world of art. For example, the pop singer Madonna has acknowledged the enormous influence that women Surrealists have had on the imagery used in her music videos and has specifically mentioned Leonora Carrington along with her close friend, the Spanish artist Remedios Varo.[3] In an ironic postmodern twist Carrington is being visually *sampled* by an audience who is still by and large unable to recognise her work. The time for a deeper and wider appreciation of this artist by the art world and the general public is long overdue and hopefully the present book will address this problem.

Her biography reads as a series of resistances to conformity: to her parents with their expectations based on class and gender; to educational institutions which repeatedly expelled her for a variety of transgressions; to being a 'Muse' to Max Ernst and other male Surrealists; to sexism where, as a feminist in Mexico, she questioned the assumed roles of wife and mother; to conventional notions of reality as her explorations into the occult led her to ascertain alternative dimensions of time and space; and even to commonly held notions concerning 'nature' for, as an early ecologist and vegetarian, she has even questioned the primacy of the human species among life forms on the planet. A crucial part of her resistance has been an adamant refusal to explicate any aspect of her creative production, declaring that her work should speak for itself. Carrington's attraction to occult traditions lay in her correlation with them to the transformational nature of art production itself as a type of magical practice. Although Max Ernst and other Surrealist artists were also interested in the occult for similar reasons, what was unique about Carrington's approach was its early feminist goal of reclaiming the central role of women within these traditions. Therefore, *The Alchemical Kitchen* is an allegory for what I perceive as one of her primary means of reclamation, which was to equate the feminine domestic sphere with the magical practices of diverse cultures. Thus the nursery, the kitchen, the kitchen garden, and so on, were transformed from sites of feminine drudgery and oppression into sites of contestation and power. Another important contribution to the Surrealist idiom by this artist was her employment of fairy-tale-like imagery which, now spiced with a sly wit and removed from any narrative sequence, differed greatly from the illustrations found in children's fairy-tale books.

This book's goal is twofold: to provide a text which outlines the artist's life and the themes involved in her visual output, and to present a carefully selected overview of the full scope of her work in painting, sculpture, drawing, printmaking, textiles and theatrical set and costume design. Alchemy, astrology, the cabbala, Tibetan Buddhism, the tarot, Celtic mythology, Mexican healing traditions and other mystical practices all have a significant place in Carrington's visionary realm, and are animated by a mischievous sense of humour that serves to subvert any potentially pedantic spiritual weight. Although at first glance her paintings, often teeming with mysterious creatures – humans, animals and combinations thereof – who perform obscure ritualistic acts, may appear impenetrably hermetic, after close and prolonged inspection they reveal an internal logic of their own – similar to the idiosyncratic language of dreams supplied by our unconscious. The great secret to Carrington's art is that there is no key with which to decipher her work easily, because there *cannot* be one. It is not that certain embedded symbols have no meaning; it is that these symbols cannot and do not 'illustrate' ideas in the manner we are accustomed to. Like the sixteenth- and seventeenth-century alchemical engravings her work at times emulates, they are profoundly personal interpretations of complex philosophical and magical ideas whose meanings have always been permeable and shifting, encouraging multiple levels of perception. Within the pictorial world of Leonora Carrington, let all those who make assumptions beware.

3
Crookhey Hall
1947
Casein on masonite
31.5 x 60 cm/12½ x 23½ in
Private collection

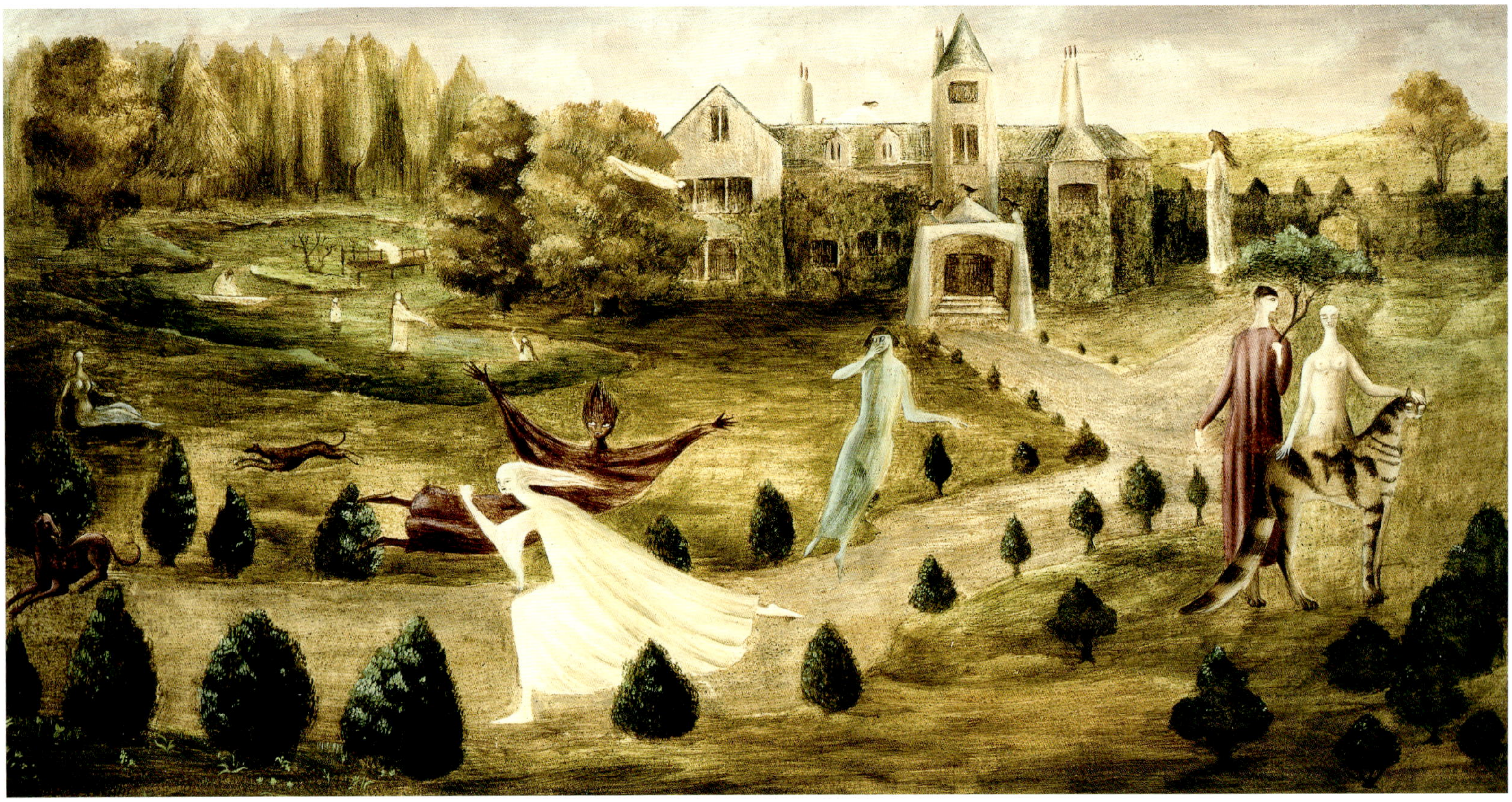

CHAPTER 1 THE RELUCTANT DEBUTANTE

Childhood: the myth begins

It appears that from the very beginning Leonora Carrington's life took on aspects of the fabulous and the uncanny, and her own droll personal recollections assist in promoting a kind of biographic mythology. It is not that she tells untruths, quite the contrary, her authorial and spoken styles are so extraordinarily dry and matter of fact that they accentuate her credibility. Carrington reveals tantalisingly brief portions of select aspects of her life in a sparse and concise manner, and it is the omission of homely detail that gives these narratives their mythic potency – less is more. It is not only what she says but how she says it, in what context, and, most importantly, what she chooses not to reveal.

Leonora Carrington was born in the north of England on 6 April 1917 in Clayton Green, near Chorley, South Lancashire. Lancashire has long been the site of textile manufacturing, and Leonora recalls that it was called the Black Country because of the sooty pollution that accompanied its industrialisation. Her father, Harold Wilde Carrington, was a textile tycoon whose entrepreneurial father was a mill hand who invented and patented a new loom attachment that subsequently led to the development of Viyella, a popular blend of cotton and wool. Harold sold the family company, Carrington Cottons, to the giant corporation of Courtaulds and then became a principal shareholder of Imperial Chemicals Industries (ICI). Her mother Maureen, née Moorhead, was Irish and the daughter of a country doctor from Moat, County Westmeath, Southern Ireland.[4] Carrington remembers that her mother was much given to fantasies about her family origins and claimed ancestry back to Irish King Malcolm, as well as Franz Joseph of Austria, whose portrait hung in the family home and subsequently turned into an 'ancestor'.[5] In the literary realm Maureen claimed to be related to Maria Edgeworth (a prolific English novelist of the early nineteenth century, writing mostly about Irish life) and boasted that her brother Harry was a fellow student and friend of James Joyce at the Jesuit Clongowes College.[6] Leonora seems to have inherited some of her mother's propensity toward fabrication, although instead of bolstering the family's position her fictions tend to deflate it.

Although the Carringtons lived in a number of stately homes, it was the cavernous and theatrical Crookhey Hall (Fig.4), with its views of the Irish Sea and Morecambe Bay, which would exert the greatest influence on Leonora's imagination and childhood memories. This Edwardian country manor was located in Cockerham, near Lancaster, and while perhaps a bit smaller than the estates owned by royalty and aristocrats in the region, it reflected the wealth of her industrialist family at the time. Leonora recalls that they had ten servants as well as a chauffeur and a nanny. A French governess and a religious tutor were also brought in. Living there from the impressionable ages of three to ten years (1920–27), Crookhey Hall would come to embody a plethora of psychological symbols for the artist, from a forbidding and restrictive prison that represented parental authority to the mysterious state of childhood itself. Carrington would depict the gloomy Gothic-revival mansion in her artwork time and again in the future, perhaps to exorcise the traumatic aspects of her youth.

Photographs of Crookhey Hall's dimly illumined grand rooms and conservatory (Figs 5 and 6), connected by labyrinthine corridors and winding stairs, gives some idea of the profound effect such a dwelling could have on an imaginative child. Leonora had an older brother Patrick and two younger brothers, Gerald and Arthur, and, as was customary for their time and class, the children were strictly relegated to certain spaces and their every activity supervised. On the occasions that they were allowed to visit their mother in her sitting room, they played with her Chinese bric-à-brac and were given chocolate at the visit's conclusion.[7] Carrington

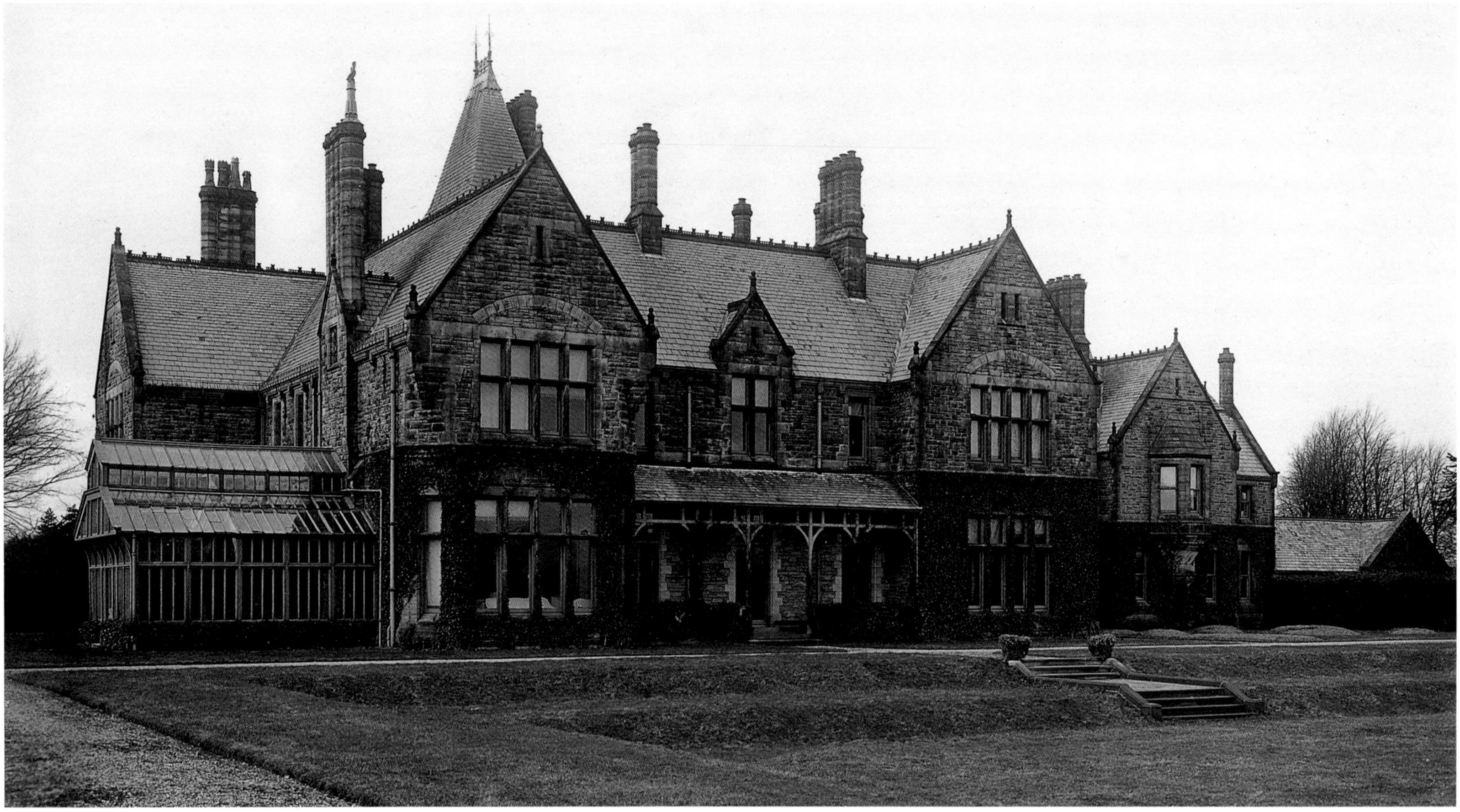

4
Crookhey Hall, exterior

has mused: 'Do you think anyone escapes their childhood? I don't think we do. That kind of feeling that you have in childhood of being very mysterious. In those days you were seen and not heard, but actually we were neither seen nor heard. We had a whole area to ourselves, I think that was rather good, actually.'[8] Marina Warner astutely elaborates on this sense of marginality and how this freedom from parental scrutiny allowed Leonora to explore dream space:

> In a sense you can see in this house the structural hierarchy which enclosed her as a child. She is much closer in all her imagery to the world that is at the margins of the house. She doesn't occupy the essential spaces, her imagination wanders in the kitchens, in the attics, where the servants and the women live.[9]

All the children were placed into the care of an Irish nanny, Mary Kavanaugh, who stayed with them through thick and thin. It was through the stories told to her by Nanny, her mother and her maternal grandmother that Leonora came into early contact with Irish folklore, an important part of her heritage. Of the strongest Irish influence on her life and work, that of her maternal grandmother, Grandmother Moorhead, Leonora would later remark:

> My love for the soil, nature, the gods was given to me by my mother's mother who was Irish from Westmeath, where there is a myth about men who lived underground inside the mountains, called the 'little people' who belong to the race of the 'Sidhe.' My grandmother used to tell me we were descendants of that ancient race that magically started to live underground when their land was taken by invaders with different political and religious ideas. They preferred to retire underground where they are dedicated to magic and alchemy, knowing how to change gold. The stories my grandmother told me were fixed in my mind and they gave me mental pictures that I would later sketch on paper.[10]

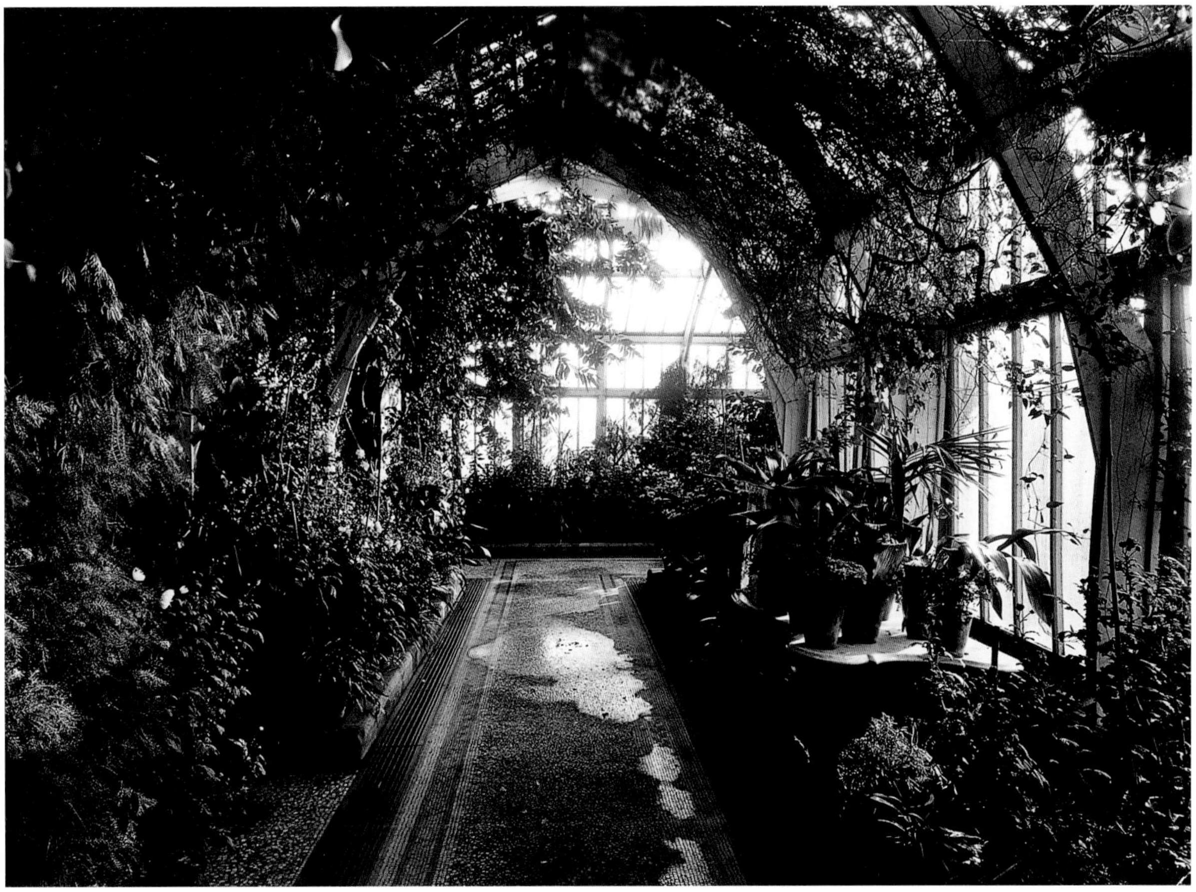

5
Conservatory at Crookhey Hall

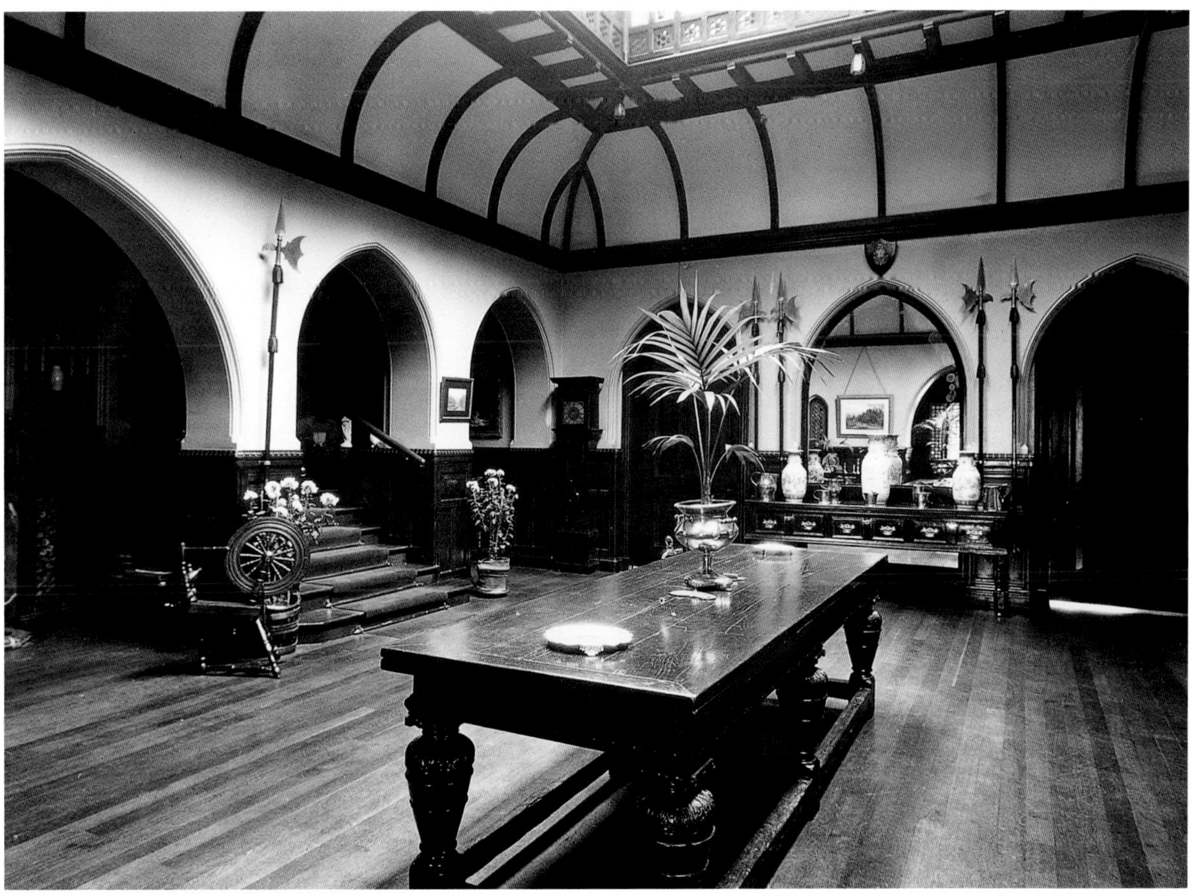

6
Great Hall at Crookhey Hall

7
Leonora Carrington on her horse Winkie, *c.*1931

8
Leonora Carrington as a young girl, *c.*1930

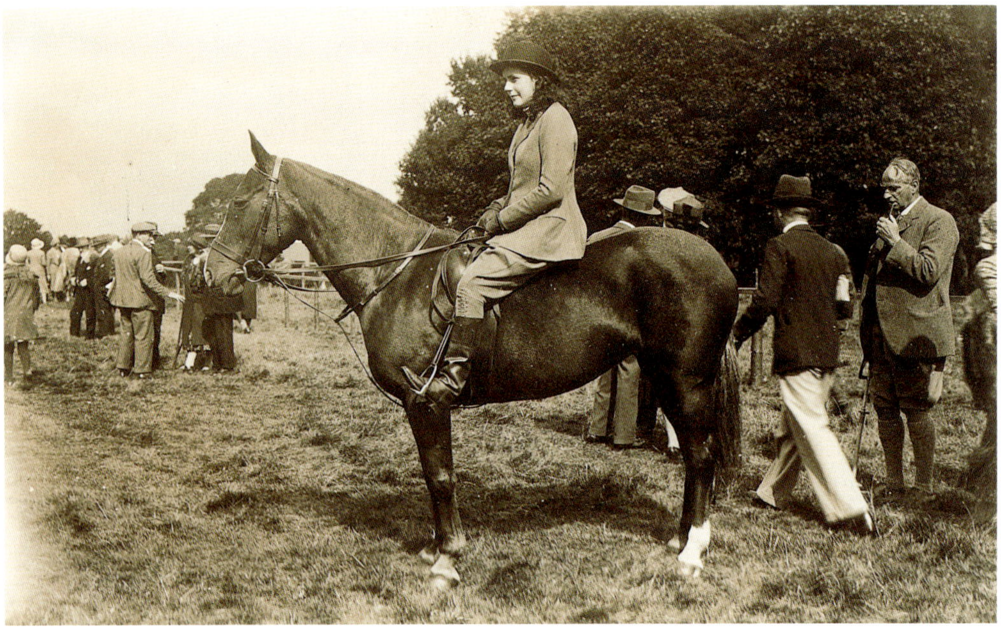

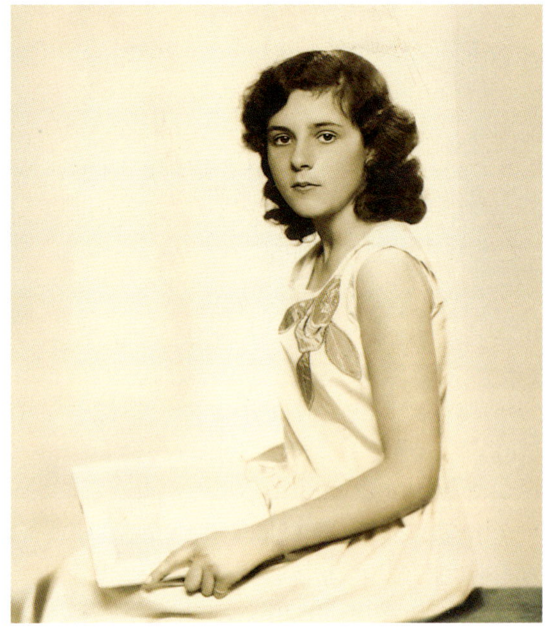

Indeed, these stories so profoundly impacted upon their young listener that they surface throughout her adult life, not only in her artwork and stories, which abound with images of the Sidhe, but also in the development of her personal belief system and, ultimately, her unique and peculiar brand of feminism.

Leonora began to draw by scribbling on the walls as soon as she could, around the age of four. 'Everybody scribbled. My mother used to paint murals, or what looked like murals, on boxes for jumble sales, and they looked like Joan Miró. I used to draw horses. I just loved it.'[11] It is interesting to note that her two great early loves, horses and drawing, were linked together. Leonora and her mother were the only members of the family to ride and that must have created a bond between them. A photograph taken in London in 1931 (Fig.7) shows a smiling and confident 14-year-old Leonora atop her mare Winkie, clad in equestrian garb. In fact she was passionately attracted to all animals, both tame and wild, and has said that she was 'born loving them'.[12] She also recalls that as a treat to celebrate her first communion her mother took her to the small local zoo in Blackpool, a nearby English seaside resort. The reason this memory stayed with her is that, first, it was a rare treat to be with her mother and not Nanny, and second, she was able, during these visits, to see the wild animals that she often dreamed about.

The nursery library was full of English children's classics: Lewis Carroll, Jonathan Swift, Beatrix Potter and Edward Lear. Carroll's use of parody and his 'nonsense' rhymes, such as those in *Alice in Wonderland* and *Alice Through the Looking Glass* would be accessed later as a prototype in her early Surrealist short stories and in her cryptic titling of works of art throughout her career.[13] Her father exposed her to the Gothic tales of W. W. Jacobs, best known for his macabre *The Monkey's Paw*, while her mother used to read aloud the books of her favourite Irish writer, James Stephens, especially from *The Crock of Gold* (London: MacMillan, 1912),[14] still one of Leonora's favourite books. At age six Leonora began to write stories, in particular ghost stories and animal fables, influenced by the Irish tales told to her by her mother and Nanny. That writing and drawing began more or less at the same time and at a very early age for Carrington is a fact of some significance. First it reveals that these two talents began on equal footing, and second, that they sprang from the same imaginative source.

Carrington remembers as a small child seeing ghosts and being afraid, but also seeing 'visions' that were amusing, such as one where a wild tortoise would sometimes cross her path or a large cat would sit in an empty dog kennel. Surrounded by tales of ghosts, fairies and the ancient races of Ireland, Leonora grew up in an environment where the magical and unseen were forces to be contended with. In looking back at her childhood paranormal experiences, Carrington also places them within the context of Catholic mysticism, another aspect of her Irish inheritance. So, fuelled by fantastic literature, Catholic mystical traditions and the Irish fables told to her, Leonora's imagination developed along certain lines that must have seemed 'natural' to her.

In addition to her family environment, strange legends surrounding the area where she grew up also influenced her. Lancashire has a reputation for being a centre for witchcraft since the seventeenth century; however, neolithic stone circles and other remains attest to its pagan past as well. The most infamous incident was in 1612 in the remote region of Pendle Hill. Twelve people were accused of witchcraft, ten of whom were found guilty and hanged.[15] The city of Lancaster, a short distance from Cockerham and Crookhey Hall, had a dungeon where witches were imprisoned before execution; although the building that housed the dungeon was mainly used as a nunnery and not open to the general public, Carrington knew of its existence.

Boarding schools: verdict 'ineducable'

In spite of their enormous wealth, Mr and Mrs Carrington were far from being aristocrats, but they enthusiastically adopted all the social customs of the upper classes in order to conform to the lifestyle of those in their economic bracket, and this included sending their children to boarding schools. At the age of nine, Leonora was sent away to the convent of the Holy Sepulchre near Chelmsford, Essex, which was housed in a castle built by Henry VIII. Her parents were soon asked to take her away as she was deemed 'mentally deficient'. This was to be the first in a series of expulsions, for it was apparent that Leonora took no interest in any of her studies or in communal sports. But more than the academic failure it was her 'eccentricity', usually a combination of antisocial tendencies and certain 'supernatural' proclivities that propelled schools to be rid of her.[16] For example, at Holy Sepulchre Leonora wanted to become a saint or a nun like her Aunt Leonora.[17] This desire did not manifest itself as extreme piety, but rather a fascination with the 'miraculous', occurrences that went beyond the everyday. Later in life she admitted, 'I probably overdid it. I liked the idea of being able to levitate, mainly.'[18]

The Bishop of Lancaster intervened on behalf of the Carrington family and Leonora was accepted into a second Catholic convent, St Mary's in Ascot. She hated this school and was yet again expelled in less than a year. Her cousin Patricia Paterson recalls Leonora's behaviour at school:

> We were both at St. Mary's at Ascot and she was a rebel. She was anti any discipline and rather inclined to go her own way. She was rather musical, as well as artistic, and the great craze was to have a saw and she would play on it and we were caught and there was trouble. She just didn't fit into school.[19]

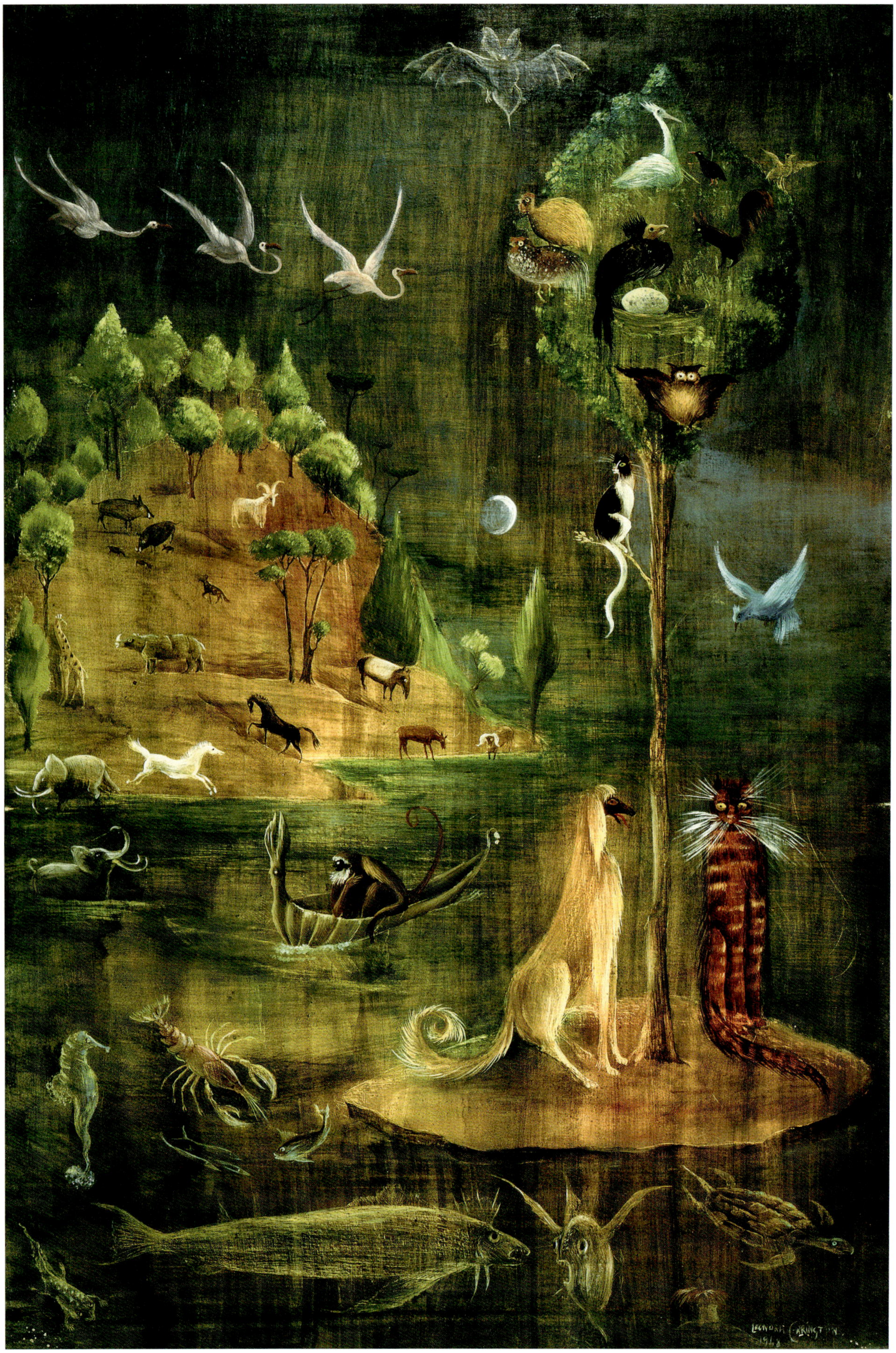

9
Untitled
*c.*1949–50
Oil on canvas
61 x 46 cm/24 x 18 in
Private collection

10
Figuras Miticas: Bailarin I
1954
Oil and gold leaf on masonite
30.5 x 22.5 cm/12 x 9 in
Private collection
Photograph: Christie's Images

11
Figuras Miticas: Bailarin II
1954
Oil and silver leaf on masonite
30.5 x 22.5 cm/12 x 9 in
Private collection
Photograph: Christie's Images

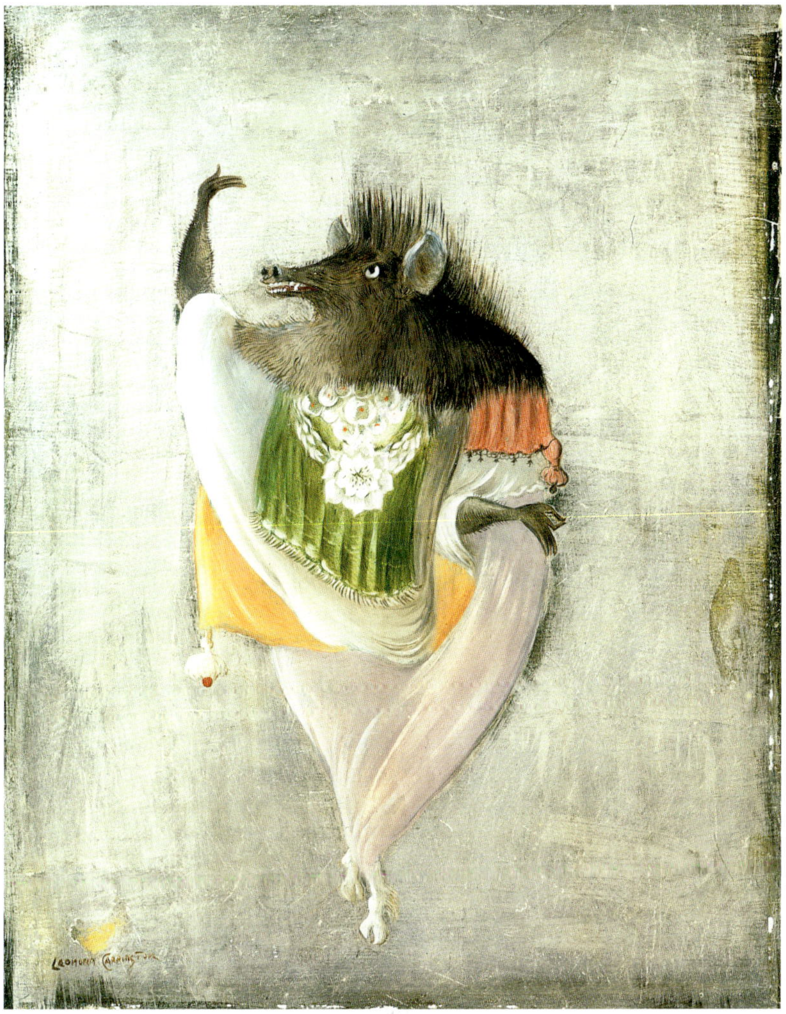

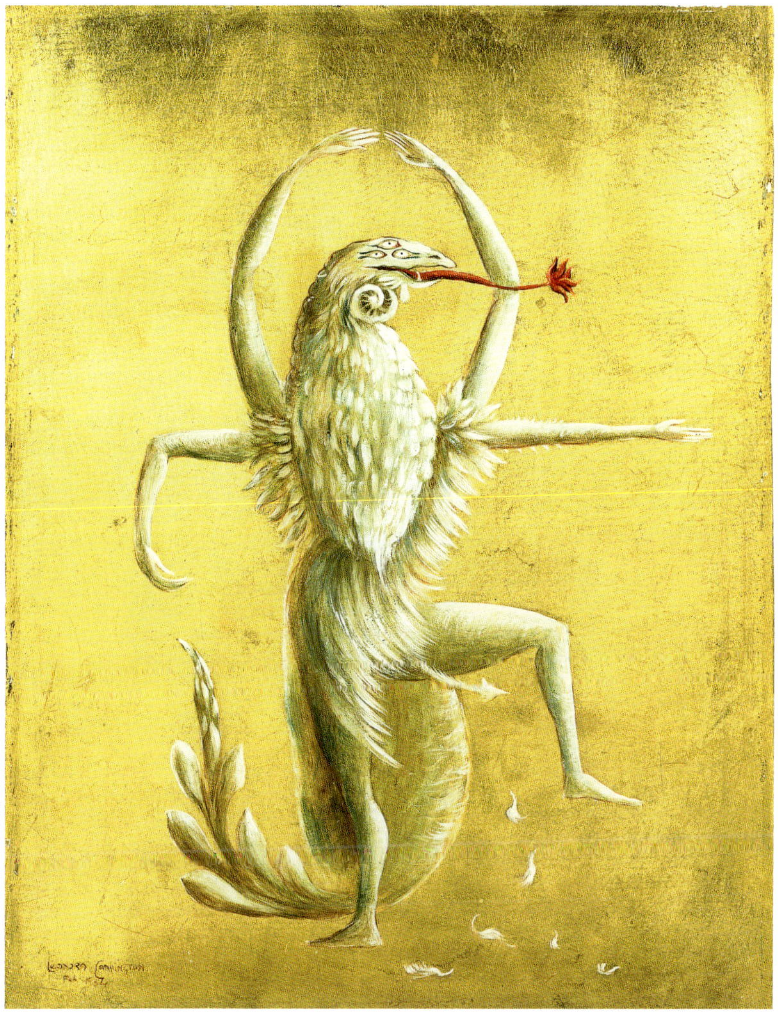

12
Leonora Carrington with Saint-Bernard dogs in Switzerland, *c.*1932

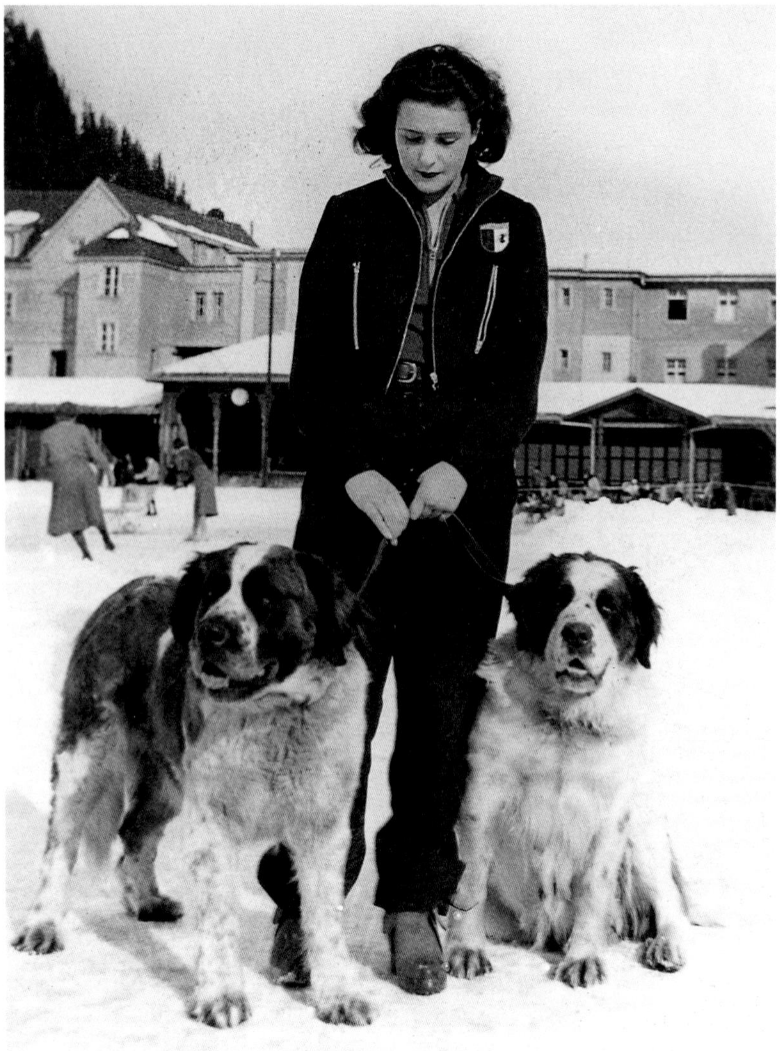

In addition, the nuns thought something was 'wrong' with Leonora because she could write with both hands and preferred to write with her left, backwards.[20] Carrington recalls their reaction to her backwards writing: 'I think it is called dyslexia, I was told it was a disease, but people were a bit less curious about what was going on in the brain and they did tend to think that anything like that was a bit diseased.'[21]

If Leonora was really dyslexic, then it is not surprising that she had learning problems at school. Made to feel abnormal, she was punished and pronounced ineducable. To this day she still practises mirror writing and paints ambidextrously, sometimes with both hands at the same time. It was perhaps in reaction to these repeated rejections at school that her distrust of the Catholic Church began. This antipathy would last a lifetime, fuelled later by Surrealism's anti-clerical stance, and would manifest itself in bitingly satirical depictions of priests in both her writings and artwork.

Carrington also believes she was punished for her inability to conform to prevalent social standards and behaviour deemed appropriate for a girl of her class:

> I think I was mainly expelled for not collaborating. I think I have a kind of allergy to collaboration and I remember I was told, 'apparently you don't collaborate well either at games or work.' That's what they put on my report. They wanted me to conform to a life of horses and hunt balls and to be well considered by the local gentry I suppose.[22]

After her second expulsion, the family reluctantly took her back, while her mother tried to figure out how to 'civilise' her. This led to a family conference, presided over by her father, in which it was decided to send Leonora to Miss Penrose's boarding school in Florence, followed by a year of finishing school in Paris, in preparation for her presentation at court. In 1932, a 15-year-old Leonora was sent off to Miss Penrose's in the Piazza Donatello. Speaking satirically about the education she received at Miss Penrose's, Carrington commented in the Mexican press: 'Later my parents sent me to Florence to a school for aristocratic children that only taught useless activities like how to behave socially, horseback riding and fencing. They said I needed to have a great education so I could be presented at the court of George V.'[23] However, she developed appendicitis for which she was operated on in

13
Leonora Carrington and her mother at their presentation at the court of King George V, 1934

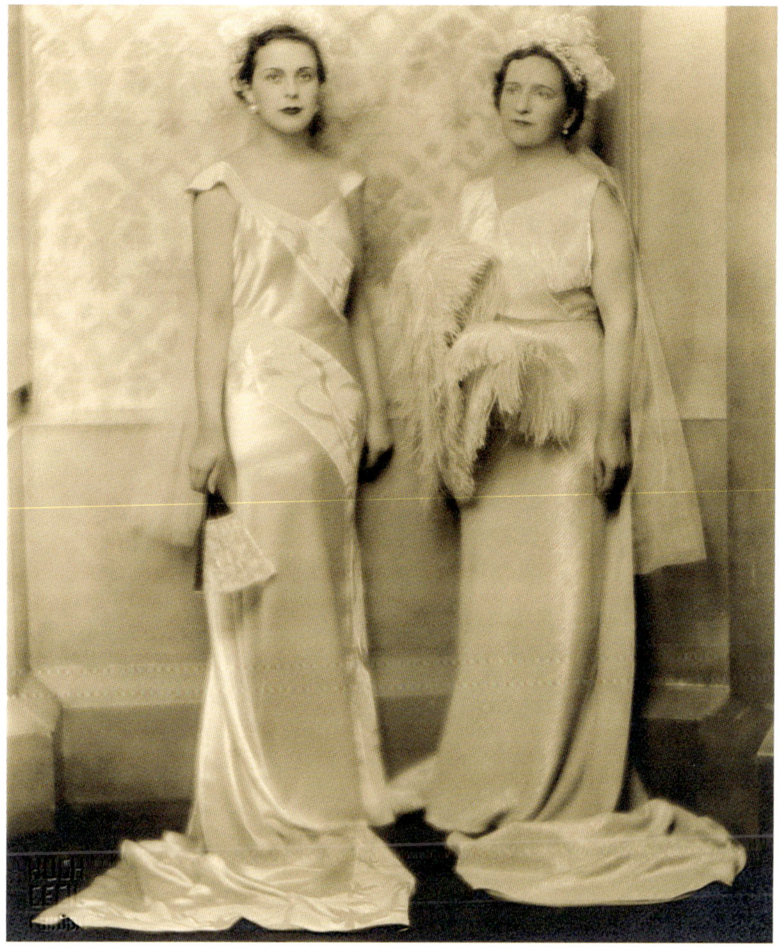

Bern, and once again was sent back home. Although her stay in Florence was brief (approximately one year), it was important for her later career for it was there that she first came into contact with artists who would later have a great impact on her painting. 'Florence amazed me with its museums, but not with the school. I loved to see the paintings of Uccello, Archimbaldo, Pisanello ... and I also became familiar with cities like Padua, Venice and Rome.'[24] The work of Sienese artists in particular, such as Sassetta, Francesco di Giorgio and Giovanni de Paolo, contributed to her later love of tempera painting and influenced her composition, palette and style.

In 1933, as planned, Leonora was sent to a finishing school in Paris. She had already learned French at home as a child from her French governess. This time she lasted only a few months and was once again expelled for unruly behaviour. Her angry father decided to send her somewhere 'really tough' and so she was packed off to Miss Sampson's in Paris where she had a little room over a church graveyard.

> I didn't like it, so I escaped at night. I went to a family that I'd heard of, only heard of, through some friend of the family's. Their name was Simon. M. Simon was a professor of *beaux arts*. I'd never met them, but they took me in, nevertheless. God only knows why. And there I stayed until I was presented at court. That was the last court of George V. I was on the marriage market.[25]

The reluctant débutante

In 1934, while her mother dreamed of a royal wedding for her daughter, Leonora attended the London season balls. She was given a débutante ball at the Ritz Hotel[26] by her parents (Fig.13);[27] went to Ascot where she viewed the races from the royal enclosure, and in 1935 was presented to the court of George V. Numerous photographs, including a particularly glamorous one by Cecil Beaton,[28] attest to Leonora's great beauty which, with her father's great wealth, must have made her quite eligible for marriage. Carrington was less than enthusiastic about her presentation, later commenting:

> So I went through the season, in London, the royal garden party, which is tea in a tent at Buckingham Palace, and you go around with a teacup. You have a different dress for that, very expensive. Then you go to Ascot, the races,

14
Leonora Carrington, 1934

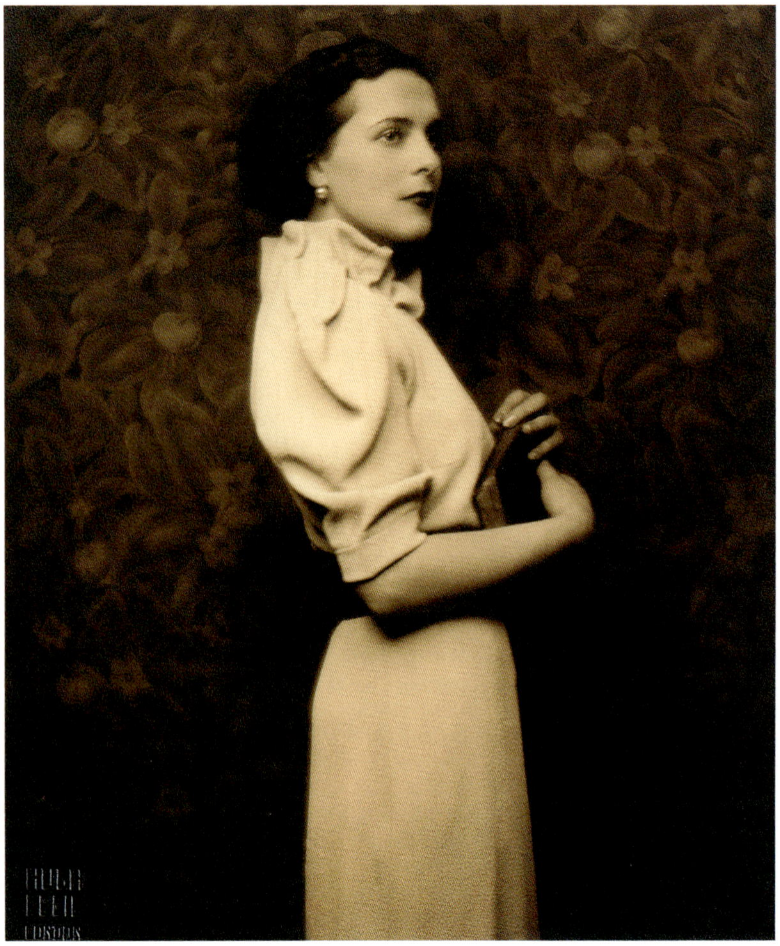

> and you're in the royal enclosure. And, if you please, in those days, if you were a woman, you were not allowed to bet. You weren't even allowed to the paddock, where they show the horses. So I took a book. I mean, what would you do? It was Huxley's *Eyeless in Gaza*,[29] which I read all the way through. And then, thoroughly fed up, I was dispatched back to the North of England.[30]

Leonora had no intention of being, as she so succinctly put it, 'sold to the highest bidder'.[31] Instead, she informed her family that she intended to go to art school. Her parents vehemently opposed this idea and her father told her that she could stay at home and paint in the house and even suggested that she take up breeding fox terriers.[32]

In 1965 Leonora wrote a bitingly satirical essay called 'Jezzamathatics or Introduction to the Wonderful Process of Painting' (see p149), which was included in numerous exhibition catalogues, presumably in place of, and most definitely a subversion of, the artist's statement. Bordering on the unintelligible and written in the exaggeratedly serious tone of one full of pompous self-importance, it gives a decidedly Surrealist account of her birth and childhood. The second paragraph begins: 'The only person present at my birth was our dear and faithful old fox-terrier, Boozy, and an ex-ray apparatus for sterilizing cows.'[33] The inclusion of the fox terrier may, in this case, indicate more than her usual love of animals and refer to the bizarre career alternative given her by her parents when she asked to go to art school. Harold Carrington had no patience with his daughter's interest in art, thinking painting was 'horrible and idiotic' and that 'you didn't do art – if you did, you were either poor or homosexual, which were more or less the same sort of crime'.[34] Nevertheless, Leonora proved immovable on her decision and in 1935 moved to London to study at the Chelsea School of Art.

As Leonora has often stated, she began drawing at the age of four and never stopped. A childhood outing that had a profound effect on Leonora was her first trip to the British Museum where she recalled seeing the Egyptian mummies.[35] Fortunately, a small number of sketchbooks and other works survive from her youth, allowing us to confirm her early interests. A small sketchbook (13 x 18 cm, 5 x 7 in) from 1929, executed when she was 12 years old, is filled with pencil drawings of horses in stables and pastures, and although she would later adopt the horse as her totemic animal, these domesticated creatures, such as those she probably saw at home, seem ordinary enough for an adolescent girl with equestrian leanings. Sketchbooks from 1931 and 1933 contain numerous pencil drawings, in varying degrees of execution, of her classmates and fanciful characters resembling book illustrations.[36] Carrington appears to be experimenting with a number of styles and subjects which seem appropriate for an adolescent girl caught between fairy-tale books and fashion magazines.

Leaving home: art schools

In 1935, at the age of 18, Leonora left for London and headed for art school. Her parents, particularly her father, were strongly opposed to this course of action. It is, therefore, not surprising that they offered her little financial support. Leonora attended the Chelsea School of Art[37] in London for approximately one year, taking classes in painting and drawing, but her most vivid memories of this time are not of school but of freedom, and of her changed circumstances of living: 'From the Kings Court I went to a pigsty. I lived in a basement and didn't have money. I barely had enough to eat but my painting and classes distracted me from this.'[38]

In another interview she was somewhat less dramatic and simply stated: 'I had scrambled eggs on a gas range, and I did a lot of painting.'[39] Carrington said she studied with Jean de Botton from whom she learned to draw busts and some other objects without colour so that she could concentrate on form.[40] Serge Chermayeff, a friend of her father's, looked in on her weekly, and Carrington considered him a 'spy'.[41] Apparently, in spite of their lack of financial support or approval, her family was keeping tabs on her. Chermayeff was concerned with the quality of her education at the Chelsea School of Art, exclaiming, 'You'd better at least try and learn to draw.'[42] His knowledge of the London art scene led him to recommend that she attend the new Ozenfant Academy. This decision would change the course of her life irrevocably.

The French painter Amédée Ozenfant opened his Ozenfant Academy in London (1935–8), although this 'academy' turned out to be a rather modest operation. In 1918 Ozenfant had, along with the architect-painter Charles-Edouard Jeanneret – called Le Corbusier – founded the movement known as Purism, a variant of Cubism. In the spirit of reform, they sought to purge Cubism of its decorative elements and of any fantastic subject matter. Instead, with subdued colour, sharp outlines, underlying grid structure and mechanical-looking still-life subjects, the work exudes an antiseptic purity. Jeanneret, as Le Corbusier, would go on to express Purist theories in his architecture whereas Ozenfant taught its principles in a series of art academies that he opened in Paris, London and finally in New York. On the surface his Academy would appear a highly unlikely environment to teach Carrington, with her propensity towards fantasy and narrative. However, it turned out to be a fortuitous match.

Carrington was, in fact, the first student to enrol in his newly opened London Academy. Of the admission process she recalls: 'So I was sent to a tiny little school in a barn in West Kensington. I brought what I had, and Ozenfant looked at it and said, "Ah ha, we begin tomorrow!"'[43] The classes were small and instruction began with an emphasis on drawing.[44]

As Carrington tells it, Ozenfant warned her from the beginning: '"Now you're going to work." Then he made me work like bloody hell.'[45] Although it was a highly disciplined environment, the formerly unruly student was now doing what *she* wanted to do and buckled down to work. The uncritical attitude of the instructor helped her to concentrate and she remained appreciative of the discipline she learned there.[46]

> You had to know the chemistry of everything you used, including the pencil and the paper. He would give you one apple, one bit of paper, and one pencil, like a 9H,

15
Portrait of Joan Powell
*c.*1936
Oil on canvas
28 x 38 cm/11 x 15 in
Private collection

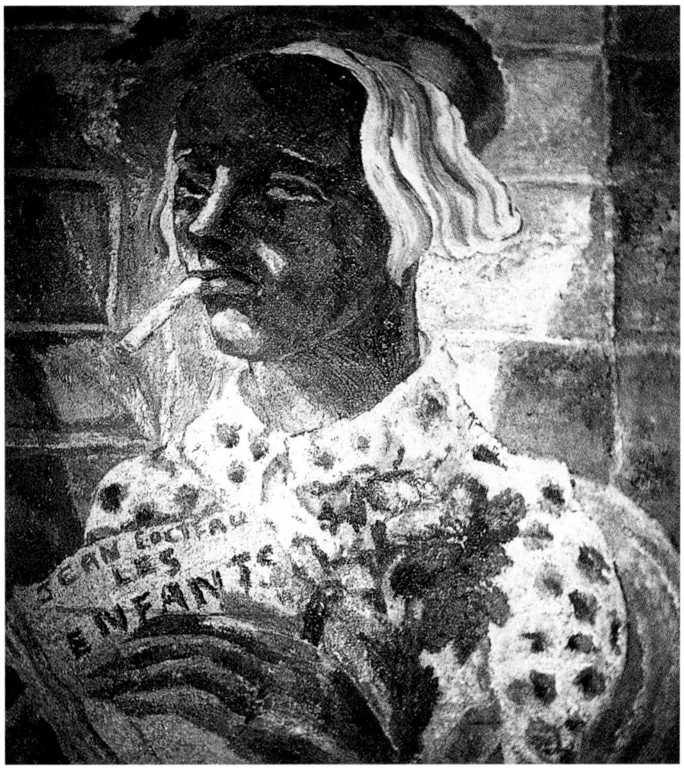

> which was like drawing with a bit of steel. And you had to do a line drawing, with one line. I was drawing the apple for six months, the same apple, which had become a kind of mummy. He was a very good teacher because he had the eye, but he never put you down.[47]

Since classes were small, we can assume that tuition was costly and that Carrington's father must have been providing financial assistance, possibly on the recommendation of Chermayeff. While at Ozenfant's Carrington met another wealthy and rebellious young woman, Stella Snead and the two remained lifelong friends.[48] According to Snead the students were primarily upper class young women, although men were also in attendance. Carrington indirectly confirmed this view by recollecting: 'Ozenfant never had more than about ten students. There was an Ursula Goldfinger there. Erno Goldfinger was a Hungarian revolutionary and an architect, but Ursula had been Miss Blackwell, of Cross and Blackwell. They make marmalade.'[49] Perhaps Carrington was getting along better with her parents at this time, since Ursula Goldfinger remarked that, at least on one occasion, Carrington stayed at the family suite with a friend and on occasion even took friends to the Carrington's home for a visit.[50]

Although Leonora at 19 was the youngest student at the Ozenfant Academy, according to Snead she was a highly charismatic individual, noted for her directness and unconventional behaviour.[51] While Carrington was learning to draw at Ozenfant's she was also painting from her imagination and doing work that was quite different from the other pupils.[52] Although we cannot know with certainty what these paintings were or where they are now, one surviving work dating from this period, *Portrait of Joan Powell* (Fig.15) is done in a rough and painterly manner suggesting that it was executed outside the school curriculum. Carrington depicts her childhood friend standing (from the bust up) in front of a brick wall reading Jean Cocteau's *Les enfants terribles*. Whitney Chadwick believes this work acted as a 'talisman' for the artist, signifying youthful rebellion with its prominent display of Cocteau's book, which, published in 1930, was adopted as a manifesto by a generation of alienated adolescents.[53] The iconic frontal pose and the unsmiling, intense expression on the girl, combined with her beret, short hair and buttoned up shirt, project an aura of masculinity and foreshadow Carrington's own self-portrait in *Inn of the Dawn Horse*, begun later in 1937 (Fig.18). The halo of light (or cigarette smoke) that surrounds Powell's head reads as an emanation of female psychic power, a power enhanced by subversive masculine posing.

In *Portrait of Joan Powell*, Carrington was invoking a transcendent androgyny that at the time she associated with her own strivings for personal autonomy and artistic freedom. The masculine attire and expression in this portrait and in other early works may have related to the appropriation of male independence and self-confidence.[54] After her involvement with the Surrealists and her further study of alchemy, she dropped this particular portrayal of androgynous feminine power. Women in trousers with scowling faces would be replaced with the adept's shapeless robe and impassive stare, both of which would serve as signifiers of the appropriation of male esoteric knowledge. Now mystically combined with female experience, this knowledge would result in the creation of a new type of female power. It is significant to note how impressed Carrington was at this time by the 'chemical' knowledge required by Ozenfant in conjunction with the production of art, and it is exactly at this point that she began to collect books on alchemy in the used-book stalls around London.[55] It was also about this time that Leonora's mother gave her a gift of Herbert Read's *Surrealism*, a book that intermittently mentioned alchemy in relation to art production in general and Surrealist art production in particular.[56] Thus her nascent feminism was connected from the beginning with occult notions surrounding art production.

Carrington spent approximately a year at Ozenfant's Academy and in interview after interview, even as late as the 1990s, Carrington will respectfully cite the Ozenfant Academy as having had an enormous impact on her.[57] Regardless of her gratitude, the fact is that Ozenfant's contribution to her art education was mainly in terms of formal painting technique. Future critics and scholars did not consider Ozenfant to have had a great influence on her work.[58] This 'influence' cannot be detected in any type of visual corollary between their work but instead can be summarised as an avid use of detailed drawing, a philosophic correlation between chemistry (alchemy) and the act of painting, and perhaps most importantly a rigorous and disciplined approach to art production.

16
Green Tea (La Dame ovale)
1942
Oil on canvas
61 x 76 cm/24 x 30 in
Private collection

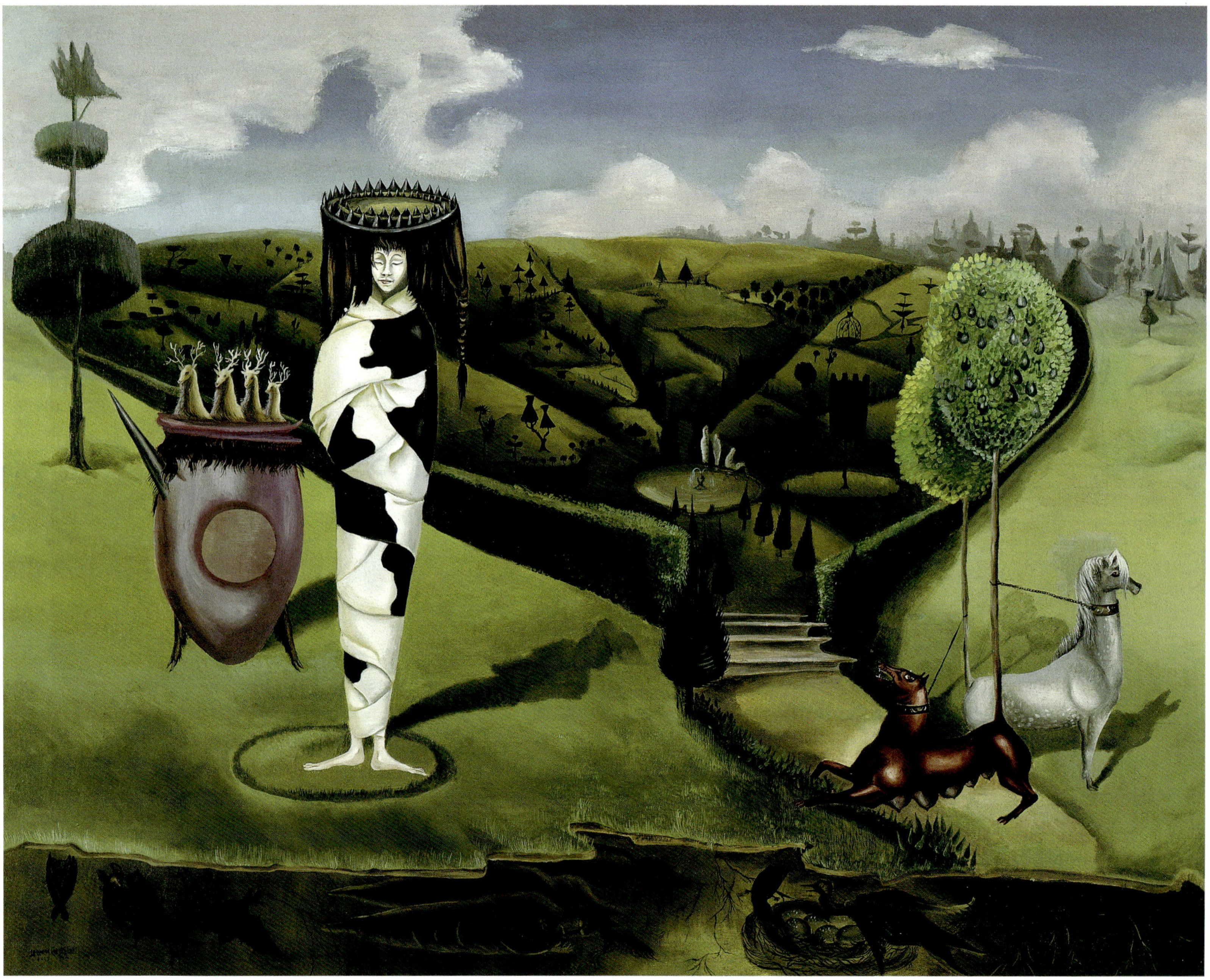

CHAPTER 2 ERNST, SURREALISM AND THE *FEMME SORCIÈRE*

Max Ernst in London

On 11 June 1936 *The First International Surrealist Exhibition* opened at the New Burlington Galleries in London. Organised by Roland Penrose and David Gascoyne, in collaboration with André Breton and Paul Eluard from France, it was a large exhibition of painting and sculpture, mixed with tribal art and 'art of the insane'. That same year Herbert Read edited a book in conjunction with the exhibition, which included essays by Breton, Eluard, Georges Hugnet and Hugh Sykes Davies. In an odd twist of fate, Carrington's mother, who thought her art-student daughter would find it of interest, gave her the book soon after its publication. This book had a great impact on the young Leonora, providing her with an introduction not only to Surrealist ideology and art, but in particular to the work of Max Ernst, whom she would shortly meet and fall in love with. The catalogue's essays would have been of interest to her, particularly Breton's lively text, 'Limits Not Frontiers of Surrealism', which discussed her favourite childhood authors, Swift and Carroll, in conjunction with his ideas on 'black humor'.[59] Illustrated were works by women artists (many of whom she would soon meet in Paris), such as Leonor Fini, Valentine Hugo, Meret Oppenheim, Toyen, as well as the British Grace W. Pailthorpe and Eileen Agar. However, it was the work of Max Ernst that most caught her attention and imagination: *The Chinese Children* (1920), *Two Children Menaced by a Nightingale* (1924), *Human Figure* (1931), *Garden Aeroplane-Trap* (1934), and *Tête Double* (1936). Carrington's response to first seeing his work was so strong it was visceral, 'like burning, inside; you know how when something really touches you, it feels like burning'.[60] But it was the reproduction of Ernst's *Two Children Menaced by a Nightingale* that left the deepest impression: 'And in the book I saw *Deux enfants menacés par un rossignol*, and it totally shocked me. This, I thought, I know what this is. I understand it.'[61] That this work in particular should speak to her so strongly is not surprising given her interest in fairy-tale illustrations and her exposure to Italian Quattrocento painting while attending boarding school in Florence. Mysterious and disturbing, Ernst's painting employs a glowing colour scheme and a meticulous eye for detail, which combined with its subtly violent narrative undertone harkens from not only the realm of dreams but also Christian martyrdom.

In the summer of 1937, Max Ernst, who had not attended the earlier Surrealist exhibition in 1936 at Burlington, had a one-man show in London at the Mayor Gallery. He stayed with the artist and critic Roland Penrose at his home in Hampstead for the duration of the show. At this time Ernst was an internationally renowned artist, hailed by Breton as the fullest embodiment of his Surrealist vision. He was 46 years old and his second marriage, to the young Marie-Berthe Aurenche,[62] was fast crumbling as she became more and more immersed in Catholicism. Ernst was irresistible to women and unable to resist them, and his life was punctuated by numerous amorous relations, often with artists or those related to the art world.[63] The meeting between Carrington and Ernst was momentous for both parties. Leonora's friend and fellow student Ursula Goldfinger and her architect husband Erno arranged a dinner party in honour of Ernst and to introduce Leonora to him.[64] As Carrington recalls: 'at that point Max was the kind of man that every woman wanted and there he was'.[65] Although Carrington was an impoverished, newly enrolled, 20-year old art student, she was also fiercely independent and rather fearless, as testified by her school history. Raised in extreme economic and social privilege she was also used to getting what she wanted and had even thwarted her powerful father's plans to marry her and had instead gone off to art school. These aspects of Carrington's history made her different from the other *femme enfants* and, although he didn't know it at the time, Max Ernst was going to get more than he bargained for.

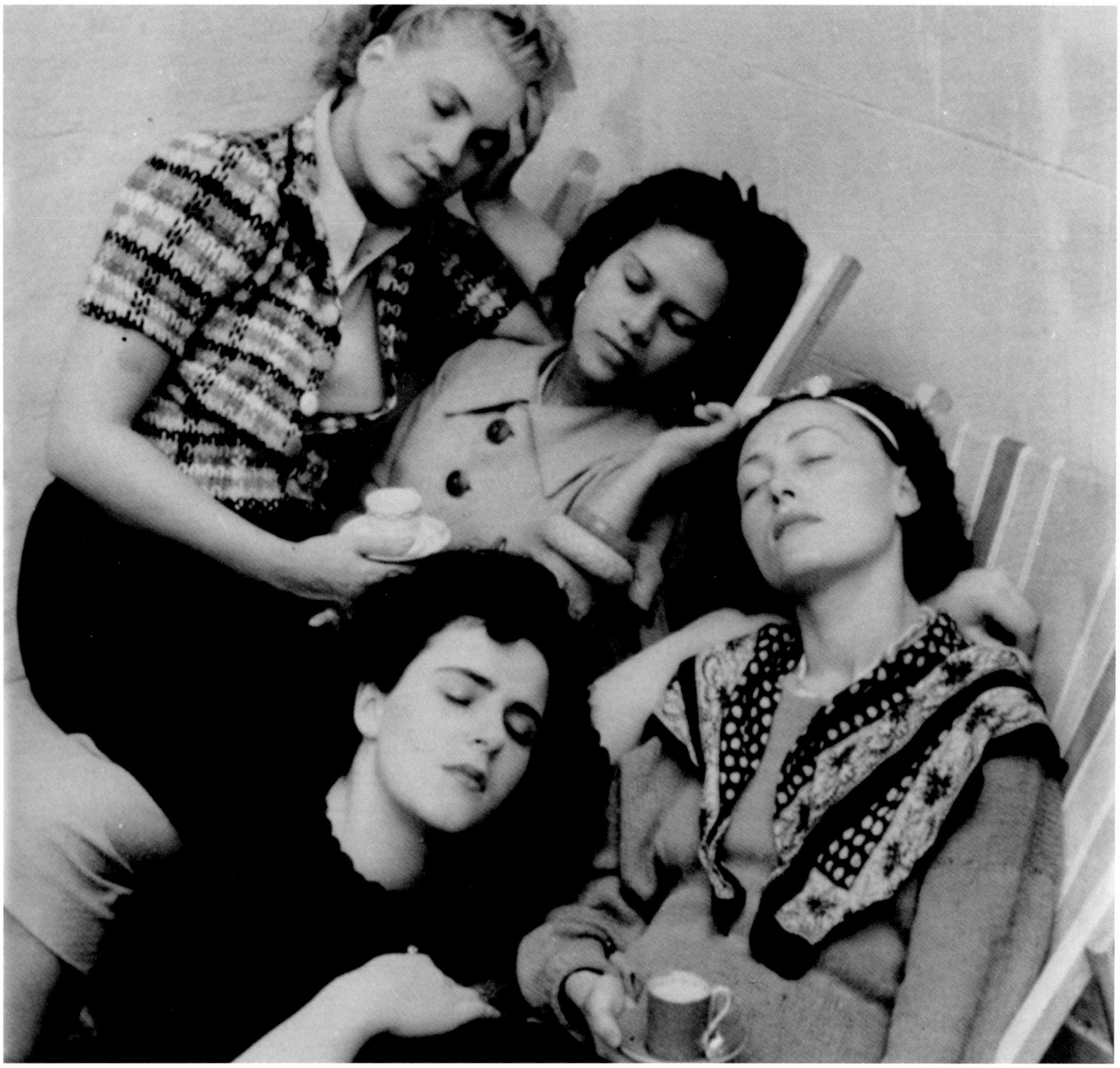

17
Lee Miller, Ady Fidelin, Leonora Carrington, and Nusch Eluard, Lambe Creek, Cornwall, England 1937

At the Goldfingers' dinner party, things proceeded according to plan and Ernst was immediately attracted to Leonora, who returned his attentions. Always with a taste for the sardonic, Carrington recalls their first meeting thus: 'I met Max while still at Ozenfant, it was love at first sight. I was holding a beer and it was starting to go over and Max put his finger on it, that way it doesn't go on the table. That was the story of my big love.'[66] They quickly became involved and much later Carrington would muse on the magic of sexual attraction: 'I think chemistry has something to do with alchemy and I think sexual attraction has something to do with chemistry, and it's a trio.'[67] Soon after their initial meeting, Max and Leonora joined Penrose for a period of time at Lamb Creek, a country estate in Cornwall belonging to his family:

> Max Ernst was to visit London and stay with me in Hampstead during his exhibition at the Mayor Gallery. It was then that he met Leonora Carrington, a brilliant girl whose talent as a writer was only exceeded by her gifts as a painter. Her arrival in his life rapidly extinguished the waning influence of Marie-Berthe, who was using every possible means to redeem his soul from the devils of Surrealism.[68]

Although this excerpt from Penrose's memoirs was written many years later from hindsight (published in 1981), what is still remarkable is the enormous respect he pays to Leonora, a young woman of 20, who as yet had not written any stories or really painted much of any worth. Impressions of Carrington by Surrealist veterans often tended to run high, with descriptions of 'brilliant' often following 'beautiful'. Carrington's initial sojourn into the heart of Surrealism appears to have been a success.

A photograph taken by Penrose reveals the playful and sensual nature of Max and Leonora's first weeks together. In a carefully staged scene (Fig.17), which reveals much about the role of women in Surrealism, Leonora, Lee Miller, Ady (Adrienne) Fidelin (a dancer) and Nusch Eluard are depicted as sleeping beauties with their eyes closed. As if some powerful magician had waved a magic wand, they have collapsed in the middle of having tea (as two of the women hold cups and saucers in their hands) – simultaneously dreaming and as objects of the male dream.[69] This was Carrington's introduction to the role of 'the Muse' that women involved with Surrealism were expected to play. It was a role that Carrington would soon recognise and categorically refuse.

Meeting Ernst was a profoundly transformational experience for Carrington, who, literally overnight, was freed from a lifetime of familial restrictions and was propelled into an artistic community and lifestyle that promised the sorts of freedoms and creative expression she had always longed for.[70] Similar to her feelings of gratitude and indebtedness to Ozenfant, Carrington would credit Ernst, first and foremost, with expanding the parameters of her world by providing her with a new means of perceiving what was around her and of accessing her creativity. 'Living with Max Ernst changed my life enormously because he saw things in a way I never dreamed was possible. He opened up all sorts of worlds for me.'[71] Speaking specifically of their first few weeks together, she explained:

> I remember we [she and Ernst] spent a day in the country, and this for me was a whole world opening. He showed me how he did what he called a 'frottage' with a pencil and paper, grass and whatnot, leaves and such. And then we were all invited to Cornwall, and we had a wonderful time there, for a week or two. But then Hitler was becoming a menace. Time wore on, it must have become winter, and I was still in England, in London.[72]

Ernst returned to Paris and waited for her to join him. Meanwhile, Carrington prepared to make the final break with her family, with England, and with life as she had known it. Although the primary reason Carrington decided to leave London was to follow her new lover, other reasons came into play as well. One was her dissatisfaction with the London art scene, which seemed stodgy and out of date when compared to what was going on in Paris:

> Art in London didn't seem quite modern enough; I wanted to study in Paris, where the Surrealists were in full cry. Now Surrealism is no longer considered modern. Even Buckingham Palace has a large reproduction of [René] Magritte's famous slice of ham with an eye peering out. It hangs, I believe, in the throne room. Times do change, indeed.[73]

Another reason, of course, was to escape her family and in particular the far-reaching influence of her father. Although her parents viewed attending art school as a regrettable delay to the more important business of getting married, Leonora's romantic involvement with a notorious and already married artist was another matter entirely. When Carrington informed her parents that she would join Ernst in Paris and that, furthermore, she would never marry him, her father excommunicated her with the admonishment: 'My door will never be darkened by your shadow.'[74] When she recalls the move to Paris she often refers to her departure as either 'escaping' or 'running away' such as in this statement: 'Then I ran away to Paris. Not with Max. Alone. I always did my running away alone.'[75] Not simply a romantic elopement,

Carrington was fully aware that her flight was a significant step towards autonomy.

The move to Paris

In 1937, at the age of 20, Leonora Carrington moved to Paris and became an active member of Breton's Surrealist circle. Being young, precocious, beautiful and talented, she didn't really have to try to impress them – they were already impressed. That she had supposedly abandoned her financial and social status for the love of an artist over 26 years her senior made her not only a great heroine but also living proof of their cherished belief in *l'amour fou.* Leonora Carrington was indeed remarkable for turning her back on all that her background entitled her to financially and socially. But it was not a random act of passion, she had been preparing for it for some time and she did it for herself, not for Max Ernst. For her it was a question of freedom, as she understood clearly and correctly that her parents meant to control every aspect of her life. She also understood, certainly after many expulsions from upper-class private schools, that she did not possess a conventional nature and, moreover, if she wanted to become an artist she must remove herself from her family's orbit of influence. One thing Carrington did not abandon was the self-confidence her upbringing afforded her. This inheritance from her privileged background would prove of the utmost benefit to her, enabling her to interact with a certain ease and lack of self-consciousness with the older male members of the Surrealist circle. I believe this attitude contributed to her early acceptance into the group, whereas many other women artists were relegated to the artistic periphery of the movement. Carrington did not have to demand her rights, it never occurred to her that she was inferior. Because she had radically rejected her background, Breton, who was a Marxist, did not view her as a 'poor little rich girl'. Instead, she managed to impress upon him another sense of her as wild and magical, simultaneously epitomising free-spirited, modern femininity and archaic feminine supernatural power. She embodied two powerful Surrealist archetypes – the *femme enfant* and the *femme sorcière.*

When Carrington arrived in Paris, Ernst soon separated from Marie-Berthe Aurenche and joined Leonora in an apartment, in one of the old houses on the rue Jacob. They spent a lot of time socialising both at home and at the Café Flore on the boulevard Saint-Germain where Leonora met a wide assortment of artists then working in Paris.

> There were always friends in our house and we had constant visitors such as Breton, Paul Eluard, Luis Aragon, Marcel Duchamp, and Yves Tanguy. We had formidable evenings where we would write, paint, compose poetry, communicate ideas and feelings. During one of these evenings Picasso introduced me to a young Mexican named Renato Leduc who would later play such an important role in my life. On that occasion Picasso and Renato brought me a jar of Spanish wine.[76]

Dating from the time of her first arrival is one of the often-recounted stories about Carrington that demonstrates the type of uninhibited and eccentric behaviour that immediately enamoured her to the Surrealists. As Gloria Orenstein told it to *Ms. Magazine*:

> [Ernst] later invited her to a party in Paris to be given by couturier Marcel Rochas. Leonora left immediately for France, arriving without a proper party dress. She asked the advice of a friend and clothing designer, Princess Maria de Gramont, who in appreciation of Leonora's natural beauty, replied: 'My child, you don't need a thing.' When 19-year-old Leonora Carrington arrived, she was draped in a sheet, toga style, but when the party warmed up, she dropped the sheet on an impulse and stood naked

before the scandalized guests. She and Max were instantly ushered out.[77]

Alongside Ernst she did a lot of writing and painting: 'While we were in Paris Max taught me a new way to live – to be myself. He made me develop the ideas and visions I had had since childhood and he introduced me to Surrealism. He gave me his support and his love.'[78] While Carrington found herself stimulated and even exhilarated by her new artistic milieu, she also found herself at the centre of an emotional maelstrom created by Ernst's complicated love life. There were numerous public and unpleasant confrontations with Ernst's wife who was having, needless to say, a difficult time reconciling herself to his new relationship. Comparing her new-found life to what she had known in England, Carrington noted: 'It was so much better than a convent in England. It was a very exciting time in Paris and seemed incredibly free.'[79] Ironically, Marie-Berthe, whom Ernst had married upon her graduation from convent school, was entertaining ideas of returning to it permanently in response to her abandonment.

Jimmy Ernst, Max's son by his first wife, Lou Straus, is the best source for untangling the labyrinthine romantic attachments surrounding his father. His memoirs, *A Not-so-still-Life* (St Martins: 1984) shed some light on this particular time period, beginning with his own awkward initial encounter with Carrington in 1937. Only three years her senior, he first learned of her existence when he went to visit his father on the rue Jacob and Leonora answered the door. [80] Max's ex-wife Lou had, in the meantime, befriended Marie-Berthe for whom she felt a great deal of sympathy (no doubt stemming from an understanding of her position since Ernst had abandoned her for Gala Eluard); the two women even contemplated living together for mutual consolation.[81] Another story told by Jimmy Ernst highlights the intensely public life Carrington and Max were leading at the time, which involved the constant interaction with significant artists, and the ensuing personal melodramas that always seemed to occur. As he tells it, Ernst and Leonora were giving him a send-off drink at the Café Flore in the spring of 1937, as he was about to leave for the United States. While Leonora and Man Ray were giving him English lessons, Paul Eluard, Hans Arp and Alberto Giacometti, who were strolling by, joined the party. Their fun was shattered by the arrival of Marie-Berthe who went into a jealous rage and had to be mollified by Jimmy and his mother Lou, also present. Entranced with his new lover, Max had no sympathy for his wife's position or her emotional well-being and appeared only irritated that she would not magically and immediately disappear from his life.[82]

Jimmy Ernst is also the only source that states that Carrington was having difficulties with her parents who were apparently trying to cause trouble for Ernst. As Jimmy tells it:

> They [Carrington's parents] never ceased in their efforts to separate the two in any way possible. They had gone so far as to influence British authorities to issue a warrant for Max's arrest, on charges of exhibiting pornographic paintings in London while he was on his way there. It was only with the help of Roland Penrose that he escaped discovery by the police during what had to be a secret stay there.[83]

Thus, not quite free of their influence, in 1937 much of Carrington's energies were still focused on rebelling against her family.[84]

Inn of the Dawn Horse

Although there was much in her new life to distract her, such as the emotionally volatile situation surrounding Ernst and his wife Marie-Berthe, frequent café socialising with its dazzling array of artist personalities, as well as adjusting to both a new city and a new relationship, Carrington appears to have found time for her own creative endeavours. In fact, her meeting with Ernst ushered in a period of intense productivity that would last through 1939 when the events of the Second World War and her resulting nervous breakdown would change the course of her life yet again. In addition to painting and drawing, Carrington began to develop her writing and completed a number of short stories and plays that delighted Breton and other Surrealists, who were eager to include them in their various publications.

Begun in London in 1937 and completed in Paris in 1938, her painting *Self-Portrait (Inn of the Dawn Horse)* (Fig.18) is the first fully realised expression of Carrington's personal vision, containing ideas that she would spend a lifetime developing more fully. It is a pivotal painting within her œuvre, where she first sought to transcend mere representation in order to create an image that elevated painting to a magical act, within the context of a specifically feminine domestic arena. *Self-Portrait (Inn of the Dawn Horse)* marks a qualitative leap in her artistic development, displaying an increased technical ability and a greater iconic clarity and strength. That Carrington's breakthrough work would be a self-portrait seems no accident and, indeed, could be viewed as a kind of manifesto of independence, functioning as a token of her rite of passage into the Surrealist realm.[85]

Self-Portrait (Inn of the Dawn Horse) provides us with a view into the corner of a room where two walls, part of the ceiling, and a large expanse of tiled floor demarcate a quietly dramatic space where an intense and multi-layered drama unfolds as if on a stage. This interior is vaguely reminiscent of the cut-away spaces of the Italian Renaissance paintings she so admired from her stay in Florence, especially the terracotta brown of the tiled floor with its carefully delineated recession into space. This is her first attempt at using the cut-away view and it is a compositional ploy that later, in Mexico in the 1940s, she will develop into a signature aspect of her style. In contrast to the rich brown of the floor, the back wall is a cool blue-grey, the side wall a pale grey, and the ceiling off-white. Seated on a chair, situated slightly off-centre, the artist gestures to a hyena standing to her right while above her head floats a white rocking horse. Behind the hyena an ornately curtained window affords a garden vista complete with a white horse galloping into the distance. These four elements (hyena, woman, rocking horse and window) create a rotating compositional circle, leading the eye to travel from one to the next over and again as if caught in a visual vortex.

The psychic centre of this engrossing whirlwind is clearly Carrington who, through gaze and gesture, both conjures and commands the other characters. Dressed in closely fitted riding clothes, she is seated with legs spread in a pose whose masculinity is reinforced by the absence of breasts under her shirt. Her jacket is a sylvan green, her shirt an earthy brown and her bright white pants accentuate the curves of her muscular but feminine thighs. Forgoing utilitarian paddock boots, her pointy, black lace-up boots hint at Victorian fetish and a menacing female sexuality, in direct contrast to the rest of her outfit. Her frontal gaze holds the viewer in a lock of wills, her unsmiling lips demand a stern attention while around her face swirls a mane-like shock of hair animated by hidden supernatural forces emanating from her person. This androgynous Leonora is perched on a chair facing a lactating hyena – both chair and animal serving to reveal aspects of her subversive rebellion against traditional femininity. The upholstered and skirted, boudoir-style chair marks yet another first in this painting – anthropomorphic, sentient furniture. In future works (particularly later in Mexico) animate and 'living' furniture will make their appearance. In Mexico, the Spanish painter Remedios Varo will also feature 'living' furniture, under Carrington's influence. The carved armrest is hand-like,

18
Self-Portrait (Inn of the Dawn Horse)
1937–8
Oil on canvas
65 x 81.2 cm/25½ x 32 in
The Metropolitan Museum of Art,
The Pierre and Maria-Gaetana Matisse Collection, 2002
(2002.456.1)

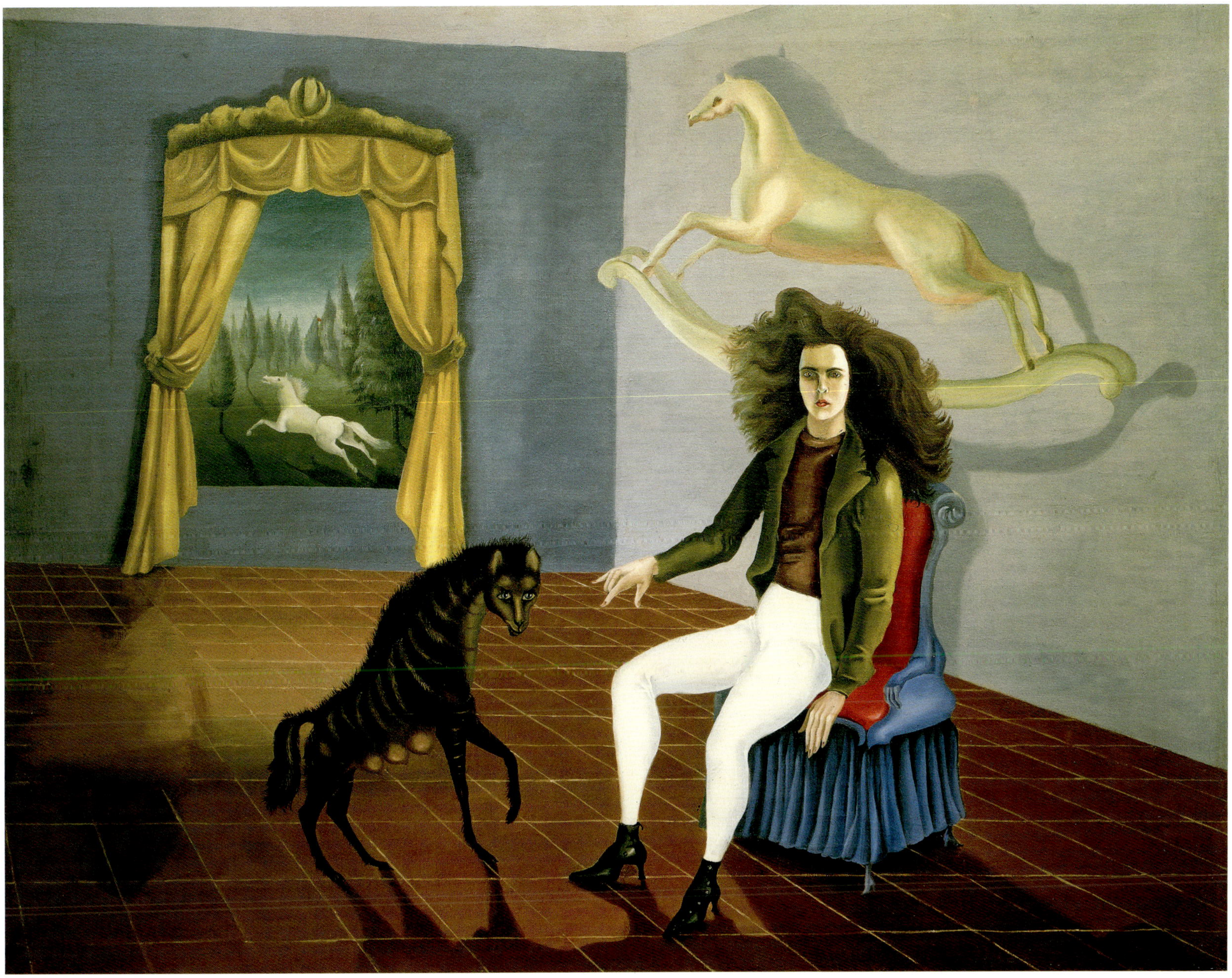

mirroring the figure's left hand, while the legs terminate in small, carved boots like the real ones in close proximity. Another unusual aspect of this chair is that its seat and back are a glowing ember-red. A white brushstroke on a lower corner seems to indicate the sheen of a sumptuous fabric, perhaps silk, making the sensual allusions even more overt. The opposite of a piece of ladylike bedroom furniture, it mocks decorum like an open red mouth or a protruding tongue. Taking things a step further, the red seat atop the skirted bottom of the chair could be viewed as the artist's genital doppelgänger. Enthroned within the chair's vaginal centre, Carrington announces and owns her newly found sexual power.

The hyena to her right, representing the intrusion of the wild into a domestic space, is unsettling and startling. Even more disquieting, however, is their intimate communion, expressed through mirroring gestures and similar staring countenances. For here Carrington not only aligns herself with the forces of nature, but also with her own animal nature, and in this context the hyena is a highly telling choice. Animals, of course, had always been important to her, both personally and artistically, but on the choice of hyena Carrington would later reflect: 'Hyenas particularly attracted me in the zoo ... Their great virtue is that they eat garbage.'[86] The 'zoo' and 'garbage' are the key concepts here and seem, on some level, related to her mother and familial expectations. One only has to think back to her vivid childhood memory of going to Blackpool zoo with her mother as a reward after her communion. The pleasure was dual and inexorably linked, that of being with her mother alone (and not her nanny) and of being able to see wild animals. Carrington explains: 'I'm like a hyena, I get into the garbage cans. I have an insatiable curiosity.'[87] Without venturing too deeply into the psychological, this comment affords us some insight into the symbolic meaning of the hyena for the artist. Like herself, it is a wild creature and therefore cannot be domesticated, and the 'garbage' that it feeds on, by her parents' standards, is specifically her artistic aspirations and her extramarital relations with Max Ernst. Leonora then reverses this 'natural' order by turning that wildness into a *virtue*, an indictment of the hypocrisy and falsity of the life she was expected to pursue. Her lifelong 'insatiable curiosity' led her to see behind appearances and to delve into the hidden and discarded ('the garbage cans') in order to seek the truth.

In addition to its unwholesome eating habits, the hyena is hairy, smelly and possesses a 'laughing' cry that eerily mocks human sound. In the painting, three swollen, lactating teats add to its effrontery, suggesting taboo bodily functions *and* an unsettling maternal role toward the artist. It is an abject and monstrous stand-in for an 'unclean' femininity and, in fact, has human eyes that stare ahead, defiant. 'In everybody,' Carrington has said, 'there is an inner bestiary.'[88] Two other creatures are present, a white rocking horse that rises above her head as if alive and a real white horse that gallops away outside the window. Windows were a symbol of freedom to the artist and here she makes a point of further mystifying this space by omitting the windowsill and surrounding it with ornate draperies like stage curtains. The garden is also mysterious with topiary-like trees reminiscent of certain Italian Renaissance paintings, such as Leonardo da Vinci's 1472–5 *Annunciation* hanging in the Uffizi since 1867 and presumably seen by Carrington while living in Florence in 1932.[89]

Horses occupy a central role in Carrington's entire œuvre, from her first known drawings from 1929 through to the present day. Epona, the Celtic goddess that appeared to her followers on a white horse, would be an important feminine archetype for Carrington later on in Mexico, particularly after reading Robert Graves's 1948 Celtic study *The White Goddess*. Although it is uncertain if she specifically identified the white horse with Epona at this early date, it is certainly a possibility, considering her mother's and grandmother's great interest in Celtic legends. That she depicts herself in equestrian gear with white pants that echo that of both horses is indicative of some level of identification with the Celtic deity. Like the hyena, horses are another aspect of her animal self, representing her love of freedom and her desire to escape the stultifying class background that her outfit implies and perhaps satirises.

Returning to the lower portion of the canvas, her hand gesture is of the utmost importance. Made with the right hand, the index and little fingers are extended in the age-old sign of malediction[90] and thus transform this image from a fairy-tale-style narrative into something decidedly different. The two fingers carefully mark two corners of a floor square, as if establishing the unit of measure of this psychically charged space. The hand itself is located at the intersection of the floor and two walls – an intersection of different planes of the room, perhaps indicating a rupture between two worlds, or different planes of existence (or multiple levels of consciousness). Pointed in the direction of the hyena, it binds the two in an occult pact, transforming them into the witch and her familiar. All of the characters in this work have carefully delineated shadows, even the trees outside the window. This brings us to the most startling portrayal in the work, which is the area to the left of the hyena, below the window. A scumbled section of paint clearly disrupts the clear geometry of the floor tiles and from it rises a nebulous mist, casting a conical shadow. What we are witnessing is the magical act of materialisation, the formation of an entity from another realm, conjured forth by the gesture and the combined concentration of woman and animal. Not yet visible, it is only beginning to coalesce; tellingly its shadow shows first. Likewise, we can read the transformation of the rocking horse into a live horse above as completing the circular compositional whirl of magical activity.

Much later, in the 1980s, both Carrington and Chadwick use the term 'liminal' to describe the sense of suspended time and magical play present in many of the artist's compositions. This term is taken from Victor Turner's anthropological theories regarding the ritual significance of performance and play that he first used to describe aspects of his field research in Africa. This concept was later expanded to include rites of passage in western culture.[91] Speaking of Carrington's later work, in a way that is applicable here, Chadwick explains:

> Carrington's recent paintings depend on a vibrant metalanguage to overcome the limitations of linear space and time and communicate the interdependence of all aspects of the phenomenal world. She often refers to these paintings as 'liminal,' a word used by anthropologist Victor Turner to describe the way communities are formed through ritual or process 'which is betwixt-and-between the normal, day-to-day cultural and social states and processes ... Since liminal time is not controlled by the clock it is a time of enchantment when anything *might*, even should happen.' Enchantment comes naturally to Carrington whose images have for many years belonged to a magical realm between sleep and waking, conscious and unconscious.[92]

Turner posits that during certain 'rites of passage' or public festivals, those who are marginal to society take on a threatening and menacing aspect in order to call into question the established social order. For example, in discussing the 'liminal domain' of carnival, he notes that performances of feminine unruliness represents the 'perilous realm of possibility' and thus: 'The powers of the weak – to curse and criticize – set limits on the power of the strong – to coerce and ordain.'[93] In light of this then, we can read *Self-Portrait (Inn of the Dawn Horse)* as a menacing performance of female sexuality meant to disrupt parental (and therefore societal) order, complete with an inverted maternal totem (the lactating hyena) that Carrington invokes as both protector and signifier of a wild mother more appropriate to her new-found 'bestial' sexuality.[94] Carrington's masculine appearance in the painting adds yet another dimension to her rebellious and socially disruptive performance of gender. Poised on the border between dream and reality where the animate and inanimate are indistinguishable, *Self-Portrait (Inn of the Dawn Horse)* is a record of Carrington's triumphant psychological transition from girl to woman.

The sub-title *Inn of the Dawn Horse*, like so many of the titles to both Carrington's pictorial and written work, is not so much ambiguous as arcane. In a literal sense a 'dawn horse' (Eohippus) was a small, dog-sized creature that lived 50 million years ago and was proposed as the ancestor of the modern horse in school textbooks teaching Darwinian theories of evolution. Is this a comical allusion to her own evolution? The 'dawning' of her freedom? Always intensely private, her titles tend to pique the imagination but remain impervious to interpretation. Here Warner's interpretation rings true: 'The hyena embodies the young woman's sex and fertility, the horse her dynamism and speed and sovereignty.'[95] 'A horse gets mixed up with one's body ... it gives energy and power', says Carrington. 'I used to think I could turn myself into a horse.'[96] If both the rocking horse and the horse in this work are identified with the artist, then photographs taken around this time of Ernst are pertinent to this discussion. In 1937 Carrington purchased a rocking horse in Paris and had it brought to their rue Jacob apartment where Homer Saint-Gaudens took a series of photographs with Ernst astride it for a *Life* magazine story. This is undoubtedly the rocking horse used in the painting, and the sexual connotations of Ernst 'riding' it make for an added interpretation of this horse as, indeed, indicative of her newly embodied sexual freedom.

Carrington's writings have vital correspondences to her visual work and provide insight into her visual 'language'.[97] *La Maison de la peur* (*The House of Fear*), written in French, was her first published story, put out by Henri Parisot in Paris in 1938.[98] It was accompanied by three collage illustrations and a preface by Ernst. The story includes many horse characters, including the character of Fear who was depicted by Ernst as a horse-headed circus girl in a collage that merged portions of popular prints similar to his earlier 1934 collages for *Une semaine de bonté*. In 1939, Editions G. L. M. in Paris came out with a collection of five of Carrington's short stories under the title *La Dame ovale*, which included seven collages by Ernst. Written in French, the stories included were (in English): 'The Débutante', 'The Oval Lady', 'The Royal Summons', 'A Man in Love' and 'Uncle Sam Carrington'. Lucretia, the protagonist in 'The Oval Lady' is not only able to transform herself into a white horse, but also has as a playmate a rocking horse named Tartarus. Lucretia's father destroys Tartarus in an act of punishment for her rebellious behaviour – that of transforming herself into a horse and thereby partaking of freedom. Reminiscent of Lewis Carroll, the beloved author of her childhood, the tone is mocking, understated and unsentimental, hiding deeply subversive messages of revolt against patriarchy behind a grisly humour.

Carrington is well known for 'La débutante', a spoof of her coming-out into London society. The characters in this auto-biographical black comedy bear a direct relationship to those in *Inn of the Dawn Horse* and the story recounts an ultimately disastrous role reversal between a young woman and a hyena.

> When I was a débutante, I often went to the zoo. I went so often that I knew the animals better than I knew girls of my own age. Indeed it was in order to get away from people that I found myself at the zoo every day. The animal I got to know best was a young hyena. She knew me too. She was very intelligent. I taught her French, and she, in return, taught me her language. In this way we passed many pleasant hours.[99]

The young woman convinces the hyena to take her place at her débutante ball and so it kills and eats the woman's maid, saving her face as a mask-like disguise. While the girl happily stays at home and reads *Gulliver's Travels*, the hyena attends the ball, but its pungent odour gives it away. At the end of the tale the girl's enraged mother discovers the charade and the hyena escapes with one great bound out of an open window. 'The Débutante' functions on a multitude of levels: as an exorcism of the traumatic events of Carrington's coming-out experience; as a malicious and vengeful adolescent wish-fulfilment; and as a gleefully wicked cautionary tale to parents everywhere.[100]

Annette Shandler Levitt correctly surmises: 'Her final image of the hyena leaping through the window links 'The Débutante' unequivocally with *Inn of the Dawn Horse*, in which the horse is bounding through the field just outside the open doorway, thus reinforcing the clear contrast between inside and outside in both painting and story.'[101] The hyena's most revolting and therefore subversive attribute in 'The Débutante' is her wild smell; since this characteristic could not be translated into painting, Carrington emphasised another part of the hyena to be gross and offensive – its swollen, lactating breasts. Thus in both forms, the hyena's main function is to signify the abject, as a symbol of the artist's anger and resentment at being objectified for the marriage market. The French psychoanalyst and semiotician, Julia Kristeva, writes in 'Approaching Abjection': 'It is thus not lack of cleanliness or health that causes abjection but what disturbs identity, system, order. What does not respect borders, positions, rules.'[102] By juxtaposing beauty (herself) and the beast(s) in both 'The Débutante' and *Inn of the Dawn Horse* Carrington indeed 'disturbs identity, system, order'.

Carrington's identification with animals removes her from the realm of the *femme enfant* and reveals her powers as a *femme sorcière*, challenging the traditional role of Muse prescribed by the Surrealists. Chadwick best explains how Carrington manipulates the 'natural' to disrupt the Surrealists' notions of the role of the feminine Muse:

> Carrington's animals identify the instinctual life with the forces of nature. The hyena belongs to the fertile world of night; the horse becomes an image of rebirth into the light of day and the world beyond the looking glass. As symbolic intermediaries between the unconscious and the natural world, they replace male Surrealists' reliance on the image of woman as the mediating link between man and the 'marvelous', and suggest the powerful role played by Nature as a source of creative power for the woman artist ... Carrington also suggests a redefinition of the image of the *femme-enfant* from that of innocence, seduction, and dependence on man, to a being who through her intimate relationship with the childhood worlds of fantasy and magic is capable of creative transformation through mental rather than sexual power.[103]

Perhaps this is why, in an œuvre both compelling and extensive, one of Carrington's best-known paintings is *Self-Portrait (Inn of the Dawn Horse)*, and 'The Débutante' one of the most studied and quoted of her stories.

19
The Horses of Lord Candlestick
1938
Oil on canvas
61 x 93.3 cm/24 x 36¾ in
Private collection

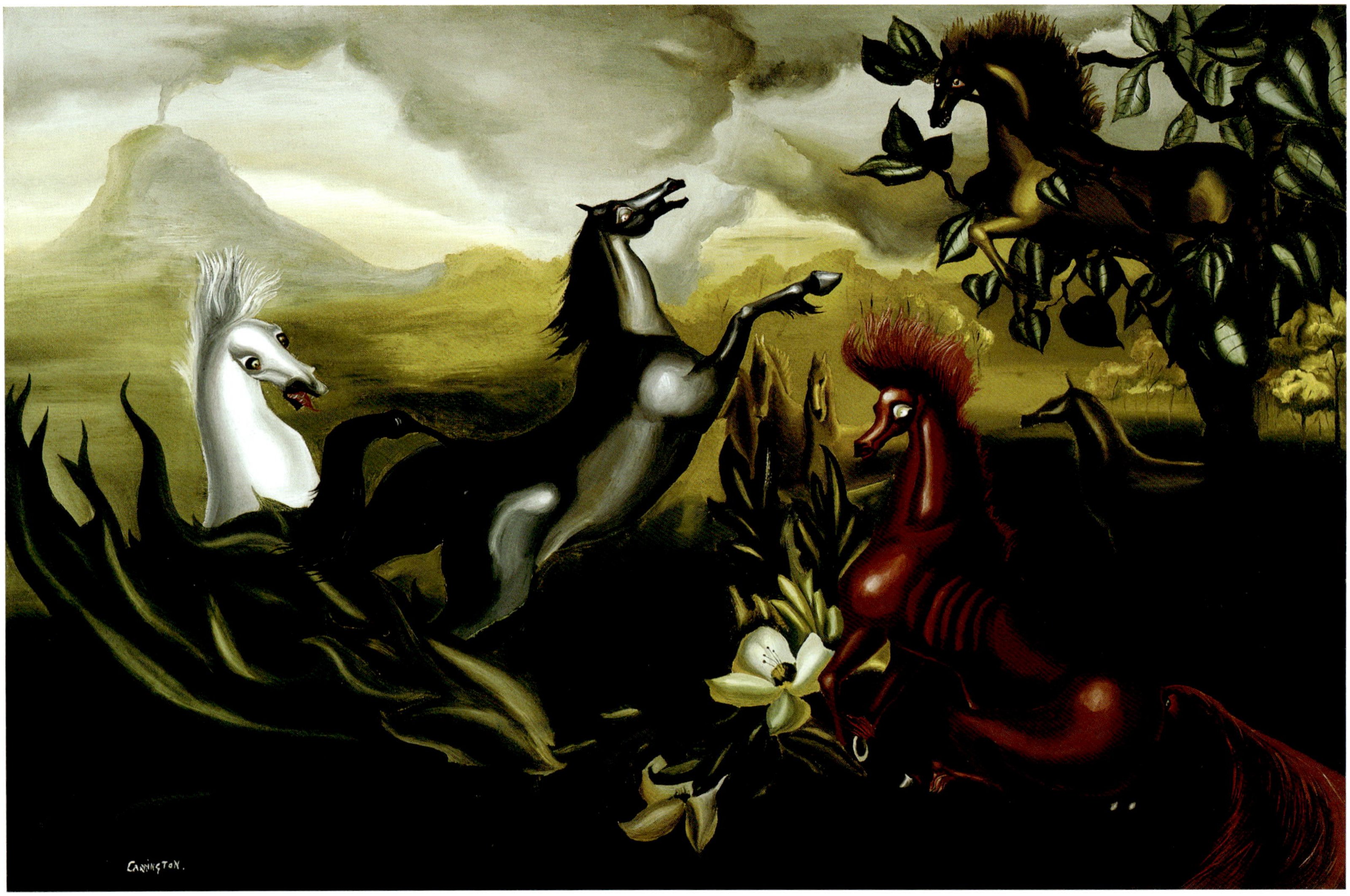

CHAPTER 3 HEAVEN AND HELL: WARTIME EXPERIENCES

Surrealist acceptance

Two major Surrealist exhibitions in 1938 included works by Carrington. The first was the *Exposition Internationale du Surréalisme* held in Paris at the Galerie Beaux-Arts, which showed two of her works from 1937. The show was organised by Breton and Marcel Duchamp, and of the 60 exhibitors there were a number of women: Remedios Varo, Meret Oppenheim, Sophie Taeuber-Arp, Ann Clark, Nina Negri, Elsa Thoresen, Toyen, Eileen Agar and Leonora Carrington. The second was the last Surrealist exhibition held before the Second World War in Amsterdam, at the Robert Gallery in April, which featured contributions from about 40 artists, including Carrington's *The Meal of Lord Candlestick* (Fig.20) and *Lord Candlestick's Horses*, both from 1938. 'What desire for extravagance!' exclaimed a delighted Breton on seeing *The Meal of Lord Candlestick*.[104] Although Carrington's involvement with Ernst undoubtedly served to bring her to the attention of the Surrealists, it was her work that earned her a place in their circle. During a visit to Ernst's studio in the winter of 1938–9 Peggy Guggenheim ended up purchasing a Carrington instead: 'She was a young pupil of Ernst and not well known but very good and full of imagination in the best Surrealist manner and always painted animals and birds. This canvas, which was called *The Horses of Lord Candlestick*, portrayed four horses of four different colors in a tree.'[105]

Guggenheim's *The Horses of Lord Candlestick* (Fig.19) is so similar to *Lord Candlestick's Horses*, painted the same year, that they could be considered a diptych. Both feature a group of horses of different colours with human eyes in a stormy landscape. One of the horses is oddly positioned in a tree, as if a bird. All of the wild and wide-eyed expressions of the creatures give it an emotionally charged atmosphere that hints of a disturbing and inexplicable confrontation. That the scene had personal meaning is implied not only by the fact that she painted it twice, but that horses always had symbolic resonance for the artist.

Carrington's rebellious attitude toward authority made no exception for Breton and his Surrealist circle and she defiantly claimed: 'I was never a Surrealist, I was with Max.'[106] This antipathy to being absorbed into a group identity was, however, coupled with a genuine appreciation for the artistic support and stimulation they offered her.[107] In addition to the many male artists she met and befriended she also met women artists such as Lee Miller, Gisèle Prassinos, Meret Oppenheim and Leonor Fini, whom she would soon become close to.

The problematic role of Muse

The problematic role of 'Muse' that many women artists within the Surrealist movement were cast to play, unwittingly or not, has been a central focus of feminist scholarship on Carrington and other women artists associated with the movement. As for the role of 'Muse', Carrington has this to say: 'The women Surrealists were considered secondary to the male Surrealists. The women were considered ... people there to inspire, aside from doing the washing, cooking, cleaning and feeding ... I never thought of myself as a muse. I thought of myself as being carried away by my lover.'[108]

The young Carrington most potently embodied the notion of the *femme enfant*, defined by Breton as the woman-child who through her naiveté is in direct connection with her own unconscious and can, therefore, serve as a guide for man.[109] Warner has astutely observed:

> Leonora Carrington was a very striking young woman with her oval face and black eyes, her long black hair and slender limbs; in her artlessness and innate, innocent

20
The Meal of Lord Candlestick
1938
Oil on canvas
46 x 61 cm/18 x 24 in
Private collection
Courtesy of the Museo de Arte Contemporáneo de Monterrey, Mexico

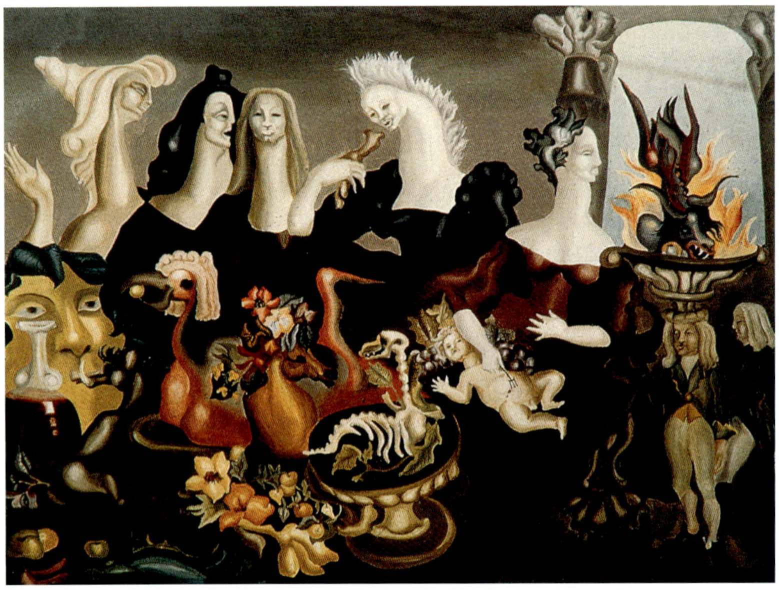

> perversity she seemed to have sprung out of the dream world as if directly summoned by the voices of the Surrealists at their automatic séances, a real-life *femme-enfant* who speaks of desire and has not yet grown up enough to grasp the full implication of what she says.[110]

Independent and defiant, as attested by her school expulsions, Carrington was *not* going to be transformed into a passive *femme enfant*: 'I never considered myself a *femme enfant* like André Breton wanted to see women. Nor did I want to be understood by this, nor did I try to change the rest. I fell into Surrealism like that. I never asked if I had the right to enter or not.'[111] Once again, it was this attitude of entitlement, born partially of the self-confidence of social class that helped her to win the respect of Breton and others. 'If you are in a condition of social inferiority, I think it affects you very much creatively', Carrington has observed. 'You might have incredible visions but you might be too bashful to show them. Your creativity becomes inhibited.' She then added dryly, 'I've always found women as individuals as stupid or as intelligent as men. I've never had any reason to find them otherwise.'[112] Carrington was well aware that her 'grand romance' with Ernst, complete with objecting Catholic parents and dramatic age difference, was a repeat performance for him. When he met her, Ernst was at the tail end of his last great *amour fou* with his previous *femme enfant*, Marie-Berthe Aurenche who, although now still in her twenties, had obviously outgrown her role. As Carrington herself summed it up: 'Once you were over 25 you were pretty well out.'[113]

St. Martin d'Ardèche

In the summer of 1938 Carrington and Ernst escaped from Paris and moved to a house in the town of St. Martin d'Ardèche. Both wanted some respite from the jealous confrontations with Marie-Berthe, Ernst was tired of the constant infighting between Breton and the other Surrealists,[114] and Carrington preferred the country to an urban environment. They originally planned to spend the summer, but ended up staying longer, and together they renovated a group of dilapidated dwellings to suit their creative needs. The move ushered in the most idyllic period of their relationship, lasting a year and a half until Ernst's incarceration as an enemy alien in a French concentration camp in 1939. Jimmy Ernst quotes his father as saying at the time: 'All I want now is to leave Paris for a long time and live with Leonora in Ardèche ... and to love her ... if the world will only allow it.'[115] They worked together and alone in their respective studios, and also shared their literary interests: 'Max would teach me romantic German literature, read me Archim von Arnum and I would teach him about Black British literature.'[116] In addition to painting, Carrington tended their vineyards and garden, took care of the animals on the property and reconnected with nature. In a rare instance of nostalgia she recalled: 'It was an era of paradise.'[117]

21
Max Ernst at St. Martin d'Ardèche, sitting with sculptures, 1938

22
Leonora Carrington at St. Martin d'Ardèche, 1938

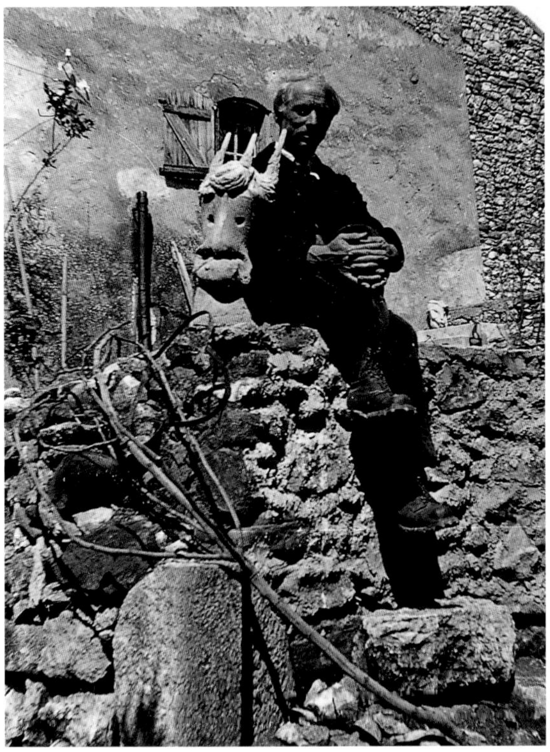

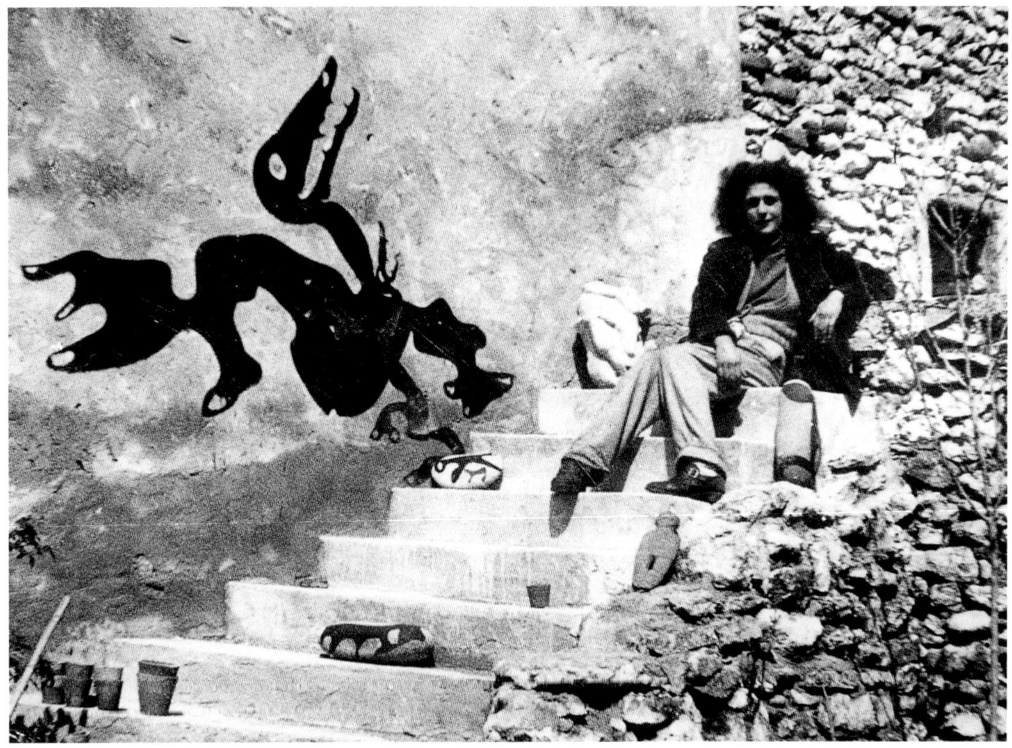

Ernst was happily engaged in decorating the exterior of their farmhouse with a series of large-scale cast cement sculptures of human/bird hybrids and even Carrington made a plaster sculpture of a horse's head. The choice of guardian animals, the bird and the horse, had long been totemic stand-ins for Max and Leonora but the horse had further resonance for them as a couple since it was Ernst's poetic evocation of her as his 'bride of the wind'. All of these sculptures were meant to function as protection against ex-wives, hostile parents and disgruntled Surrealists, but to the real threat of impending war and its consequences, the two seemed stubbornly oblivious.[118] Roland Penrose, travelling with his companion, the photographer Lee Miller, commented on these sculptures:

> On our way south we stayed for a few days at St. Martin d'Ardèche, where Max Ernst had found a new home with Leonora Carrington in an old farm house. They had both decorated it with paintings and great concrete sculptures that emerged from the walls like vigilant monsters, guardians, whose power, however, when the imminent catastrophe arrived was unhappily zero. Only a few weeks later Max was to be led off by the gendarmes to a concentration camp for enemy aliens.[119]

Sometime in 1938 Carrington painted *The Meal of Lord Candlestick* (Fig. 20) in which she introduced a theme that would feature prominently in subsequent paintings, a ritualistic meal atop an altar-like table. With Catholic school a bitter memory still fresh in her mind, the artist presents us with an unholy cannibals' banquet in lieu of the Eucharist; this is Carrington at her most blasphemous and satiric. A group of grotesque female characters, spectre-like in their

23
Leonora Carrington and Max Ernst at St. Martin d'Ardèche, France, 1939
Photograph: Lee Miller

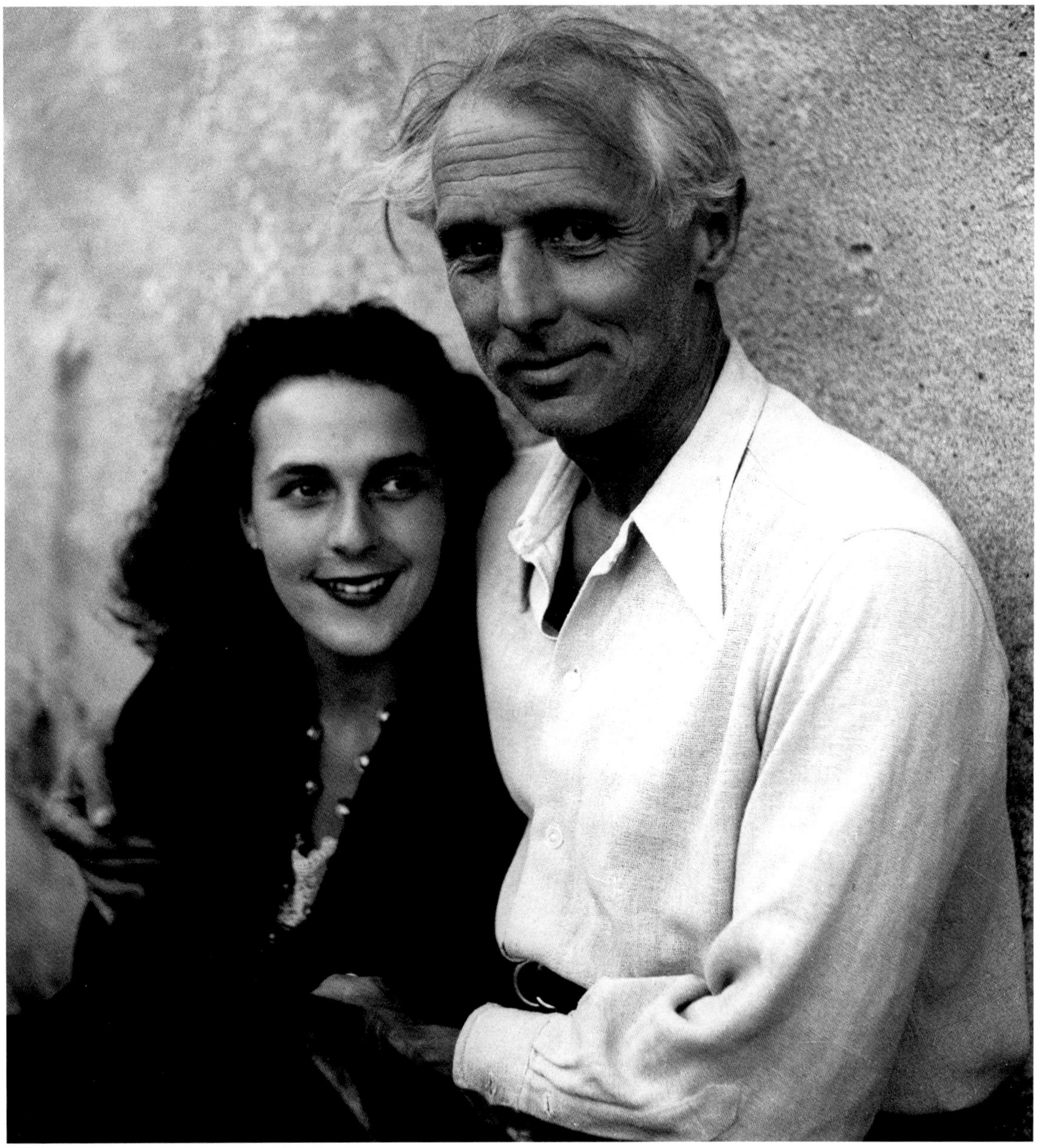

24
Leonor Fini
Portrait of Leonora Carrington
1939
Oil on canvas
64 x 53 cm / 25¼ x 20¾ in
Private collection
Courtesy of Weinstein Gallery, San Francisco

25
Leonor Fini
The Alcove: An Interior with Three Women
*c.*1939
Oil on canvas
91.5 x 71 cm / 36 x 28 in
Private collection

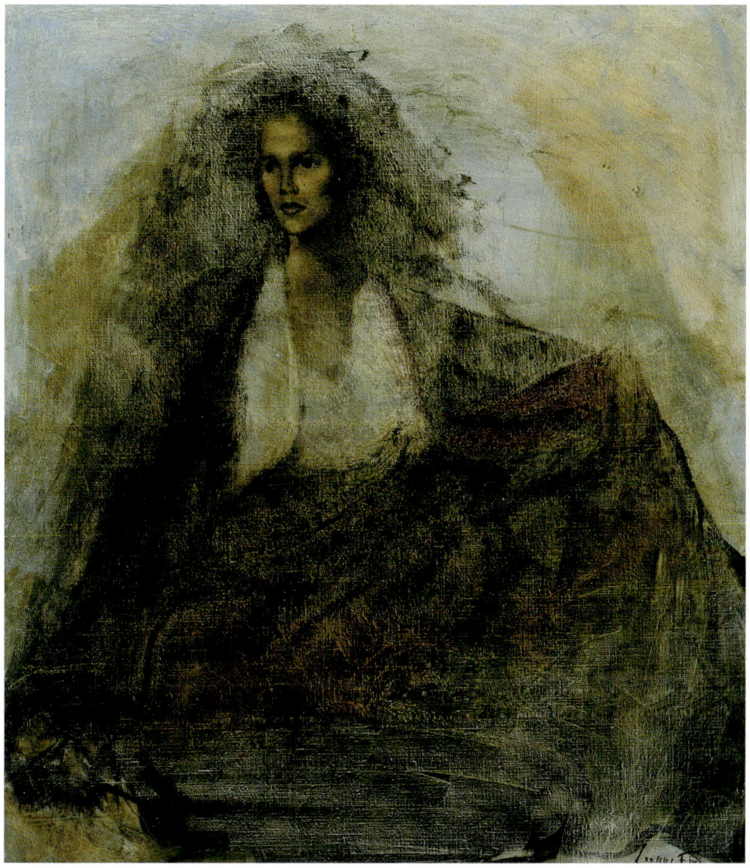

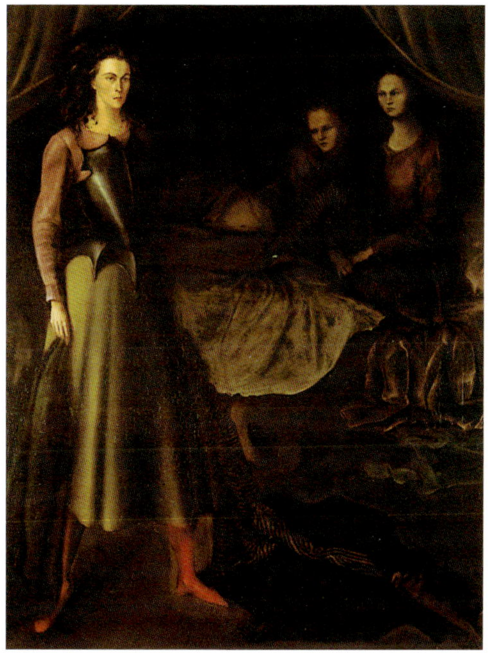

whiteness and possessing heads both phallic and horse-like, are seated above a table overflowing with perverse and inventive dishes. Although presented on elaborate platters, the food is more alive than dead: a pink flamingo sports abarrister's wig, a pony wears a wreath of flowers, a duck skeleton sits upright and alert, and a reclining boar sprouts vines from his anus. This is the hallucinatory realm of Hieronymus Bosch, with all of the internal logic of a nightmare. On the far right of the picture is a window framed by foliate capitals, enclosing a serene blue sky. Are we in an enchanted banquet chamber, high up in the tower of a castle? Or are we in Crookhey Hall, as seen through the looking glass of Carrington's rebellion? 'Candlestick' was the code name she invented for her family, and so the 'Lord' in the title presumably refers to her father. He is present in the lower left portion of the painting in the form of a bloated green head with leaves for hair and wide staring eyes, but with no mouth he cannot partake of, or criticise, the revelry. The woman in red is temporarily distracted from her meal by an exotic goat flambé on a dish poised on the head of a male servant in eighteenth-century attire. Her fork has begun to dig into a live male baby, his tender flesh forming droplets of blood. Crowned with grapes reminiscent of the Eucharist, the sacrificial child on the table calls to mind both scenes of the nativity and the rites of Holy Communion. *The Meal of Lord Candlestick* inverts the established order of things, questioning notions of class, religion, gender, maternity and the bestial.[120] While Ernst cast his hybrid guardian figures in concrete, Carrington formed hers in paint. Although both artists were simultaneously engaged in creating monstrous figures meant to repel evil, their respective demons were different.

Friends, mostly other artists, often interrupted their romantic idyll in the country and these visits were full of fun and pranks. Carrington remembers playing culinary practical jokes on guests, such as serving them up an omelette full of their own hair, cut while they slept the previous night.[121] Leonor Fini spent part of the summer of 1939 at St. Martin d'Ardèche and would dress Carrington up in elaborate lace blouses and a bell-fringed shawl, most likely from her own fantastic wardrobe. Fiercely independent, Fini refused to join Surrealism officially, although she exhibited with the group during the 1930s and early 1940s. Not only did she maintain that she and Carrington were never Surrealists, but she also viewed Carrington as a 'true revolutionary'.[122] During this time Fini executed two portraits in oil of Carrington, *Portrait of Leonora Carrington* (1939–40) (Fig.24) and *The Alcove: An Interior with Three Women* (*c.*1939). Dressed in the lace blouse, long skirt and shawl previously mentioned, the portrait shows Carrington seated on the floor filling up most of the canvas like a monumental Sibyl. The paint throughout is roughly scumbled; only her delicate face emerges from a halo of black hair, sensitive and alert. But the second work, *The Alcove* (Fig.25) reveals some of the fascination the painter felt for her subject and records Carrington's emerging public persona. Typical of many of Fini's paintings, this presents a mysterious tableau of androgynous young women engaged in a quiet drama. In the background is an alcove with a bed with theatrical curtains drawn to reveal two women on it, holding hands, who gaze with awe at another woman standing to the left: Carrington. Slender and elegant, she strikes a Gothic S-curve pose which, combined with her simple garment covered with an armoured breastplate, brings to mind medieval depictions of Christian knights, even down to her pointed fitted boots. Again Carrington's delicately featured white face emerges from a cloud of dark hair, unsmiling as if seeing a vision.

Portrait of Max Ernst (1939) (Fig.26) is Carrington's tribute to her lover, and in ways neither could foresee it is her farewell eulogy, comparable to the written one she would complete a few years later in New York, 'The Bird Superior: Max Ernst'. This painting can be seen as the companion piece to *Self-Portrait (Inn of the Dawn Horse)* done roughly a year and a half earlier, perhaps most obviously because like that earlier work, it is one of the rare serious portraits Carrington has done in her lifetime. The mantle he wears can be read as feathers or fur and terminates in a fish tail, while his only visible foot wears a yellow striped sock – one could see this as a playful parody of Ernst's own hybrid creatures decorating the façade of their St. Martin d'Ardèche home. Ernst's cloak of downy feathers resembles the robe Carrington will wear in his painting *La Toilette de la mariée* (*The Attirement of the Bride*) of 1940. Fiona Bradley claims the work could be said to reverse traditional roles of artist and Muse:

> Carrington's *Portrait of Max Ernst* recreates the male artist as a mystical figure of transformation and rescue. Bird-like and also fish-like, Ernst is a vivid splash of colour, capable of liberating and reviving both the frozen horse behind him and the one trapped in the glass of the lantern he carries. If the bird and the horse may be read as totemic substitutions for Carrington and Ernst, the picture perhaps reverses conventional Surrealist male/female behavior: Carrington may be claiming Ernst as her 'muse.'[123]

It seems plausible that he intended this to be a kind of companion piece to her portrait of him, especially since the robe opens to reveal a slender nude female body that resembles Carrington's. Warlick interprets the work as a complex alchemical allegory of the 'chemical wedding' of sulphur and mercury, and indicates his continued interest in such esoterica, which Carrington shared.[124] I believe this does much to explain the profusion of alchemical references made in her later account of her experience of madness, *En bas* (*Down Below*), recorded in 1943.

26
Portrait of Max Ernst
1939
Oil on canvas
50.2 x 26.7 cm/20 x 10½ in
Private collection

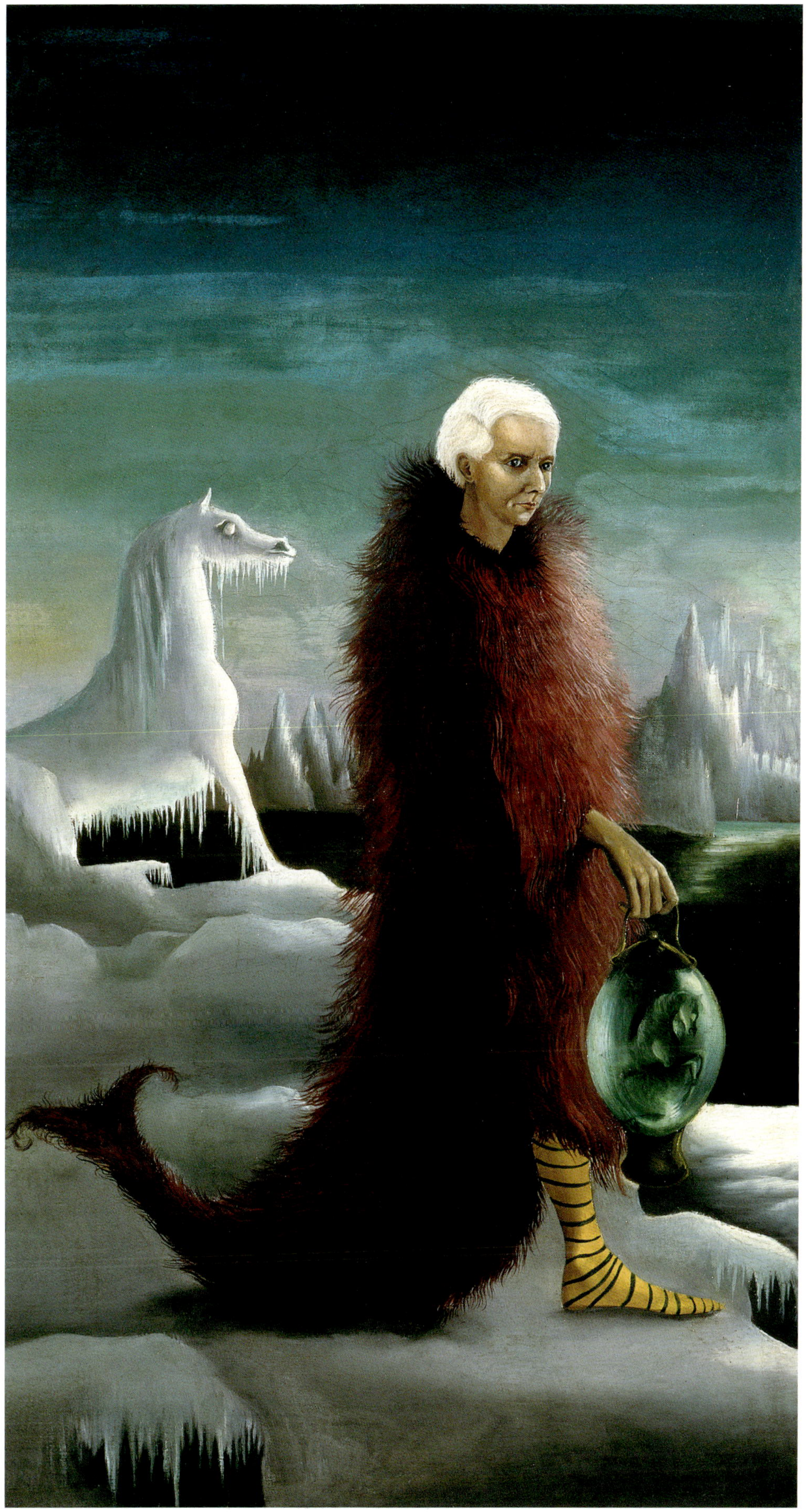

In contradistinction to *Inn of the Dawn Horse*, *Portrait of Max Ernst* is an outdoor scene and the white horse in the background (presumably a self-portrait) is here frozen instead of galloping freely. Witzling has observed that there is a correspondence between Ernst and a character in one of Carrington's stories: 'In 'Fly, Pigeon', Célestin, with his white feathery robe and striped stockings, seems remarkably similar to the painted shamanic image of Ernst.'[125] Written sometime between 1937 and 1940, 'Fly, Pigeon' contains many disturbing references to Carrington's and Ernst's relationship. The character Célestin is an elderly man with white skin, striped stockings, and a feathered cloak – the reference to Ernst could not be clearer. The young female protagonist, Agathe, feels a great repugnance towards Célestin, her husband, who is slowly turning into a bird. Meanwhile, she is slowly disappearing and can barely see her own reflection in the mirror. Her husband, in his narcissism, seems not to see: 'Célestin came. He didn't notice anything, but he touched my face with those smooth hands of his ... much too smooth ... He said, "You will always be a child, Agathe. Look at me. I am terribly young, aren't I?"'[126] Carrington's stories often reflect autobiographical content, and in this case the parallels seem all too obvious.

Later on in 1941, when reunited in Lisbon after their forced separation, Carrington refused to return to Ernst. Despite his pleadings she felt she could no longer live with him unless she became his 'slave'.[127] Suleiman has suggested that while Carrington lived with Ernst and reaped the many positive effects of their relationship, she was able to suppress her oppressive sense of dependency upon his opinion. Once they were separated by the war, the more negative aspects of their relationship came to the fore and she realised that she must separate from him. There are some indications, visible in *The Portrait of Max Ernst*, that this realisation had begun even before the events of the war shattered their existence together at St. Martin d'Ardèche. Sometime in 1940, presumably before their separation, Ernst painted a luminous tribute to Carrington, *Leonora in the Morning Light*. Peering out at the viewer through tangled grapevines like a nature spirit, surrounded by mythical creatures (a unicorn and the Minotaur), Carrington is as transcendently beautiful as any fairy princess. Yet in this work there is an ominous hint of her future vulnerability and madness as well, for a small skeleton lurks in the foreground, and a large tear is visible in the sleeve of her dress from the cruel thorns on the vines.

War and separation

While lost in the romance of country life, Ernst and Carrington chose to ignore the dangerous signs of the impending war. It is perplexing that Ernst, who had lived through the miseries of the First World War, did not pay more attention to his precarious position as a German living in France[128] and indeed, his son Jimmy expressed his frustration: 'my suggestions to him concerning his personal safety in Europe evoked nothing more than a slightly quizzical annoyance'.[129] Even when Jimmy's admonishments took an urgent turn, Ernst blithely ignored them:

> I had written to Max, who by now was living happily with Leonora Carrington in St. Martin d'Ardèche near Avignon. He did not reply to my pleas to leave Europe before it was too late. Instead, he sent me photographs that showed him in the process of embellishing the walls and doorways of the sixteenth-century buildings he'd bought with grotesque cement bas-reliefs and sculpture.[130]

Consequently, when war did break out, the repercussions were swift for Ernst and their effect on Carrington's mental stability would have lifelong ramifications.

27
Jacques Hérold (standing), Max Ernst and Danny Bénédite, Varian Fry's co-worker, hang paintings by Ernst and Leonora Carrington from a tree, for an auction of artworks, Villa Air Bel, 1941
Photograph: André Gomes

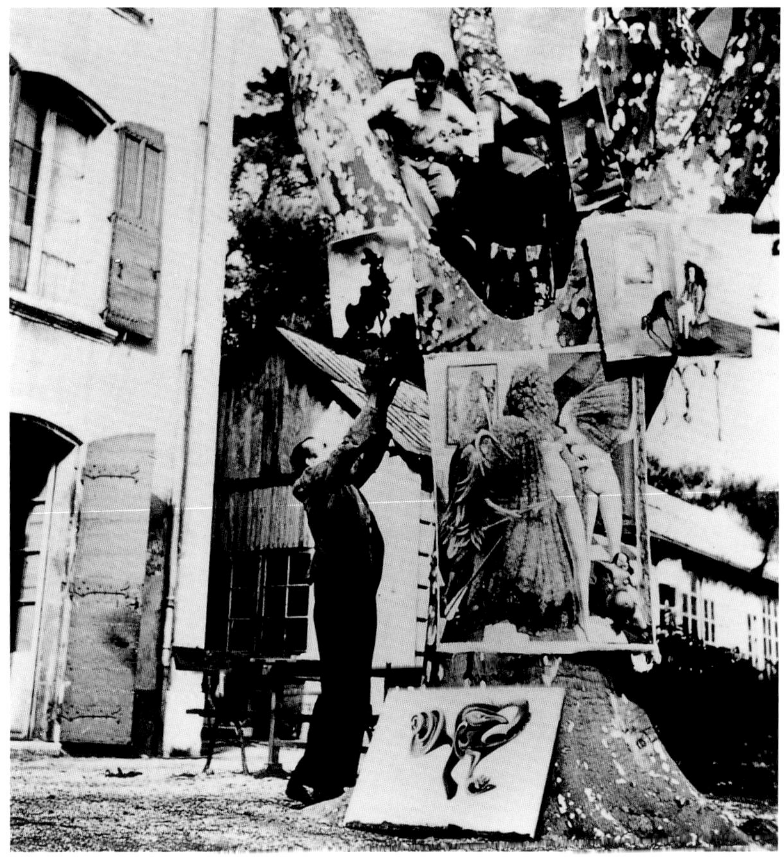

In 1939, after the French declared war on Germany, Ernst was interned at Largentière, not far from St. Martin d'Ardèche, along with 100 or so other German nationals. Carrington could visit him and brought him clothing, provisions and art supplies but soon he was transferred to the Les Milles camp near Aix-en-Provence where the conditions in an old brick factory were crowded and unsanitary. According to Marcel Jean, he stayed there for three months and was freed only at Christmas 1939 thanks to the intervention of Paul Eluard who pleaded his case personally with the appropriate minister.[131] In May, 1940, at the start of the German offensive, Ernst was again taken away, this time as a 'suspect', to an internment camp at Loriol (Drôme), then once again to Les Milles. When the collapse of the French army seemed imminent, the prisoners in Les Milles camp were sent in the direction of Bayonne, then rerouted to Nîmes, where the armistice set them free and Ernst was able to return to St. Martin d'Ardèche. Also interned at the Les Milles camp was Hans Bellmer, and together, despite the terrible physical conditions, they experimented graphically with decalcomania.[132] These expressions presumably helped buoy their spirits, and, on his return to St. Martin d'Ardèche, Ernst experimented further with this technique, producing paintings such as *Europe After the Rain*, and *Dream by a Young Girl about a Lake*.[133]

When Ernst returned home he found that Carrington had left the premises and had inadvertently turned over their house to an unscrupulous farmer from the village.[134] Yves Tanguy's wife, the American artist Kay Sage, asked Peggy Guggenheim to finance Ernst's passage to America. Guggenheim, who was in Grenoble shipping her newly acquired art collection back to the United States, had financed the passage to America of a number of other 'distinguished' Surrealists, including the entire Breton family. Ernst wrote to her, in a desperate attempt to recover the contents of his house, asking for 6000 francs and a letter for a lawyer testifying that she had seen the sculptures in his house and that they were worth at least 175,000 francs. Because Guggenheim had seen these sculptures reproduced in the periodical *Cahiers d'Art*, she complied with his request and recounts that he was able to get his paintings out of the farm at night.[135] Guggenheim recalled: 'Ernst had also written to tell me how Leonora had disappeared and that he thought she was in Spain and had gone mad. It all sounded very cold-blooded. Later I was to discover just how passionately he still felt about her.'[136] His future wife, Dorothea Tanning, was told later by her husband that all he found at their villa was a note hastily scrawled by Carrington before fleeing: 'Dear Max, I have gone with C. and will wait for you in Estremadura ...'[137]

Ernst came to Marseilles in December 1940; by that time he had spent roughly a year in and out of internment camps and was fearful that the Gestapo were after him. Marseilles had become crowded with antifascists from all over Europe who were desperately waiting at the port for passage out of Europe. The Vichy government became increasingly paranoid and its 'surrender on demand' law, which allowed it to deport aliens and other suspects with impunity, made Marseilles a dangerous place for Ernst to stay. He became a resident at the Villa Air Bel (nicknamed by its inhabitants the 'Villa Esper-visa'), a dwelling located in the suburbs of Marseilles where a number of Surrealists, among them Breton, were camped while waiting to leave. One of the many activities employed to keep the artists' spirits up were garden auctions; a 1941 photograph by André Gomes (Fig.27), who for two years recorded with snap-shots the residents of Air Bel, shows Jacques Hérold helping to hang paintings by Ernst and Carrington on a tree. Identifiable are Ernst's *The Attirement of the Bride* and an untitled decalcomania painting featuring Carrington, as well as Carrington's *Inn of the Dawn Horse* and *Portrait of Max Ernst*. The two paintings by Carrington were presumably rescued by Ernst along with his own work from their home and must not have been sold since he brought them with him to New York later.

When Guggenheim arrived in Marseilles, sometime in 1941, Ernst sold her a large portion of his artwork for her collection. Always attractive to women, Ernst found it easy to slip into casual sexual relationships, and she was no exception. In this case, given future events, there was perhaps an ulterior motive since he needed her money and her protection as an American citizen to guarantee his safe conduct to the United States. They travelled together, accompanied by her children, ex-husband (Laurence Vail) and others to a variety of cities in France, ending up ultimately in Lisbon, Portugal where they were to embark for New York. It was there that he was unexpectedly reunited with Carrington, but we will return to that later.

Down Below

Only 23 years old, disowned by her family, living in a foreign country with an illegal alien who was then forced to abandon her, and powerless against a terrifying and swiftly approaching war, it is understandable that Carrington lost her hold on reality and began to suffer a nervous breakdown. The account of this time in her life is inextricably interwoven with her written record of it entitled *En bas* (*Down Below*) from 1943 and can be supplemented by information obtained later from the artist. When Ernst was arrested and Carrington was left alone at their villa she found herself in such a terrible emotional state that she attempted to counteract it with periodic fasting and hard physical labour in the gardens and vineyards on their property. Towards the end of June 1940 an old British friend, Catherine Yarrow, arrived with her Hungarian companion, Michel Lukas. Alarmed by both the approaching Germans and Carrington's erratic behaviour they begged her to accompany them by car to Spain, where they hoped to secure a visa for Ernst in Madrid. During the course of this nightmarish journey Carrington became seized with growing anxiety and delusions that culminated finally in an episode in Madrid where she was apprehended by the police at the British embassy.[138] Through the intervention of her family she was ultimately incarcerated in a Spanish mental institution.[139] Diagnosed as marginally psychotic, she was treated and cured with three doses of the drug Cardiazol, which chemically induced convulsive spasms similar to electrical shock therapy. Over 50 years later Dr Luis Morales, the Spanish doctor who treated her at the Santander Mental Asylum, remembered his patient perfectly. He wondered if her diagnosis by the conventional Catholic doctors was influenced by her 'Surrealist' world-view, which stressed a disturbing belief in the magical, primitive and illogical, and rejected notions of a noble humanity and of civilisation in general. 'Surrealism was a prophylaxis' Morales asserted, and he wondered if Carrington, in 1941, was actually sane in her

28
Down Below
1941
Oil on canvas
40 x 60 cm/15¾ x 23½ in
Private collection

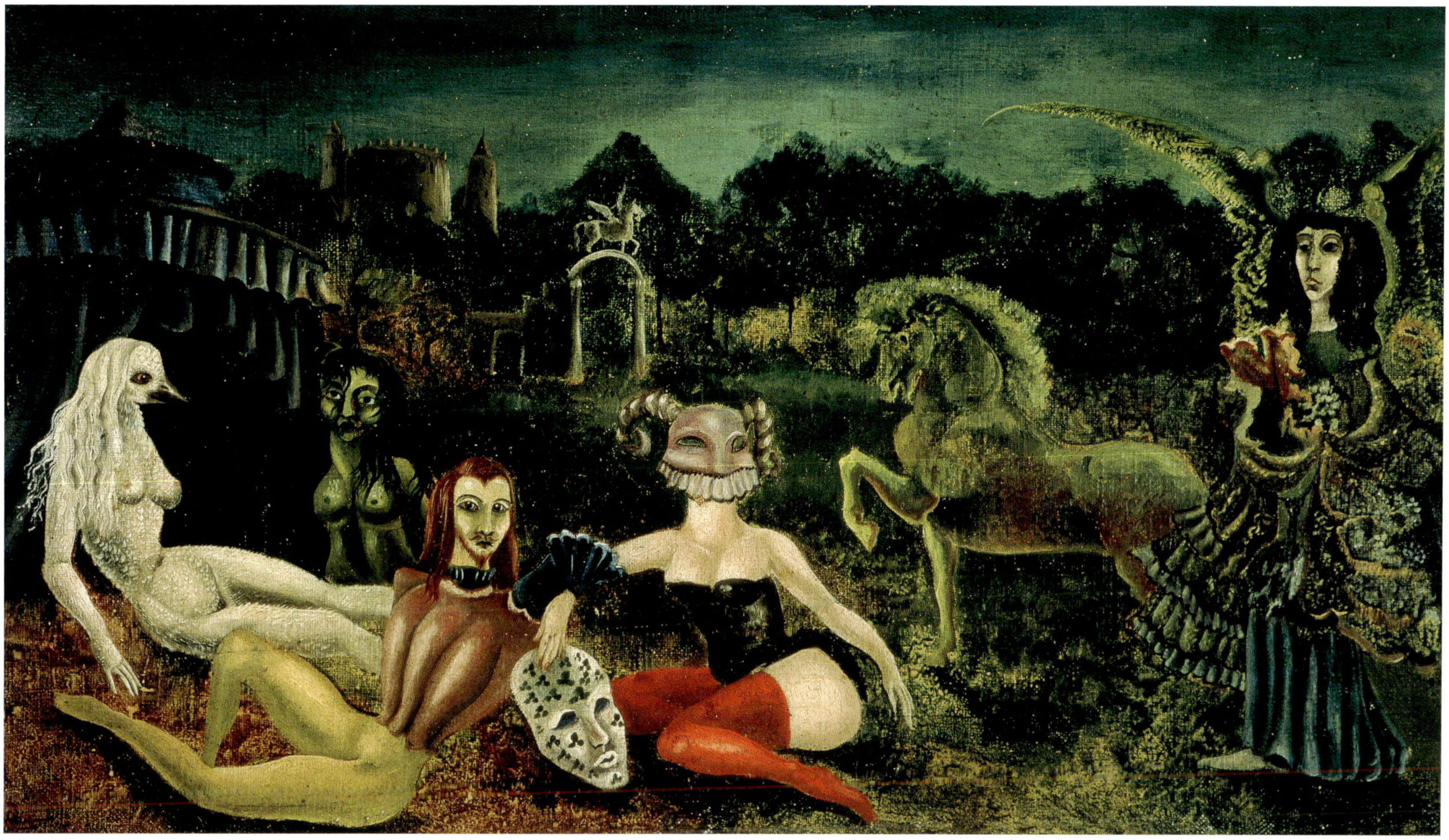

adaptation to society as it was at that time and if now she would even be classified as ill.[140]

With this harrowing experience Carrington's youth was formally at an end. She now saw herself as physically vulnerable, among other things: 'I suddenly became aware that I was both mortal and touchable and that I could be destroyed. I didn't think so before.'[141] The negative flip side of the naive *femme enfant* was revealed: psychological fragility and naivety were no match for the strains of separation and war. The following year in New York, Breton, excited by the artistic potentialities of Carrington's experience with madness, urged her to write about it. From his first *Manifesto of Surrealism* (1924) he had written on the societal injustice of the incarceration of the insane: 'We all know ... that the insane owe their incarceration to a tiny number of legally reprehensible acts and that, were it not for these acts their freedom (or what we see as their freedom) would not be threatened ... I could spend my whole life prying loose the secrets of the insane.'[142] As Chadwick explains:

> it was the research of the French psychiatrist Pierre Janet, with whom Breton had studied while a medical student, which provided Surrealism with a model for the sexual basis

> of ecstatic discourse. In his study of Hysteria, Janet called the ecstatic states of his female patients *l'amour fou,* or mad love; his vision became the basis for Breton's belief in the transformative power of the ecstatic state, at once erotic and irrational. Breton was content to maintain the identification of woman with this image of convulsive reality; once again, she completes the male vision by absorbing into herself those qualities that man recognizes as important but does not want to possess himself.[143]

Carrington may have found Breton's theories on women and madness disturbing, perceiving a gulf between his romantic vision of 'convulsive beauty' and the agony she experienced during her all too real Cardiazol-induced convulsions. At the very least she was aware of the safety of his position as voyeur and astutely commented: 'Not Breton or anyone has ever seen the inside of a Spanish madhouse. But I don't regret my life.'[144] Nevertheless, she did take his advice and wrote a short version of her experience, which was unfortunately never published and subsequently lost, during her move to Mexico.

While in the abandoned Russian Embassy in Mexico City, where she and other Surrealist refugees were temporarily living, she began to record it again in August 1943, on the third anniversary of her incarceration. Pierre Mabille, the surgeon and Surrealist intimate, was instrumental this time in its recreation. She met him at the home of the poet Benjamin Péret in Mexico and although still haunted by those painful memories, was convinced at his urgings to exorcise the experience. As Mabille tells it, he gave her a copy of his book *Mirror of the Marvellous*, which was a compilation of numerous folk traditions that focused on magic: 'By reading many folk stories she found again the same symbolic images that had been part of her own experience of insanity. She also found planetary and numerological symbols with which things, even the most insignificant ones, transformed into symbols because she had the habit of seeing them more transcendently than utilitarian.'[145]

This fact is critical to understanding the mythological tone of *Down Below*, which was conceptualised, apparently, immediately after reading *Mirror of the Marvellous* and which must have exerted some influence on her. First she talked it through with Mabille's wife, Jeanne Megnen, who later edited the original version, which was written in French and published in Paris by Editions Fontaine in 1946. Again, Mabille offers a crucial insight into her creative process:

> The reading of this book [*Mirror of the Marvellous*] made her start to think that a person should not try to repress themselves. She should exteriorize what she had gone through and examine what she could keep as valuable. Spotlight all that mess that was on her, keeping her in sorrow and anxiousness. In four days she wrote it, spent night and day straight and this explains the many mistakes and omissions in the text, important details are still unknown.[146]

Down Below was first published in English in the Surrealist journal *VVV* (no. 4, February 1944), in a translation by Victor Llona. Warner considers *Down Below* distinctive among Carrington's writings as lacking her characteristic dry sense of humour, which she attributes to its many transmutations – from oral to written and from French to English:

> It's as if, in her dementia, she vacated her own being, becoming for a while other, uttering in a different voice, to a different pace, using another sentence structure. Leonora herself, who has since studied Tibetan Buddhism, does not adhere to a classical Western notion of the fixed self and considers the person of *Down Below* another member of her disparate inner population. On a literary level, however, *Down Below* belongs more closely to the genre of autobiographical record advocated by Breton and practiced by him in both *Nadja* and *L'Amour fou*.[147]

29
Portrait of Dr. Morales
*c.*1943
Taken from the Surrealist periodical *VVV*, No.4, February 1944.
Drawing on paper

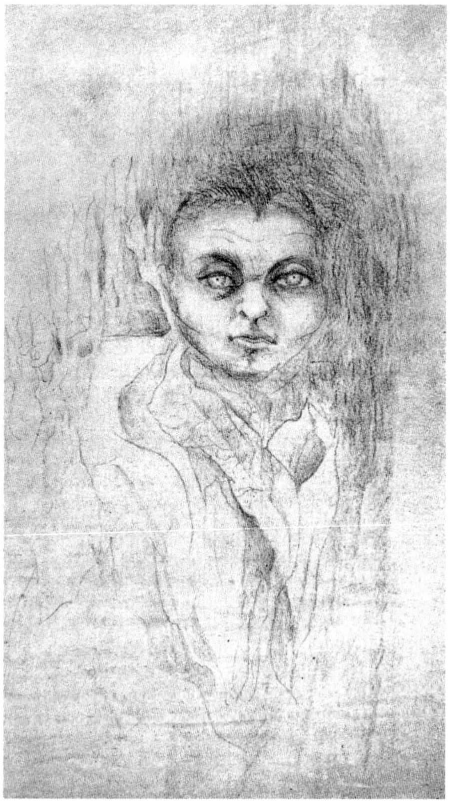

However, it differs radically from Breton's *Nadja* (1928), a rather detached account of a woman's descent into madness. Contrary to Breton's cherished images of women who, free from the restraints of logic, delve into a poetic realm of divination, Carrington's story is intensely personal, visceral and relentless in its litany of pain. *Down Below* was hailed as an almost clairvoyant glimpse into the very heart of madness while Carrington herself was viewed as a visionary victimised by the conformity of the medical establishment.

Written a full three years after her time at the asylum, Carrington had plenty of time to ruminate on this experience and to engage in further alchemical readings. In spite of its narrative structure, the many mystical references in *Down Below* form it into a kind of hermetic text similar, for example, to the famous alchemical allegory *The Chymical Wedding of Christian Rosenkreutz.*[148] Throughout *Down Below* alchemical references are mixed with Christian ones, a practice that persisted later in Mexico in her paintings. A good example of this melding, inevitable perhaps after all those years of Catholic schools, and also part and parcel of many alchemical texts, is this excerpt:

> With a few pieces of paper and a pencil José had given, I made calculations and deduced that the father was the planet Cosmos, represented by the planet Saturn: The son was the Sun and I the Moon, an essential element of the Trinity, with a microscopic knowledge of the earth, its plants and creatures. I knew that Christ was dead and done for, and that I had to take His place, because the Trinity, minus a woman and microscopic knowledge, had become dry and incomplete. Christ was replaced by the Sun. I was Christ on earth in the person of the Holy Ghost.[149]

Carrington has renamed Dr Luis Morales 'Don Luis' and throughout *Down Below* he acts as her tormentor, against whom she is powerless. *Portrait of Dr Morales* (Fig.29), an undated drawing by Carrington which I believe was executed in 1943 while writing *Down Below*, shows a sensitive young man whose face is etched against a sfumato background. The doctor's salient feature is his enormous, mesmerising eyes: 'I thought that the Moraleses were masters of the Universe, powerful magicians who made use of their power to spread horror and terror.'[150] This drawing was reproduced in *VVV* along with another, a 'map' of *Down Below* (Fig.30), a euphemism for the asylum, that displays further occult imagery. Suns, crescent moons and other planetary symbols abound, as well as gates, caves, spirals, orchards, crosses, snakes and coffin-like shapes – all the stuff of antique alchemical illustrations but executed in a loose, free-hand manner that eschews direct copying.

30
Map of Down Below
*c.*1943
Taken from the Surrealist periodical *VVV*, No.4, February 1944.
Drawing on paper

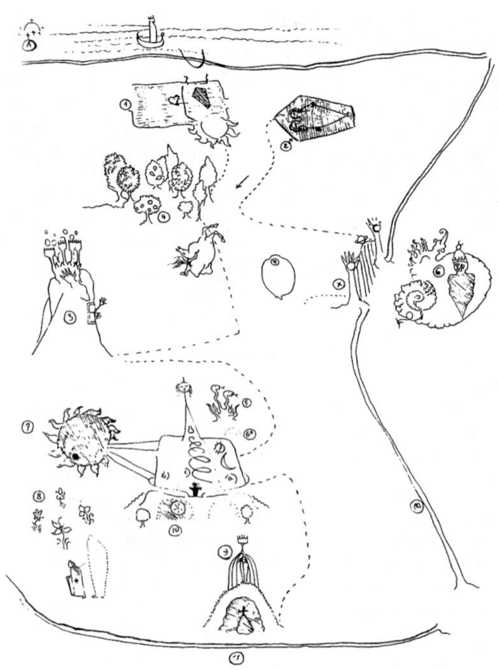

Of particular interest on this map is item number two, labelled 'Radiography' that marks the place where she received her distressing Cardiazol treatments. Here we see a coffin shape in which a body with two heads rests, the whole covered in parallel dark lines permitting an X-ray view into what is a solid and enclosed space, such as a casket with its lid on. For Carrington the Cardiazol treatments were agonising psychological torture that caused her to experience a dissolution of the ego: 'Have you an idea now of what the Great Epileptic Ailment is like? It's what Cardiazol induces. I learned later that my condition had lasted for ten minutes; I was convulsed, pitiably hideous, I grimaced and my grimaces were repeated all over my body.'[151] Was this 'treatment' to her a kind of death and thus the coffin image with its implications of transformation and resurrection?

Carrington also alludes to her personal boundaries by picturing the asylum at Santander as a map where the 'outside' world exists beyond the border of her 'inside' world, signified by a series of arcane symbols. In addition to its perimeters circumscribing the physical space of her internment, the internal pictographic elements also act as a diagram outlining the various components of her mental state. It is a liminal space, as is the text itself, where Carrington is painfully aware of vacillating between sanity and madness. In her article 'Beyond the Border: Leonora Carrington's Terrible Journey', Conley investigates the notion of mapping: 'This preoccupation with maps, with their precision, and with borders and liminal space betrays the healthy wish on Carrington's part to keep in mind the way back.'[152] Perhaps this is the original of Carrington's future visual preoccupation with the labyrinth and its implications of the confusing and multi-dimensional spaces one has slowly to find one's way out of. In light of this, a painting by the artist in 1941 entitled *Down Below* (Fig.28) must also allude to her experience in Santander, and may have been executed there or shortly after her release. Under a dark and brooding sky, which could be read as night-time, an assortment of characters convene within an enclosed garden that can be interpreted as the asylum, complete with the entry gate in the centre. The dark-haired woman with wings on the far right is Carrington who, led by a guardian white horse, approaches a group of reclining figures that could represent the other inmates, the institution orderlies, or both. They are a frightening cast of human and human/animal hybrid entities, reminiscent of Bosch in their pseudo-sexual intensity and hinting of medieval torture and nightmarish visions.

31
Group photograph of *Artists in Exile*, New York, 1942
Left to right, first row:
Stanley William Hayter, Leonora Carrington, Friedrich Kiesler, Kurt Seligmann.
Second row:
Max Ernst, Amédée Ozenfant, André Breton, Fernand Léger, Berenice Abbott.
Third row:
Jimmy Ernst, Peggy Guggenheim, John Ferren, Marcel Duchamp, Piet Mondrian
Courtesy, Philadelphia Museum of Art, collection of Mme Duchamp

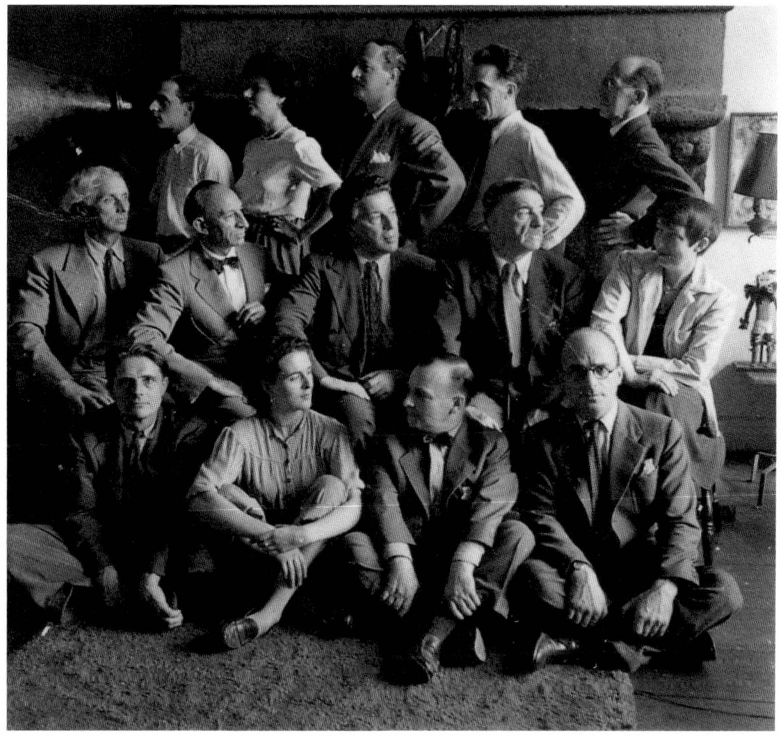

Down Below (the text) signalled Carrington's triumphal return to Surrealism, this time on her own terms, out from under the aegis of Ernst. In his *Anthology of Black Humor* Breton waxed enthusiastically: 'Michelet, who so beautifully did justice to the *Witch*, highlights among her gifts two that are invaluable, because granted only to women: "the illuminism of lucid madness" and "the sublime power of *solitary conception*"... Who today could answer that description better than Leonora Carrington?'[153] Such descriptions would haunt her painting career, for better or worse, for the rest of her life. A telling example is the 1948 brochure produced in conjunction with her one-person show at the prestigious Pierre Matisse Gallery in New York. It included an eight-page essay on the artist by the rich and eccentric British art collector Edward James, then one of her major patrons and promoters. James captions his essay with a quotation taken from Greek mythology that is meant to speak for Carrington: 'I am armed with madness for a long voyage.'[154]

Reunion with Ernst and departure to New York

As luck would have it, a distant cousin of Carrington's, Guillermo Gil, was a doctor in the medical hospital in Santander and, being family and a doctor, was granted permission to visit her. Intervening on her behalf he wrote to the British ambassador in Madrid to arrange her release and departure to England. She was sent to Madrid, accompanied by a nurse from the sanatorium, where she met with an official from Imperial Chemicals. While she was 'recuperating' in Santander, her family had made arrangements to send her to another mental institution in South Africa.[155] The nurse was sent back and Carrington was put on a train to Lisbon, Portugal, from where she would depart for South Africa. Her family placed her in the care of a guardian in the village of Estoril, a few miles from Lisbon. Under the pretext of needing to buy gloves, Carrington convinced her guardian to accompany her to Lisbon. On arrival she faked a stomach ache, asked to use a café lavatory and immediately ducked out of the back door. Hailing a cab, she went directly to the Mexican Embassy where she knew that her old friend Renato Leduc was the Mexican Ambassador.[156] Using his position as Ambassador, Leduc was able to offer her asylum; although in order to take her out of the country she would have to marry him. This way she would be under diplomatic immunity and so her parents could no longer commit her. She had always found Leduc sympathetic and the two formed an alliance built of friendship if not romantic love.

By an uncanny chance one day she ran into Ernst in a Lisbon market with his Guggenheim caravan. According to Peggy Guggenheim, Ernst was still in love with Carrington and very jealous of Leduc, whom he referred to derisively as an *homme inférieur*.[157] Next followed two emotionally volatile months

32
Brothers and Sisters Have I None
1942
Drawing on paper
Page from *First Papers of Surrealism*, exhibition catalogue, 14 October–7 November 1942. New York: Coordinating Council of French Relief Societies, Inc.
Alchemical drawing included by André Breton

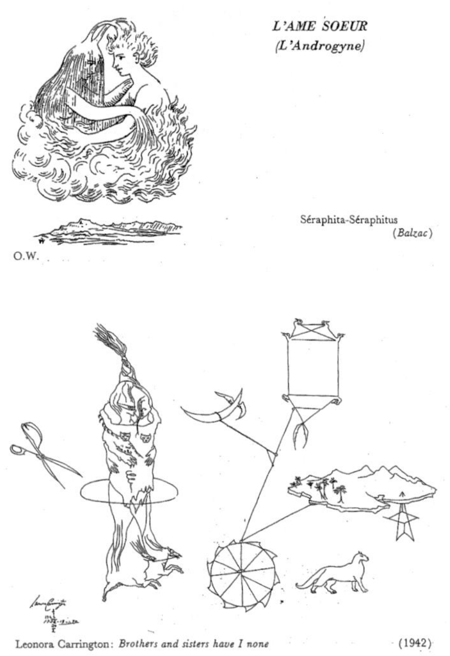

where, although married to Leduc, Carrington spent time with Ernst talking, drawing, riding horses, and in many ways resuming where they had left off, although Carrington maintains that their romantic relationship was over. When asked by Paul De Angelis if she felt confused by these events she replied: 'Yes, the situation was so ambiguous, everything was like an historical comedy, so absurd, like a soap opera.'[158] Although devastated over the loss of Ernst, she could not go back to him; Santander had changed her irrevocably. Ernst was also distraught over the loss of Carrington and constantly tried to persuade her to return to him. Nevertheless, he remained with Guggenheim whom, it was tacitly acknowledged, was necessary for his survival in those war-torn times. This state of affairs continued throughout 1941 until she and Leduc sailed for New York, just a few days before Ernst and Guggenheim did the same.

Surrealism in New York

In New York Carrington and Leduc lived on West 74th Street in Manhattan. Leduc worked for the Mexican Embassy in New York, while Carrington maintained close contact with the Surrealists. On a subway platform, Carrington ran into her old friend from the Ozenfant Academy, Stella Snead, and they would visit each other every day talking about cats, their old school friends, and art. She met Ernst in New York, again by chance, at the Pierre Matisse Gallery, although it was inevitable that their paths would cross sooner or later. She saw a lot of Breton and the filmmaker Luis Buñuel (whom she would later be close to in Mexico) and even her old teacher Ozenfant, who was now teaching and living in New York.

Masson, Chagall, Duchamp and many others were part of her social milieu, including Guggenheim and Ernst (who were married briefly in 1942): 'They had a grand mansion by the river in Sutton Place, where all the diplomats lived. Everyone gathered at Peggy's, she was very generous, always having parties.'[159] A remarkable 1942 group photograph (Fig.31) shows Leonora amidst other artists in exile. Highly staged, the three rows of individuals are arranged facing different directions alternately, while in the centre of the first row Carrington and Frederick Kiesler look at each other. Included in the photograph are, among others, Kurt Seligmann, Max and Jimmy Ernst, Peggy Guggenheim, Berenice Abbott, Amédée Ozenfant, André Breton, Fernand Léger, Marcel Duchamp and Piet Mondrian.

Max Ernst was still preoccupied with Carrington and hoped for a reconciliation, in spite of Guggenheim's jealousy: 'Leonora used to phone Max to come and take her to lunch.

Sometimes he would spend the whole day with her and they would wander around New York, something he never did with me. It made me wildly jealous and I suffered agonies.'[160] Jimmy Ernst recalled the effect that seeing Carrington had on his father:

> I don't recall ever again seeing such a strange mixture of desolation and euphoria in my father's face when he returned from his first meeting with Leonora in New York. One moment he was the man I remembered from Paris – alive, glowing, witty and at peace and then I saw in his face the dreadful nightmare that so often comes with waking. Each day that he saw her, and it was often, ended the same way. I hoped never to experience such pain myself, and I was at a loss of how to help him.[161]

To her credit, Guggenheim never let her personal feelings interfere with her admiration for Carrington as an artist, and in 1943 included her 1938 painting *The Horses of Lord Candlestick* (Fig.19) in *Exhibition by 31 Women* at her gallery Art of This Century.[162]

Carrington was suffering a sense of loss concerning Ernst as well and her autobiographical short story, 'Waiting', published in 1941 in the Surrealist magazine *VVV* does little to disguise the awkwardness and pain of her current situation.[164] Carrington also published stories in another American journal called *View*: 'White Rabbits' in 1 (1) (December 1941–January 1942) and 'The Sisters' in 1 (2) (February–March 1942). Later on, as a testament to Ernst's predilection for talented women and his generosity in promoting those talents, the March 1943 issue of *VVV* contained items on or by three of Ernst's most recent lovers. There was a photograph taken by Frederick J. Kiesler of Peggy Guggenheim seated in her new gallery, Art of This Century; Carrington had a short story 'The Seventh Horse' and a reproduction of her 1942 painting *La Dame ovale*; and finally Dorothea Tanning, his current lover, received the most attention with a short story 'Blind Date' and two paintings, *Birthday* and *Jeux d'enfants*.

Also in 1942 in New York, a Surrealist exhibition was organised in aid of French children and prisoners, held at the Co-ordinating Council of French Relief Societies at 451 Madison Avenue, called the Reid Mansion. In order to disguise the old-fashioned decor, Duchamp wove a giant spider's web made of miles of white twine, which stretched across the rooms like a giant labyrinth. Carrington's drawing, *Brothers and Sisters Have I None* and her painting *La Chasse* (both 1942) were shown in good company, for the exhibition included the work of many of the prominent artists of the day: Ernst, Tanguy, Magritte, Arp, Matta, Chagall, Giacometti, Lam, Delvaux, de Chirico, Oppenheim, Breton, Miró, Klee, Masson, Moore, Picasso, Brauner, Bellmer, Baziotes, Motherwell and Calder. The catalogue of the exhibition, designed by Duchamp, was called *First Papers of Surrealism*[164] and featured 'compensation-portraits', his solution to the unavailability of photographs for many of the artists. Anonymous documentary images were used in lieu of photographs of the artists: Carrington's was a Works Progress Administration photograph of a gaunt female sharecropper by Walker Evans.

The title for Carrington's drawing, *Brothers and Sisters Have I None* (Fig.32), comes from an old Irish riddle that plays upon one's own reflection in the mirror.[165] Combining her love of word play and children's rhymes, this sharp line-drawing contains a fascinating grouping of iconographic elements. The composition is roughly broken into two parts, with elements flowing into each other or connected together in an organic yet illogical way exemplifying the best of automatism. The right section shows a wheel with spokes edged with flames, reminiscent of the sun symbols in the *Down Below* map, connected to this by two lines are: on the right an island pierced by a pentagram (five-pointed star), and on the left string are a kite with bird heads, and a crescent moon with wings; a striding feline, perhaps a panther, is autonomous in the lower right corner. On the lower left side is an embracing couple held aloft on two horses galloping through the air. Above, their hair is twisted and knotted together, around them is a feline skin complete with claws and two heads, in the centre of which is a spiral, again like that found in the *Down Below* map. In minute handwriting, above the left claw, are words that can roughly be made out to say 'This is past, is past.' Around the hips of the couple, where they are most symbolically joined, is a circle; a huge scissor on the left is approaching, to sever their connection. Under her signature on the lower left corner are some calculations, which appear to be numerological. A cross between a personal drawing and a hermetic diagram, the details coalesce to chart an inner topography, one concerned with the loss of love, change, and the mysterious workings that may have caused them. Throughout the catalogue Breton, as a kind of annotation, provided his own mythological correlations next to certain works of art: Carrington is associated with the 'Soul-Sister' and the page with this drawing is labelled as such.[166] Under 'L'âme soeur' Breton has placed, in parenthesis 'L'Androgyne' and a few lines below that 'Séraphita-Séraphitus' and under that in parenthesis 'Balzac'. This last item refers to his *Seraphita* (1834), a metaphysical novel concerning an angel, half-man/half-woman, going through its final earthly transformation in Norway, which opens with a disclaimer that it was written by a Rosicrucian adept.[167] As if to illustrate this point, as well as his other headings, Breton has included on the upper left an alchemical drawing showing the combining of water and fire visualised as an embracing woman and man. By doing this Breton excavates Carrington's alchemical symbolism, albeit in a much more direct and pedagogical manner.[168]

Some of Carrington's eccentric behaviour while in New York became the stuff of legend, lent more notice perhaps because of her recent bout with madness. One often-told story has her inexplicably and calmly spreading mustard on her feet while at a restaurant.[169] Another anecdote, recounted by the film-maker Luis Buñuel in his autobiography *My Last Sigh* shows that Carrington's experiences in Spain were still fresh in her psyche:

> Separated now from Max Ernst, Leonora apparently lived with a Mexican writer named Renato Leduc. One day, when we arrived at the house of a certain Mr. Reiss for our regular meeting, Leonora suddenly got up, went into the bathroom, and took a shower – fully dressed. Afterward, dripping wet, she came back into the living room, sat down in an armchair, and stared at me. 'You're a handsome man,' she said to me in Spanish, seizing my arm. 'You look exactly like my warden'.[170]

Other stories involve her dinner parties with their elaborate feasts made from archaic recipes, bordering on the inedible. Like her practical jokes at St. Martin d'Ardèche, cooking was associated with art production, and she would elaborate on this practice later in Mexico. Breton recalled these gastronomic experiments:

> Of all those whom she invited to her home in New York, I believe I was the only one to try certain dishes on which she had spent hours and hours of meticulous preparation, an English cookbook from the sixteenth century in hand – compensating by sheer intuition for the lack of certain ingredients that had become unobtainable or exceedingly rare since then. (I will admit that a hare stuffed with oysters, to which she obliged me to do honor for the benefit of all those who had preferred to content themselves with its aroma, induced me to space out those feasts a bit.)[171]

The March–April 1942 issue of *View* was devoted to Max Ernst concurrent with his one-person show at the Valentine Gallery where some 30 of his paintings (from 1937–42) were on view.[172] The issue contained a reproduction of Carrington's 1939 painting *Portrait of Max Ernst* together with her text 'The Bird Superior: Max Ernst'. This one-page essay, which brings together one last time their shared iconography of the horse and the bird, can be construed as a goodbye tribute to the man who had changed her life irrevocably. It also acts as a segue to future themes she would elaborate upon in Mexico, for here she introduces the kitchen and the magical cauldron of transformation:

> Love-Birds, Night Birds, Birds of Paradise and Devil-Birds are all clasped in each other's wings in the Subterranean Kitchen of The Bird Superior. He stirs his pot in the shape of a man and watches his bare arms hypnotically while overhead droves of houseflies and bluebottles, perched on the hanging joints of meat, teach their young to fly.[173]

The haunting tale ends with a fierce dream of mystical union and love eternal, a dream from which she had awoken long ago:

> The Bird Superior preens his arms which have now become wings, unties Fear from the fire and ties himself on her back with her mane. They escape through the four winds which leap out of the pot like smoke, like hair, like wind. Only seven little fishes like eyeless zebras lie suffocating on the fire in the bottom of the big black pot.[174]

Although Carrington was productive in New York, writing and painting, eventually Leduc tired of the city and wanted to return to Mexico. The emotional drain on Guggenheim caused by Leonora's presence had been wearing: 'Max was so insane about Leonora that he really could not hide it ... He always protested and said he was no longer in love with Leonora, and that I was the person he wanted to live with and sleep with. But I was never reassured and I was very happy when she went to Mexico.'[175] Her romantic victory in the form of Carrington's departure was to be short-lived, however, since Max would take up with yet another *femme enfant* in 1943, the American painter Dorothea Tanning.

33

Les Distractions de Dagobert

1945

Egg tempera on masonite

74.9 x 86.7 cm/29½ x 34 in

Private collection

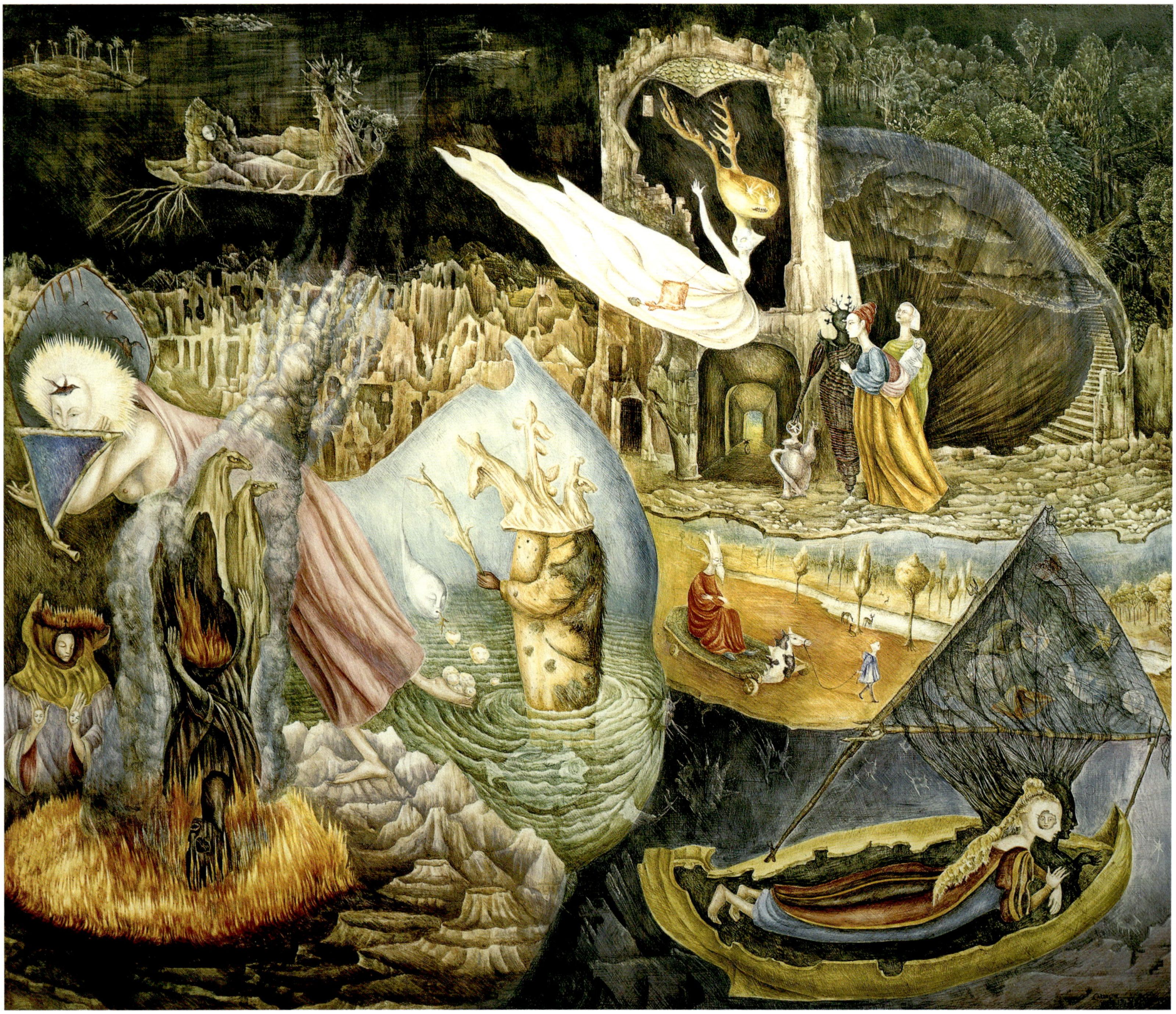

CHAPTER 4 THE ALCHEMICAL KITCHEN: DOMESTIC SPACE AS SACRED SPACE

Mexico and Surrealism

Moving to Mexico in 1943 provided Carrington with another chance to transform her life. Liberated from the constraints of her relationship with Ernst, far from the controlling machinations of her father and Imperial Chemicals, and immersed in a new country rich with dynamic cultural and religious hybrids, she was now positioned to develop her creative visions in a manner that would ultimately lead to artistic recognition and success. Although when she first arrived she was still recuperating from the traumatic events of her stay in Santander, she would come to terms with them by writing *Down Below*. Emotionally and psychologically vulnerable at this point, Carrington was fortunate to be welcomed into the existing émigré Surrealist community living in Mexico City, and through their support and encouragement was able to achieve a new kind of personal and creative autonomy. Mexico's leftist government under President Lázaro Cárdenas del Río (1934–40) instituted a generous policy towards European war refugees and granted asylum and citizenship to those who made it to their country.[176] One of the reasons that Mexico became such a popular sanctuary for artists was that the government did not pry into their previous political backgrounds; consequently, Mexico City had a significant émigré community of artists and writers.[177] As Janet Kaplan notes, Mexico was unique in its generosity considering that most other countries were enacting increasingly restrictive laws to limit immigration. More remarkable still was that many of these émigrés were Spanish while this post-revolutionary country was celebrating its indigenous roots, not its colonial Spanish heritage. Breton and his wife Jacqueline Lamba had travelled to Mexico in April 1938 to deliver lectures and to meet the exiled Leon Trotsky, who was then living with the Riveras. Dubbing Mexico the 'Surrealist place *par excellence*'[178] he enthusiastically elaborated on the country further in his 1939 article 'Souvenir du Mexique' in *Minotaure* and in a booklet entitled *Mexique* published that same year.[179] During this trip he became enchanted with Frida Kahlo and wrote the introduction for the brochure that accompanied her New York debut at the Julien Levy Gallery in 1938. In Mexico the influence of the muralist movement was waning and artists such as Antonio Ruiz, Julio Castellanos, Rufino Tamayo and María Izquierdo were exploring fantasy, folklore, myth and self-portraits that utilised personal allegories. Although to a European eye these works may have superficially resembled those of Surrealism, the Mexican art historian Ida Rodríguez-Prampolini defines them instead as 'fantastic' and reflective of a world-view that incorporates elements of the unexpected.[180] In 1940 Surrealism was officially introduced to Mexico in a show called the *International Surrealism Exhibition*. Held at the Galería de Arte Mexicano in Mexico City, the exhibition was jointly organised by Breton and two influential émigrés who had moved to Mexico in 1939: the Austrian-born artist Wolfgang Paalen and the Peruvian painter and poet César Moro, who had already spent many years in Paris where he participated in Surrealist circles. The cover displayed a photograph by the Mexican Manuel Alvarez Bravo but the exhibition itself was clearly divided into a European and Mexican section, with Rivera and Kahlo, at their own request, placed in the European section.[181] The reasons for this division reflected the complex politics surrounding European–Mexican artistic relations at that time that resulted in a hesitancy on the part of most Mexican artists (other than Rivera and Kahlo) to align themselves with a European-based movement.[182] As Kahlo wryly pointed out: 'I never knew I was a Surrealist until André Breton came to Mexico and told me I was ...'[183]

Carrington and Leduc moved into the old centre of Mexico City and their apartment on Rosa Moreno was in the abandoned Russian Embassy building that, although in partial ruin, possessed aspects of its past grandeur. Just a few blocks away lived her two new friends, the French poet

top:
34
Leonora Carrington and Emerico 'Chiki' Weisz at their wedding, Mexico City, 1946
Photograph: Kati Horna
© Kati Horna Foundation

bottom:
35
Leonora Carrington and Chiki Weisz on their wedding day, Mexico City, 1946
To the right of Carrington are Benjamin Péret and Miriam Wolf.
In back row are Gerardo Lizarraga, José Horna, Remedios Varo, and Günther Gerzo.
Photograph: Kati Horna
© Kati Horna Foundation

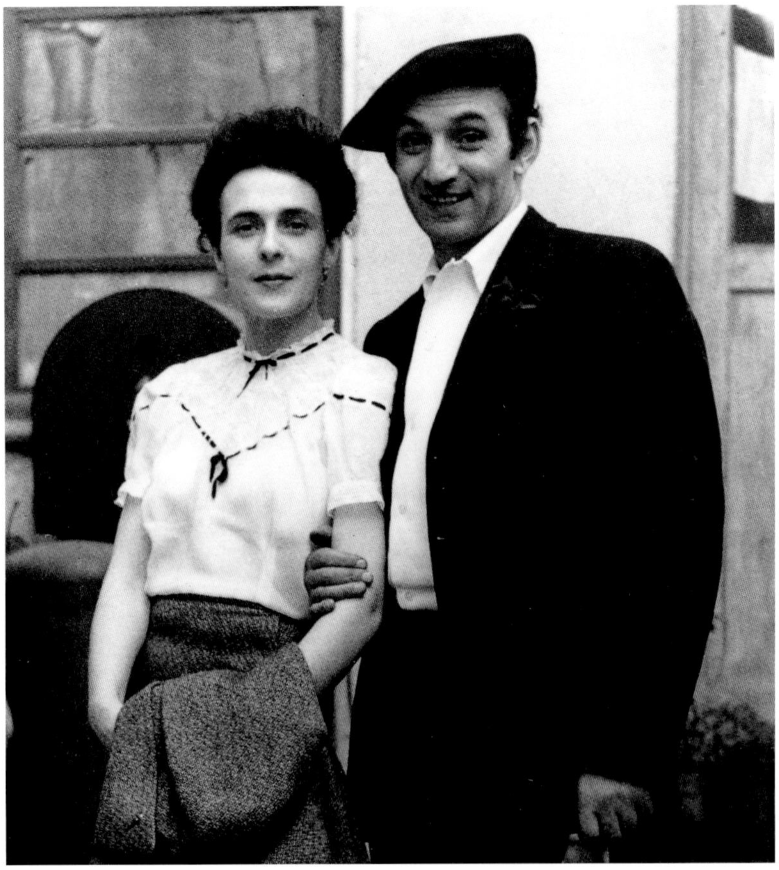

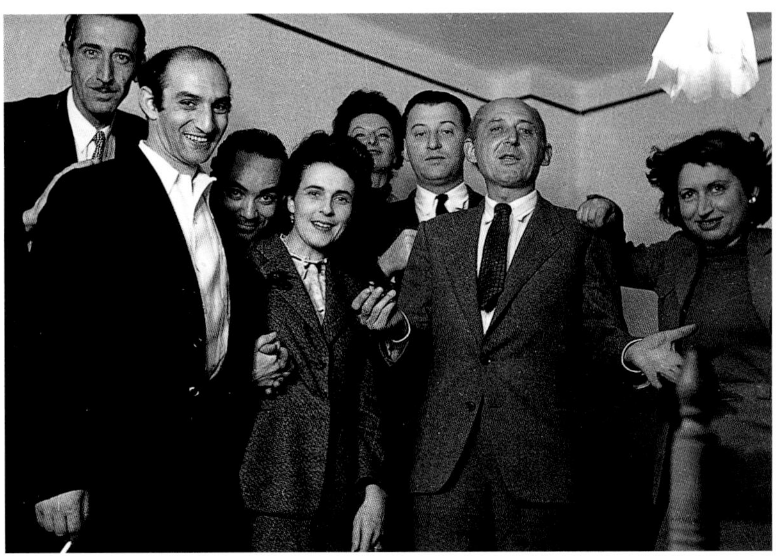

Benjamin Péret and his Spanish companion Remedios Varo, who had arrived in 1941. Carrington's wider circle of friends, however, included both Mexican and European artists, as she recalled:

> There was also Remedios, Péret, Octavio Paz, Diego Rivera, and for a little while Frida Kahlo. Diego and I would every now and then see [José Clemente] Orozco. Diego and Frida got remarried and I helped with the wedding. It was a huge party. I had a long conversation with Diego who told me a lot of gossip. He was very animated; he was a lot of fun, full of life, exuberant. But Frida was going through a rough patch, she was becoming seriously ill so I barely saw her.[184]

Once back in Mexico, Leduc became immersed with toreadors and politicians in the social life he had left behind, and their three-year marriage of convenience came to an end. After Carrington and Leduc were divorced she met Emerico 'Chiki' Weisz, through Péret and Varo, and they were married in 1946. The photojournalist Weisz was a friend of Breton and had arrived in Mexico together with other war refugees on a Portuguese ship that had departed from Casablanca. A Hungarian Jew, Chiki had been deeply marked by his wartime experiences, walking across Europe to escape the Nazis. Photographs taken at their wedding party (Figs 34 and 35), by another Hungarian émigrée and close friend, the photographer Kati Horna, shows Carrington and Chiki surrounded by friends and fellow artists, such as Péret, Varo, the Mexican-born but European-educated painter Günther Gerzso, José Horna – husband to Kati and a Spanish sculptor – and the Spaniard Gerardo Lizarraga (Varo's ex-husband).

Many of the émigré artists maintained contact with the art world outside of Mexico. Interested in ethnography and Amerindian art, Paalen founded the magazine *Dyn* (1942–4) and his circle, including his wife the French painter Alice

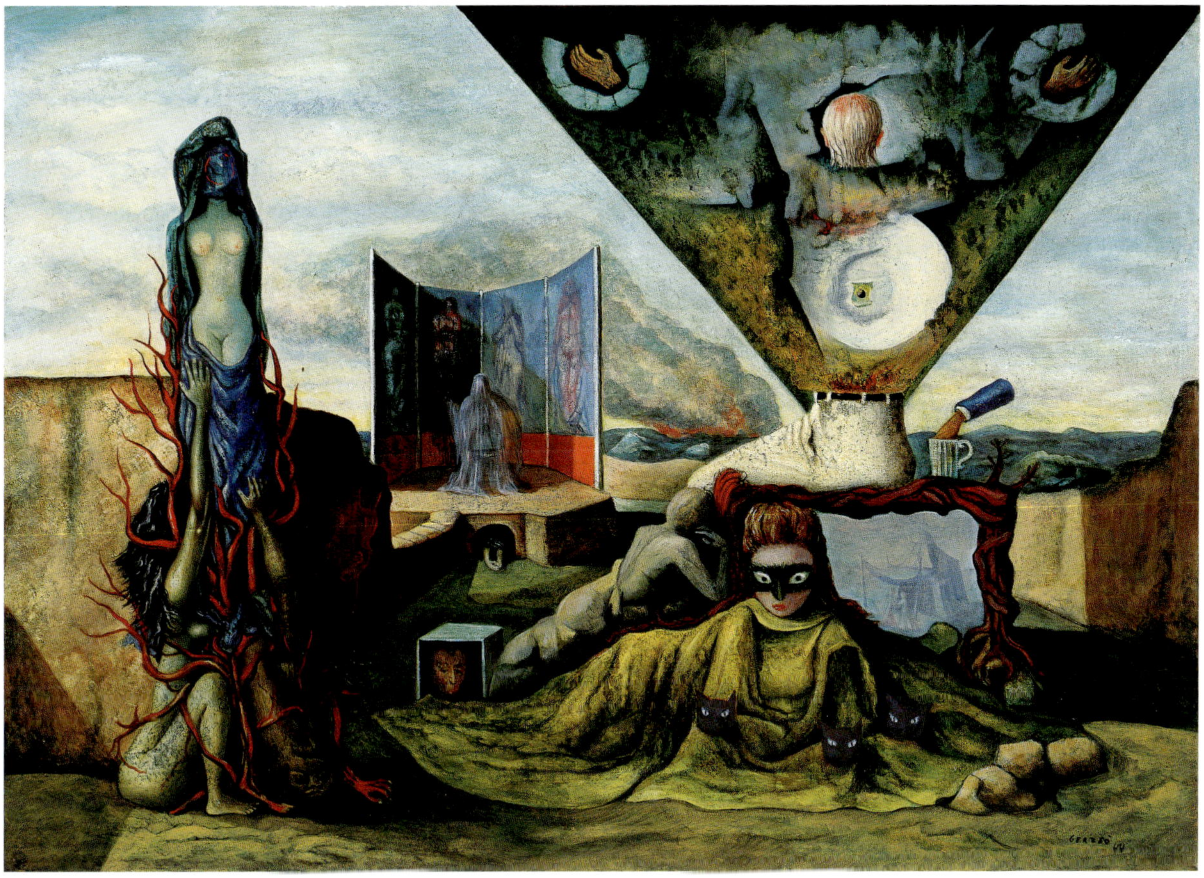

36
Günther Gerzso
The Days of Gabino Barreda Street
1944
Oil on canvas
40.6 x 55.5 cm/16 x 22 in
Private collection

Rahon, had strong Surrealist affiliations. *Dyn* had a wide distribution and became influential to Surrealists and Abstract Expressionists in New York, although in Mexico he distanced himself from Breton's more dogmatic positions and began to eschew the descriptive and metaphysical in his own work. Carrington aligned herself with Péret's circle, partially because she preferred its less formal atmosphere, but primarily due to her burgeoning friendship with Varo. Varo was a strong force in this group and who, despite the hard living conditions, was able to keep spirits up with her sense of play and spontaneity. Sawin expounds on the role of Varo: 'It was Remedios who was the principal support of the household, finding work as a decorator of furniture, a costume designer, a builder of small dioramas, and an illustrator of promotional literature for the Bayer pharmaceutical company.[185] Although Varo and Carrington had met briefly in France, their friendship now became central to Carrington's creative life: 'Remedios' presence in Mexico changed my life.'[186]

In spite of the cross-cultural stimulation clearly experienced and enjoyed between the Mexican and the European artists, socially the two groups kept some distance.[187] Freed from the traditional mores of home, united by a perilous poverty, and sharing a degree of cultural isolation (more so for those who did not speak Spanish), the émigré Surrealists formed a close-knit group that was characterised by a high level of intellectual stimulation and creative experimentation. Their social gatherings continued in spirit the sense of play and fun of those they had left behind in Europe and New York. There were costume parties, provocative all-night story-tellings, Surrealist games, practical jokes, and on occasion a fantastical meal prepared by Carrington and Varo. The unofficial headquarters of these events was Péret's and Varo's apartment on the calle Gabino Barreda which, although dilapidated, was filled with a marvellous array of artwork by Picasso, Tanguy, Ernst and others that they had managed to bring with them. An early painting by Gerzso, a frequent visitor and comrade, *The Days of Gabino Barreda Street* (1944) (Fig.36), is a Surrealist-style portrayal of the goings-on there. Varo crouches on the floor surrounded by cats and looking like one, Esteban Francés plays guitar in the background, Péret sits at a table while his disembodied head floats in the clouds and Gerzso portrays himself peering out at the scene from a small box. To the far left, Carrington's 'dual' portrait is composed of a crouching nude woman (entangled in leafy vines) who holds aloft a female nude torso with her head draped. The effect is semi-monstrous and grotesque and her covered face and nude torso also seem reminiscent of Ernst's decalcomania paintings of Carrington. Although Gerzso would gradually veer from Surrealism stylistically, developing a unique architectonic abstraction, he and Carrington would remain close friends for many decades.

Varo and Carrington formed an intense friendship and artistic partnership that enabled them to develop a new pictorial language. Carrington responded strongly to the magical atmosphere of Varo's home on the Gabino Barreda, filled with cats and her specially placed talismans of stones, shells and crystals. 'Meeting almost daily for years, they shared their dreams, their nightmares, their obsessions, and their deepest secrets.'[188] Kaplan goes on to explain: 'Varo and Carrington shared an intensity of imaginative power that each found in no one else.' Varo served as a model for the Spanish character, Carmella Velásquez, in Carrington's novel *The Hearing Trumpet* completed in 1950, but not published until 1976.[189] According to Carrington, when they first met, Varo was painting in an abstract style that, over the course of their relationship, changed to figuration and explored many of the same subjects as those in her work. However, any thematic similarities between Carrington's and Varo's paintings are overshadowed by their distinctive styles, colour palettes and paint handling.[190]

Together they began to experiment with cooking and, with a penchant for experiment and a taste for the ludicrous, they conducted pseudoscientific investigations using the kitchen as their laboratory.[191] Cooking, always important for Carrington, became one of their avenues for exploration into the occult:

> Using cooking as a metaphor for hermetic pursuits they established an association between women's traditional roles and magical acts of transformation. They had both been interested in the occult, stimulated by the Surrealist belief in 'occultation of the Marvelous' and by wide reading in witchcraft, alchemy, sorcery, Tarot and magic. They found Mexico a fertile atmosphere where magic was part of daily reality; traveling herb salesmen would set up on street corners with displays of seeds, insects, chameleons, special candles, seashells, and neatly wrapped parcels with such mysterious labels as 'sexual weakness:' all used for the practice of witchcraft by the *curanderas* (healers), *brujas* (witches), and *espiritualistas* (spiritualists) who outnumbered doctors and nurses. Mexico proved a vibrant influence on Varo and Carrington, for whom the power of spells and omens was already very real.[192]

Mexico's markets deeply impressed Carrington with their antiquity and breadth of commodities: 'I always liked markets, Mexican markets, it goes back to the start of humanity, the

37
Chiki, ton pays
1947
Oil on canvas
90 x 60 cm/35½ x 23½ in
Private collection

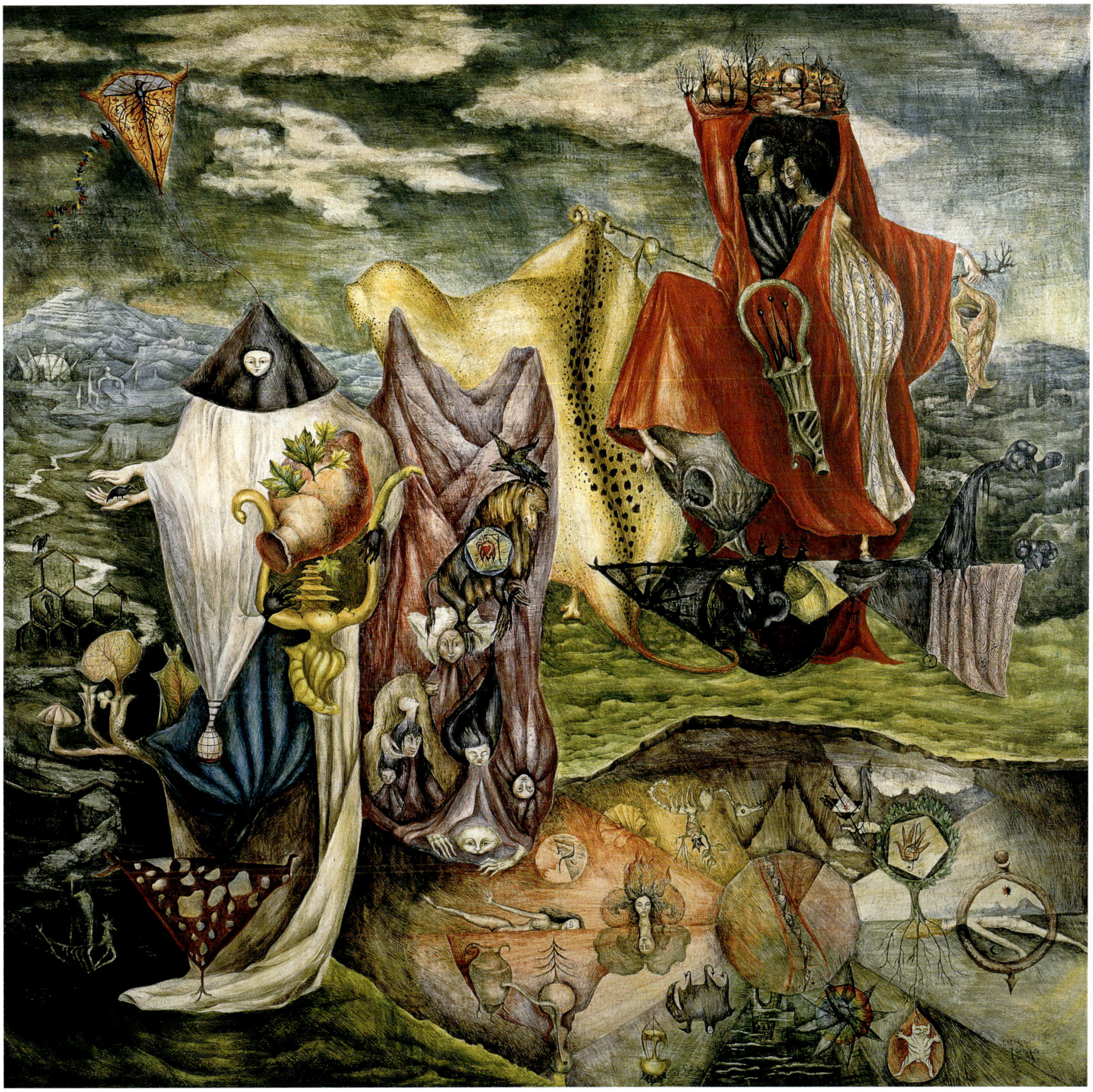

38
Mujeres Conciencia
1972
Offset
71 x 48.5 cm/28 x 19 in
Private collection
Courtesy of Galerias Grimaldi
Photo credit: Artechnia

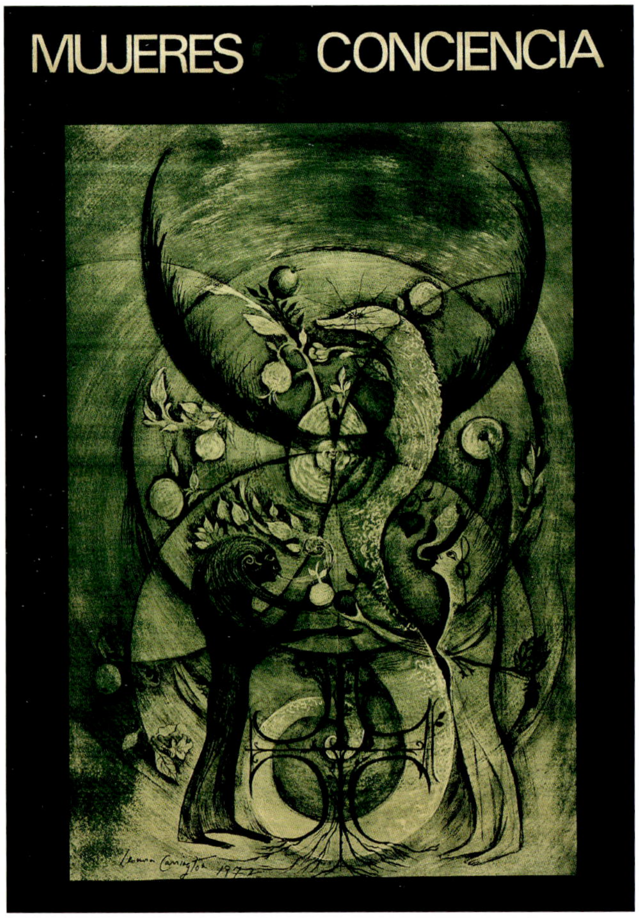

marketplace. In Mexico they used to sell what they called the "delicious little fruit of the gods" and they were people they were going to eat afterwards, you know, good looking young people, males and females who were sold in the market.'[193] She also became acquainted with the traditions of Mexican healers: 'I used to go to the *curandero* ... they are people who have a knowledge of herbs and the medicine that goes back to ancient times and of course at night they do witchcraft but that's up to whether you believe it or not.'[194] An aspect of Mexican culture that the Surrealists relished in particular, and which would catalyse Carrington into mixing cultures in her work, was the paradoxical intermingling of the colonial Spanish with the surviving pre-Hispanic Indian culture. Remnants of earlier Mesoamerican worship were embedded in the nation's Catholicism, and the Surrealists found the physical manifestations of this, such as in the decor of churches, subversive.[195] Carrington befriended the Mexican anthropologist Ignacio Bernal, Director of the Institute of Anthropology, and together they visited many archaeological sites where she became acquainted with the rich myths and images of pre-Columbian civilisations such as the Aztec goddess Coatlicue and the war god Huitzilopochtli. Her initial response was mixed; although Mexico seemed extraordinarily exotic, particularly the indigenous people and their customs, she was also repelled by the ancient practice of human sacrifice. Reflecting on the effect Mexico's past has on her psyche, Carrington has said: 'Once you cross the border and you arrive in Mexico you feel that you are coming to a place that's haunted.'[196]

Public reception in the 1940s and 1950s

It was not until Carrington had relocated to and settled down in Mexico that she began to receive notice for her painting. She had been living there for five years when in 1947 the London-based periodical *Horizon* discussed her in two separate issues. In January she had a brief, nevertheless significant, mention in Victor Serge's 'Letter from Mexico':

> After several years of hesitation ... Carrington has resumed her writing and painting, in a narrow little room in old Mexico, the most dream saturated place I know here. Her present work, clearly revealing the influence of the Primitives, is, in my opinion, an astonishing example of the direct projection on to canvas of an intense, anguished, yet luminously adolescent inner life.[197]

In the August issue Gustav Regler's article 'Four European Painters in Mexico' presented two pages of glowing and astute praise, accompanied by two reproductions of Carrington's work.[198] Carrington next appears in the catalogue published in conjunction with the Bel Ami International Art Competition, which consisted of eleven paintings by American and European artists submitted in competition to be featured in the Loew-Lewin[199] film based on Guy de Maupassant's novel *The Private Affairs of Bel Ami*.[200] The subject to be portrayed was The Temptation of St Anthony, and Max Ernst won first prize. Next to an illustration of her entry was a page explaining the painting by the artist at her humorous best along with a brief biographical paragraph accompanied by a photograph of her.

Aside from the Galería de Arte Mexicano in Mexico City, owned and operated by the legendary Inés Amor, there were few venues at the time in Mexico for artists to exhibit their work, and the art scene as it existed in New York and other urban centres in Europe was non existent. Carrington and other artists in her Mexican circle often looked to New York to show their work – to galleries such as Knoedler, Levy and Pierre Matisse who promoted their work. In letters written in 1944 by Péret and Esteban Francés, Carrington's work is mentioned as being impressive, proving once again that Carrington was perceived as being an artist in her own right, not dismissed as a peripheral talent or a companion to a male artist.[201] It was Francés who introduced the English art collector Edward James to Carrington and it was he who arranged for her substantial one-person show (27 works) at the Pierre Matisse Gallery in New York in 1948, which included a small brochure. Now one of Carrington's major patrons and promoters, James wrote an eight-page essay on the artist, and the exhibition was briefly reviewed in *Time* and *Art News*.[202] Later that same year she was the only woman included in a group exhibition at Pierre Matisse, called *Carrington, Chagall, Dubuffet, Giacometti, Lam, MacIver, Matta, Miro, Tamayo, Tanguy* with a painting reproduced in the brochure.[203] Her painting, *The Giantess* (also called *The Guardian of the Egg*), appeared in conjunction with a story by Jean Malaquais ('Day One') in the January 1949 issue of *Town & Country* magazine.

Chadwick has stated that neither Carrington nor Varo ever believed that they would have professional careers and that furthermore Carrington told her: 'I painted for myself. I never believed that anyone would exhibit or buy my work.'[204] This was a rather telling pronouncement on the part of Carrington since she had early on received recognition for both her written and visual work and always thought of herself as a professional artist worthy of an active career. Such low expectations, for Carrington at least, were most certainly based on what she perceived as a pervasive gender bias, but she continued to work at a prodigious pace regardless. An early and staunch feminist, Carrington has repeatedly and adamantly voiced what she perceived as the difficulties and challenges facing women pursuing a career in the arts in terms of securing shows, finding the time to work while raising children and running a household, and in being taken seriously by a patriarchal art world. (An outspoken advocate for women's rights in Mexico, in 1972 she designed a poster promoting women's liberation entitled *Mujeres Conciencia*. Carrington believes that it is the lack of opportunities available for women that often cause them to stifle their talents.)

In February 1950 Leonora was given her first one-person show in Mexico at Clardecor, an interior design showroom in Mexico City which served as her introduction to a Mexican audience: 'After the Matisse Gallery show, the critics mentioned me. Inés Amor, the owner of a gallery [Galería de Arte Mexicano] took an interest in me thanks to the press, and she provided a lot of publicity for me.'[205] A veritable avalanche of positive reviews followed in the Mexican press raving about her technique, mysterious subjects, Renaissance influences, and so on, and many carried reproductions of her work and even photographs of the artist from the opening.[206] *Novedades* declared it 'one of the most important events of our artistic life'[207] while the *Excélsior* announced that although Carrington was British and had lived in Mexico for a while: 'her temperament is not of one who is limited by geographic environment, but the world in which she breathes is one of extraordinary amplitude.'[208] Indeed, the importance of Inés Amor's support and guidance cannot be over-emphasised. Soon she would take Carrington into her Galería de Arte Mexicano where for many decades she provided the artist with exhibitions, patrons and some degree of financial security. The two women became close friends and Leonora would come to trust Amor's astute judgement and critical eye. Through the Galería de Arte Mexicano, Carrington also came into contact with contemporary Mexican artists that she admired, in particular Antonio Ruiz.

She had a number of French publications during the 1950s: her short story *Une Chemise de nuit de flanelle* was printed in 1951 by Librairie les Pas perdue; the stories 'La Chameau de sable' and 'La Mouche de Monsieur Gregoire' were both included in the 1953 issue of *Bizarre* (no.2); and in 1957 'L'Homme neutre' was included in *Le Surrealisme même*. In 1955 Donald Cordry, the Mexican folk-art specialist, reported on Carrington's experiments in weaving in *Craft Horizons* as part of his 'Mexico Weaves' article,[209] and in 1957 a small brochure was printed for her exhibition at Galería de Antonio Souza in Mexico City, 'Tapices de Leonora Carrington'. In 1958 one of her paintings was included in an exhibition at the Contemporary Arts Museum in Houston entitled *The Disquieting Muse: Surrealism*, but only written details and no illustration appear in the catalogue. In 1959 she received mention in the *News* (an English-language newspaper published in Mexico City) for her stage sets and costumes in a production of Shakespeare's *The Tempest*. The decade ended with Marcel Jean including her in his survey *The History of Surrealist Painting* published in New York by Grove Press in 1959. Jean doesn't just mention her in passing but respectfully discusses her origins, relationship with Max Ernst, her mental breakdown and the ensuing *Down Below*, and ends with her relocation to and work in Mexico.

The alchemical kitchen

Supported by her new artistic partnership with Varo, and stimulated by living in Mexico, Carrington embarked on a series of paintings that displayed new directions of interest and technique. Chiki and Leonora had two sons, Gabriel (born in 1946) and Pablo (born in 1948), and in addition to her Surrealist activities she now found herself being a mother of two and running a household. Although there were challenges, this in no way diminished her creative output. Motherhood was a profoundly positive experience for Carrington; however, she objected to the workload that fell on women with child rearing:

> I always continued to paint, even when the children were very small. Only when they were ill I dropped everything and my children became my priority. But often I said to my friend Remedios: 'We need a wife, like men have, so we can work all the time and somebody else would take care of the cooking and the children.' Yes, men are really spoiled![210]

It was at this time that she became preoccupied in her work with the transformation of the feminine domestic sphere into a site of magical power, specifically through a correspondence between food preparation, magic and painting. Carrington began a full exploration into different mythological and esoteric traditions and the inclusion of certain symbols in her paintings served to elevate the homey everyday into the realms of the sacred. The transit of food from the kitchen to the table to consumption was, in particular, likened to

39
The House Opposite
1945
Tempera on panel
33 x 82 cm/13 x 32½ in
Private collection

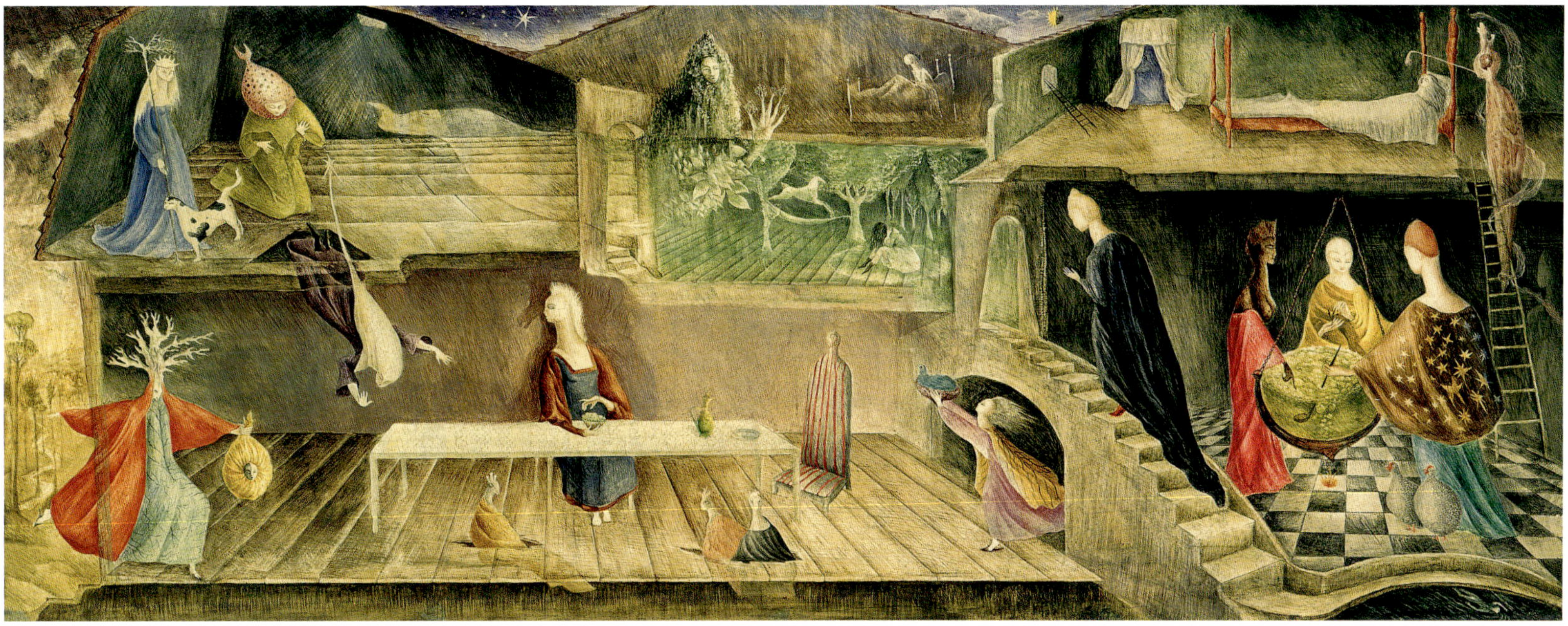

alchemical processes of distillation and transformation, which in turn led to associations involving art production. Carrington had a history of pairing cooking and art production, and this confluence was now reanimated through the lens of her growing feminist consciousness. In a letter to Edward James of 1946 Carrington mused on the salutary influence that eating had on painting, which to her was one of the benefits of pregnancy: 'Inspired painting, I find, favors a rather bucolic and opaque frame of mind on a continually replenished stomach – preferably with heavy and indigestible foods such as chocolate, sickly cakes, marzipan in blocks ... That is why I painted so beautifully when I was pregnant, I did nothing but eat.'[211]

Ozenfant's emphasis on the importance of technique was not lost on his pupil and Carrington began to experiment with a new medium that greatly excited her: egg tempera. 'What I needed was technique. I didn't want ideas. Each one of us has those. Technique, however is something that is learned. That is why I went about acquiring the recipes for painting. For me it was very important.'[212] One of the reasons that Carrington began to paint with the medieval technique of egg tempera was to create jewel-like tonalities, but according to her friend Gerzso: 'The fact that mixing egg tempera seemed to mimic culinary procedure further enhanced its use in her eyes.'[213] With painstaking attention to building her technical acumen she dedicated herself to perfecting her craft and the resulting complexities of composition, subtleties of colour and delicacies of draughtsmanship soon became apparent.

These new directions were driven and supported by a reconnection with the iconographic traditions of her past. At the time of the opening of her one-woman show at the Pierre Matisse Gallery (1948), she was 31 years old and giving birth to her second son, Pablo, in a Mexican hospital. Motherhood served to awaken dormant memories of her own childhood with its flights of fancy and sense of wonderment. Her newly adopted country provided yet another opportunity for reintegration, this time with the Catholicism of her upbringing. Freed from its pedagogical, philosophical and sexual restrictions as a result of her Surrealist involvement, Carrington could now use its conceptual language as the underlying structure on which to build her own, multivalent symbolic visual system. Mexico is first and foremost a Catholic country where pre-Conquest ancient practices had combined with the new Spanish religion to create a hybridised and unique manifestation of the Catholicism of her past. Speaking of her childhood Catholicism Carrington recalled its magical side:

> Well, ever since I was an infant, and I think this is common among many, many more people than you'd think, I had very strange experiences with all kinds of ghosts and visions and things that are generally condemned by orthodox religion. So I can't tell you if it was because I was brought up by Catholics, or because we were brought up with Celtic mythology, but I do have that kind of mentality. It's certainly been natural to me.[214]

By 'that kind of mentality' she is referring to her childhood inculcation into a particular brand of hybrid Catholicism practised by her Irish mother who freely mixed the Christian with the Celtic, not seeing them as mutually exclusive belief systems.[215] This upbringing provided Carrington with two essential elements for the development of her artistic vision: a foundation in traditional religious symbolism and the ability to mix cultural references. While in Paris she had met Kurt Seligmann and the two had become good friends in New York in 1942. His knowledge of the occult was profound; in 1948 he published *The History of Magic* (New York: Pantheon Books) and through this friendship, and later his book, she had ready access to multiple esoteric traditions upon which to draw. Not only did she embed alchemical symbols into

40
Tuesday
1946
Egg tempera on panel
55 x 83.7 cm/21½ x 33 in
Private collection

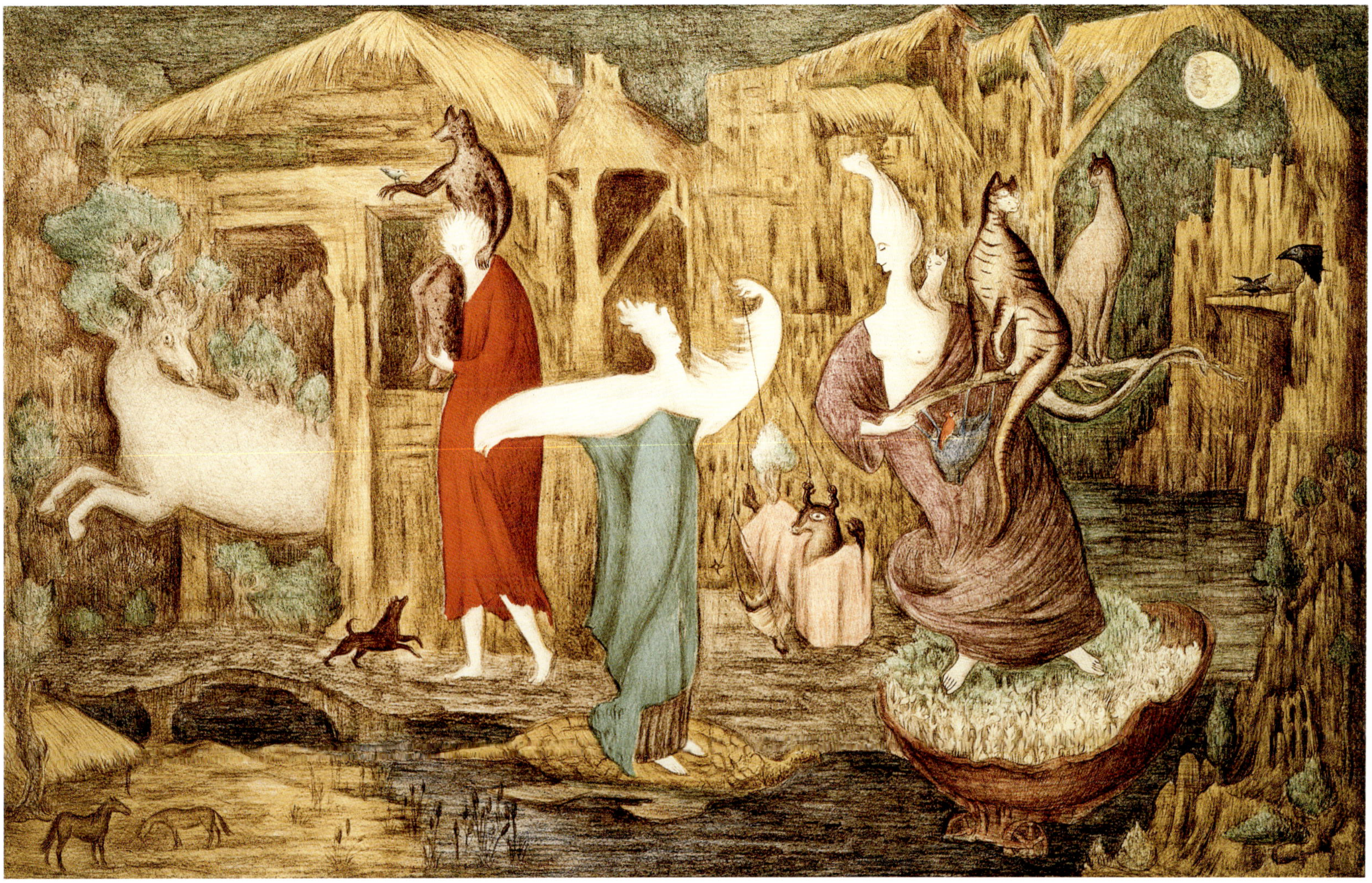

the fabric of her magical realms, but her mixing of diverse religious and pictorial influences reflect her use of a *theoretical* alchemy.

In examining her imagery from the 1940s and 1950s one can ascertain certain iconographic and conceptual correspondences to the Catholic mass, namely Holy Communion and the notion of transubstantiation. Carrington's portrayal of the table as sacramental altar was a motif that enabled her to subvert orthodox Catholicism through the insertion of symbols from other religions directly opposed to its canonical teachings. It was a perfect foil that lent an aura of solemnity and sanctity to the ordinary kitchen table and also facilitated the incorporation of compositional conventions gleaned from her fascination with trecento painting, which her use of egg tempera revealed as well. Her Catholic schoolgirl preoccupation with the saints, with levitation and other irrational miraculous manifestations, also fuelled her attraction to the paintings of Sassetta and others who carefully depicted such stories among fantastic architectural backdrops.[216] Even her heretical backwards writing, so frowned upon by established Christianity, but still a part of its sensibility, was now synthesised into a unique vision reflecting her own notions of the Surrealistic 'marvellous'.

The 1945 painting, *The House Opposite* (Fig.39), is the earliest example of Carrington's new direction and demonstrates a greater stylistic maturity and iconographic complexity. She has absorbed some of the pictorial lessons she encountered in Florence, such as the cut-away view, into a multi-chambered dwelling. The spaces teem with female figures, many of whom are busily engaged in the preparation, presentation and consumption of food. Ladder, stairs and trap doors connect these rooms in which divergent activities are occurring. According to Warner, these multiple chambers were directly influenced by the work of such Renaissance painters as Sassetta, Matteo di Giovanni and Francesco di Giorgio: 'They unfold a tale in a journey across the image, with simultaneous incidents represented in demarcated antechambers and chambers of a palace or other edifice seen in section, so that time flows in the stasis of a painted moment.'[217] The upper reaches of the canvas portray a misty liminal space where one woman sleeps while in another room a woman awakens and sits up, suggesting a dream within a dream. Below this is a grisaille scene of a young woman seated in a forest, her head bent as if weeping, while the white rocking horse from *Inn of the Dawn Horse* floats spectrally opposite and above her, an autobiographical reference to past love and broken bonds.

Dominating the composition is a centrally placed long table, the focus of everyone's attention. Looking down from a chamber above on the left is a blue-robed woman looking very much like a crowned Virgin Mary, yet accompanied by her feline familiar and holding a branch or magic wand. To the far right, three women – the Holy Trinity transformed into the three Fates – brew a special potion in a transparent magic cauldron, presumably for the table. A girl near the centre rushes to the table offering a bowl with a live hen. Seated at the middle of the table is a figure reminiscent of the horse-headed women last seen in *The Meal of Lord Candlestick*. As she eats from a bowl, strange figures appear from beneath the table, as if magically summoned by her consumption. The relation of cooking and art production, according to Chadwick, is of central concern to the artist:

> The prominent place given to the cauldron in Celtic myth and Grail legend had long fascinated Carrington, as had alchemical descriptions of the gentle cooking of substances placed in egg-shaped vessels. She has related alchemical processes to those of both painting and cooking, carefully selecting a metaphor that unites the traditional woman's occupation as nourisher of the species

with that of the magical transformation of form and color that takes place in the artist's creative process, nourishing the spirit.[218]

As the title *The House Opposite* implies, this is a reversal of the status quo, a look into a parallel dimension where mundane domestic activities are infused with the sacerdotal. Once again, Carrington has transformed the Christian altar and the performance of the sacrament from a male liturgy officiated over by priests to a female one with no hierarchy of office. This ritual meal is designed to instigate transit and transformation – from human to animal (for example some women have horse shadows), from the celestial to the terrestrial, and from the visible to the invisible. In this way the artist is alluding to earlier, non-patriarchal religions, which have been suppressed and appropriated by the Church, as Carrington notes: 'The Bible, like any other history, is full of gaps and peculiarities that only begin to make sense if understood as a covering-up for a very different kind of civilization which had been eliminated.'[219]

In both public and private domestic spheres Carrington encountered in Mexico a type of hybrid Catholicism that produced religious couplings often found surprising to the Western eye. Keeping with the Catholic calendar, holidays in Mexico are often accompanied by elaborate decorations that combine folkloric and traditional religious objects carefully arranged and supplemented with flowers, incense and foodstuffs. One spectacular example of Mexican hybrid Catholicism is the holiday known as the 'Days of the Dead' whereby on 1 and 2 November ornate altars dedicated to the deceased are constructed in Mexican homes. On tabletops covered with cloth, offerings of food, sugar skulls, flowers and other gifts are combined with Catholic religious imagery. These surfaces provide access between the realms of the dead and the living, and are where the inhabitants of the underworld can spiritually consume offerings of real food. Although she eschewed overt picturesque depictions of Mexican customs in her own work, she was still impressed by such remnants of indigenous practices. That *ofrendas* (home altars) are constructed by women, usually in the dining area, and are accompanied by a ritual meal meant as a solemn reunion of both living and deceased family members also would have impressed her. Whatever the sources of inspiration were, she began to develop her own notions about kitchens as magically charged spaces used to

41
Leonora Carrington in her studio, 1947
Photograph: Chiki Weisz

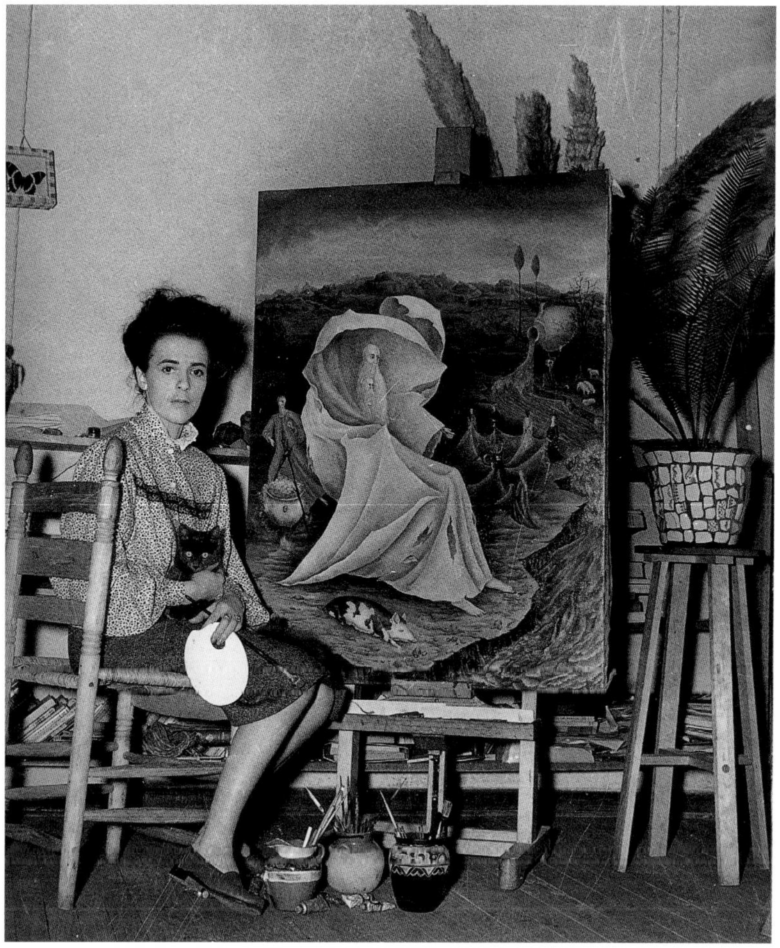

42
Hieronymous Bosch
The Temptation of St Anthony
1500s (no exact date)
Oil on panel
70 x 51 cm/27½ x 20 in
Courtesy of Museo del Prado, Madrid, Spain
Photo: ALBUM/Erich Lessing

43
The Temptation of St Anthony
1947
Oil on canvas
120 x 90 cm/47 x 35½ in
Private collection

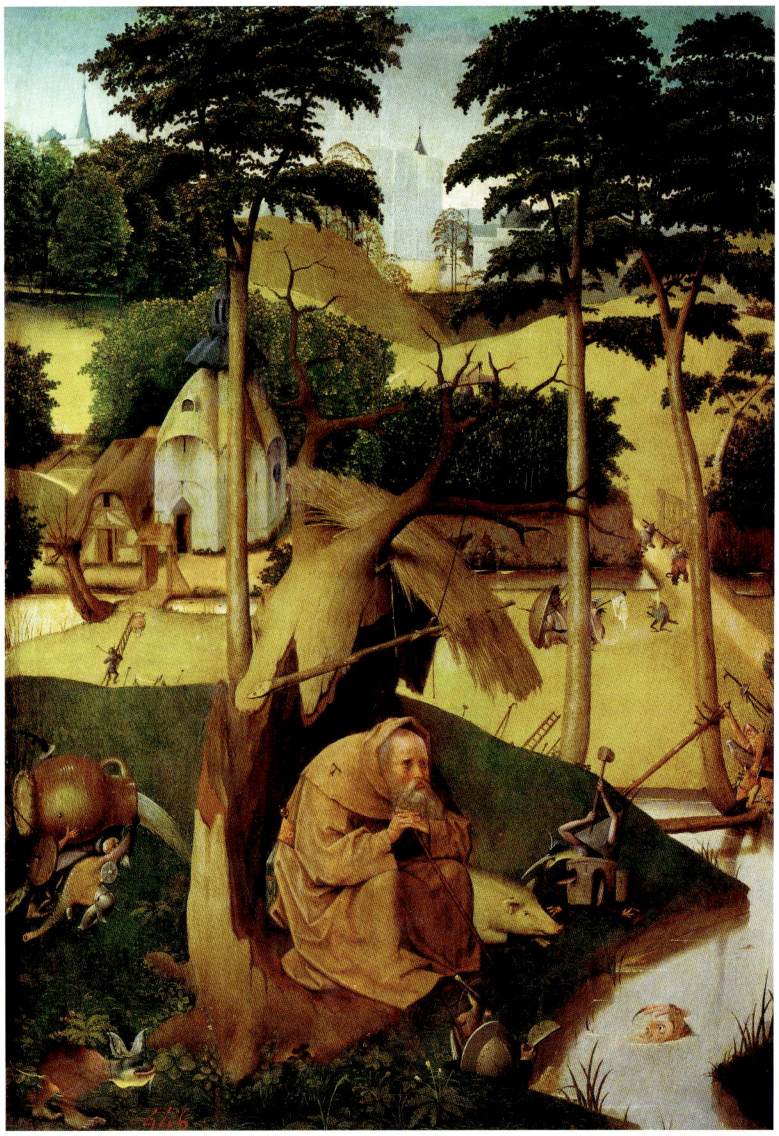

In 1941, during her traumatic travels through Spain, she had gone to the Prado in Madrid and had been deeply impressed by the works of Hieronymus Bosch and Pieter Bruegel the Elder (*The Triumph of Death, c.*1560–64). The influence of Bosch's *The Hay Wain* (*c.*1492–1503) and *Gardens of Earthly Delights* (1505–10), swarming with small figures engaged in inexplicable and arcane activities, would be particularly vivid. Both in Madrid and Lisbon (Museu Nacional de Arte Antiga) Carrington saw versions by Bosch of his favourite subject, *The Temptation of St Anthony*. When the subject for the Bel Ami International Art Competition was announced to be the Temptation of St Anthony it was to these examples that she turned for inspiration, especially the one in the Prado Museum (Fig.42). Carrington's 1947 entry (Fig.43) borrowed many elements of the Bosch composition: most notably the seated pose of the hermit with his staff, his placement on a piece of land almost surrounded by water, his companion pig, and a large ceramic jug from which water pours. It also shares Bosch's jumps in scale, attention to detail, and the inclusion of many small figures busy at their strange activities. The Bel Ami organisers must have asked Carrington for a photograph of herself for inclusion in the catalogue because an uncharacteristically formal picture exists, taken by her husband, that shows her posed by this painting with palette in hand (Fig.41). This photograph gives us a glimpse into Carrington's studio, a place that captivated Edward James in the 1940s:

> Leonora Carrington's studio had everything most conducive to make it the true matrix of true art. Small in the extreme, it was an ill-furnished and not very well lighted room. It had nothing to endow it with the title of studio at all, save a few almost worn-out paintbrushes and a number of gesso panels, set on a dog and cat populated floor, leaning face-averted against a white-washed and peeling wall. The place was combined kitchen, nursery, bedroom, kennel and junk store. The disorder was

concoct potions, weave spells, prepare herbs and conduct alchemical 'cooking' experiments. Fuelling this interest was her discovery of the large, mostly open-air markets in Mexico, which, with their women vendors and plethora of consumables for the body and spirit, instigated an exploration into the magical potentialities of food preparation.

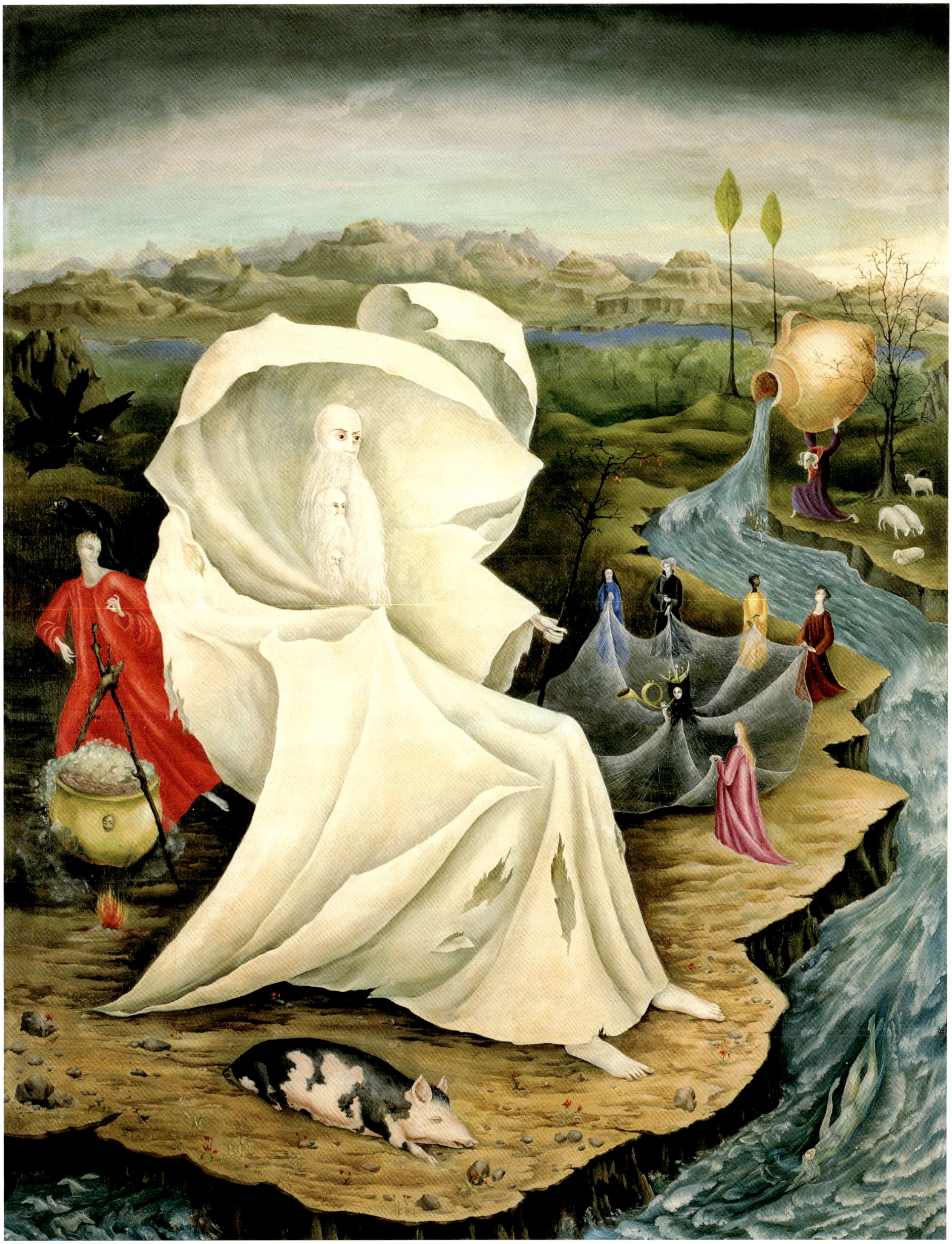

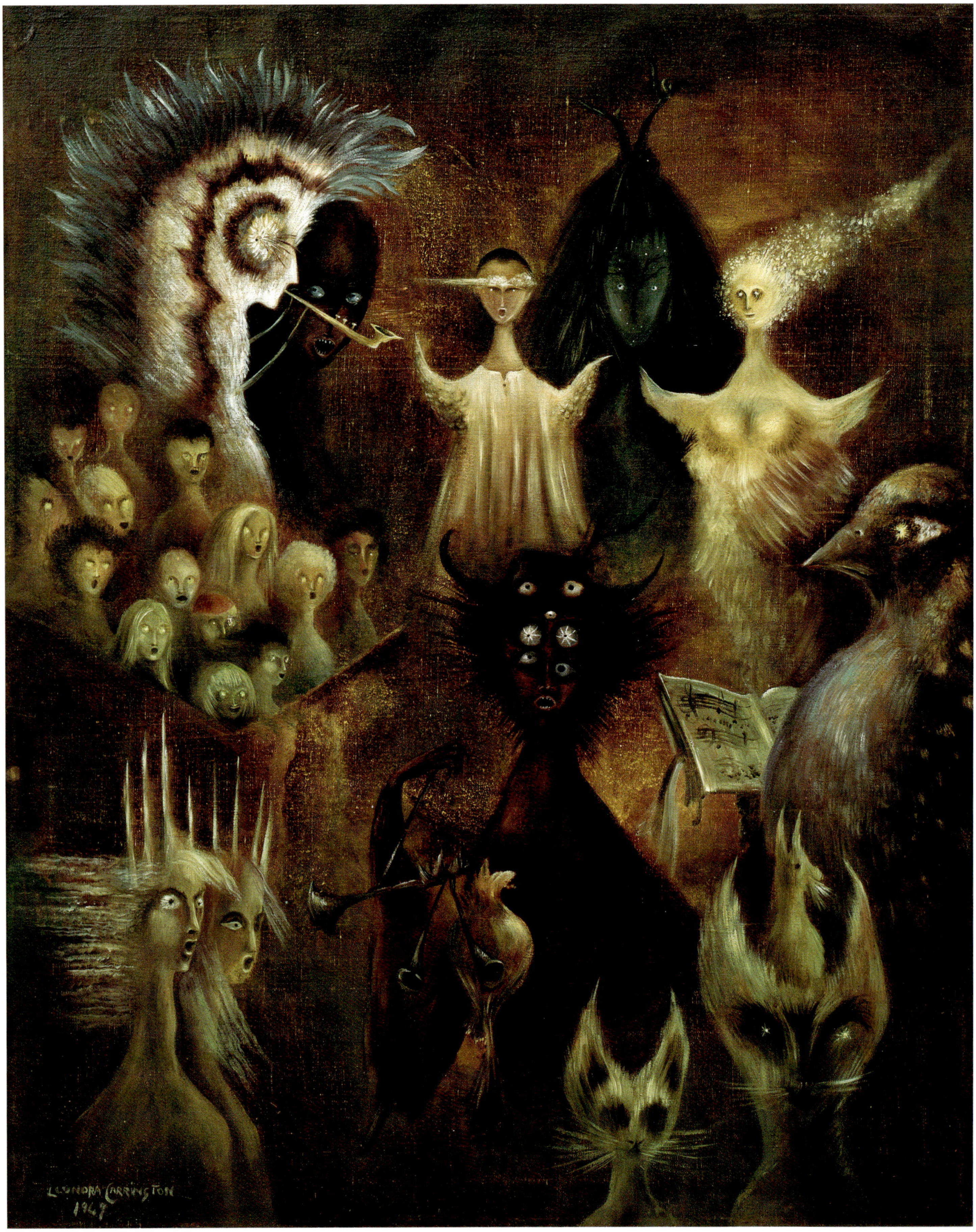
LEONORA CARRINGTON
1947

opposite:
44
Plain Chant
1947
Oil on canvas
90 x 68.5 cm/35½ x 27 in
Private collection

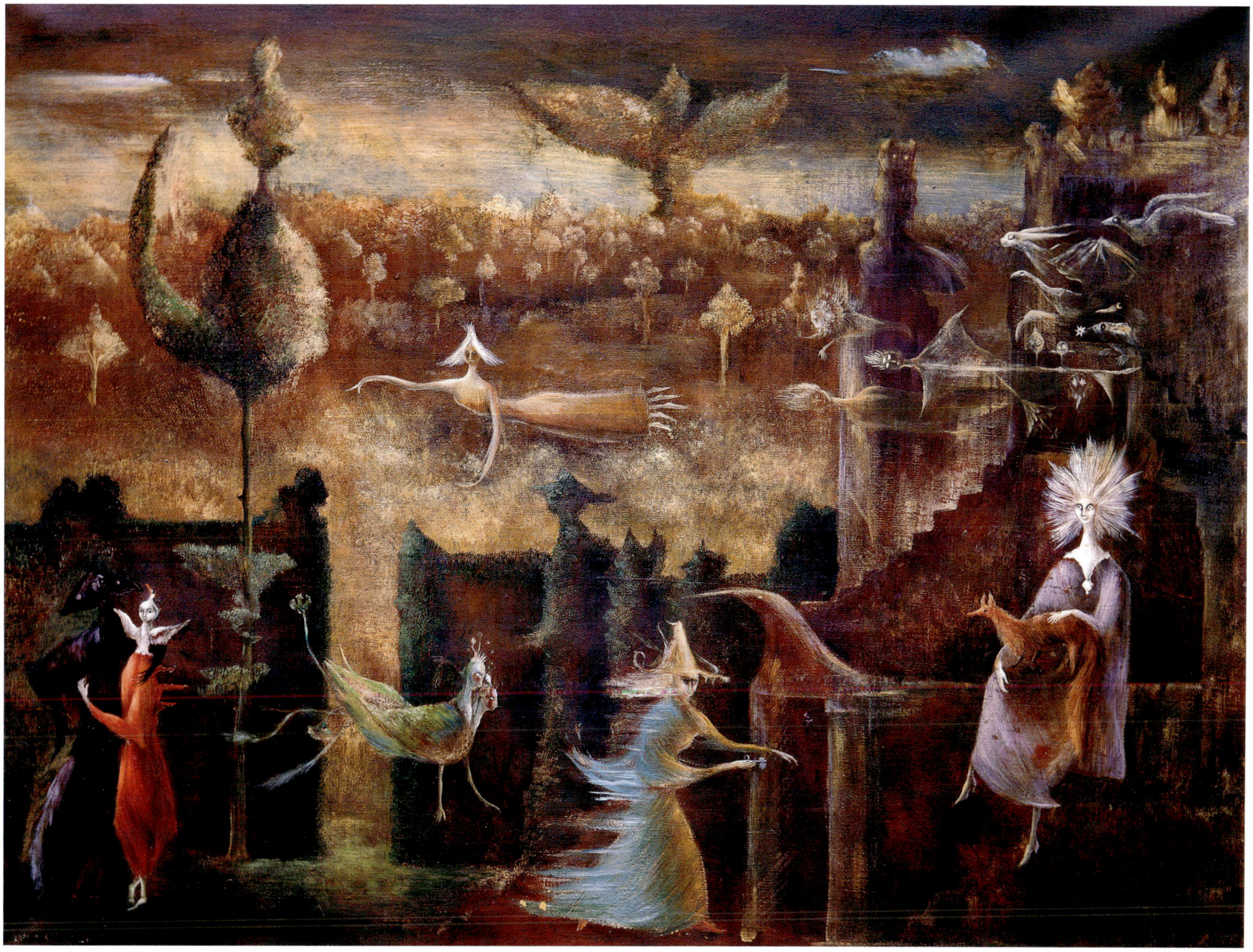

45
Nine, Nine, Nine
1948
Oil on canvas
68 x 88.5 cm/27 x 35 in
Private collection

46
The Hour of the Angelus
1949
Tempera on board
155 x 233 cm/61 x 92 in
Private collection
Photograph: Christie's Images

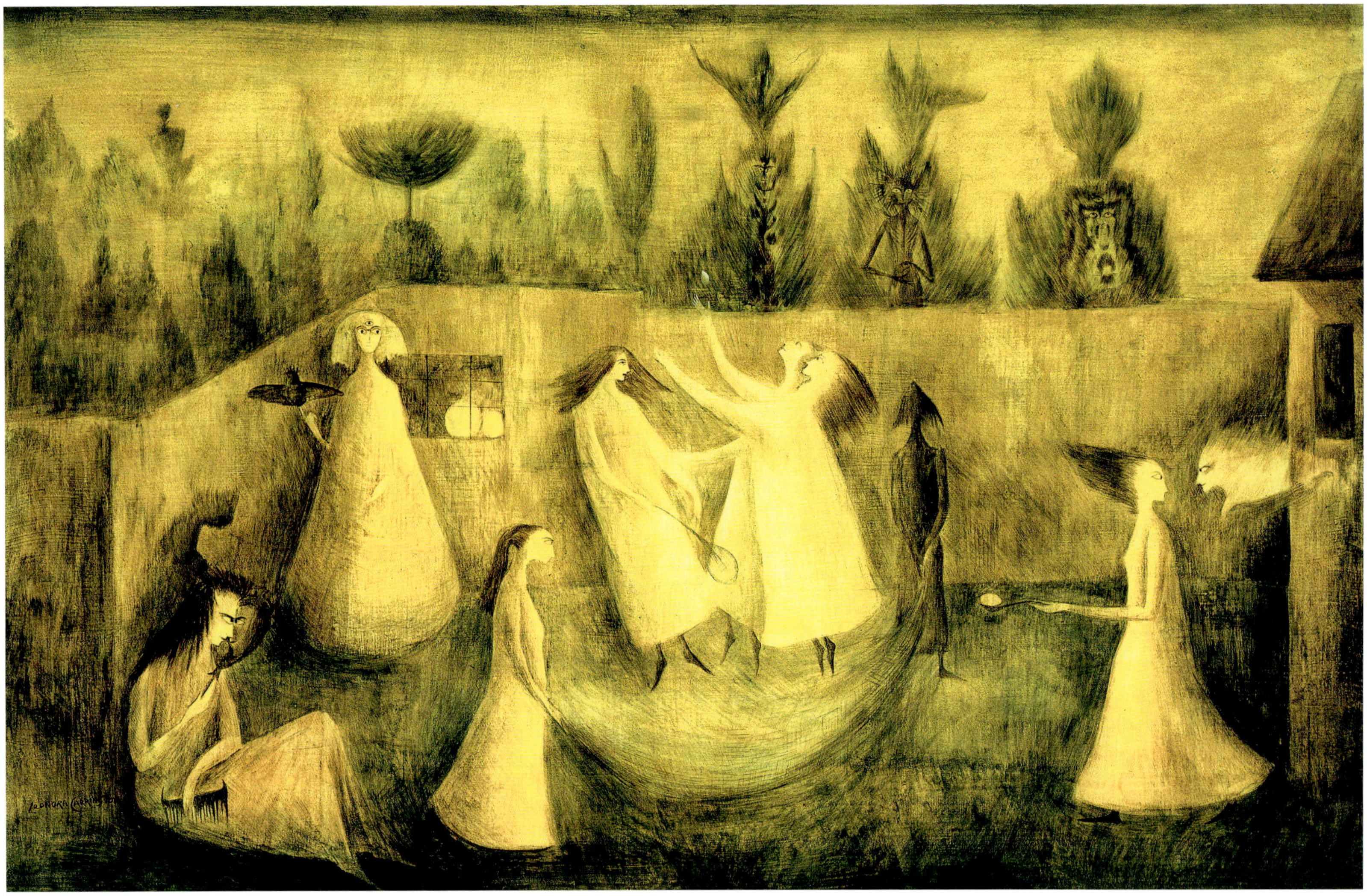

47
Bird Pong
1949
Egg tempera on panel
45 x 72.5 cm/18 x 28½ in

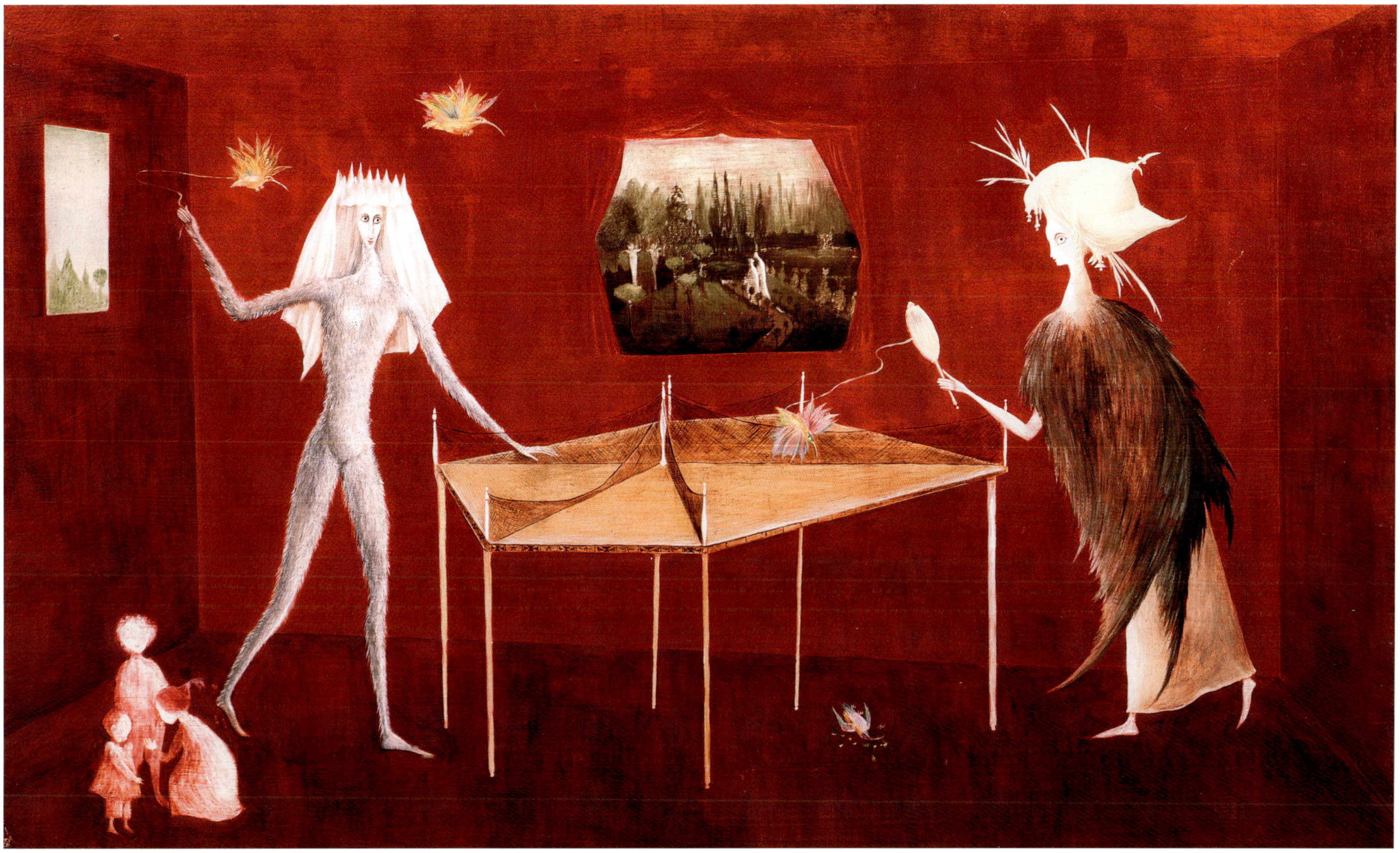

> apocalyptic: the appurtenances of the poorest. My hopes and expectations began to swell.[220]

Painted with exquisite detail in radiant, luminous colour, the *Temptation of St Anthony* is not about women's sacred domestic space, but about the survival and power of pre-Christian feminine spiritual practices. Carrington used this opportunity to combine her long-held interest in the saints and their miraculous actions with her developing feminist consciousness. To the left is a bubbling cauldron lit by a small fire, similar to that of *The House Opposite*, and presided over by a hairless, androgynous woman in a long red robe, with a vulture perched on her head. The cauldron, symbol of fertility and abundance, mystic transformations both alchemical and magical, and witches' rituals, lurks behind the saint, who, inside his billowing rags is pale and insubstantial from penitential deprivations. To the left of the three-headed, bearded saint are a group of diminutive robed women who hold up the circular garment of a crowned central queen who blows a curved horn. In the competition catalogue this work

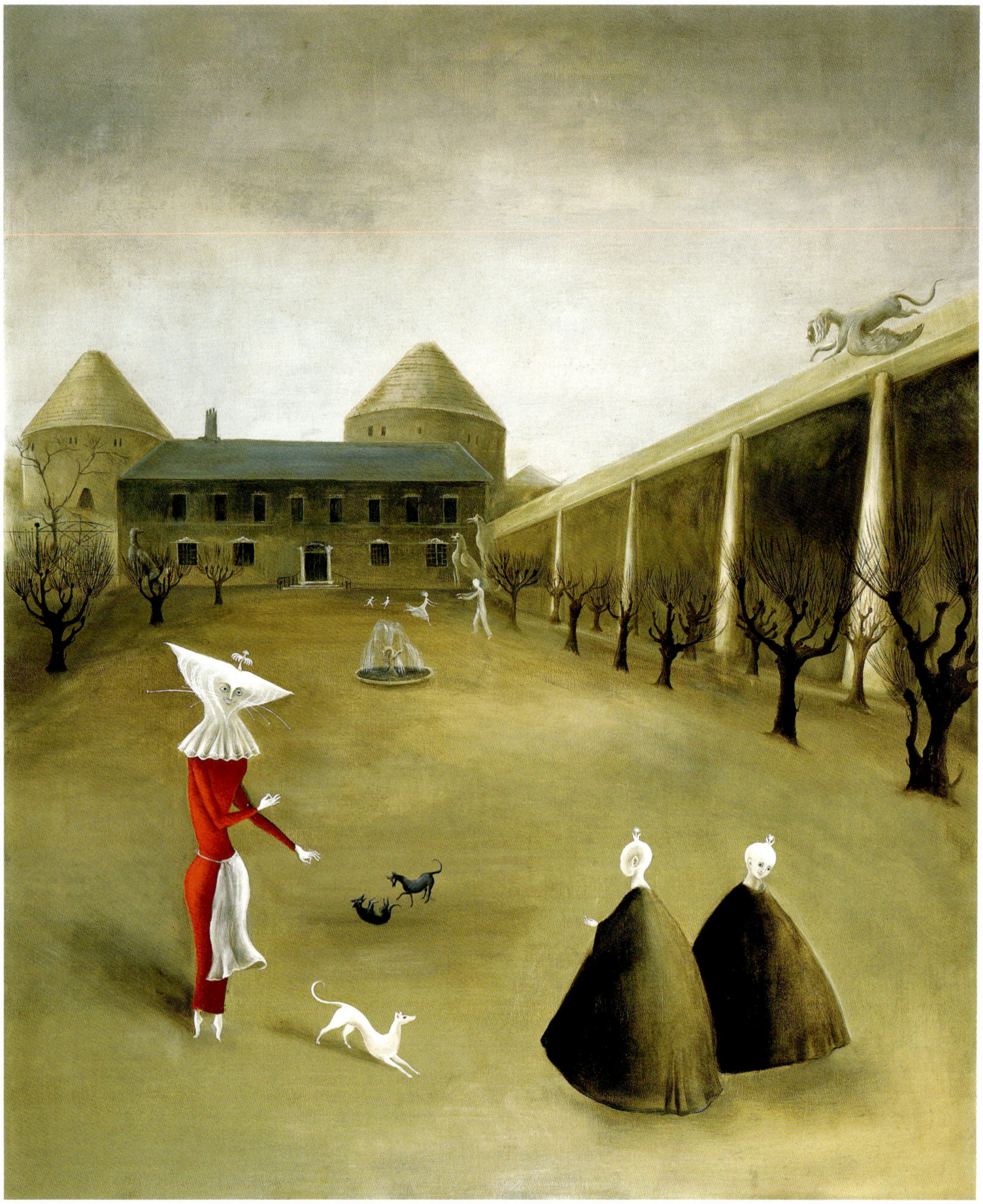

48
Darvault
*c.*1950
Oil on canvas
80 x 65 cm/31½ x 25½ in
Collection of Miguel S. Escobedo
Photograph: Willem Schalkwijk

opposite:
49
Pastoral
1950
Oil on canvas
53.5 x 74.5 cm/21 x 29½ in
Private collection

was accompanied by a remarkable explanatory statement, the only one she will ever make about her work, which resembles her short stories in its playful and satiric character. Read in its entirety, it is a sly commentary on Catholic asceticism, and places a great emphasis on the magical act of cooking:

> The picture seems pretty clear to me, being a more or less literal rendering of St Anthony complete with pig, desert and temptation. Naturally one could ask why the venerable holy man has three heads – to which one could always reply, why not?
>
> You will notice the veteran's suit to be whitish and of an umbrellaoid form which by the vagaries of the weather or that the monkish apparel had been cleverly constructed out of used mummy wrappings in umbrella or sunshade form as a protection from sandstorms and sun, practical for someone leading an open air life and given to contemplation (as Egyptologists apparently didn't exist in those days, mummy wrappings were no doubt to be gathered like blackberries and therefore to one of an economical and modest turn of mind they would provide a durable and apt clothing for the desert).

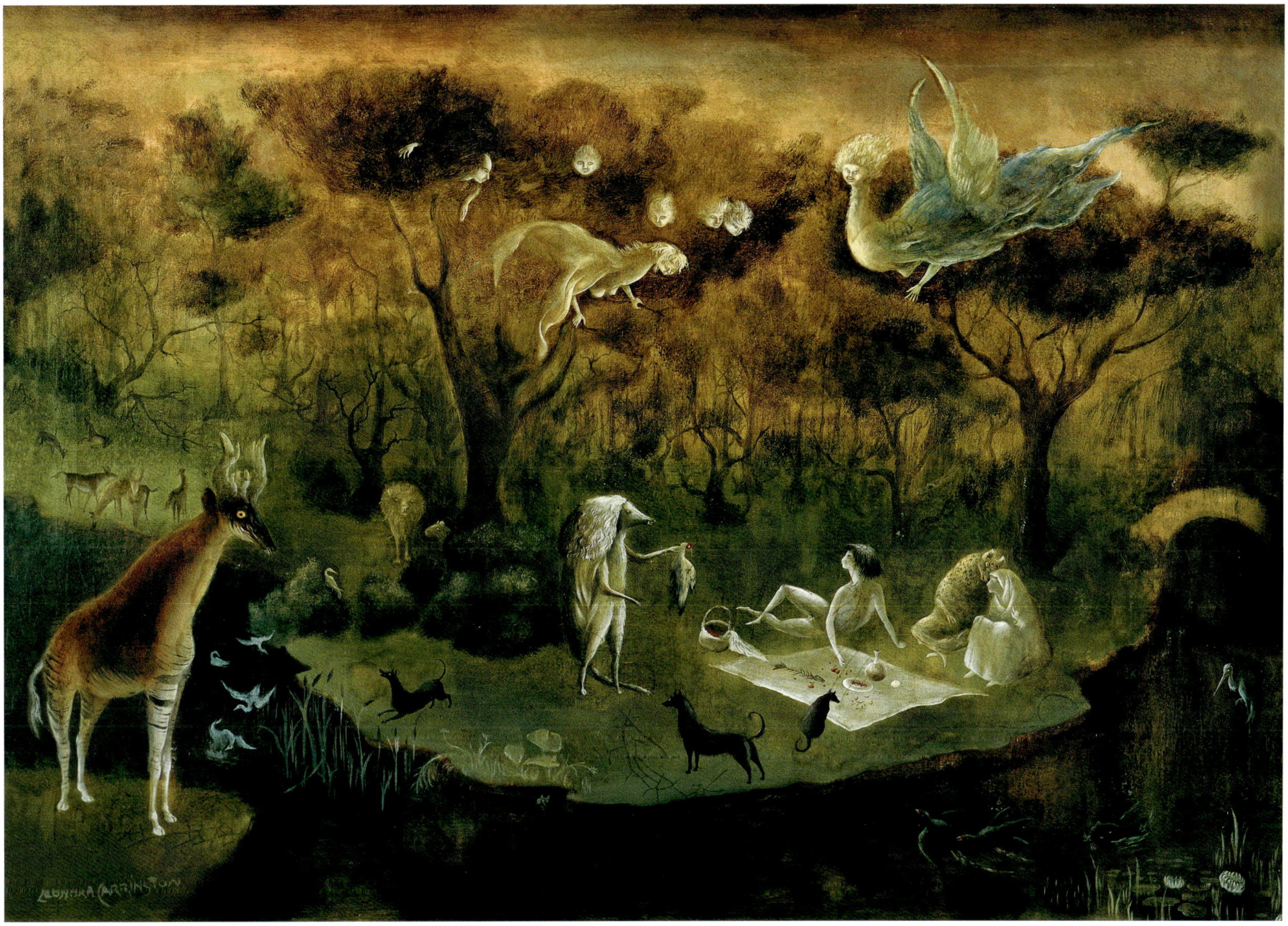

The Saint's traditional pet pig who lies across the nether half of the picture and reviews the observer out of its kindly blue eye is adequately accounted for in the myth of St Anthony, and likewise the continually flowing water and the ravine.

The bald-headed girl in the red dress combines female charm and the delights of the table – you will notice that she is engaged in making an unctuous broth of (let us say) lobsters, mushrooms, fat turtle, spring chicken, ripe tomatoes, gorgonzola cheese, milk chocolate, onions and tinned peaches. The mixture of these ingredients has overflowed and taken on a greenish and sickly hue to the fevered vision of St Anthony, whose daily meal consists of whithered grass and tepid water with an occasional locust by way of an orgy.

On the right, the Queen of Sheba and her attendants emerge in ever-decreasing circles out of a subterranean landscape towards the hermit. Their intention is ambiguous, their progress spiral.

50
The Giantess
*c.*1950
Oil on canvas
117 x 68 cm/46 x 27 in
Private collection

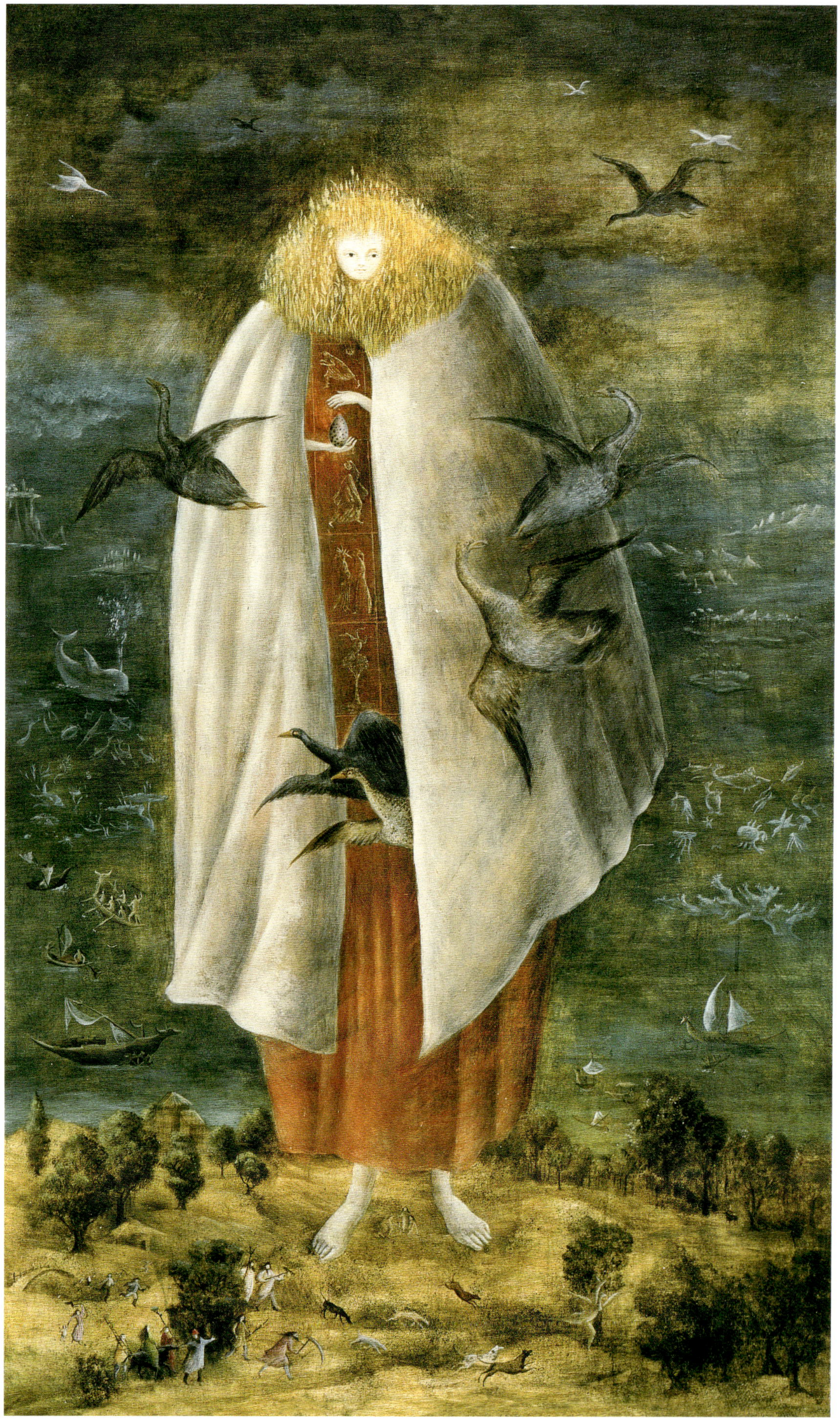

> And last to the ram with the earthenware jar one could only quote the words of Friar Bacon's brazen head: Time was – Time is –Time is past. I was always pleased with the simply idiocy of these words.[221]

The correspondence between cooking and art production was not lost upon her critics, and in the introductory essay to her one-person show at the Inter-American Relations in New York, Edward James claimed:

> The paintings of Leonora Carrington are not merely painted, they are brewed. They sometimes seem to have materialized in a cauldron at the stroke of midnight, yet for all this they are no mere illustrations of fairy tales. Hers are not literary paintings, rather they are pictures distilled in the underground caves of libido, vertiginously sublimated. Above all (or below), they belong to the Universal subconscious.[222]

This commentary astutely encapsulates many of the core concepts of Carrington's outlook on art production; her transcendent and transgressive blend of multiple symbols and most profoundly the key axiom of alchemy, 'As above, so below.'[223]

The White Goddess

Another turning point for Carrington occurred in 1949 when she read Robert Graves's *The White Goddess: A Historical Grammar of Poetic Myth* (1948).[224] The effect that this monumental and scholarly study of the archaic 'goddess' religions had on Carrington cannot be overemphasised: 'Reading *The White Goddess* was the greatest revelation of my life.'[225] It was one of the first widely available books that unequivocally explored a Goddess-centred spirituality, in addition to ancient runic alphabets, druidic and bardic poetry and the Celtic lunar year. Carrington must have felt that Graves was directly addressing her desire to create an art resonating with psychic power when he wrote:

> The reason why the hairs stand on end, the eyes water, the throat is constricted, the skin crawls and a shiver runs down the spine when one writes or reads a true poem is that a true poem is necessarily an invocation of the White Goddess, or Muse, the Mother of all Living, the ancient power of fright and lust – the female spider or the queen-bee whose embrace is death.[226]

Deeply resonating with her own Irish heritage and the emerging philosophical beliefs concerning women's mysteries that she investigated with Varo, *The White Goddess* sparked a re-discovery of her Celtic roots and recalled the stories told to her by her maternal grandmother Moorhead, who had told Carrington as a child that they were descended from the legendary Irish fairy people called the Tuatha dé Danaan, the People of the Goddess Dana. Legend had it that they were a slender white race possessed of great beauty, intelligence, grace and magical powers and were renowned for their ability to shape shift. They lived underground in grassy hill mounds and were also called the Sidhe (People of the Hills). Sometimes they enticed humans to enter their realm where the passage of time, the taste of food, and sight bore no relation to normal human experience. Carrington had also read of them in James Stephens's *The Crock of Gold* (1917), a book she cherished from her youth.

51
The Dead Queens of Cockerham
*c.*1950s
Gouache on board
37 x 29.2 cm/14½ x 11½ in
Jeri L. Waxenberg Collection

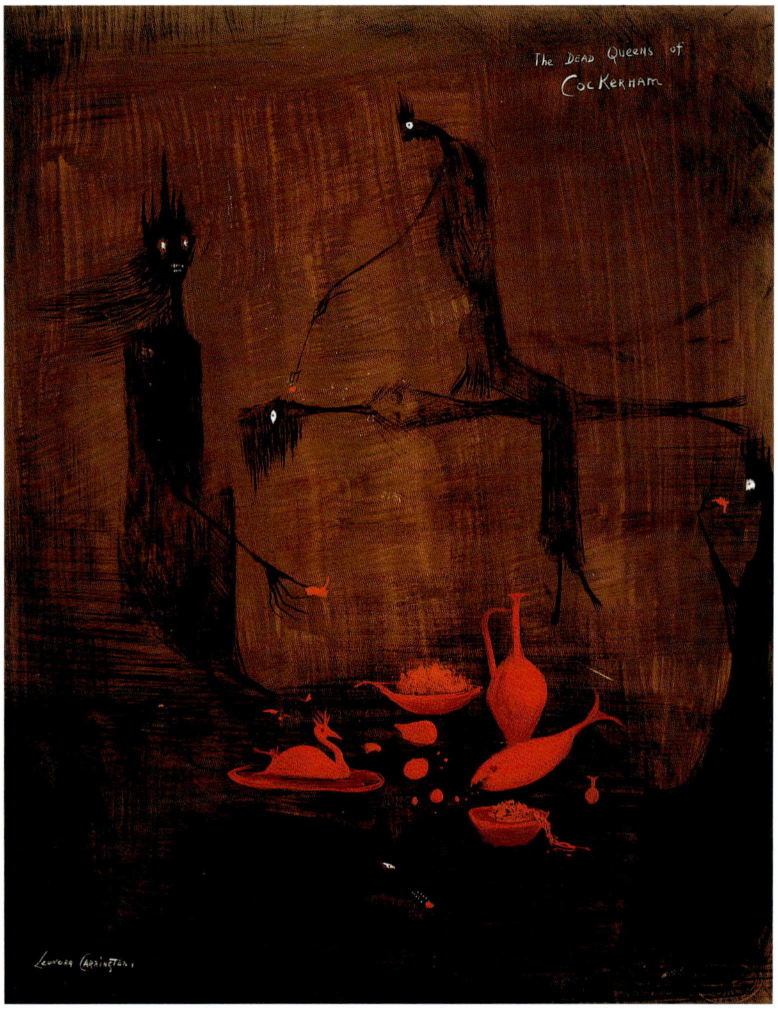

52
The Conjurer
*c.*1950s
Oil on canvas
Dimensions unknown
Private collection

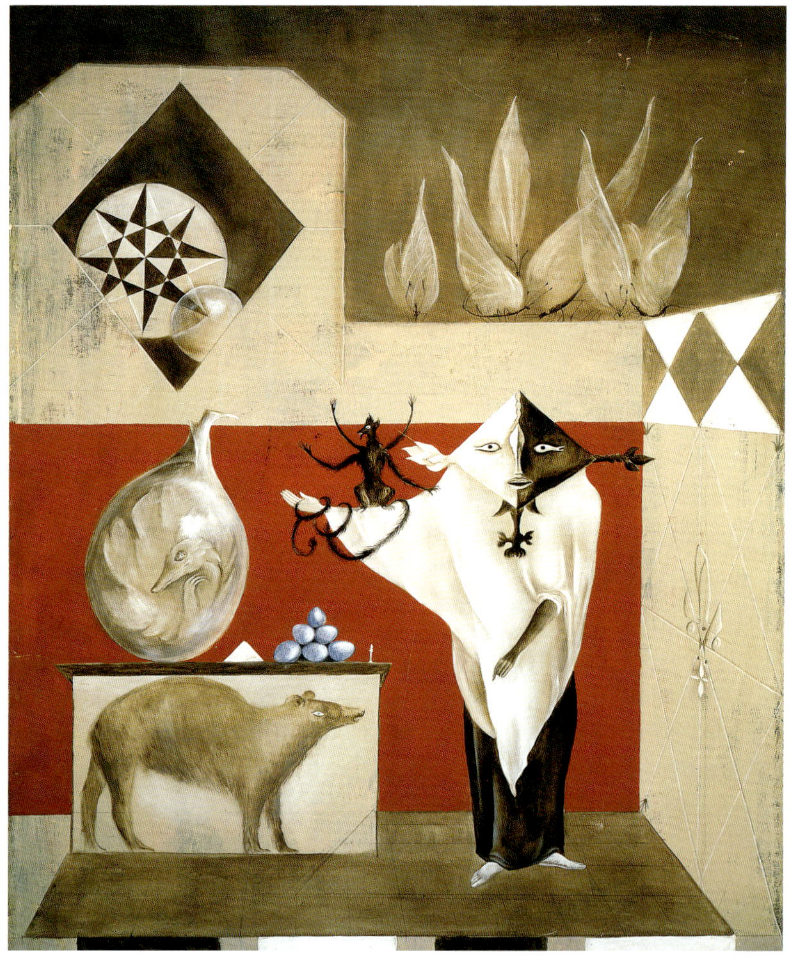

53
Red Mask
*c.*1950s
Leather
Private collection

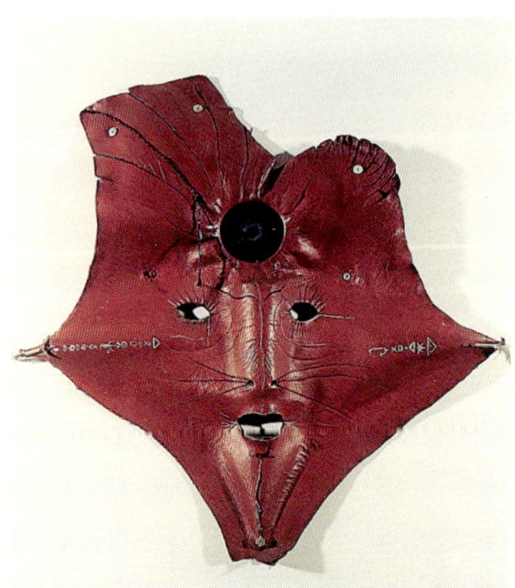

opposite:
54
Untitled three-panelled folding screen
1964
Oil on wood, painted on both sides
114 x 45 cm/44 x 18 in
Private collection

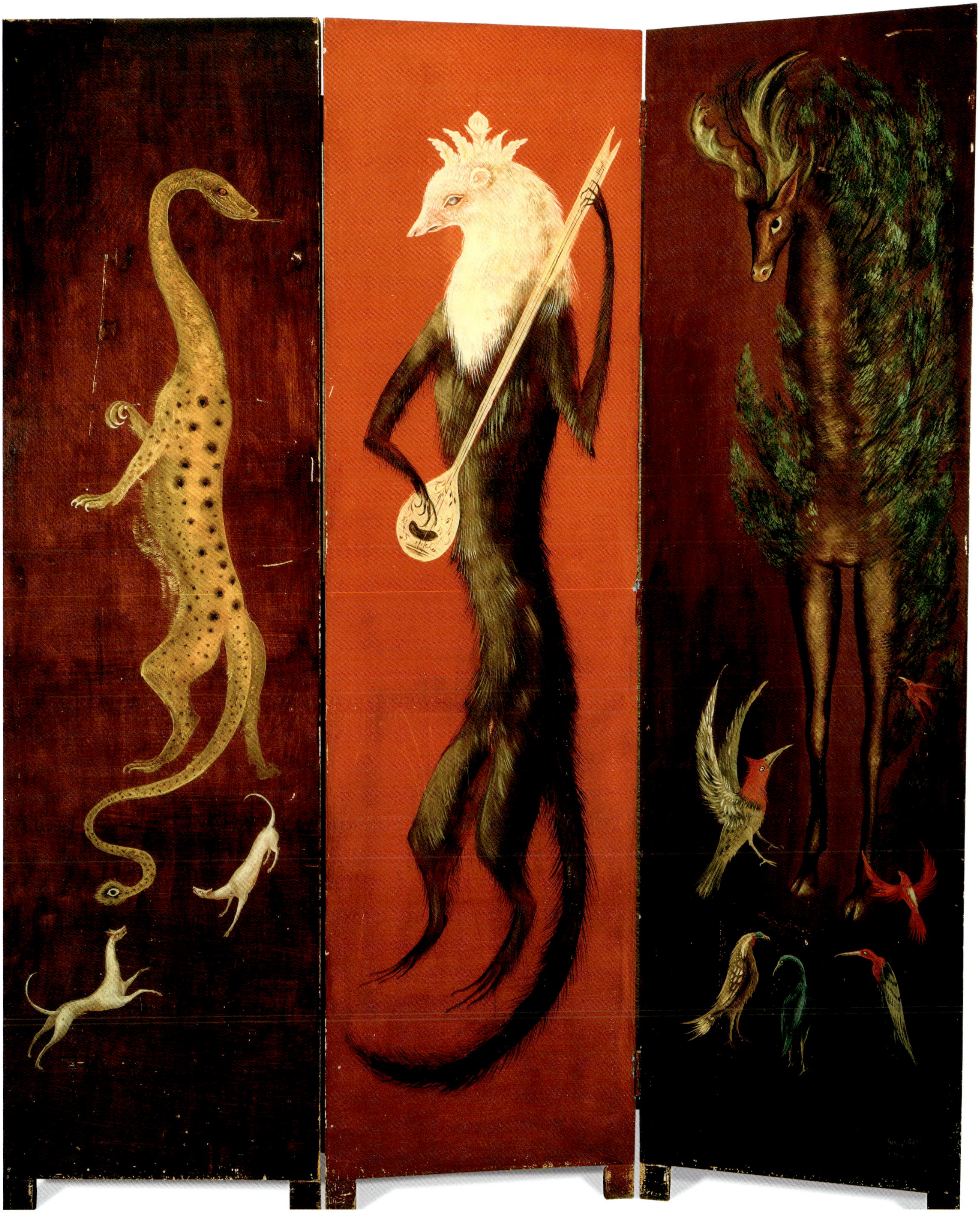

55
Hunt Breakfast
1956
Oil on canvas
40.5 x 49.5 cm/16 x 19 in
Private collection

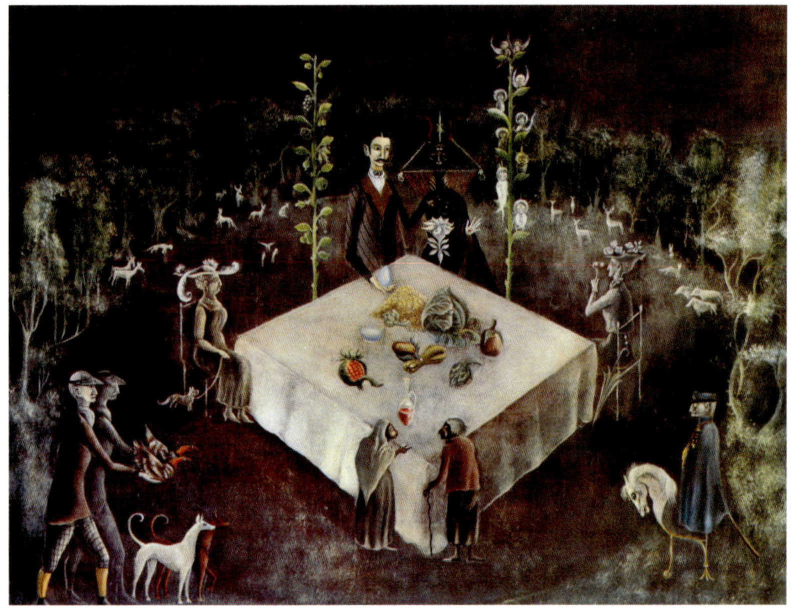

Beginning in the 1950s the Tuatha dé Danaan (Sidhe) made their appearance in Carrington's paintings, either overtly or somewhat disguised, and their depiction was at times mixed with symbols of alchemy, other goddess mythologies and even Mexican folklore. The table as altar is present in the 1954 painting *Sidhe, the White People of the Tuatha dé Danaan* (Fig.56) where spectral white faerie women have convened around a massive and weighty altar-like rectangular stone set with an earthen water jar, a soup bowl with ladle (like a small cauldron), a yam and red fruits that could be pomegranates (and thus allude to Persephone, Demeter and the underworld). To the right a standing woman juggles glowing balls of white light (one of which looks like a spider's web) while a star-burst of light emanates from her heart. To her right are a cat and a white bull, the latter a manifestation of Dana. Once again, one of the figures holds an egg, symbol of fertility and an allusion, perhaps, to the alchemical egg in tempera paint. Although entirely supernatural, it is still a domestic realm presided over by feminine entities, and the main focus is the sacerdotal meal.

A transcendent occult work, *The Chair, Daghda Tuatha dé Danaan* (1955) (Fig.68), is pictorially and iconographically complex, a rousing example of Carrington's ideal of the magical art of painting. The title is key to understanding the meaning of the work. The Daghda is the Celtic 'Good God', the High King of the Tuatha dé Danaan, whose wife and female counterpart is the triple-aspected goddess. The glowing red room refers to his epitaph as 'The Red One of Perfect Knowledge' and the chair, with his name carefully inscribed in the lower left of the back, is his throne. The black and white checked floor is echoed in the black and white designs on the chair, which is full of solar symbols such as full and half-circles with rays, a face in a multi-petalled flower, and a round orb on the seat containing a radiating star shape. Above the round table to the right hovers what appears to be a large egg with a white rose growing from the top, and below the table is a strange tableau of two severed black hands beside a small white egg. The central protagonist in this occult transubstantiation is the large egg – this is the cosmic egg of creation, which is also sometimes likened to the alchemical vessel, known as an alembic, in which the alchemist performs the distillation process. Carrington's preoccupation with the egg goes back to *Down Below* where she is haunted by the image of an egg, which she views as a kind of clairvoyant crystal: 'The egg is the macrocosm and the microcosm, the dividing line between Great and Small, which makes it impossible to see everything at once.'[227] The white alchemical rose represents the feminine principle necessary to commence transformation. The white rose is also the moon and is usually coupled with the red rose, signifying the masculine principle and the sun. Moisture drips from the ceiling (heavens) on to the rose, instigating a process of percolation, which causes water to run off the table and float through the air on to the seat of the chair. What I believe we are witnessing then is a marriage, between the Daghda and the Great Goddess, between the white rose and the red (symbolised by the red room), between opposites (black and white) – an alchemical conjoining. The Daghda was also the keeper of the sacred Celtic cauldron Undry, which was never empty and from which no man or woman ever left unsatisfied.

Carrington is at her most hermetic in the 1956 painting *AB EO QUOD* (Fig.65) – a mystical still life that is anything but still. This cloth-covered altar table holds the wine and

56

Sidhe, the White People of the Tuatha dé Danaan

1954

Oil on canvas

59.5 x 78.5 cm/23½ x 31 in

Private collection

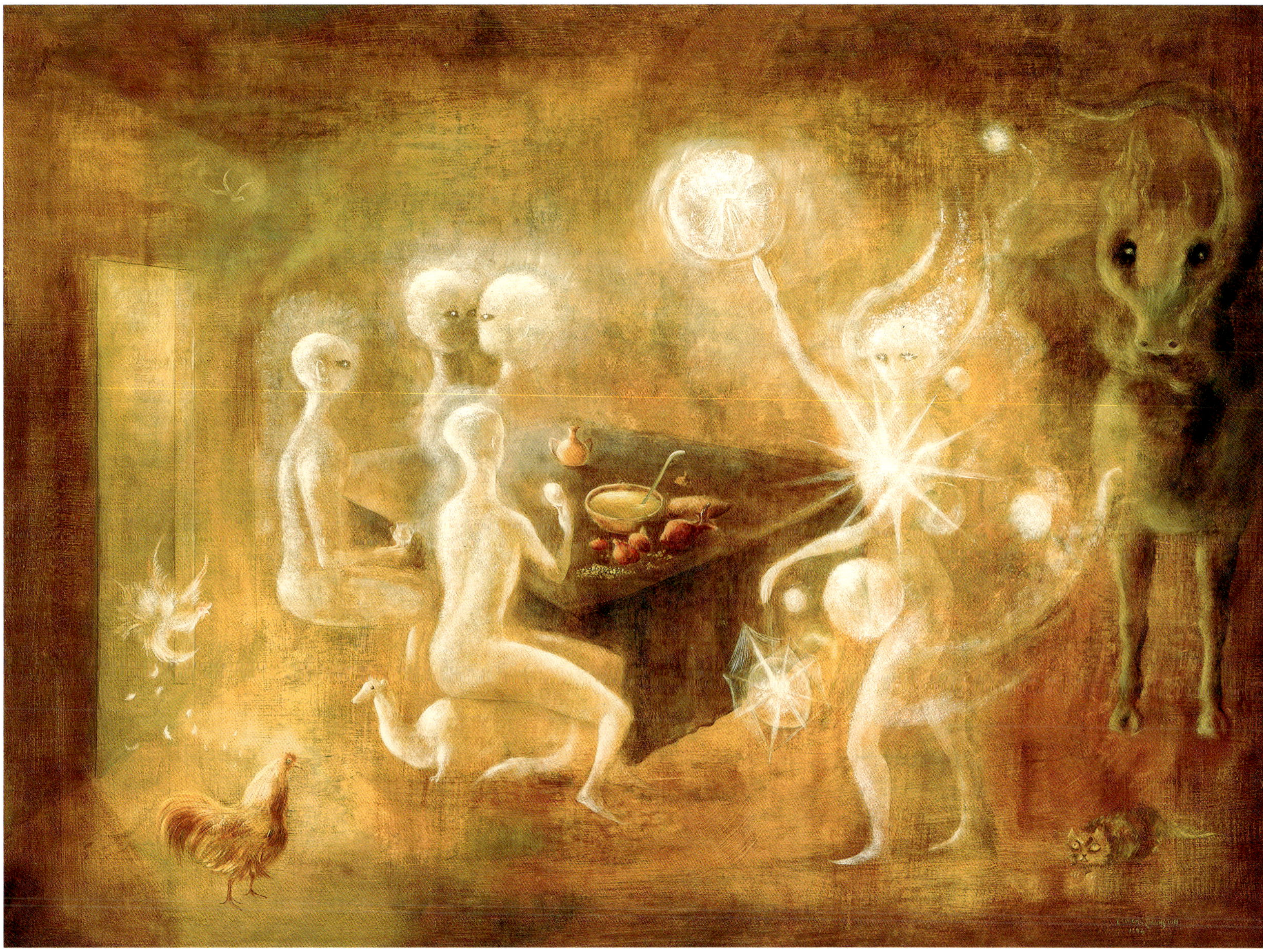

57
Ferret Race
1950–1
Oil on canvas
101.5 x 56 cm/40 x 22 in
Private collection

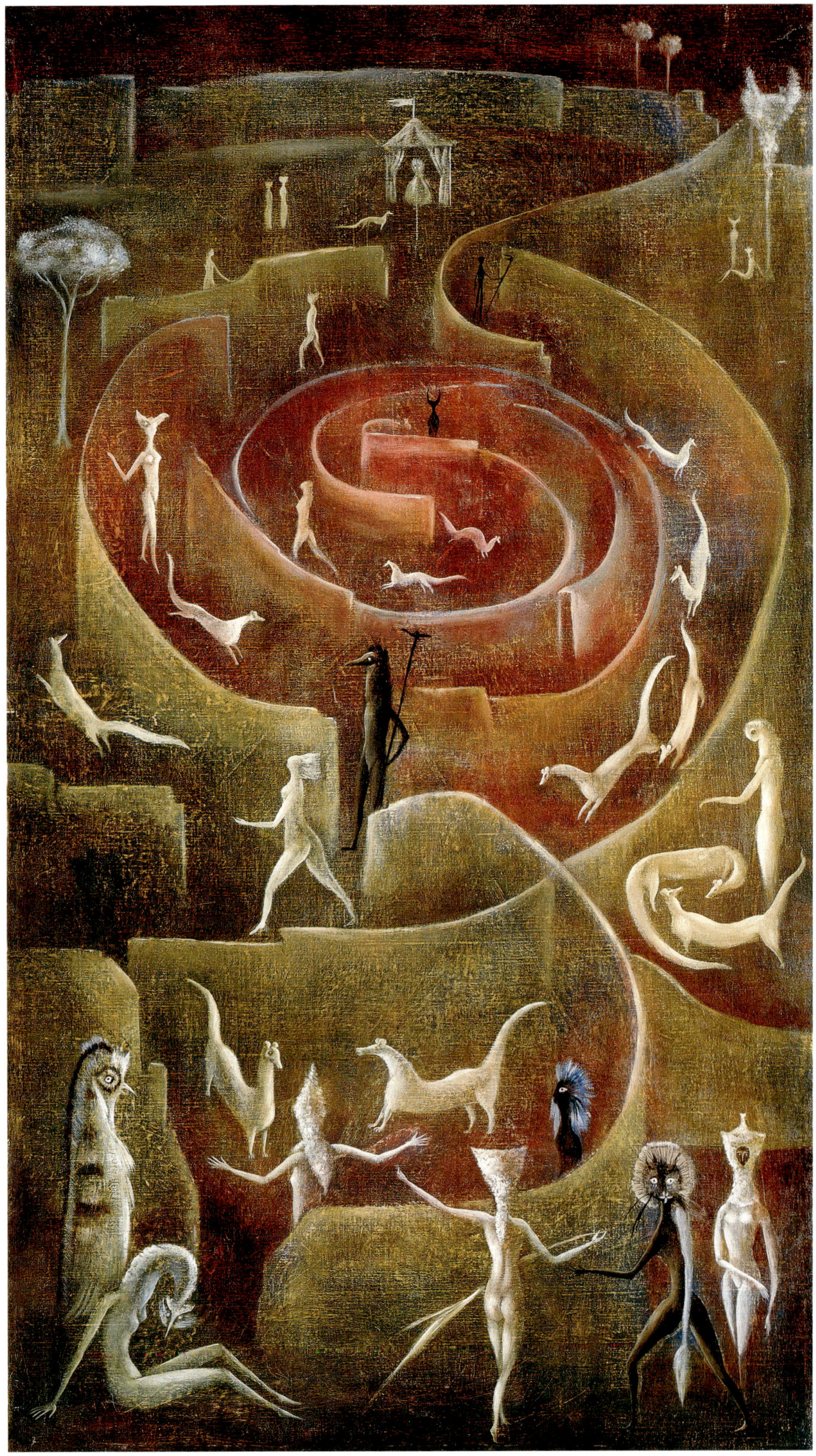

58
Samain
1951
Oil and tempera on three-ply
91 x 55 cm/36 x 22 in
Private collection

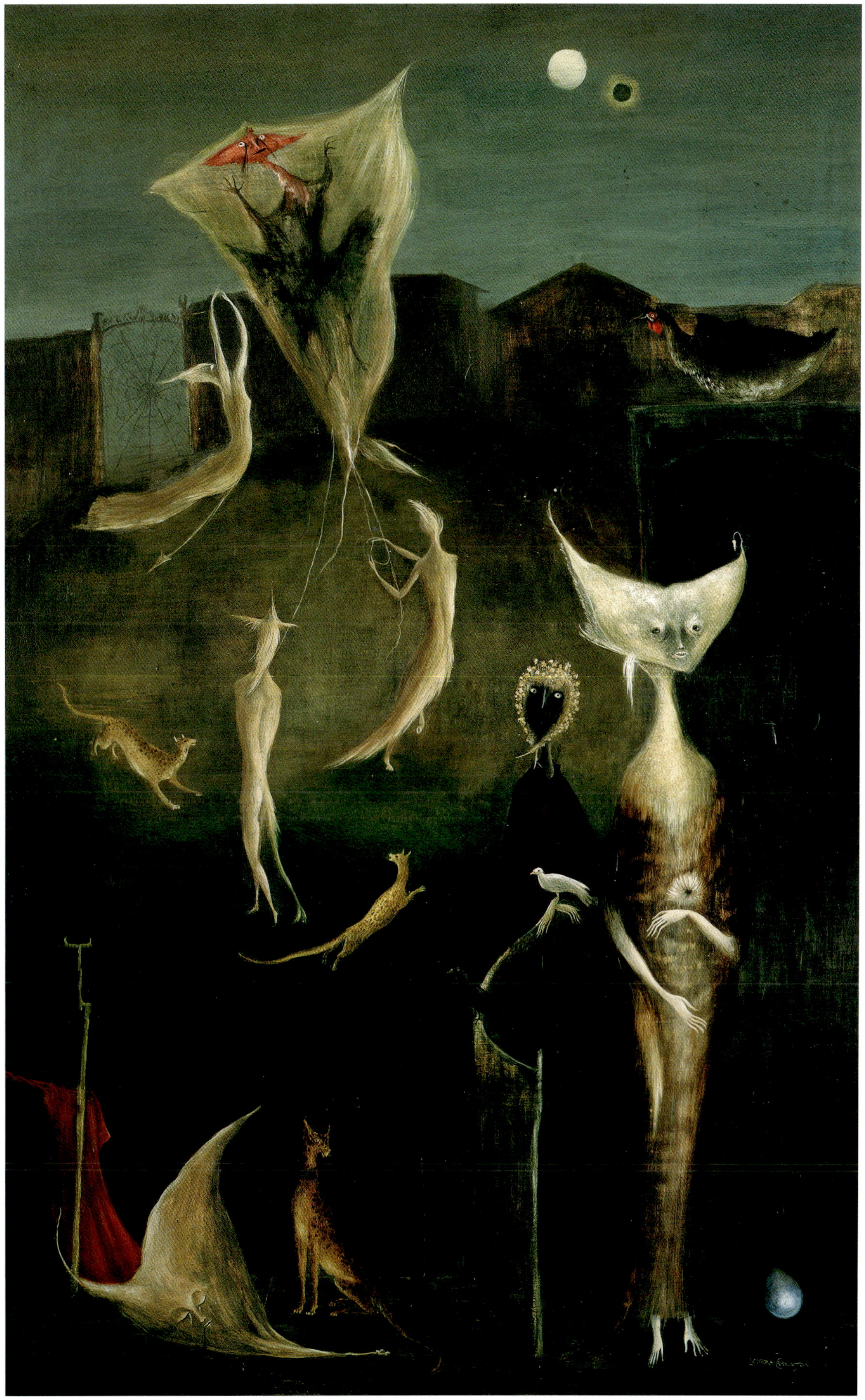

59

Good Morning Dr. Fischer

*c.*1951–2

Oil on canvas

57 x 70 cm / $22\frac{1}{2}$ x $27\frac{1}{2}$ in

Private collection

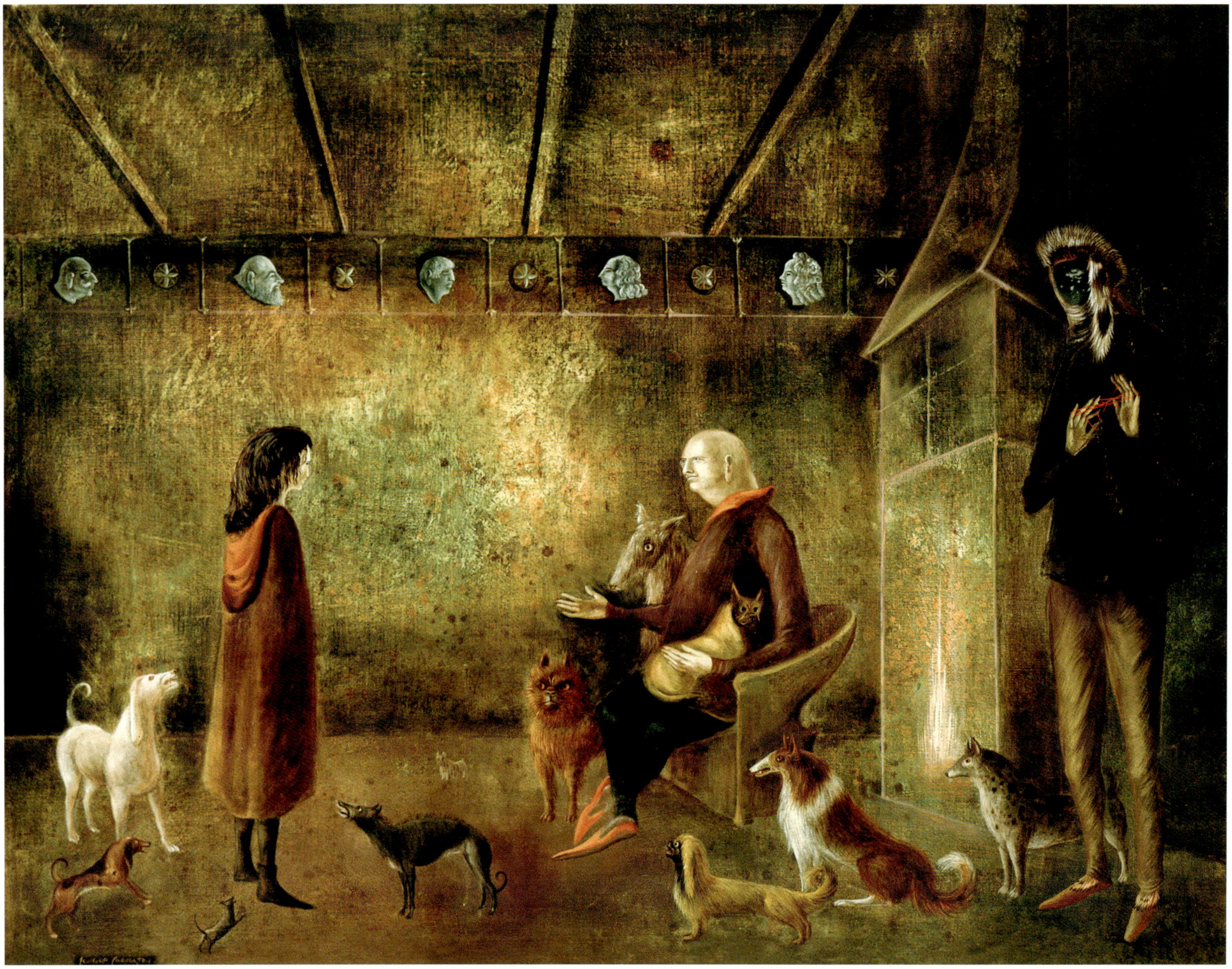

60

And Then We Saw The Daughter of the Minotaur

1953

Oil on canvas

60 x 70 cm/23½ x 27½ in

Private collection

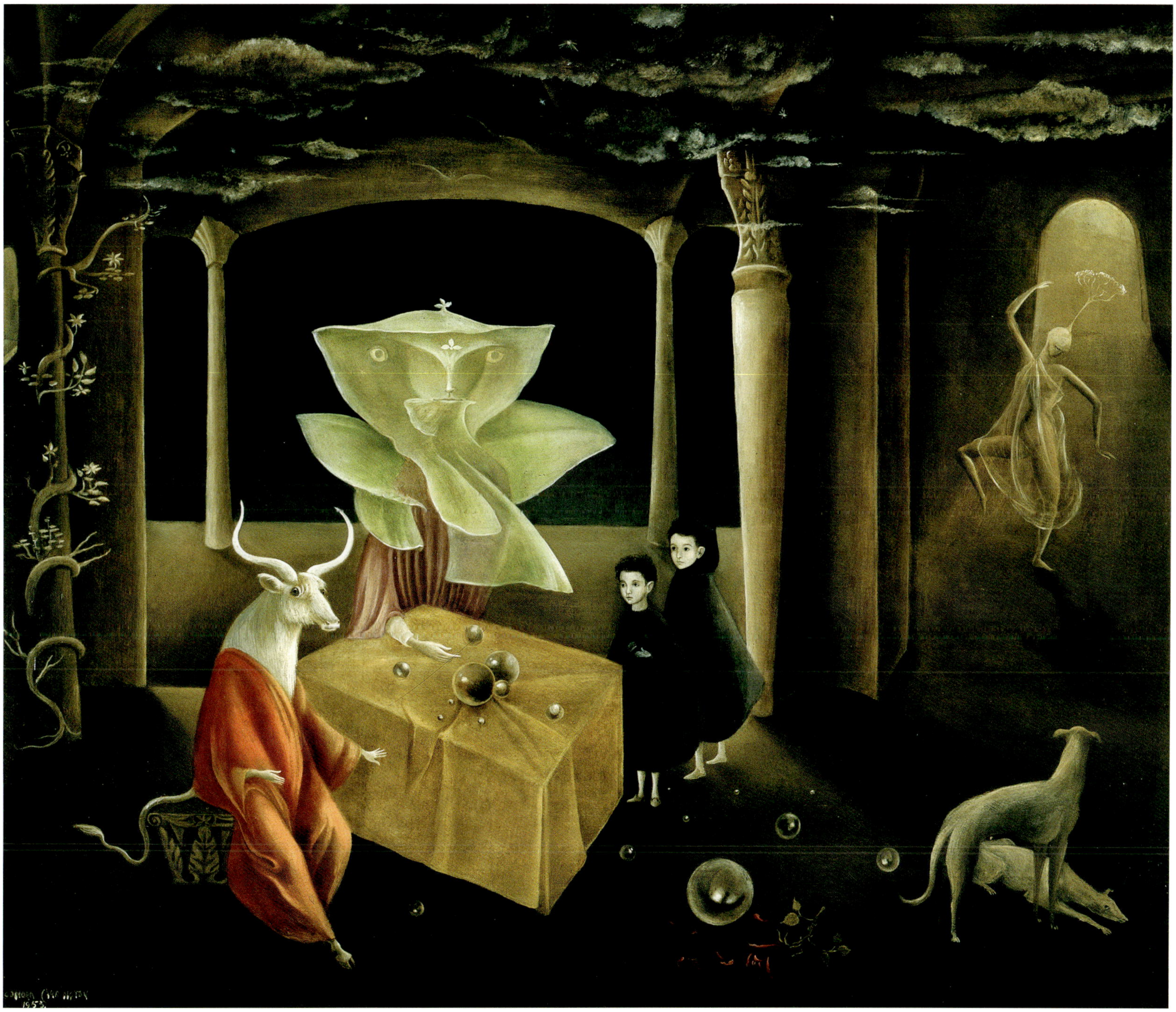

61
Are You Really Syrious?
1953
Oil on three-ply
53.5 x 91.5 cm / 21 x 36 in
Collection of Miguel S. Escobedo

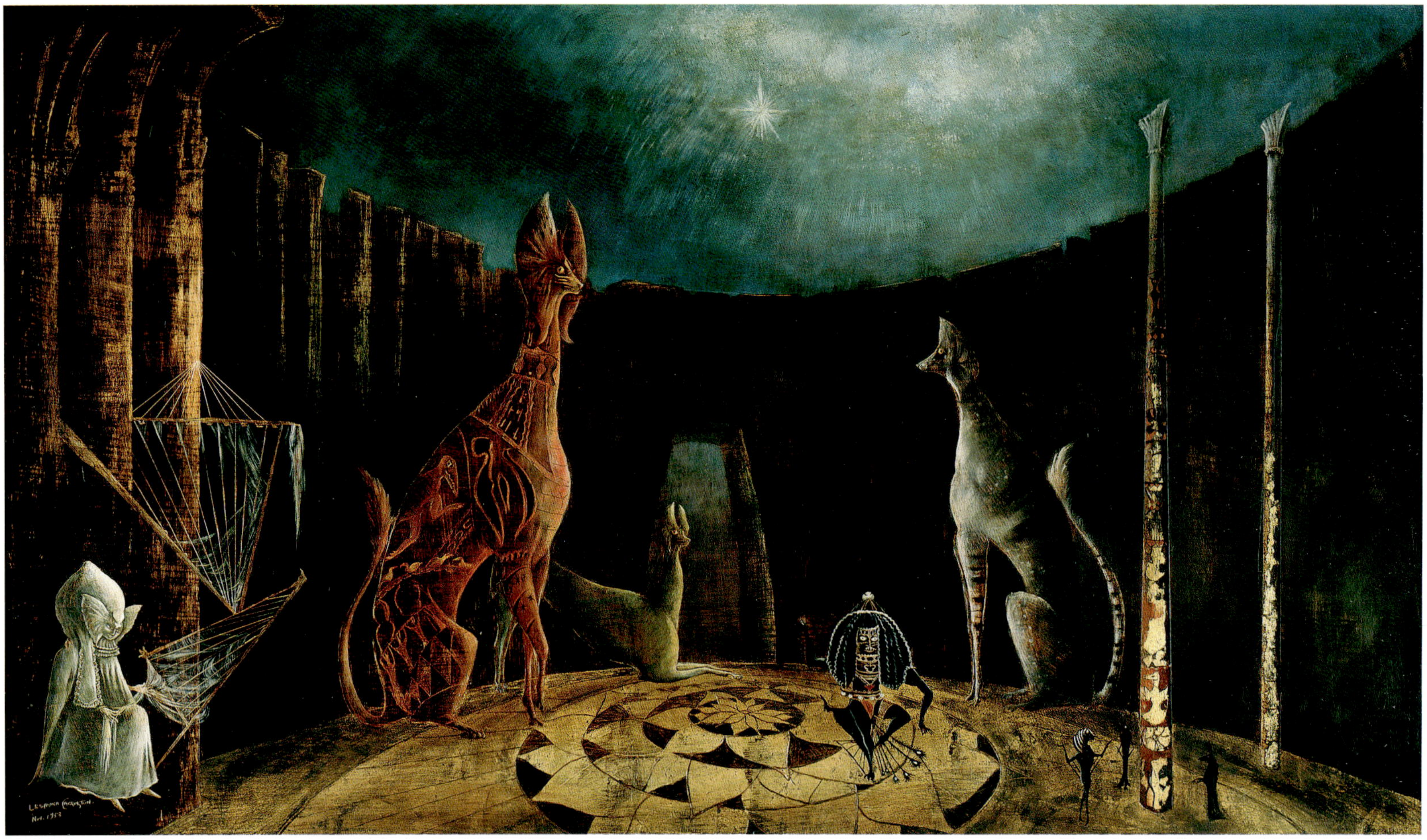

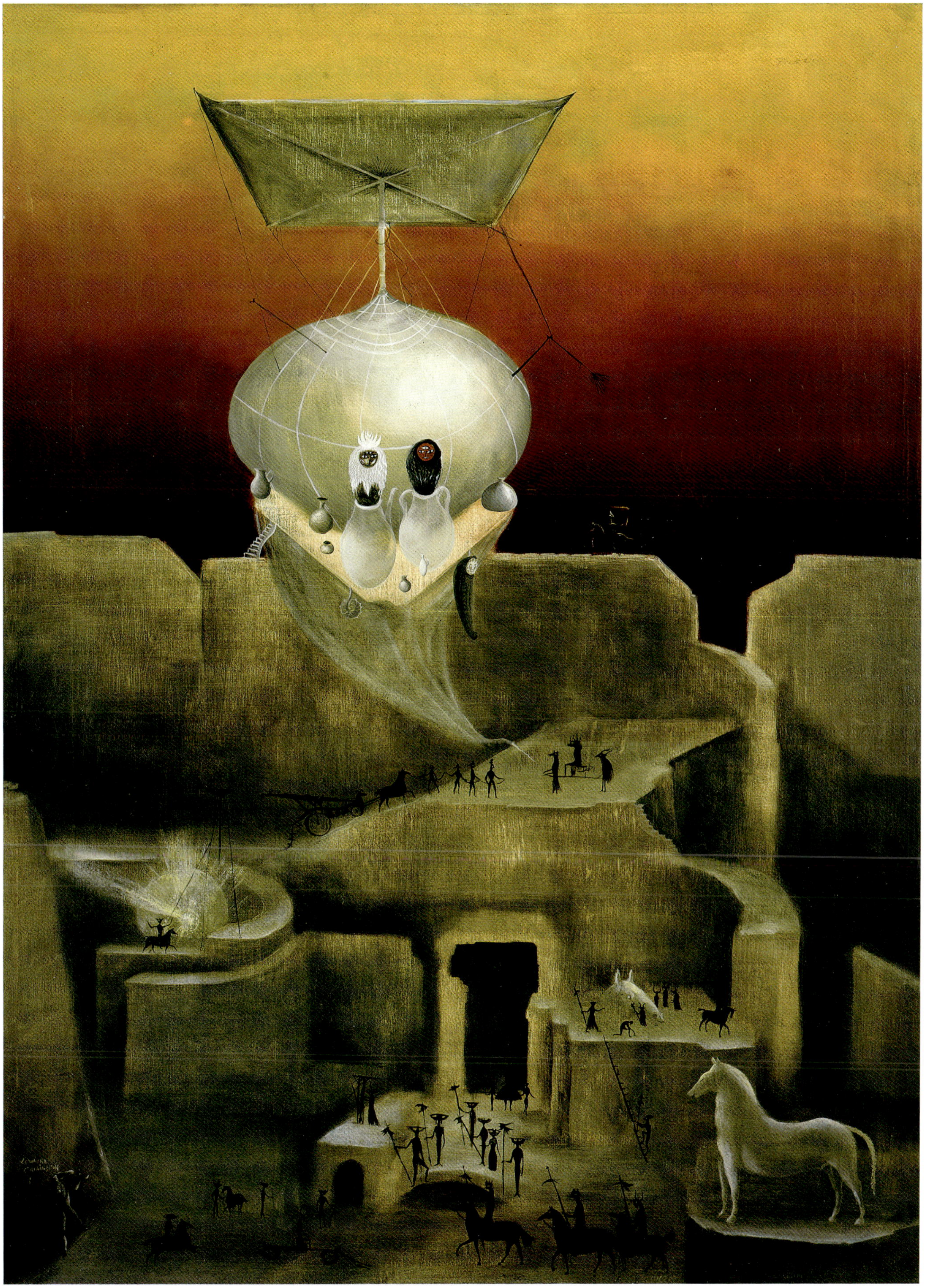

62
The Flying Ur Jar
1953
Oil on canvas
64.8 x 45.7 cm/
25½ x 18 in
Private collection

63

Casting the Runes

1951

Oil, tempera and gold leaf on panel

77.5 x 44.5 cm/30½ x 17½ in

Private collection

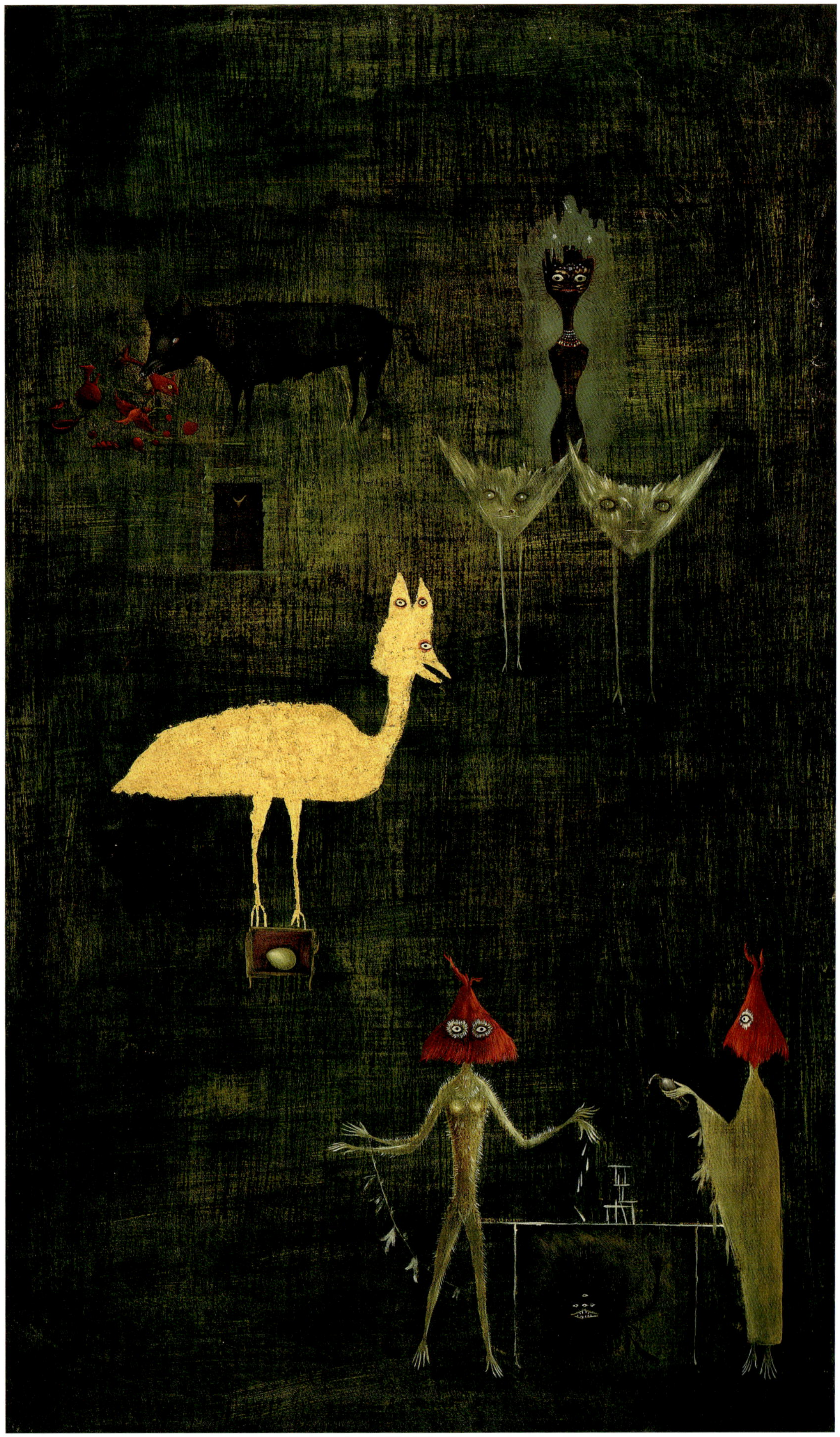

64
Untitled
1952
Painted wood
H: 40 cm/16 in
Private collection

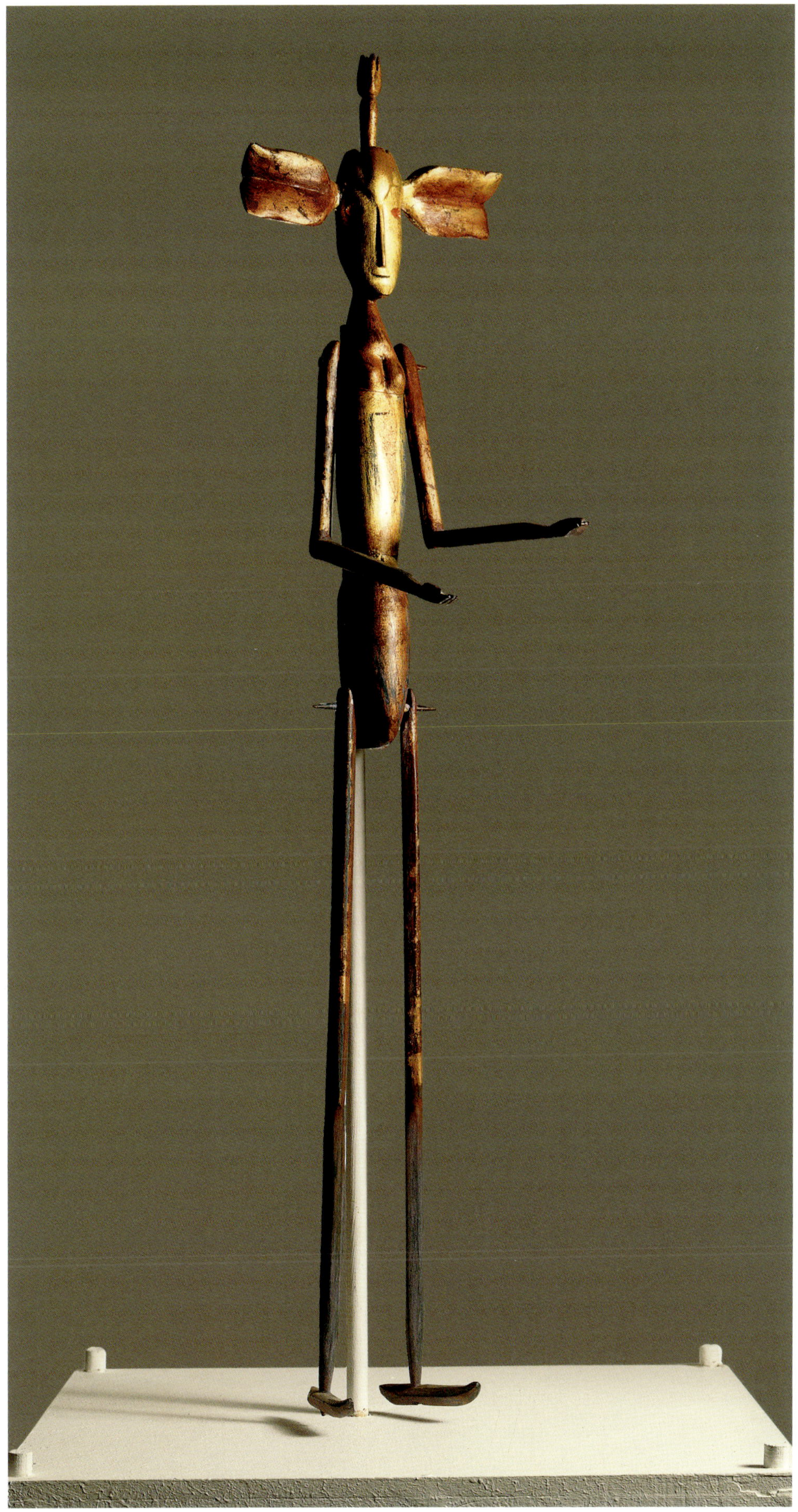

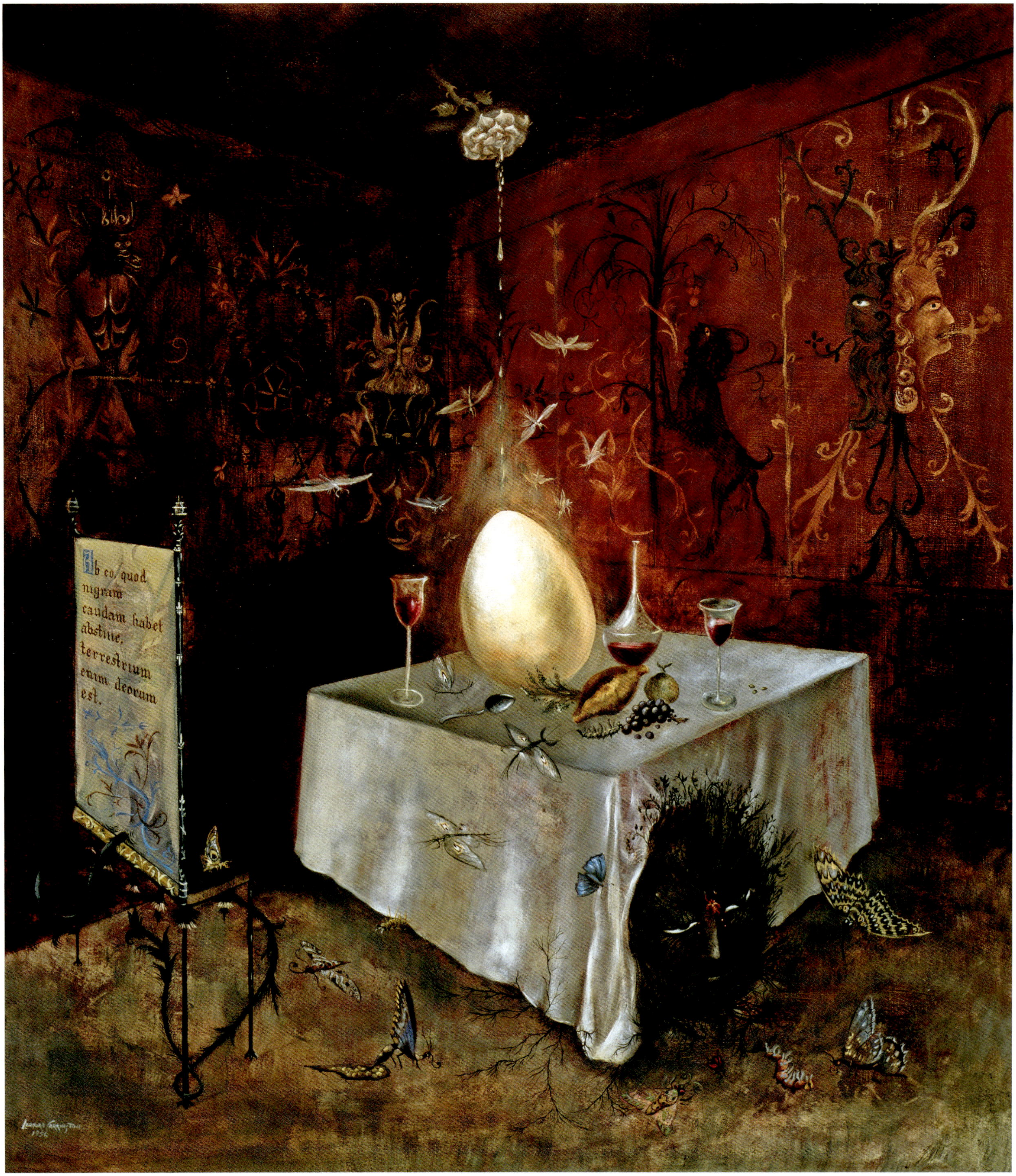
Ab eo, quod
nigram
caudam habet
abstine,
terrestrium
enim deorum
est.

65
AB EO QUOD
1956
Oil on canvas
71 x 61 cm/28 x 24 in
Private collection

66
Coitus
1628
Alchemical drawing from J.D. Mylius, in
Anatomia auri, Frankfurt

bread of the Eucharist, a symbolism reinforced by the further inclusion of a wheat-like grain and grapes. The Christian tone is offset by the addition of a pomegranate with its intimations of the underworld and the goddess. A glass beaker with wine and two full wineglasses are set to be drunk by invisible participants who are, perhaps, waiting for what appears to be an unfolding alchemical drama to conclude. Here alchemy has a direct correlation to the transubstantiation that occurs in the Catholic mass. On the ceiling of Carrington's painting is another white rose, dangling like a chandelier, that drips water on to the egg, thereby instigating the alchemical process, as the steam vaporising off the egg indicates. Other strange and unsettling things are also visible, however, that lend the scene a disturbing atmosphere. The walls are covered in arcane diagrams that highlight duality; a white woman's head joined to a black bearded man's, an Assyrian-looking goat rearing on a tree, a circle inscribed in a square, the cabbalist symbol for the spark of divine fire lying hidden within matter. An embroidered fire screen bears the Latin words 'Ab eo, Quod nigram caudum habet abstine terrestrium enim decorum est', which is a fragment from the *Asensus Nigrum*, an obscure alchemical text from 1351. This roughly translates as: 'Keep away from any with a black tail, indeed, this is the beauty of the earth.' To emphasise this point, the lower portion of the fire screen is encircled by a long and hairy black tail that grows out of the embroidery and resembles the linear designs on the wall. As if conjured from subterranean realms, peering out from below the table is the face of a creature whose 'fur' is made up, upon closer inspection, of dark grasses. Everywhere large moths (perhaps butterflies) are hatching from their cocoons and fluttering about, an allusion to processes of transformation and metamorphosis.

Also from 1956, Carrington's *Hunt Breakfast* (Fig.55)[228] continues her project of combining iconographic elements from diverse belief systems to reveal suppressed doctrines,

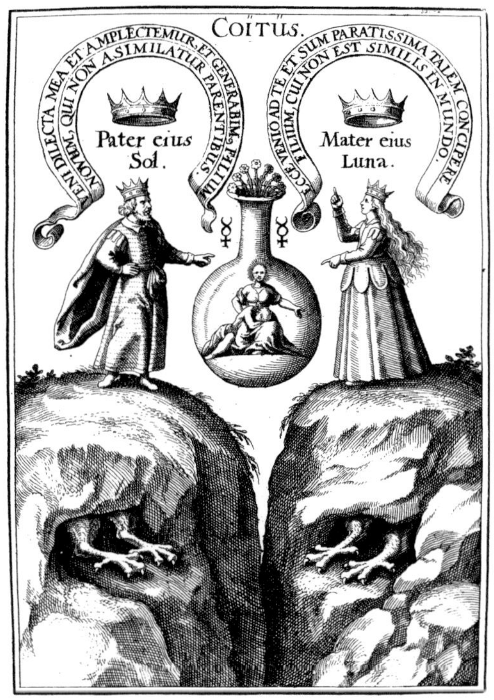

this time, however, with a certain irony. At first glance this painting appears to be a parody of the pastimes of upper-class English society, in particular the hunt. Attendants hold birds with accompanying hounds, another is on a white horse, while two sumptuously dressed matrons with overblown hats are seated at the table looking at a couple. The scene is reminiscent of the hunts Carrington herself attended while on the débutante circuit, but upon closer inspection we realise that we are witnessing a wedding. The groom is a proper Edwardian gentleman, elegantly clad with carefully combed and parted hair, but who is his strange black bride? Resisting a singular identification, she instead possesses multiple attributes. She can be identified as Artemis/Diana, the Greco-Roman goddess of the hunt, night, women, the moon and nature; the wild animals coming out of the woods into the clearing are under her protection. Her multiple breasts allude to Diana of Ephesus and the red horns

67
Gabriel, Leonora and Pablo Carrington
*c.*1959–60
Photograph: Stella Snead

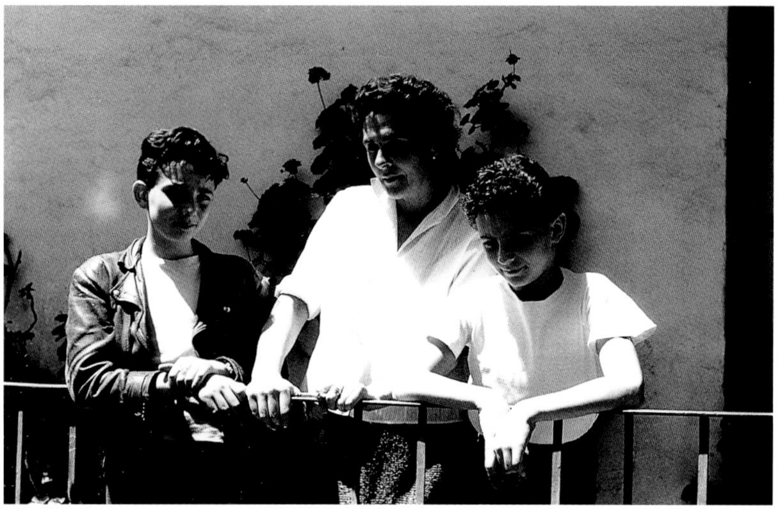

(terminating in snakes) of her headdress to her Egyptian counterpart, Isis-Hathor.[229] A large table, placed in the centre of a natural clearing forming a magic circle, is set again with the Eucharistic pile of wheat grain and wine. A variety of fruits and vegetables are strewn about the table, the two most meaningful being the pomegranate and cabbage, providing a clue as to what is transpiring. While alluding to fertility, Persephone and the periodic return of spring, the pomegranate also symbolises the Resurrection and members of the Catholic Church. The common domestic cabbage has great meaning for Carrington, who believes it to be the true alchemical rose:

> The Cabbage is a rose, the Blue Rose, The Alchemical Rose, The Blue Deer (Peyote), and the eating of the God is ancient knowledge, but only recently known to 'civilized occidental' Humans who have experienced many phenomena, and have recently written many books that give accounts of the changing worlds which these people have seen when they ate these plants. Although the properties of the cabbage are somewhat different, it also screams when dragged out of the earth and plunged into boiling water or grease – forgive us, cabbage ... The cabbage is still the alchemical Rose, for any being able to see or taste.[230]

Worn on her head like a veil is the upward-pointing triangle, the ancient symbol for the three-fold nature of the goddess and the three stages of womanhood: maiden, mother and crone. The white rose in front of her is the alchemical rose but can also link her to the Virgin Mary. The groom's left hand carefully rests on the table and holds an egg, the alchemical egg. The triangle of her head combined with her vertical body closely resembles the alchemical sign for sulphur (an upward-pointing triangle above a cross, similar to the planetary sign for Venus), which makes the groom Mercury, a favourite partner. This is a complex marriage between diverse traditions, spanning many times and places. It is a union that seeks to reconcile opposites: between man and woman, white and black, the contemporary and ancient, culture and nature. The table is now the site of a wedding banquet, an iconographic feast. Included among the guests are an elderly Mexican couple who, located in the foreground, serve as a link into the space of the painting, allowing the viewer to share in this solemn celebration, transformed from passive onlooker to active participant. Carlos Fuentes summed it up best in an exhibition essay entitled 'Leonora Carrington, or Ironical Sorcery': 'All Leonora Carrington's art is a gay, diabolical and persistent struggle against orthodoxy, which Leonora conquers and disperses with imagination, always multiple and singular, an imagination which she communicates with loving pride.'[231]

68
The Chair, Daghda Tuatha dé Danaan
1955
Oil on canvas
49 x 39 cm/19½ x 1 ½ in
Private collection

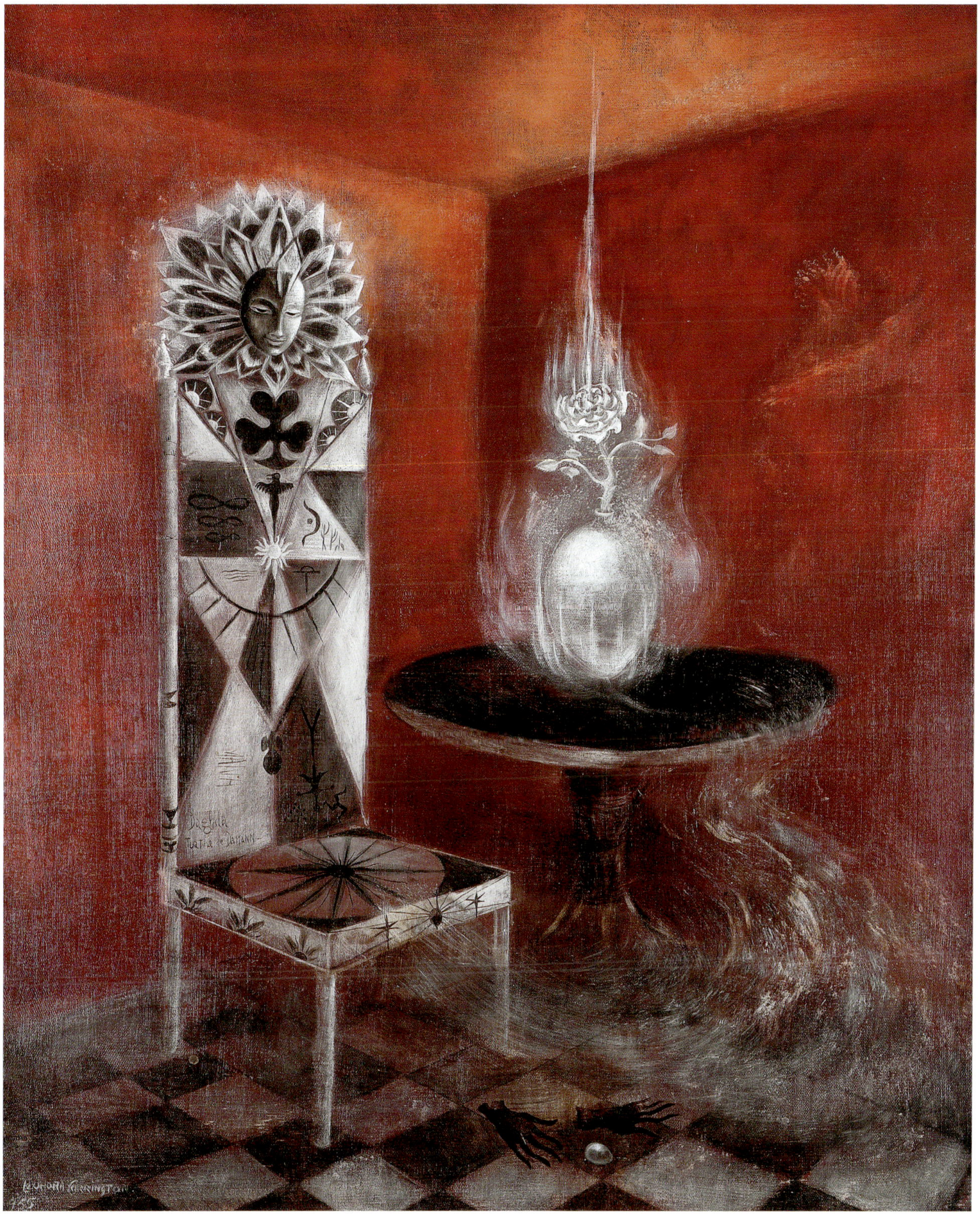

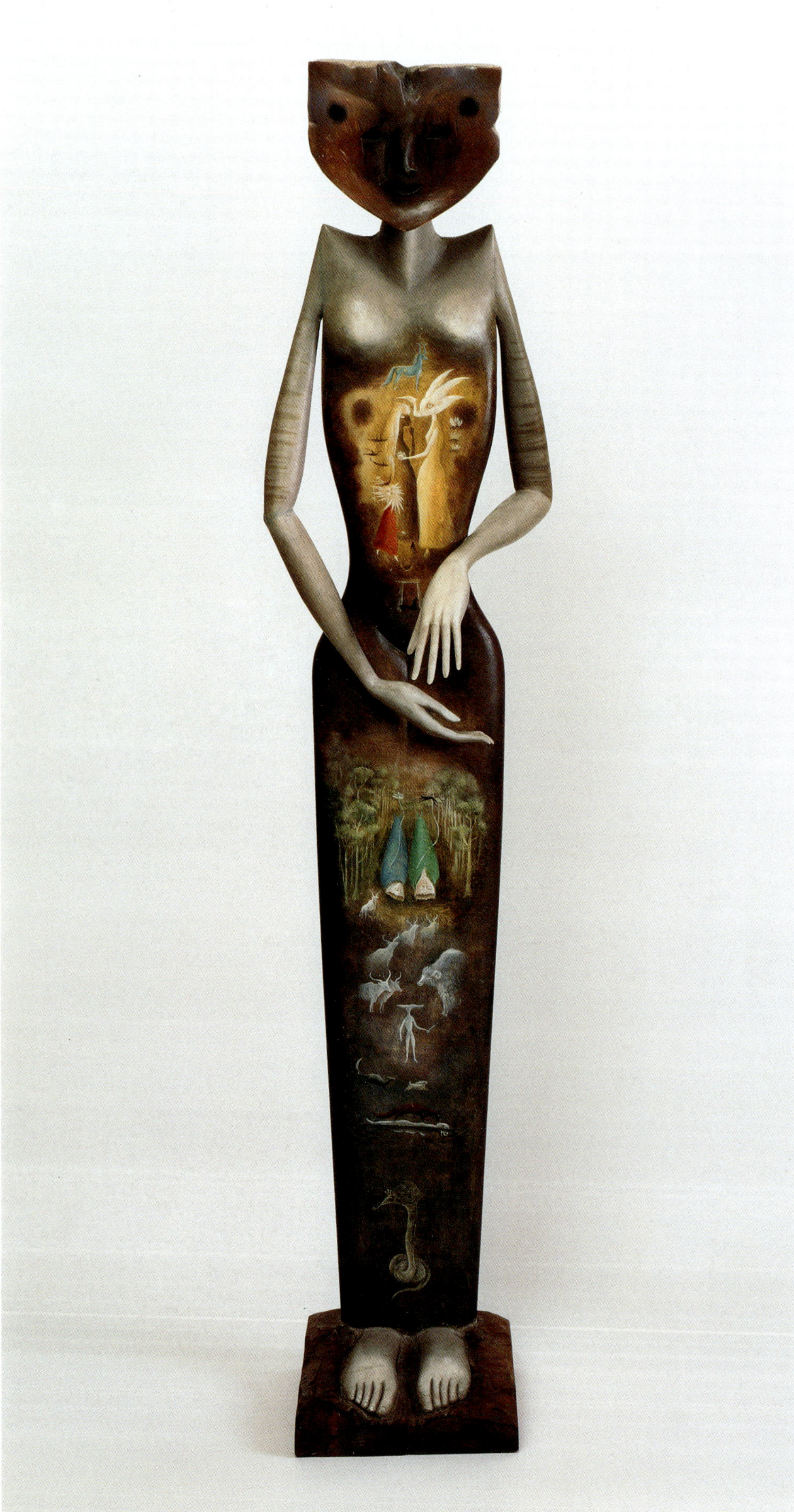

69
Cat Woman (La Grande Dame)
1951
Polychrome wood sculpture
H: 203 cm/80 in
Private collection

CHAPTER 5 ESOTERIC INTERESTS

The Galería de Arte Mexicano, the most important and influential venue for modern Mexican artists, run by Inés Amor, had become Carrington's primary dealer around 1956; for just a little over a decade from her first arrival that was quite an accomplishment. Carrington experimented with a wide variety of media, even hand-sewing and embroidering dolls. She created large-scale polychrome wood sculptures, such as the arresting *Cat Woman* (1951) (Fig.69), which stands tall at 203 cm, like an ancient Egyptian guardian figure, covered with small hieroglyphic-like painted figures. Inviting indigenous weavers into her home in 1953, she designed a set of wool tapestries covered with heraldic animals and plants (Fig.72). Like many Mexican artists in the 1950s, she delved into stage design. However, because she had a history of writing theatrical pieces Carrington was able to create the costumes and settings for her own play, *Pénélope*, in 1957 (Fig.74). A theatrical ambience enters into her painting at the time as well, for example her masterful *Temple of the Word* from 1954 (Fig.71) evokes medieval pageantry while another work from the same year, *Sacrament at Minos* (Fig.70), hints at sacerdotal mystery plays from the ancient Near East.

By the 1960s Carrington was fully versed in a number of esoteric traditions and her work fluidly employed a vast repertoire of subjects and symbols. The extent of her prodigious output was not only indicative of her creative powers but also of a commitment to her vision and a discipline in working methods: 'The real work is done when you are alone in your studio and that's it, it becomes a sense of something and then it becomes something you can see and then it becomes something you can do.'[232] A retrospective exhibition of her work in 1960 at the Museo Nacional de Arte Moderno in Mexico City, *Exposición Retrospectiva de Pinturas y Tapices de Leonora Carrington*, was substantial, with 55 pieces. Then in 1961, for the first time, she was included as a *Mexican* artist in the exhibition *El Retrato Mexicano Contemporaneo*, sponsored by the Museo Nacional de Arte Moderno and the Instituto Nacional de Bellas Artes. Not only had Mexico become her home but, more importantly, Mexico from now on perceived her as one of its own.

Ignacio Bernal became the Director of the highly acclaimed new Museo Nacional de Antropología, located in Chapultepec Park in Mexico City, which opened in 1964. A long-time friend, admirer and collector of Carrington's work, Bernal was instrumental in helping her to receive a prestigious governmental commission to paint a mural for the museum. She was one of a number of famous artists chosen to execute murals for the museum's display areas, including, among others, Rufino Tamayo, Pablo O'Higgins, Carlos Mérida, and Rafael Coronel. Entitled *El mundo mágico de los Mayas* (Fig.73), hers was destined for the section in the museum dedicated to the state of Chiapas, and to that end she travelled there in 1963 to study the region and its peoples. In San Cristóbal de las Casas she stayed with the Swiss anthropologist Gertrude Blom, whose fieldwork focused on the Lacandon Indians who lived in the area. Through Blom she was introduced to two Chiapas *curanderos* (healers) from the village of Zinacantán (called the 'House of the Bats') and, although wary of foreigners, they were so impressed by her knowledge of and respect for traditional healing that they allowed her to attend some of their ceremonies. During a six-month period Carrington executed many preliminary drawings of the villagers and also of the animals at the zoo in Tuxtla Gutiérrez.[233] When she returned home she began to study the *Popol Vuh*, the sacred book of the ancient Quiche Maya, in order to understand better the preconquest beliefs of the Chiapas Indians, descendants of the ancient Maya. In spite of the fact that Carrington in general tended to avoid the constrictions of commissions, previously had little interest in depicting Mexican scenes, and had never painted anything of this size (the mural is 213 x 457 cm), *El mundo mágico de los Mayas* presents a sweeping, vibrant panorama of the

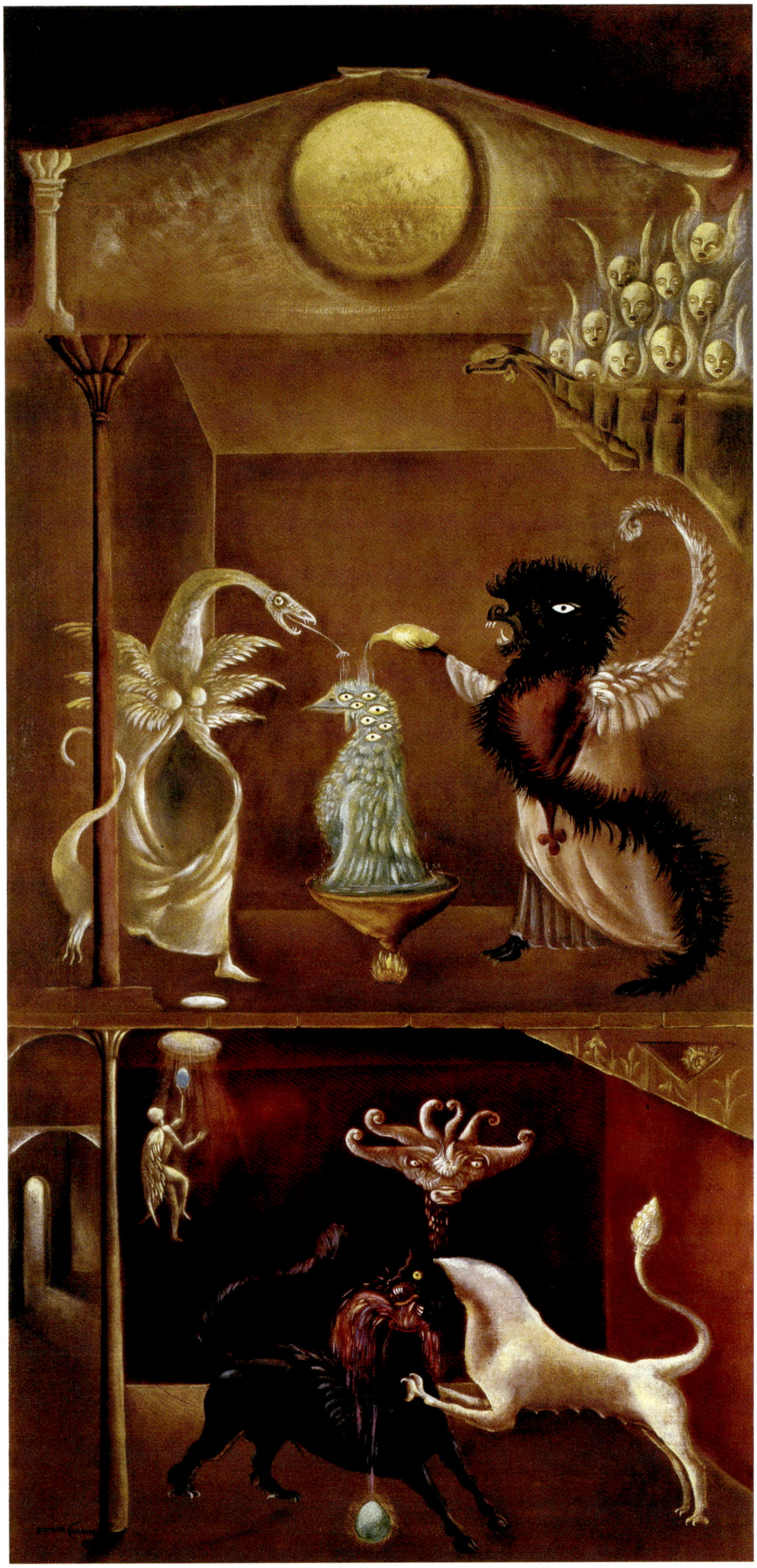

70
Sacrament at Minos
1954
Oil on canvas
96 x 45 cm/38 x 18 in
Private collection

71
Temple of the Word
1954
Oil and gold leaf on canvas
100.3 x 80 cm/39½ x 31½ in
Private collection

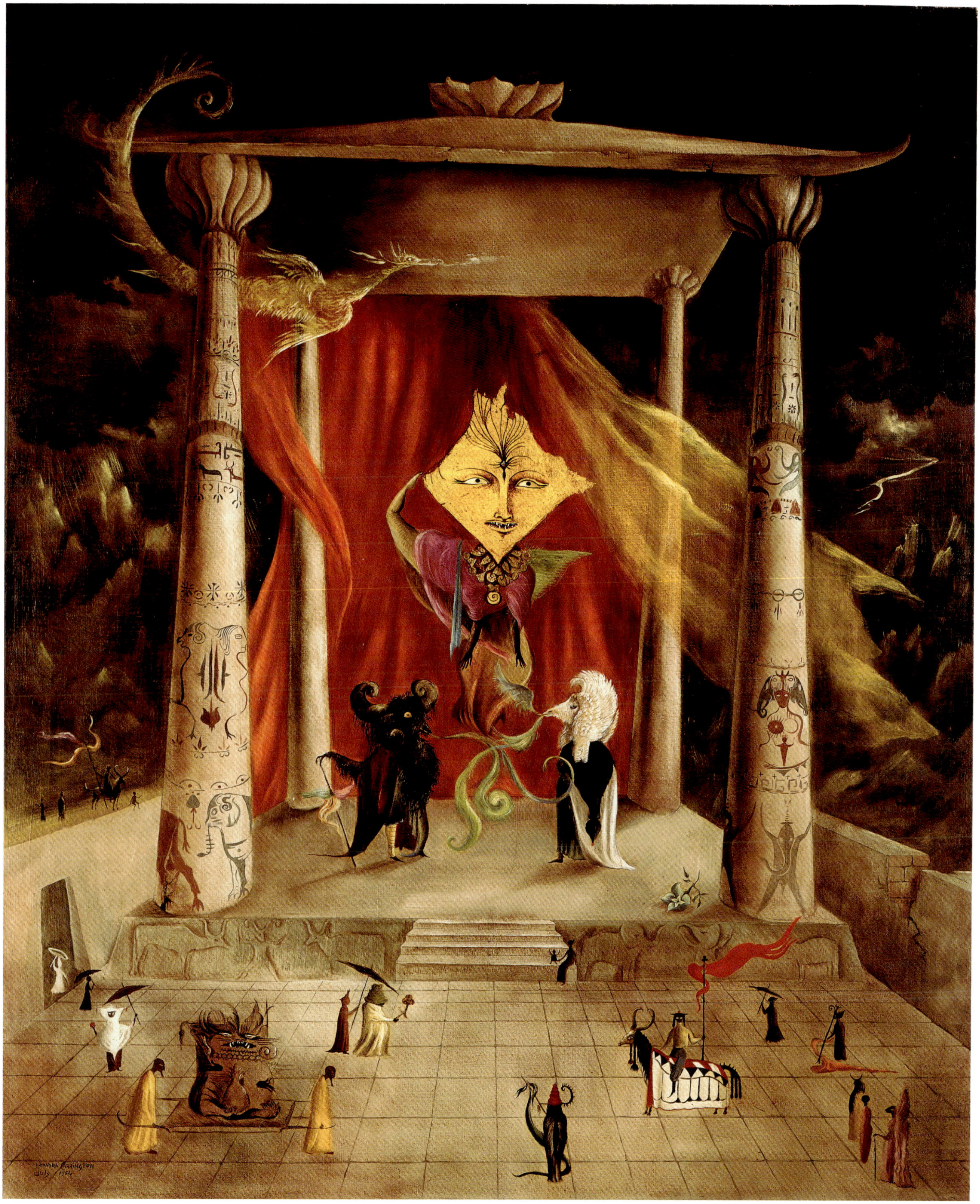

72
The Snakes
1961
Set of three tapestries, wool and metallic thread
254 x 110 cm/100 x 43 in

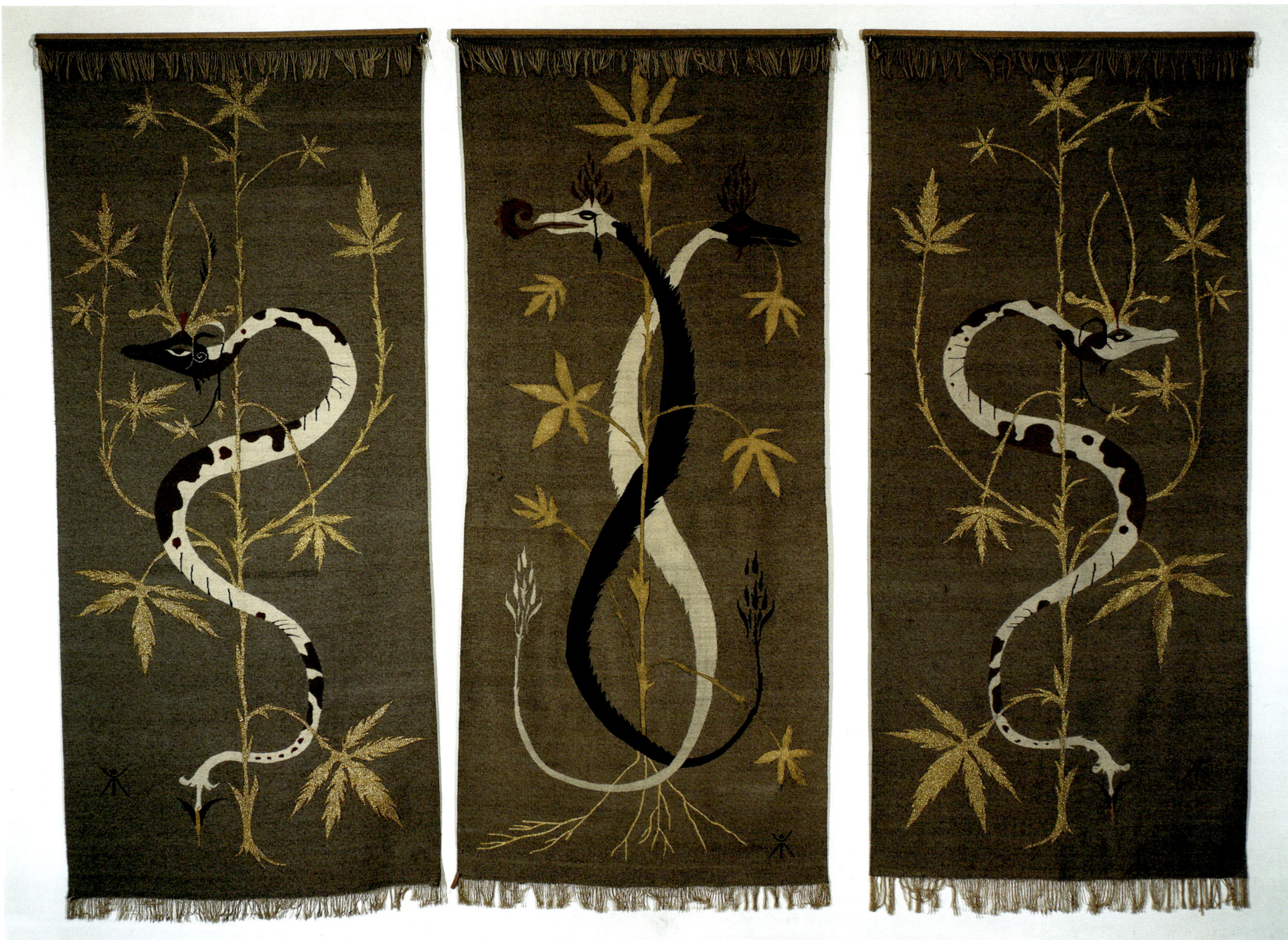

73
El mundo mágico de los mayas
1963
Casein on panel
213 x 457 cm/84 x180 in

Photo credit: Courtesy of INAH

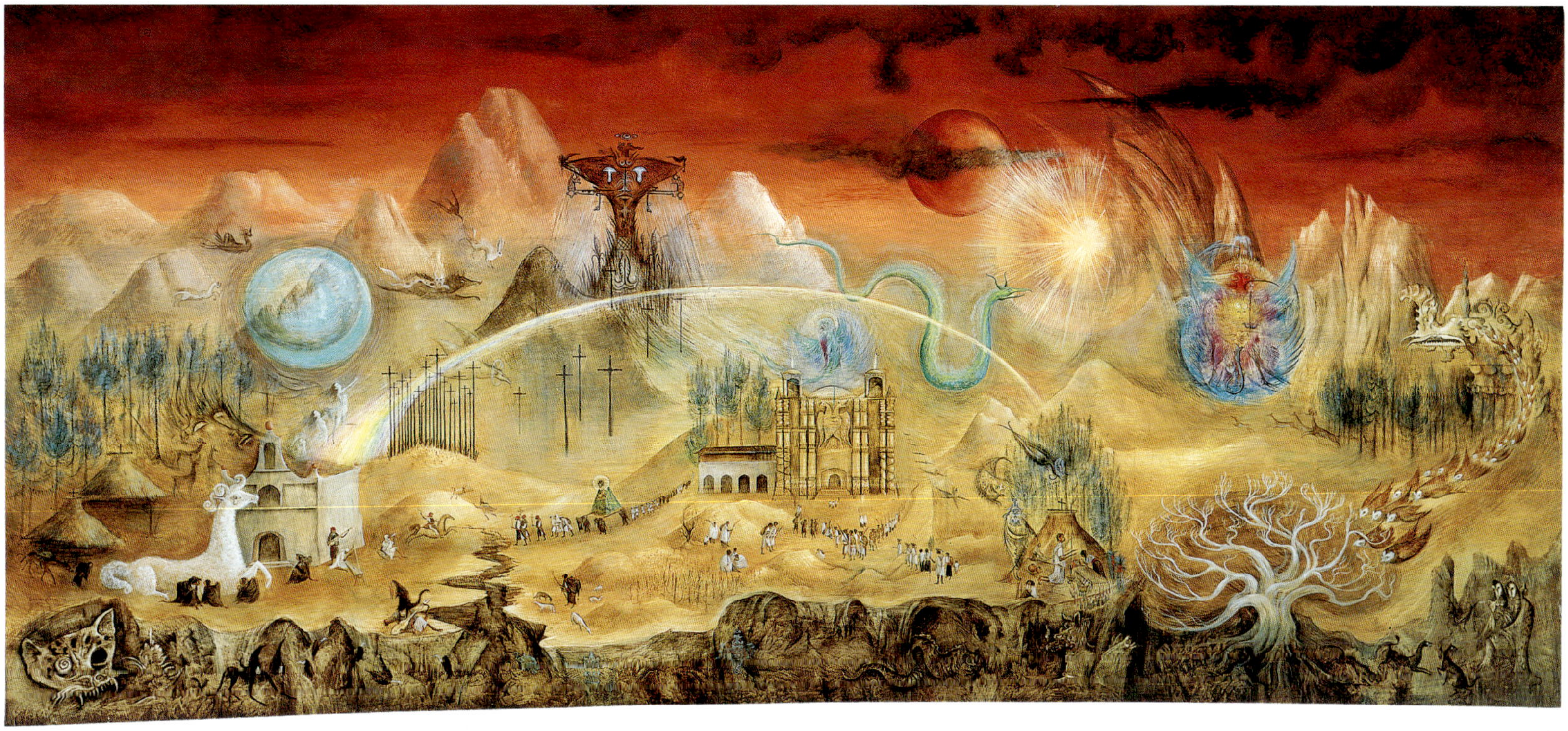

74
Pénélope
1957
Play by Leonora Carrington staged by Alexandro Jodorowsky in Mexico City
Set design and costumes designed by the artist

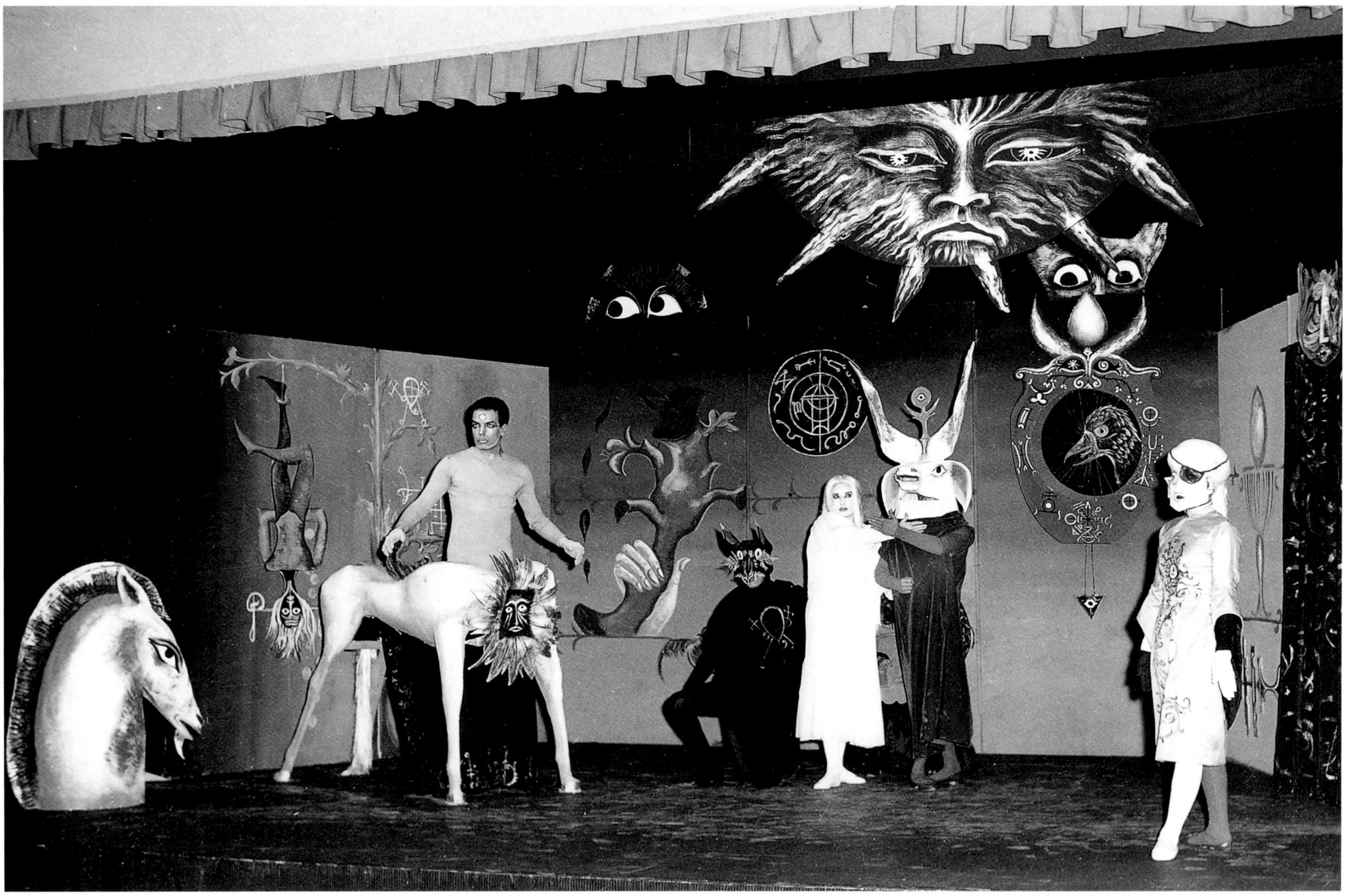

material and spiritual life of Chiapas. The composition is clearly divided into celestial, terrestrial and subterranean realms where mythological entities animate the landscape, Catholic processions take place next to indigenous healings, and animals energetically cavort, moving with ease between realms. Here the past and present, the sacred and the secular, and the seen and hidden co-exist and co-mingle as they are viewed through Carrington's visionary filter.

Themes from Jewish mysticism increasingly make their appearance throughout the 1960s in works such as *The Chrysopeia of Mary the Jewess* (1964) (Fig.76); *El Poliedro de Hod* (1965); *The Bath of Rabbi Loew* (1969) (Fig.77); as well as scenes from *The Dybbuk* (1967). The fact that Carrington's husband and a good number of her friends were Jewish may have sparked her interest in the cabbala; however, she was incapable of canonical veneration and these

75
Letter to Dana
1957
Gouache on masonite
39 x 30.5 cm/15½ x 12 in
Private collection

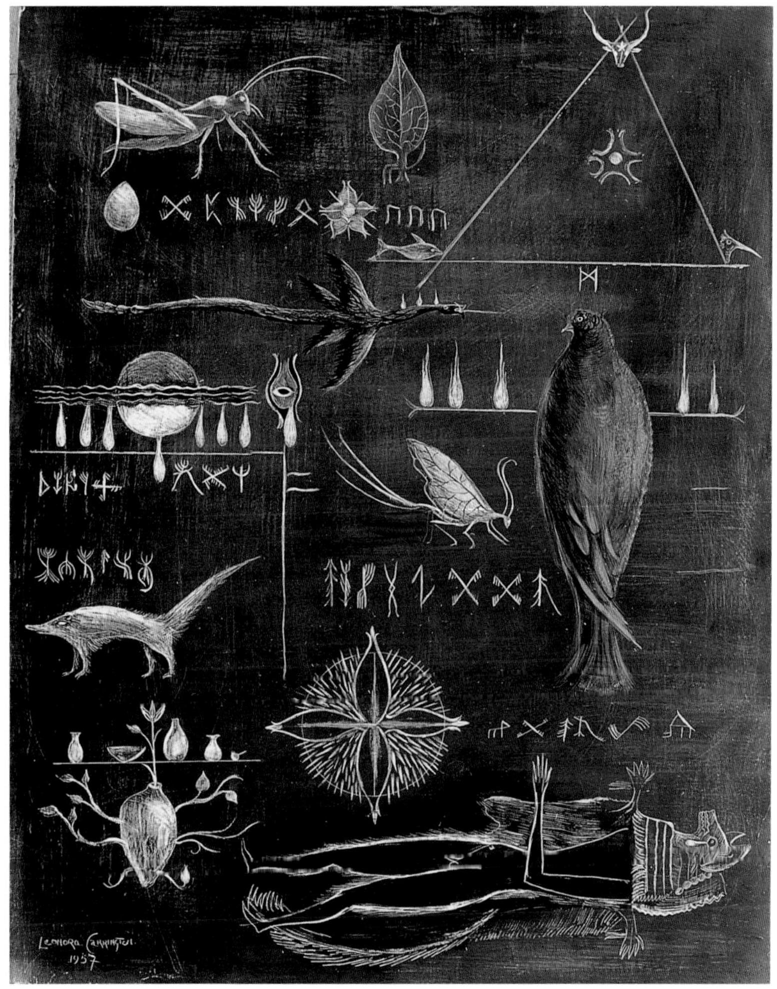

paintings can veer off into playful satire as in *Pig Rush* (1960) (Fig.78) where a group of rabbis are threatened by a herd of approaching swine. Carrington's friend, Carlos Fuentes, applauds her oppositional strategies most eloquently: 'The world is simple and life is flat when the dualities that have impoverished and simplified our lives for twenty-five centuries succeed in excluding, if not condemning, heretical multiplicity in order to install dogmatic monotony.'[234]

Beginning in 1968 and throughout the 1970s Carrington spent significant amounts of time in the United States, primarily in New York and the suburbs of Chicago. In New York she lived for a number of years in the neighbourhood surrounding Gramercy Park and became a regular visitor to the Kristine Mann Library of the C. G. Jung Center nearby. This library possesses an extraordinary collection of books that deal with not only psychology but also esoteric traditions from around the world. In addition, the Center houses ARAS (Archive for Research in Archetypal Symbolism), a remarkable collection of visual materials, arranged by subject. Carrington spent many hours there studying, with great curiosity and a desire to learn, personality traits that have defined and guided her life.[235] She was not particularly interested in either Freud or Jung and although she had long made it a practice to record her dreams, she insists that her work is rarely inspired by her dreams. It was in the 1970s that Carrington came into contact with the feminist movement, and as early as 1972, as previously mentioned, she designed a poster for Mexican women's liberation entitled *Mujeres Conciencia* (Fig.38). There was now an active political voice for all that Carrington had been philosophically and visually developing, and she began to receive attention from feminists re-evaluating her place in art history. Some of the creative isolation she had experienced was beginning to dissipate as interviewers and art historians sought her out, particularly in the United States. In 1974 Gloria Orenstein wrote a feature article 'Leonora Carrington: Another Reality' in no less than the first mainstream feminist publication *Ms. Magazine*.[236] Eschewing direct political involvements as always, her vociferous support of feminism in both the American and Mexican press constituted a risk she was willing to take, even if it meant her work being seen in an unflattering light. But the result was greater attention and appreciation, along with higher sales, and she now took on a New York dealer, Brewster Arts Ltd. Nor had they forgotten her in Mexico, for in 1974 Ediciones ERA published *Leonora Carrington*, a sumptuously illustrated book on her work written by Juan García Ponce.

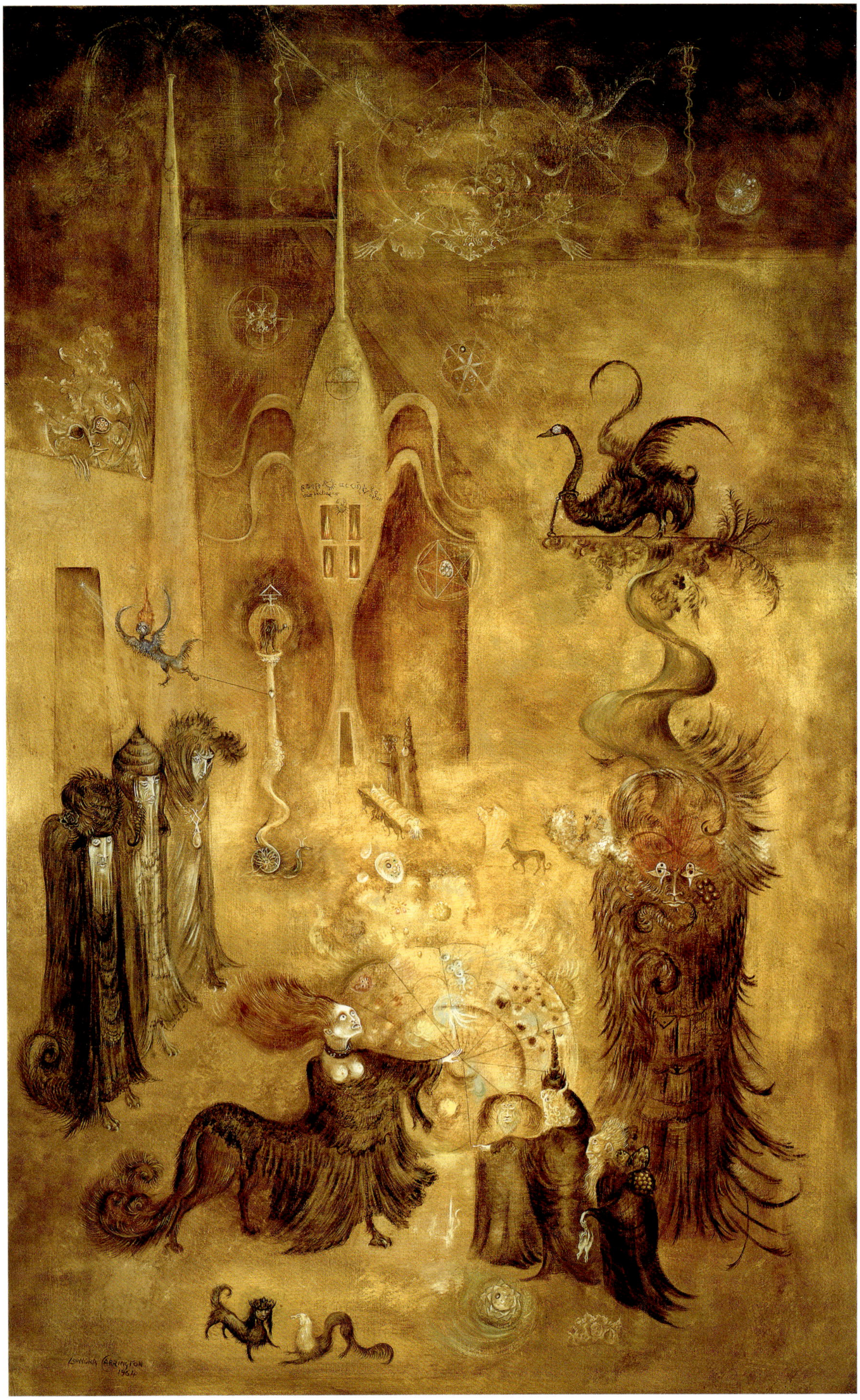

76
The Chrysopeia of Mary the Jewess
1964
Oil on canvas
150 x 90 cm/ 59 x 35½ in
Private collection

77
The Bath of Rabbi Loew
1969
Oil on canvas
45.5 x 68 cm / 18 x 27 in
Private collection

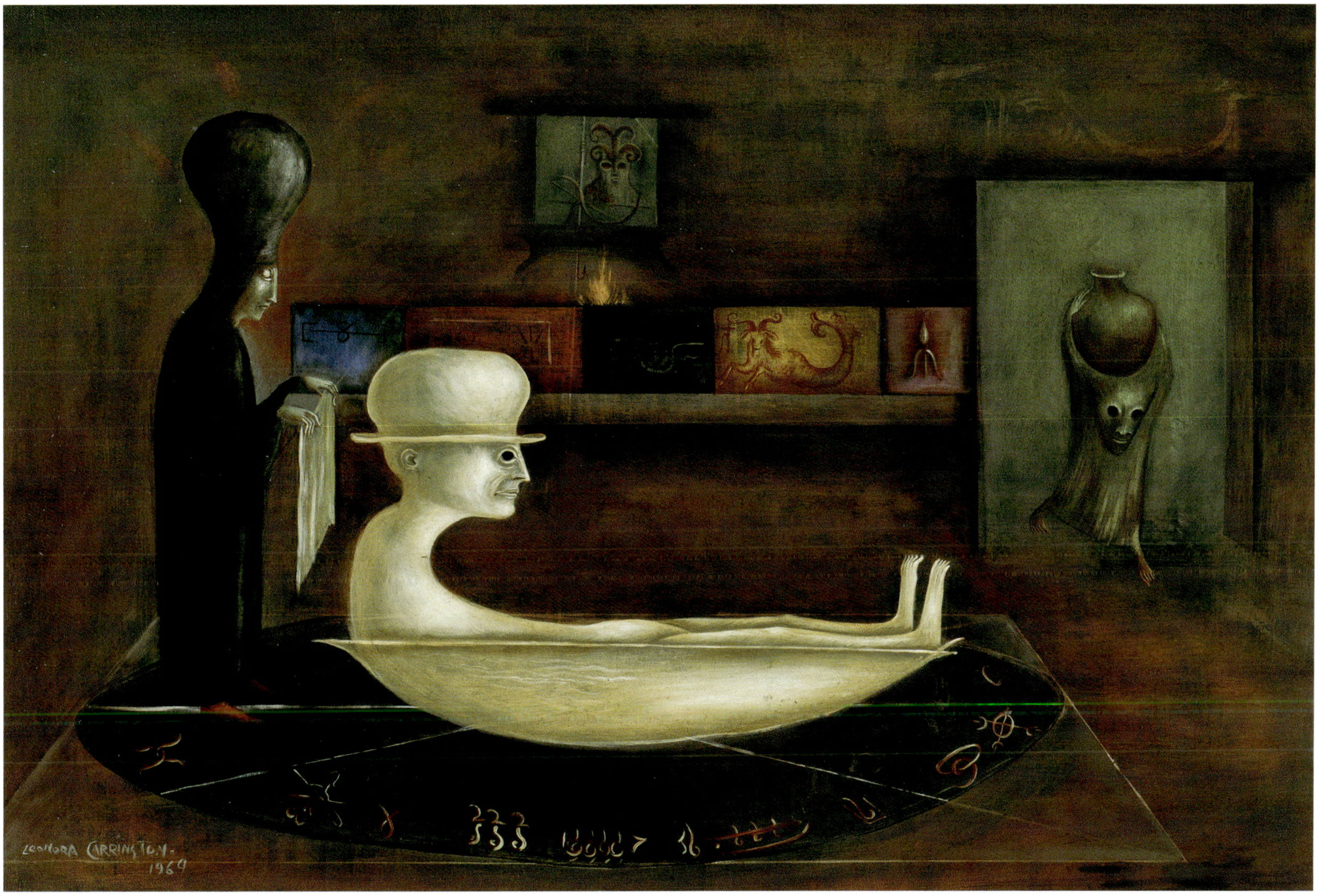

78
Pig Rush
1960
Oil on canvas
80 x 90 cm/31½ x 35½ in

79
Naturaleza Muerta (Still Life)
1960
Oil on canvas
90 x 36 cm/35½ x 14 in
Private collection

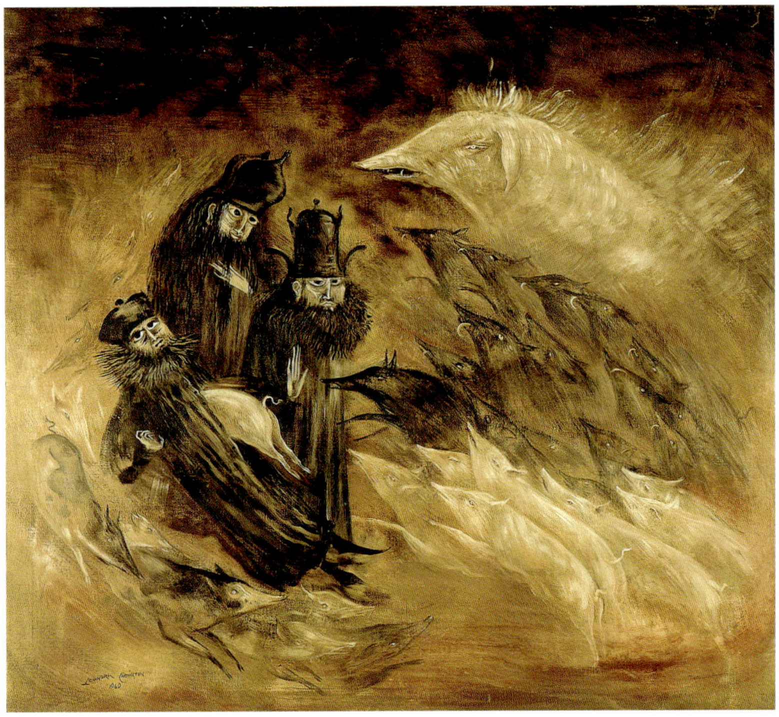

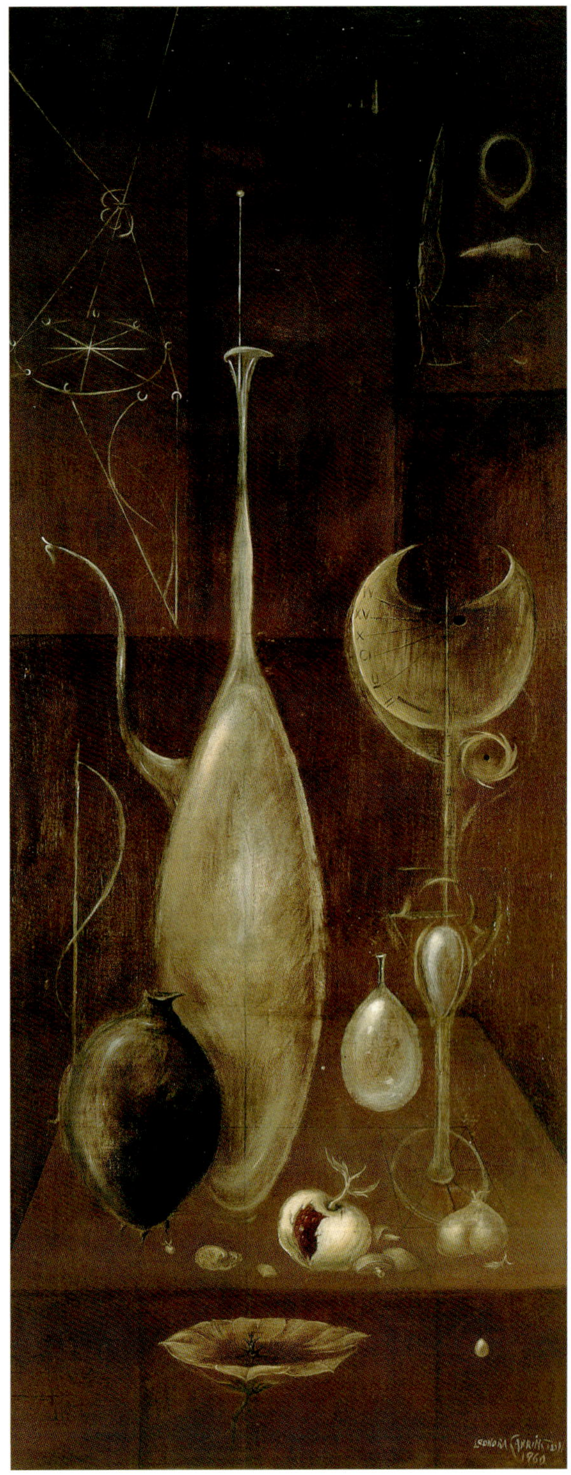

80
The Garden of Paracelsus
1957
Oil on canvas
86.5 x 120 cm/34 x 47 in
Private collection

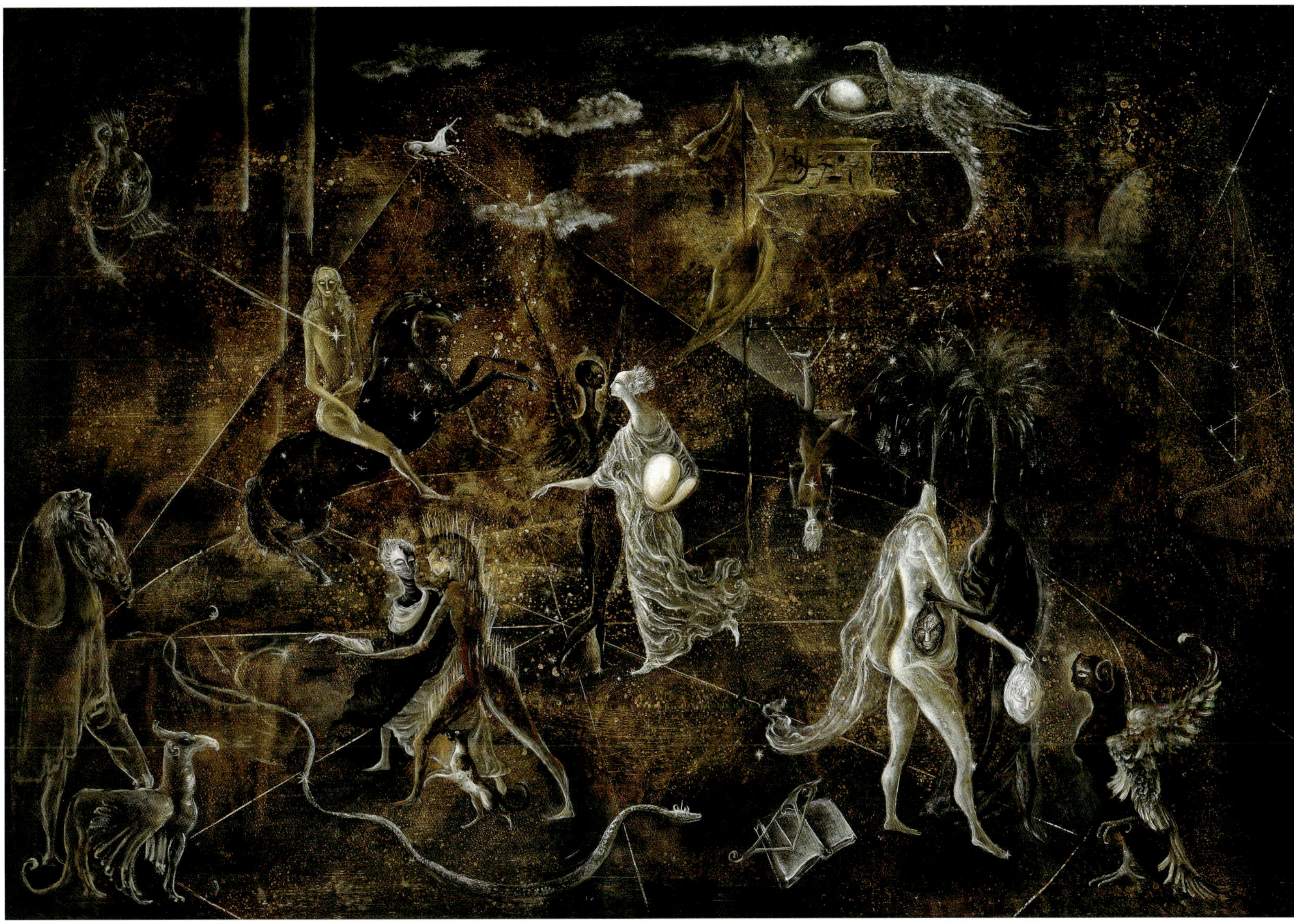

81
Syssigy
1957
Oil on board
56 x 50.2 cm/22 x 20 in
Private collection
Photo credit: Courtesy of Sotheby's

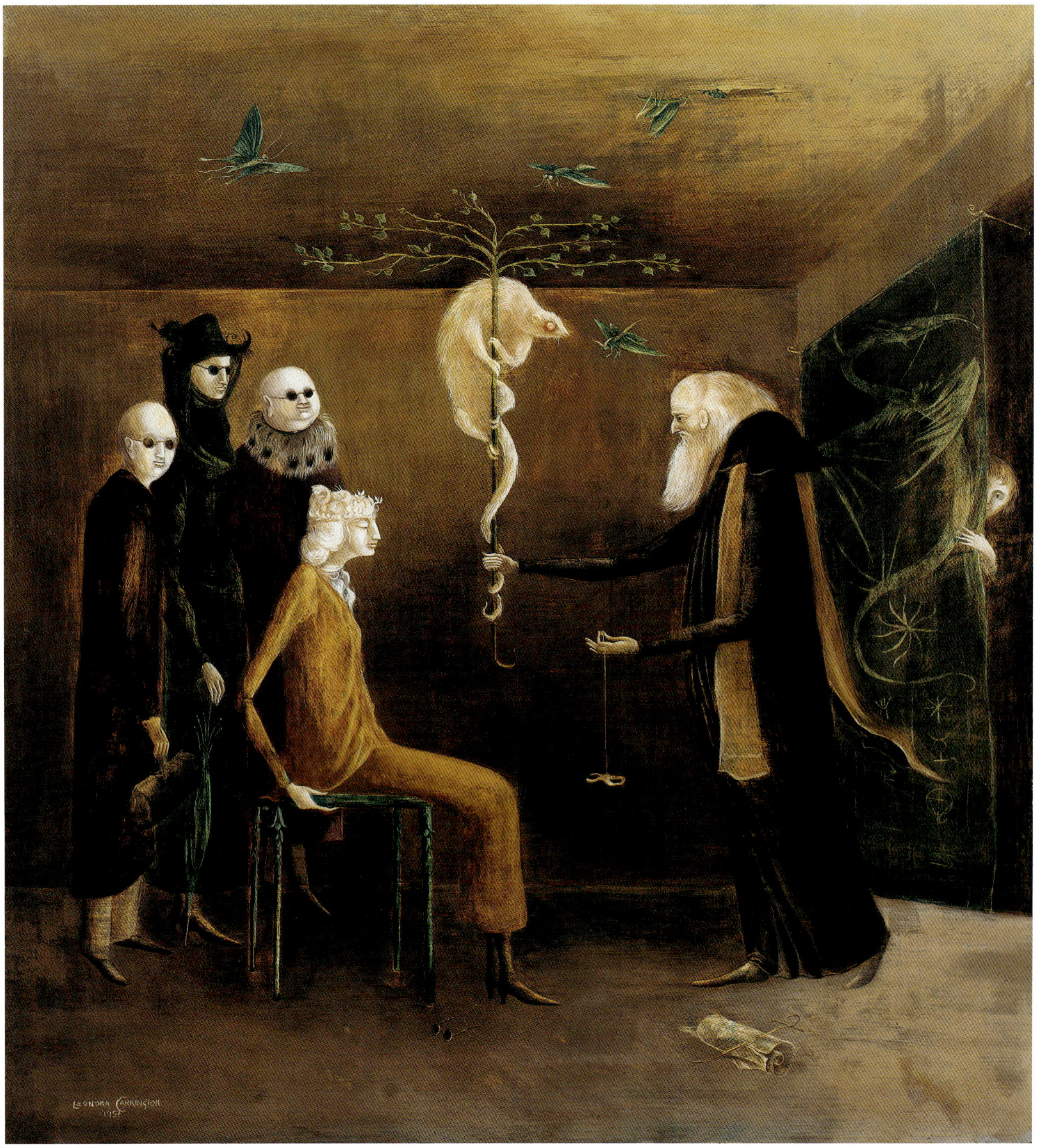

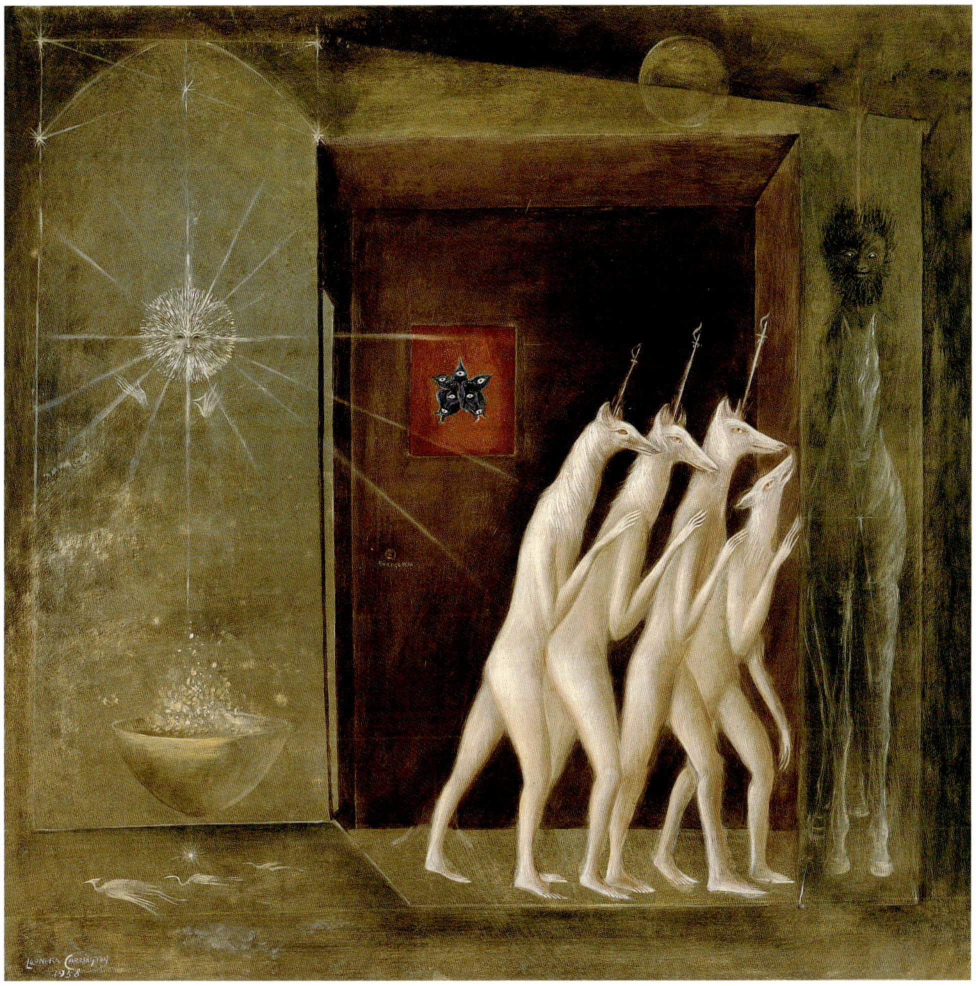

82
The Floor 4706th
1958
Oil on canvas
50.5 x 50.5 cm/20 x 20 in
Private collection

83
Le Grand adieu
1958
Oil on canvas
50.5 x 100.3 cm/20 x 39½ in
Private collection

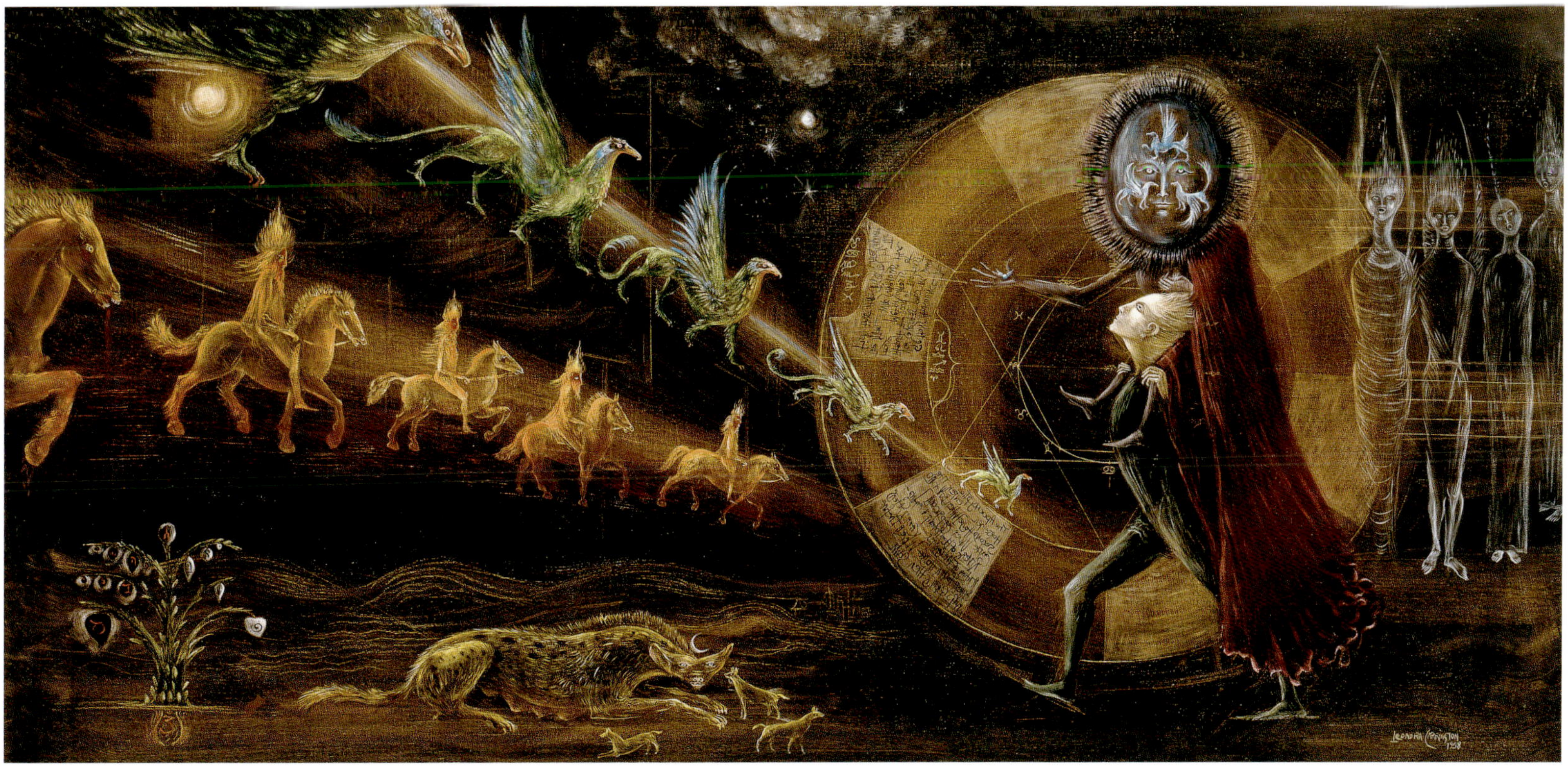

84

El Rarvarok

1963

Casein on panel

70 x 100 cm/28 x 39½ in

Private collection

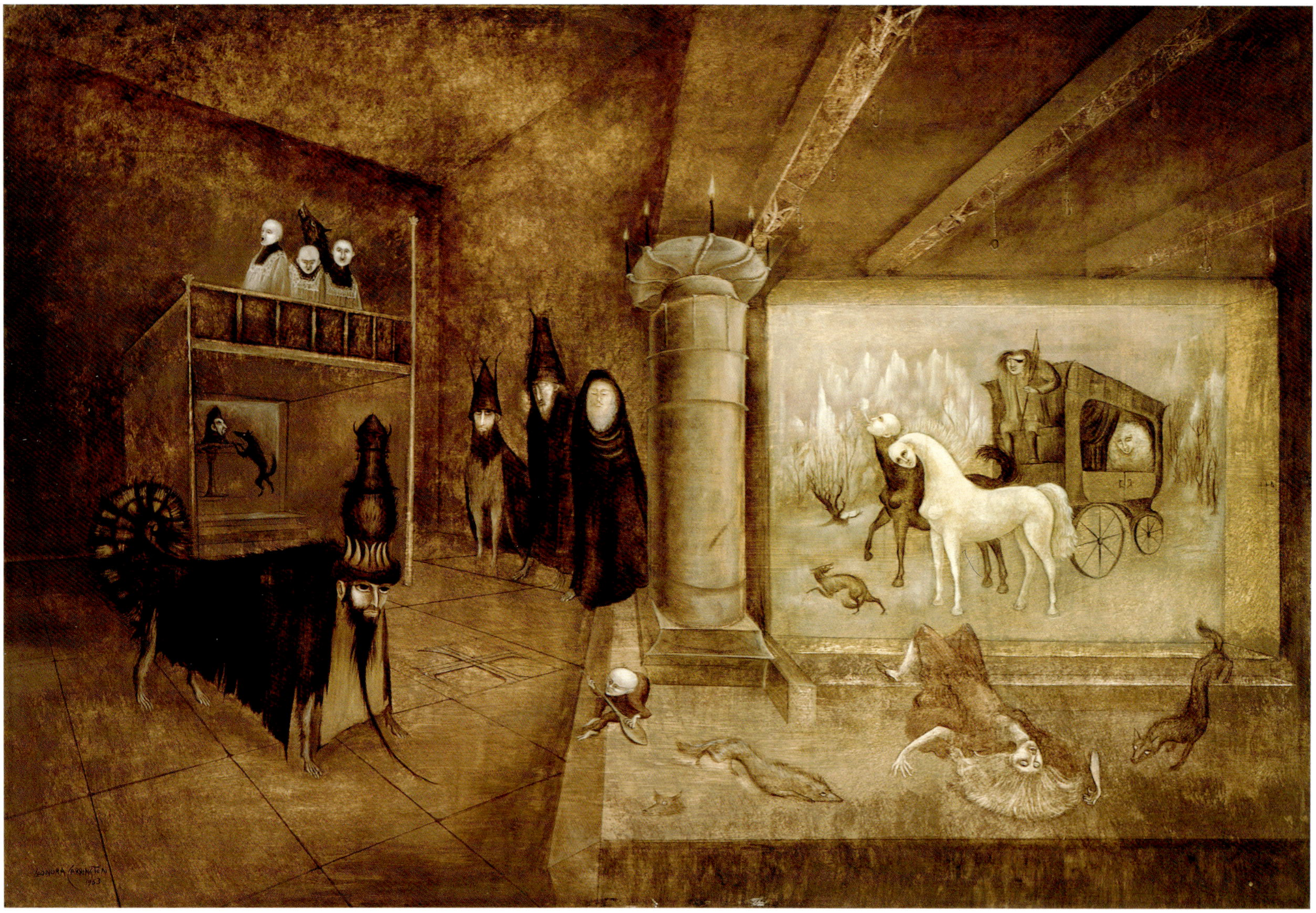

85
Litany of the Philosophers
1959
Oil on canvas
70 x 100 cm/27½ x 39½ in
Private collection

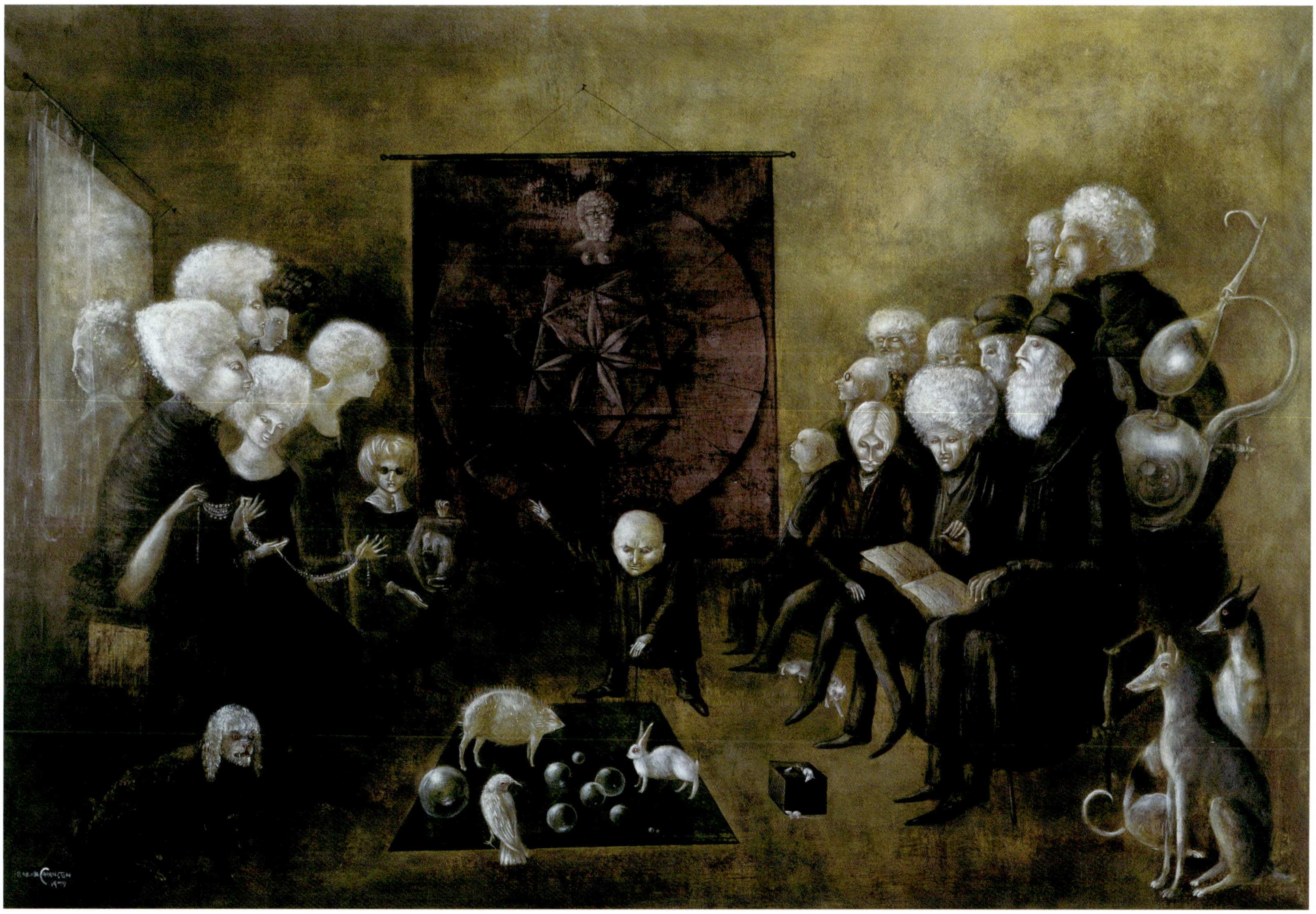

86
Reina de los mandriles
1959
Oil on canvas
47 x 38.5 cm/18½ x 15 in
Private collection

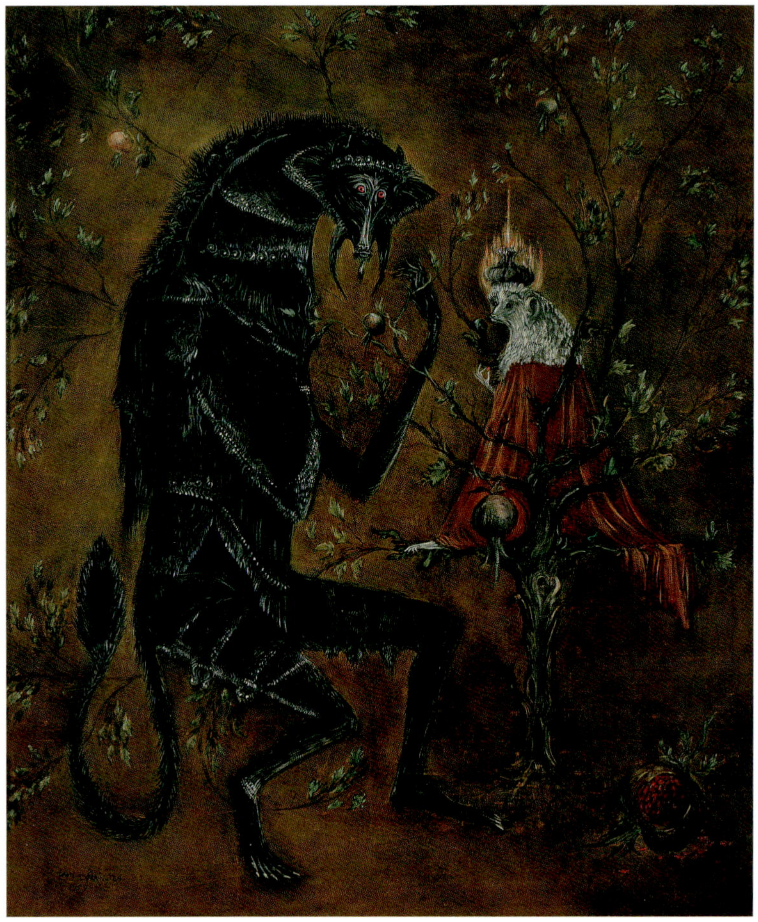

87
Who art thou, White Face?
1959
Oil on canvas
70 x 100 cm/27½ x 39½ in
Private collection

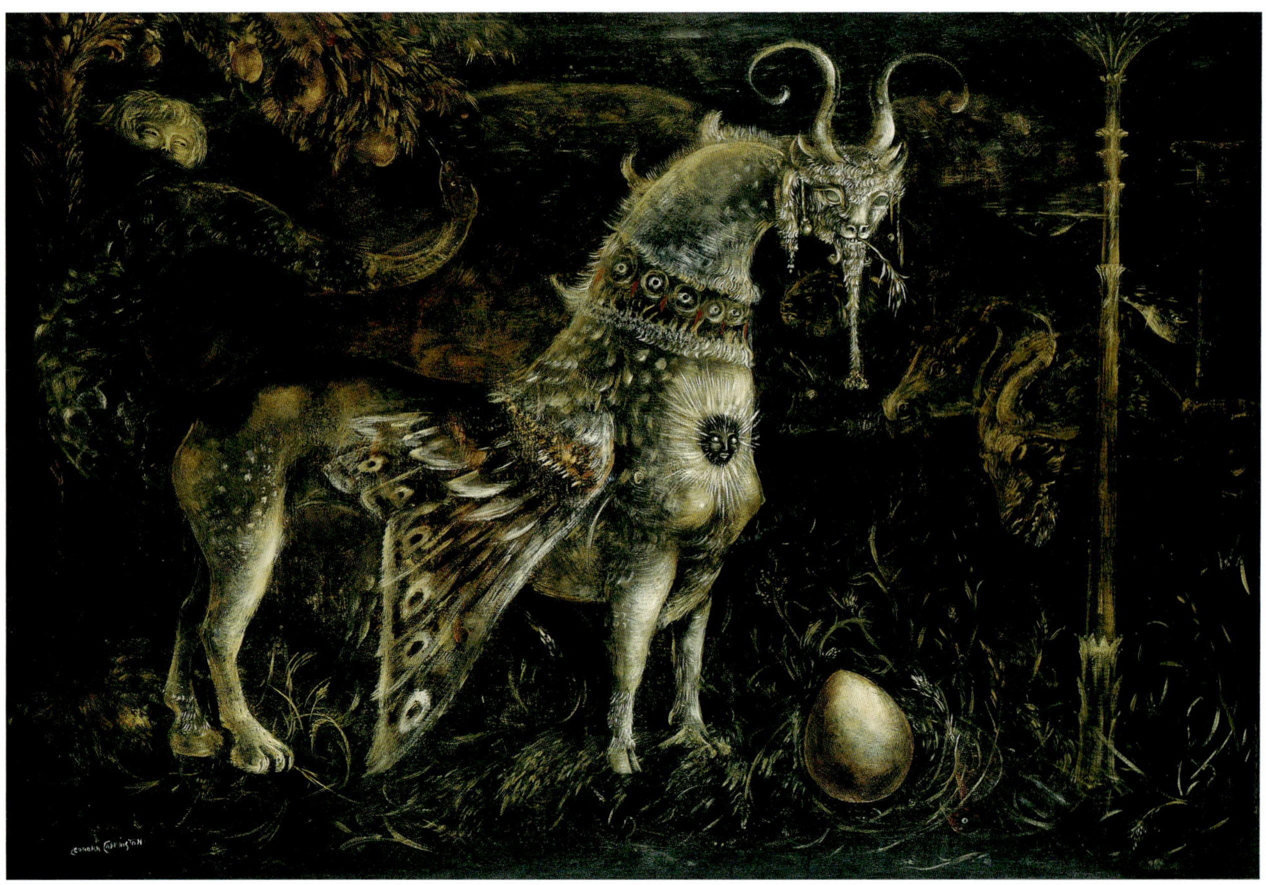

88
Animus Macquina
1962
Oil and mixed media on panel
81 x 30 cm/32 x 12 in
Private collection

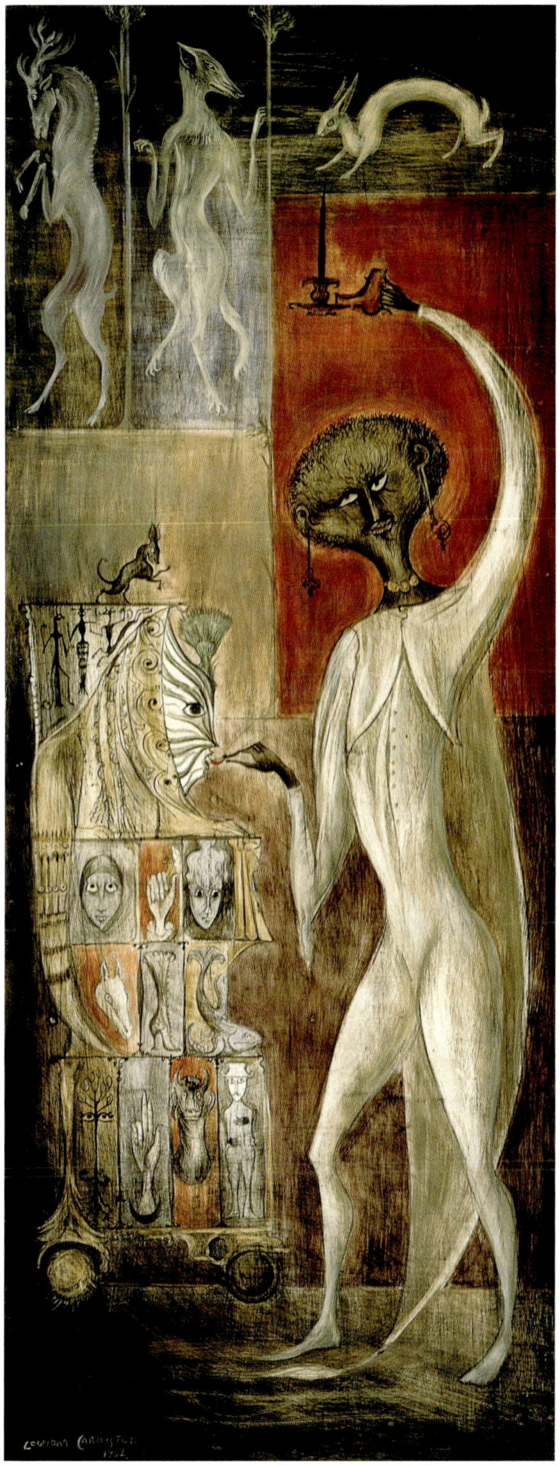

89
Friday the 13th
1965
Oil on canvas
60 x 90 cm/24 x 35½ in
Private collection

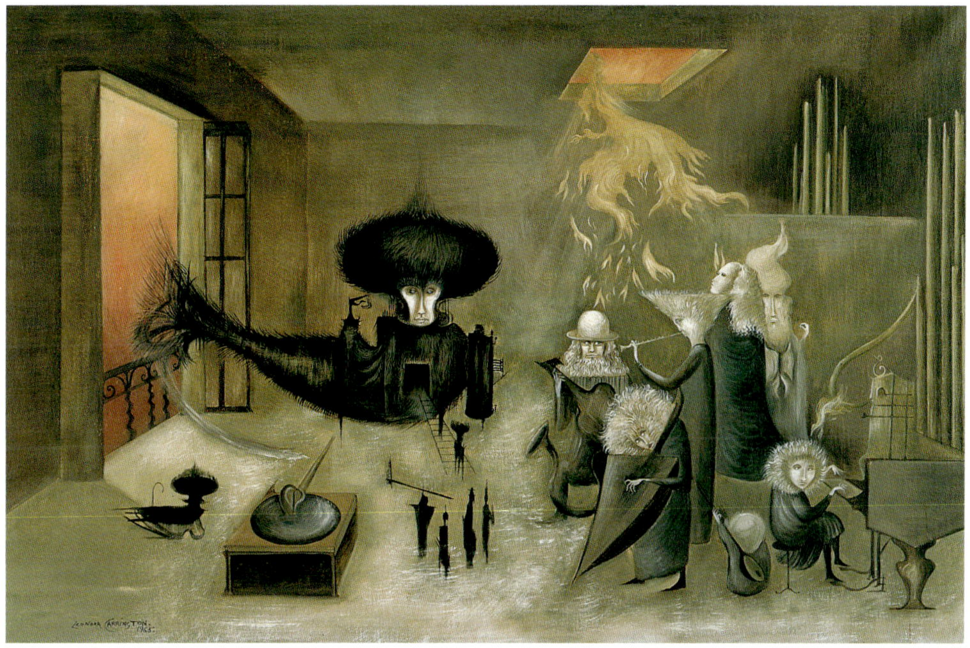

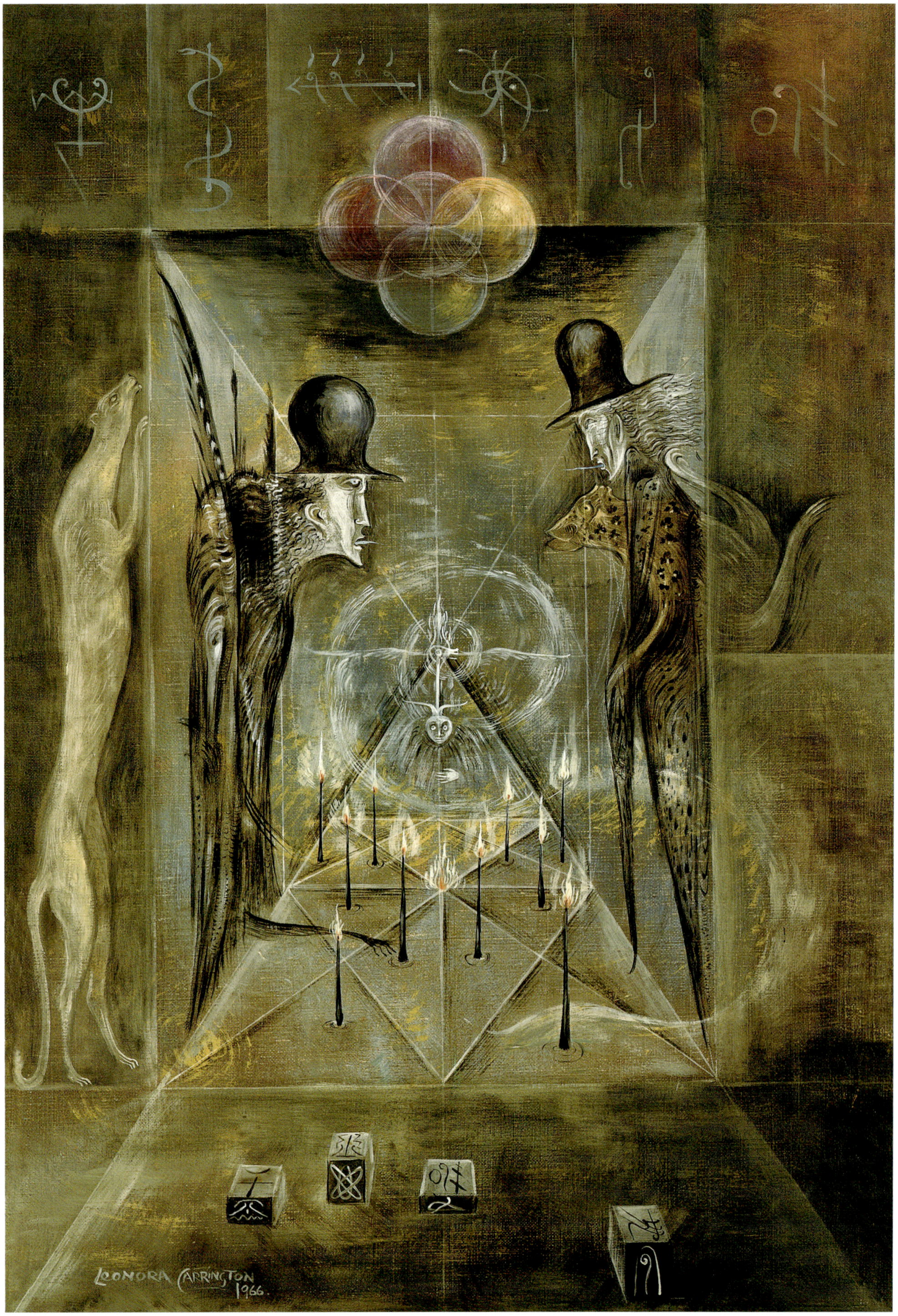

90

The Candle Game

1966

Oil on canvas

66 x 46 cm/26 x 18 in

Private collection

91
Sachiel, the Angel of Thursday
1967
Oil on canvas
41 x 60.5 cm/16 x 24 in
Private collection

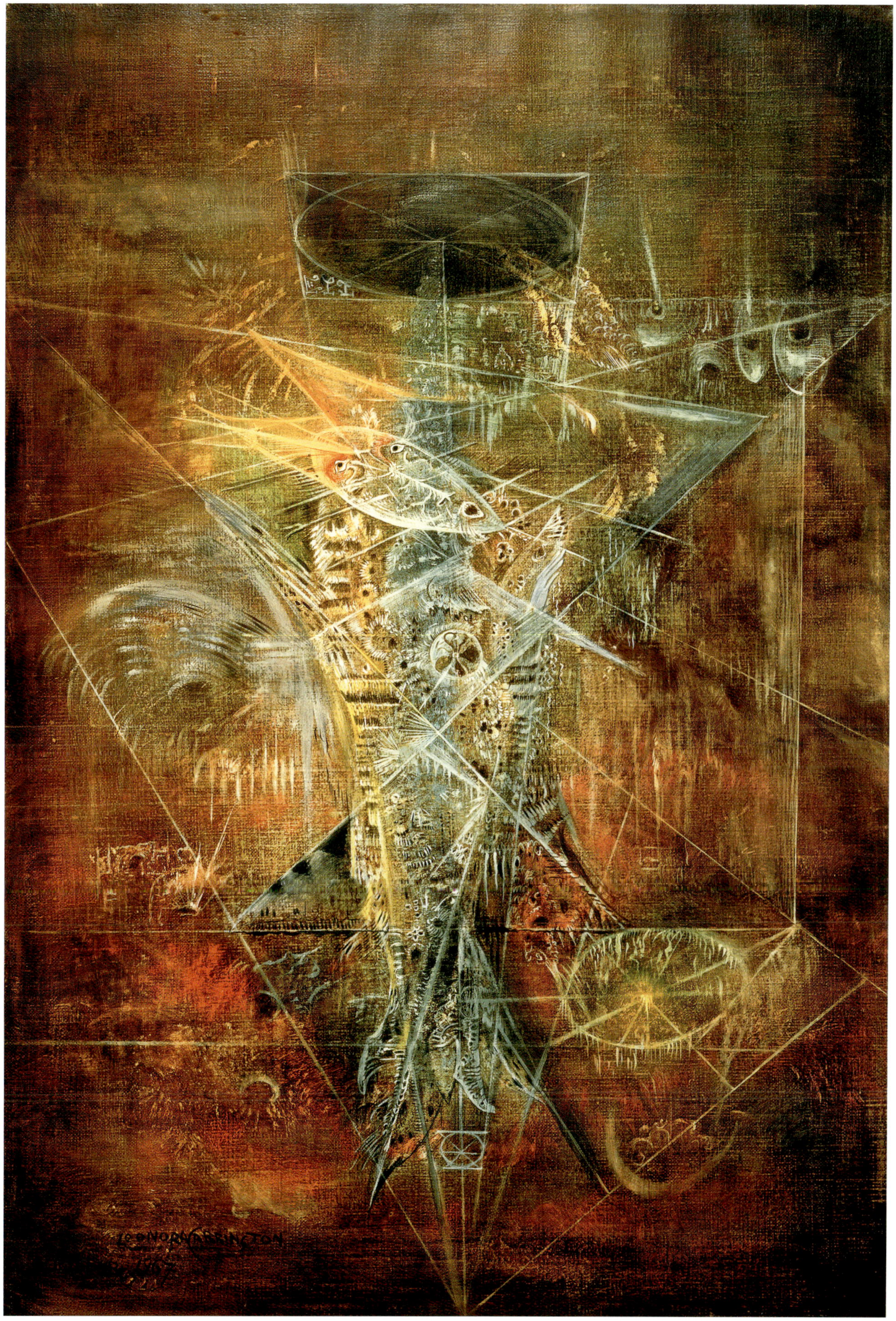

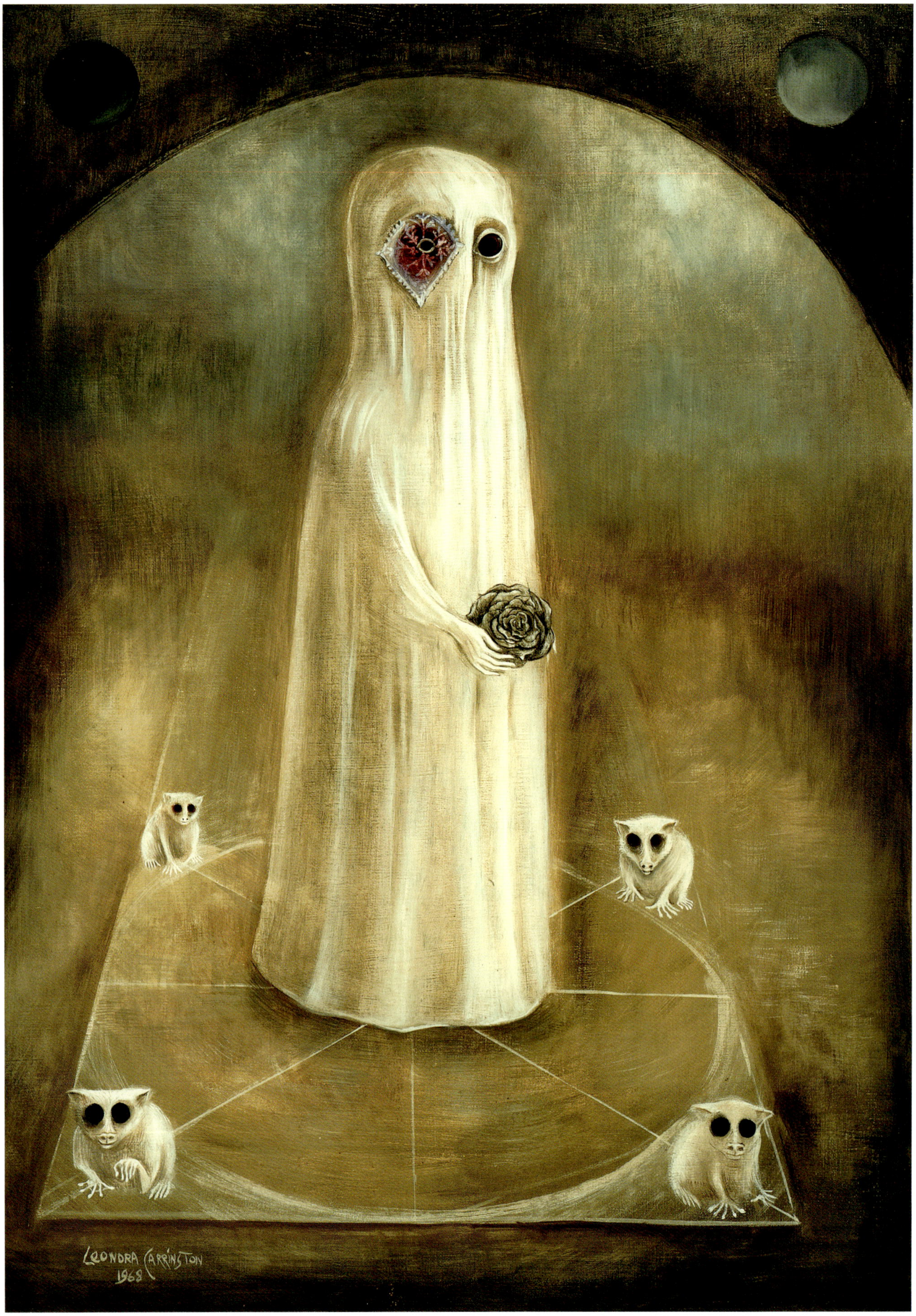

92
The Ancestor
1968
Oil on canvas
65 x 40 cm/26 x 16 in
Private collection

93
Lepidopteros
1969
Oil on canvas
90 x 90 cm/35½ x 35½ in
Private collection

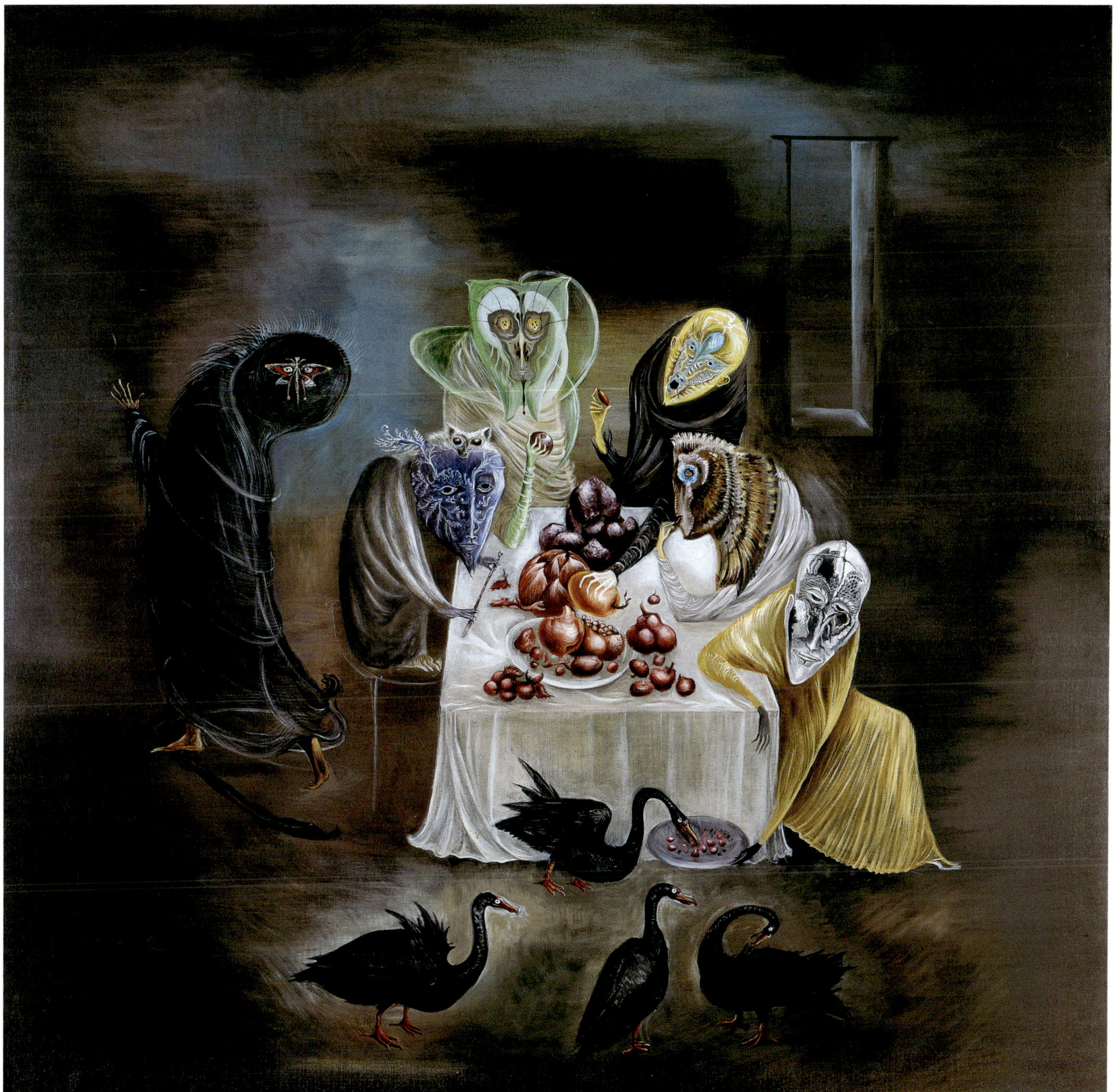

94

Forbidden Fruit

1969

Oil on canvas

49 x 46 cm/19½ x 18 in

Private collection

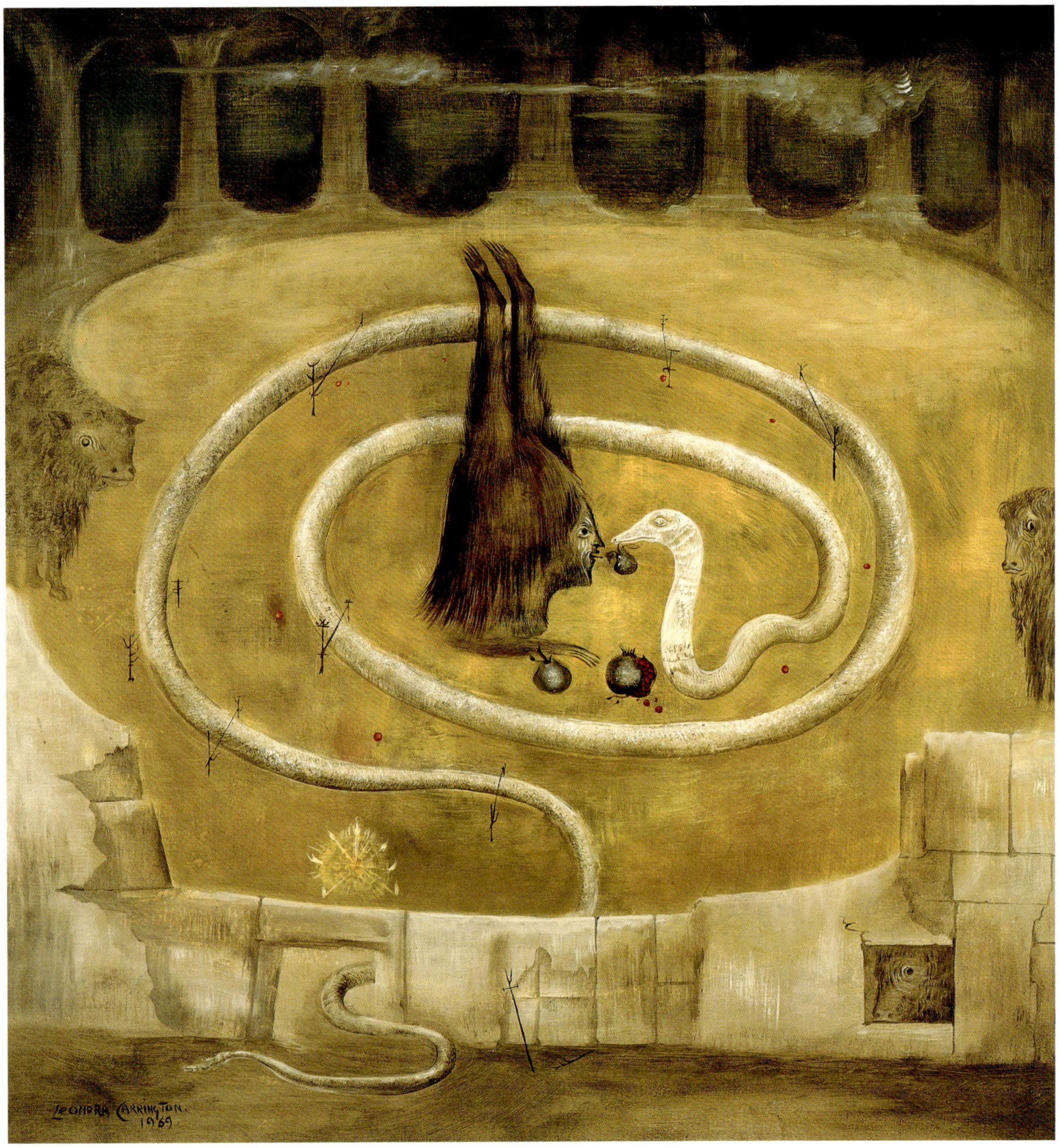

95
Untitled
One of three preparatory panels
Oncology Hospital Mural Project, Mexico City
1964–5
Oil on canvas
25 x 41 cm/10 x 16 in
Private collection

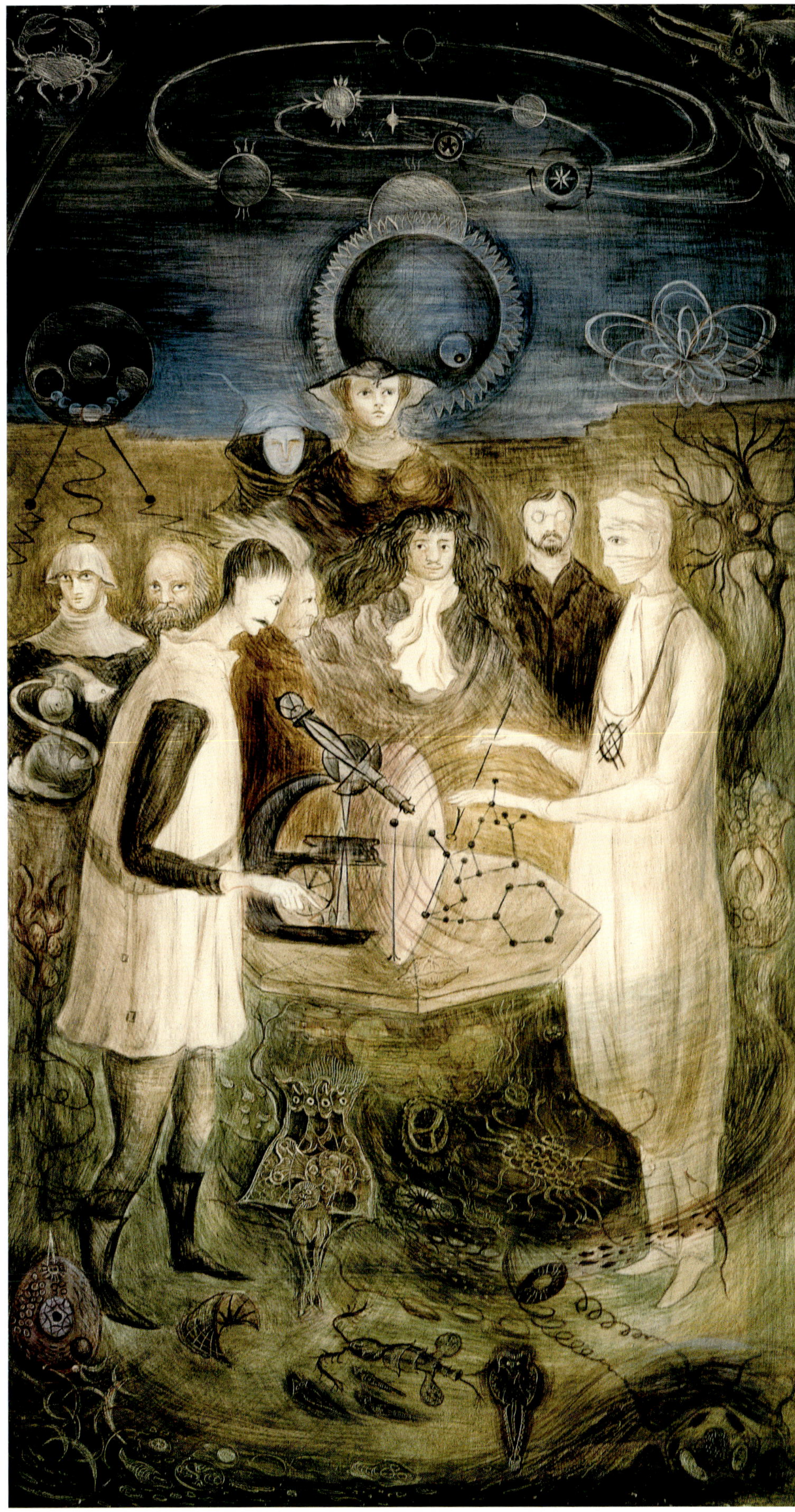

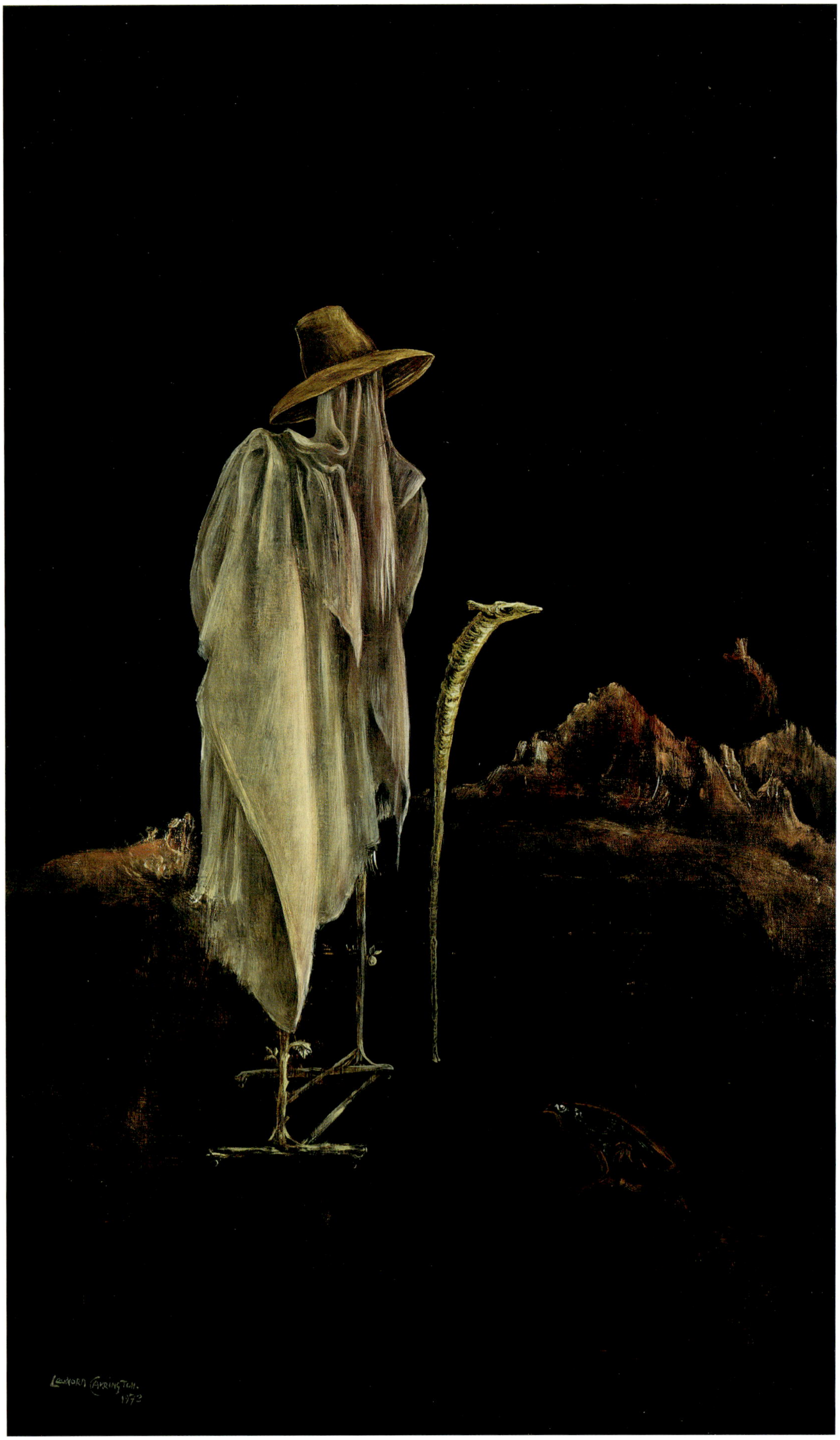

96
Self-Portrait in Orthopedic Black Tie
1973
Oil on canvas
65 x 38 cm/25½ x 15 in
Private collection

97

The Powers of Madame Phoenicia

1974

Mixed media on silk

42.5 x 44.5 cm/16¾ x 17½ in

The Vergel Foundation

Photograph: Christie's Images

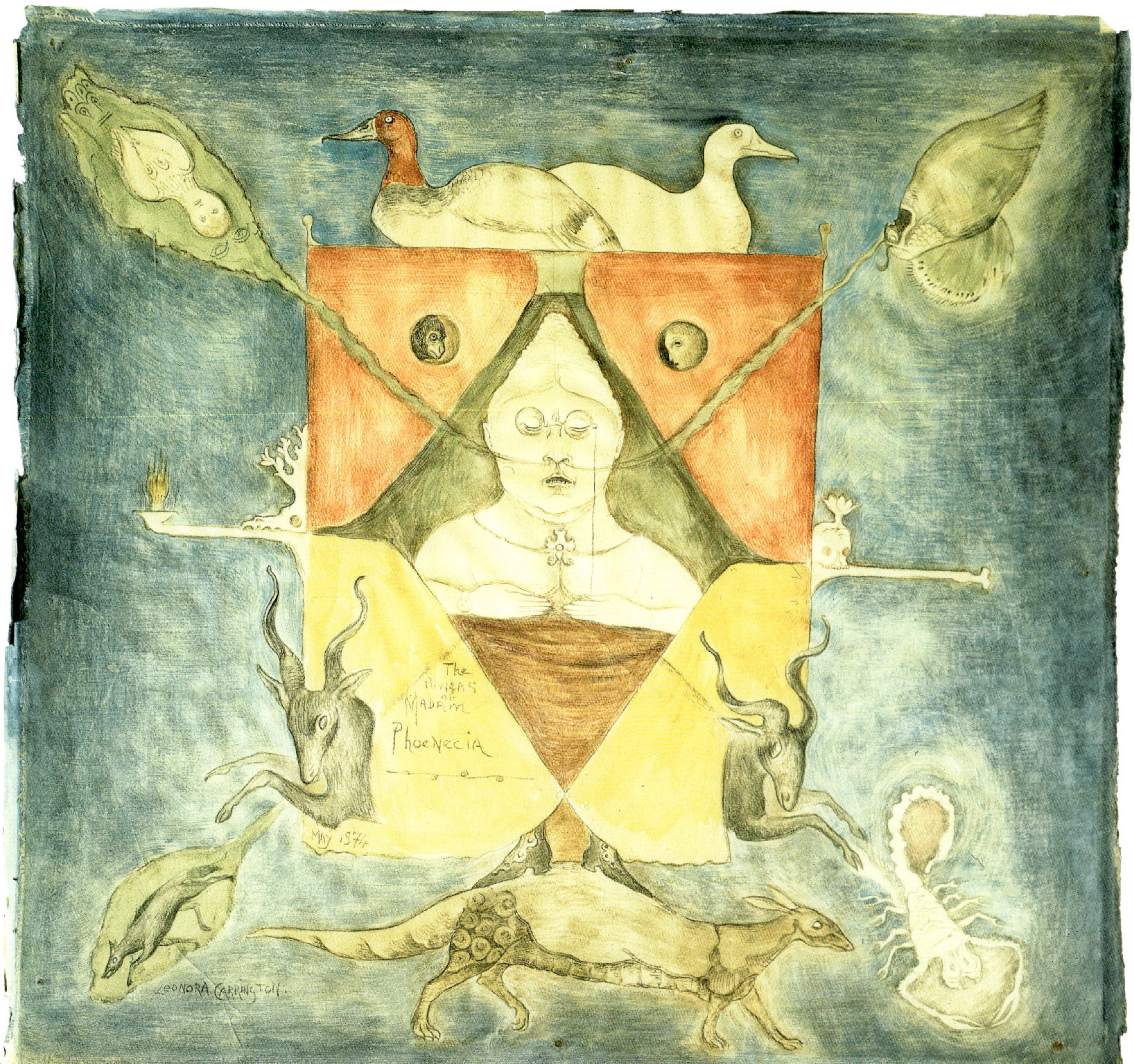

The painting *Grandmother Moorhead's Aromatic Kitchen* (1975) (Fig.98) is the penultimate example of Carrington's unique brand of pictorial feminism, encapsulating not only disparate cultural sources, but also her own past visual and stylistic inventory. It is a work of stunning, numinous power – a visual manifesto of the artist's belief in the ability of painting to transcend static representation and to enter into the realms of the magical. In a fiery red kitchen an invocation is taking place, this time within a clearly demarcated magic circle drawn on the floor. To the right an open door reveals a full moon surrounded by mists under whose pale light a dark cloaked figure appears, walking towards its opening. Near this door, in the interior, stands a horned goat-like creature holding a broom – a sign of the hearth and of witchcraft from centuries past. To the far left, also outside the circle, two robed figures are busy preparing food. The one in the upper left stirs a cooking pot on an old-fashioned Mexican stove (similar to the women stirring the cauldron in *The House Opposite* of 1945), while below a red-robed figure kneels busily grinding corn on a Mexican stone *metate* (mortar). Both figures amusingly wear sunglasses as if to protect themselves from a nocturnal radiance. Both also wear black hats; the lower figure seems to be in the act of transforming into a crow, a favourite Carrington character. The magic circle clearly demarcates a ritual space, in the centre of which is a round Mexican *comal* (griddle) upon which rest a cabbage, carrots, aubergine, corn, peppers and heads of garlic. Vessels and foodstuffs, like in the altar/tables of the previously examined paintings, are placed below the *comal* as well. Surrounding this *comal*/altar are three oddly shrouded figures.[237] The one to the left holds a knife, the middle one a bowl with something yellow in it and the third a head of garlic. Never before has Carrington so explicitly tied the act of cooking to ritual magic. All three figures are raptly gazing upon an enormous white goose, a manifestation of the Celtic mother-goddess, which is stepping into the circle as if summoned by their ritual food preparation.

Three heads of garlic – that ingredient essential to good cooking and to witchcraft – are carefully placed at intervals on the circle on the floor. Upon closer inspection the circle is a ring divided into a series of sections, and within each are inscriptions written in English and Celtic, some are inscribed backwards in the mirror-writing Carrington was always so easily able to do. One must resist the temptation to try to decipher these compelling fragments into a unified narrative and instead be content to understand that they refer to various episodes from the legends of the Celtic Sidhe, the people of the Tuatha dé Danaan. Carrington has created her own powerful incantations, designed to invoke the Goddess herself, who looks suspiciously like the Mother Goose of her beloved childhood fairy tales. The title, *Grandmother Moorhead's Aromatic Kitchen*, refers to her maternal grandmother whose name was Moorhead, and hence to her own lineage since, after all, it was this grandmother who informed her at an early age that she was directly descended from the Tuatha dé Danaan. Although it is a homage to her Irish heritage, the work utilises many Mexican culinary accoutrements and reflects her adopted nationality. A 1994 quote from Carrington helps to illuminate the spirit this work was undertaken in: 'The Mexican traditions of magic and witchcraft are fascinating, but they are not the same as mine, do you understand? I think every country has a magical tradition, but our approach to the unknown is peculiar to our ancestry. It is something that has to do with birth, your blood, flesh and bones.'[238]

In 1977 Carrington painted another powerful work redolent of initiations and travel to nocturnal realms. A triptych arranged horizontally from top to bottom, it is entitled *Took my Way Down, Like a Messenger, To the Deep* (Fig.99), and also incorporates aspects of Mexican cultural practices. The top panel features a central table at which a woman sits holding a clove of garlic. The table is round, like a magic circle, and clearly something out of the ordinary is occurring.

98
Grandmother Moorhead's Aromatic Kitchen
1975
Oil on canvas
79 x 124.5 cm/31 x 49 in
Charles B. Goddard Center for Visual Performing Arts, Ardmore, OK

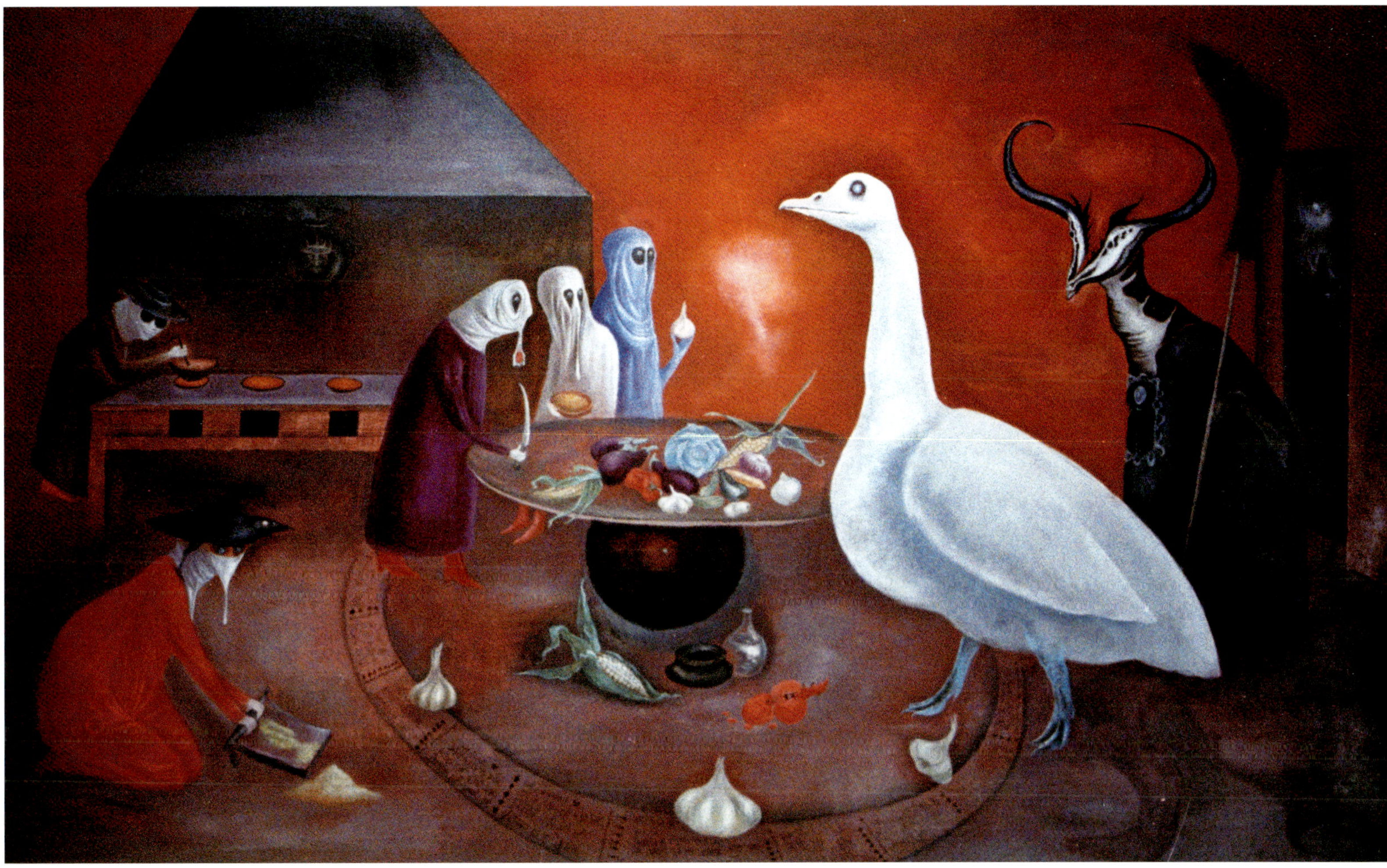

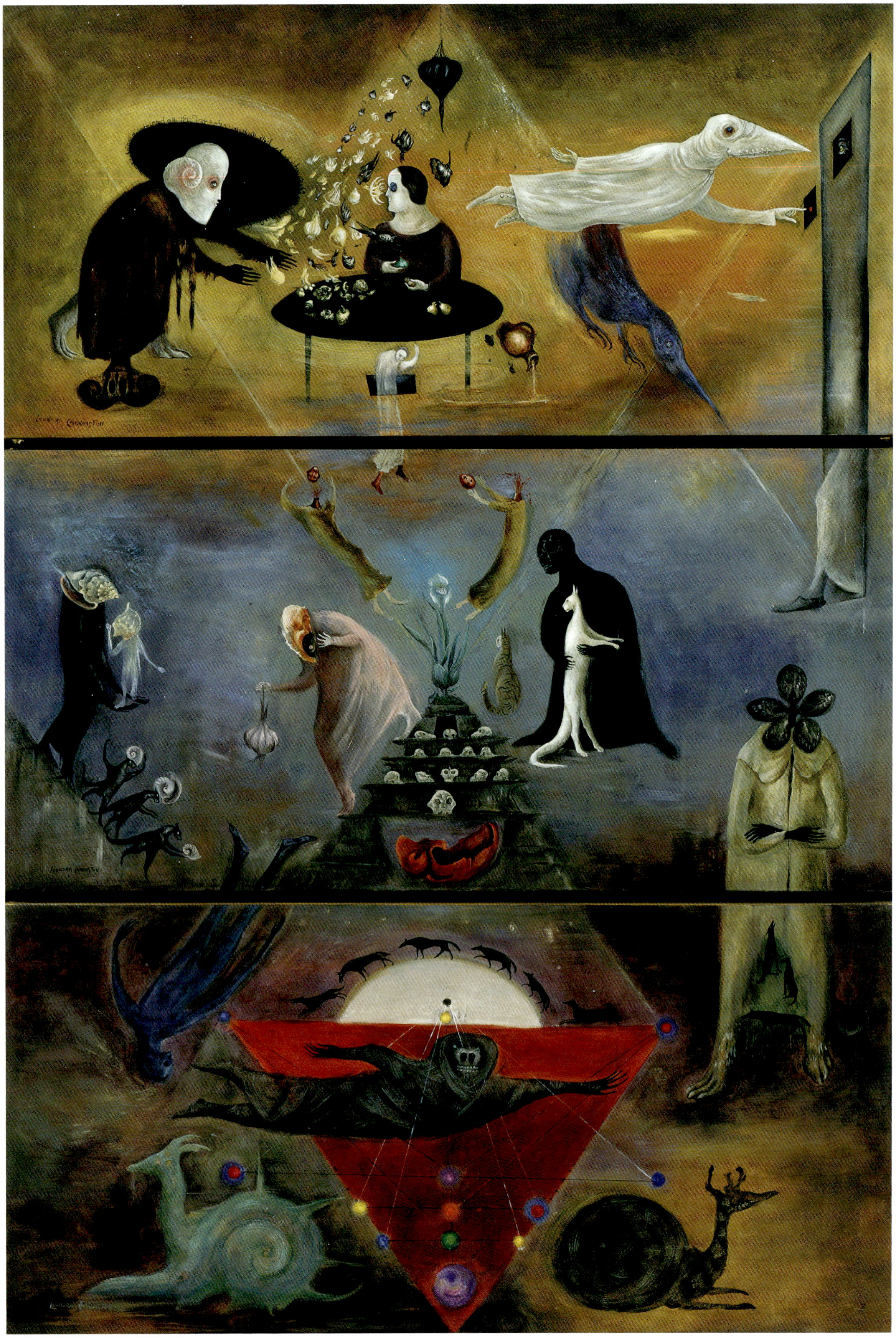

99
Took My Way Down, Like a Messenger, to the Deep
1977
Oil on canvas
181 x 120 cm / 71 x 47 in
Private collection

100
The Magdalens
1986
Egg tempera on panel
61 x 76.5 cm/24 x 30 in
Private collection

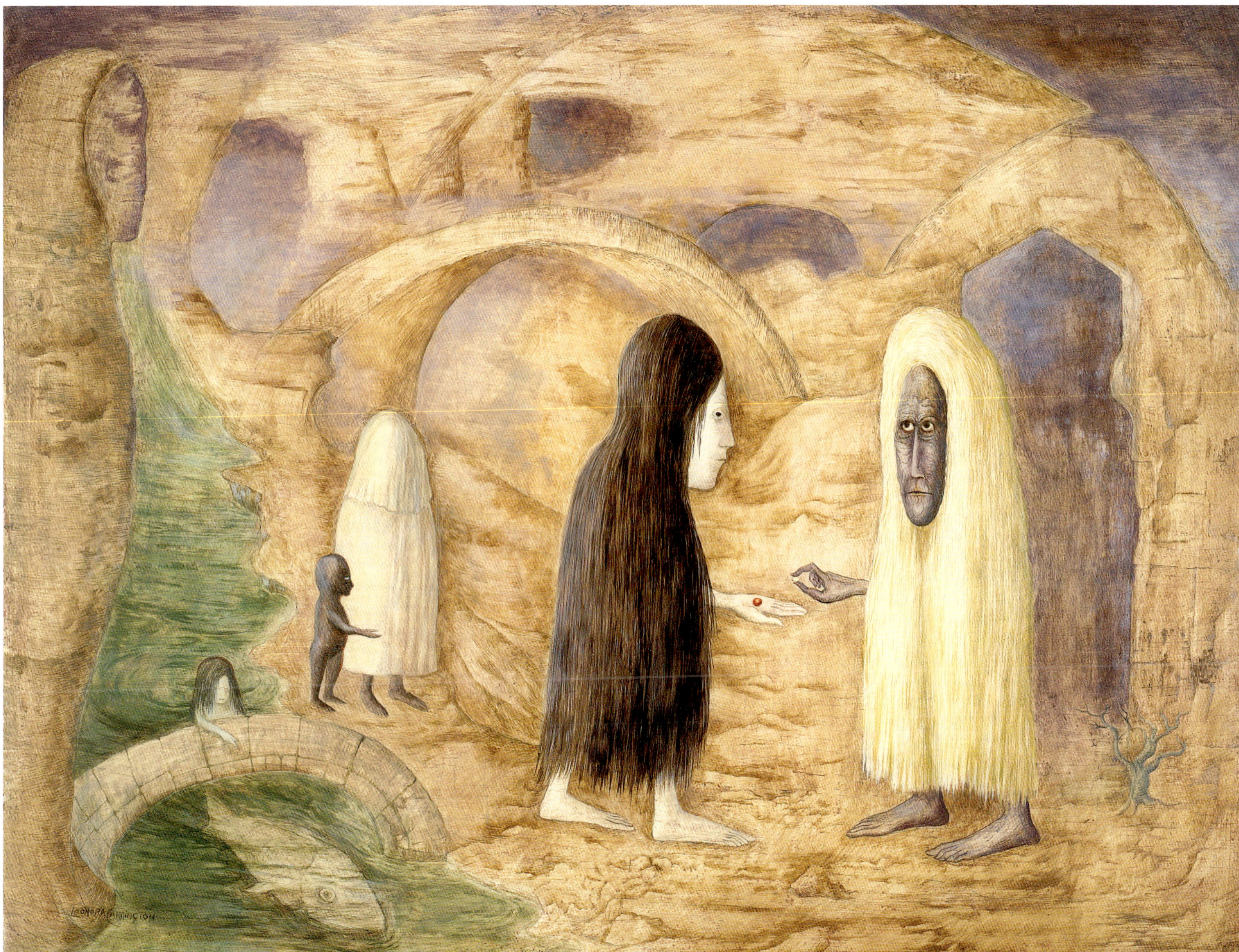

To her right an *olla* (ceramic vessel) is suspended in mid-air pouring water, while further to the right a ghostly white, crow-headed figure floats towards a door, hand outstretched to ring the doorbell beside it. To the left another ghostly creature in a brown fur-like robe stretches out both hands above the table. Apparently this causes the many cloves of garlic that were once on the table to levitate upwards into the air. Below the table a rectangular aperture opens through which an elongated white spirit passes (*I Took my Way Down*). In the centre of the middle panel is a triangular stepped structure that holds rows of skulls. This resembles both ancient Mexican pyramidal structures and a Day of the Dead altar decorated with *calaveras* (skulls). Clutching a large clove of garlic, and stuffing something in its mouth, the ghostly figure descends the pyramid, continuing down to the final panel (*Like a Messenger*). In the bottom panel the travelling soul turns blue and plummets head first (*To the Deep*). A large red triangle in the centre is filled with multicoloured orbs that resemble planets. In its midst floats a black-robed *calavera*,[239] while above him a full moon rises as a procession of black dogs traverse its curved surface. The humble kitchen table has been transformed into a magic gateway to other worlds. The foodstuffs upon it act as keys, magically animated in order to open the gate to allow progress below to the chthonic realms of sleep, dreams, the unconscious and death. Carrington has overtly paired a regular table with a Mexican altar as well as mixed her own notions of the afterlife with those of the Mexican Indians. That this work is a triptych, with all its connotations of the Christian Holy Trinity, is no accident. This combination of the heretical with the orthodox exemplifies the multiplicity of belief systems the artist is dedicated to preserving as part of the suppressed history of female spirituality. By transforming the domestic table into a sacramental altar Carrington creates a feminine sacred space that links worlds, providing access to multiple states of consciousness while collapsing the hierarchies that have prevented a more inclusive vision of spiritual possibilities.

In the 1980s, Carrington's paintings sport a brighter tone, perhaps because she began using acrylics. Now in her sixties, the artist began to tackle the question of age, and elderly women or 'crones' make their appearance. Whether examining flowers closely or energetically walking through streets, these old women exude a sense of the wonderment they still hold for the world around them. Dubbed 'Magdalens' by the artist, one surmises from an ironic reference to the medieval sisterhood of fallen women who opted for the rehabilitating influence of the convent late in life, that these recalcitrant crones are beyond caring what the world thinks of them. In *The Magdalens* (Fig.100) of 1986 a hirsute elder solemnly hands a young woman a small red berry in a penitential rocky landscape. Carrington dryly explains: 'It's a birth control pill.' In a 1988 catalogue essay for such works, Whitney Chadwick comes right to the point:

> The multiple realities that Carrington confronts in her work include the reality of old age. Aging has occupied her thoughts more and more as she considers how to live the remainder of her life. Focusing on the image of the crone, the ancient woman; she has rejected the ideals of youth and beauty that dominate both contemporary culture and most of the history of western painting ... the painting of aged and wrinkled faces – along with the restoration of knowledge and power to the elderly – are perfectly in keeping with Carrington's belief that unless women reclaim their power to affect the course of human life, there is little hope for civilization.[240]

In the 1980s Carrington also began casting sculptures in bronze, and her *La Vieja Magdalena* (1988) is a totemic standing presence whose wrinkles have been transformed into swirling decorative ridges worn as a badge of honour. The artist had previously experimented with silver casting, resulting in a delightful marionette *La Vaca* (1975) (Fig.103) whose chest has hinged doors that open up to a face where

101
La Virgen de la Cueva
1995
Bronze
120 x 18 x 48 cm/47 x 7 x 19 in
Private collection

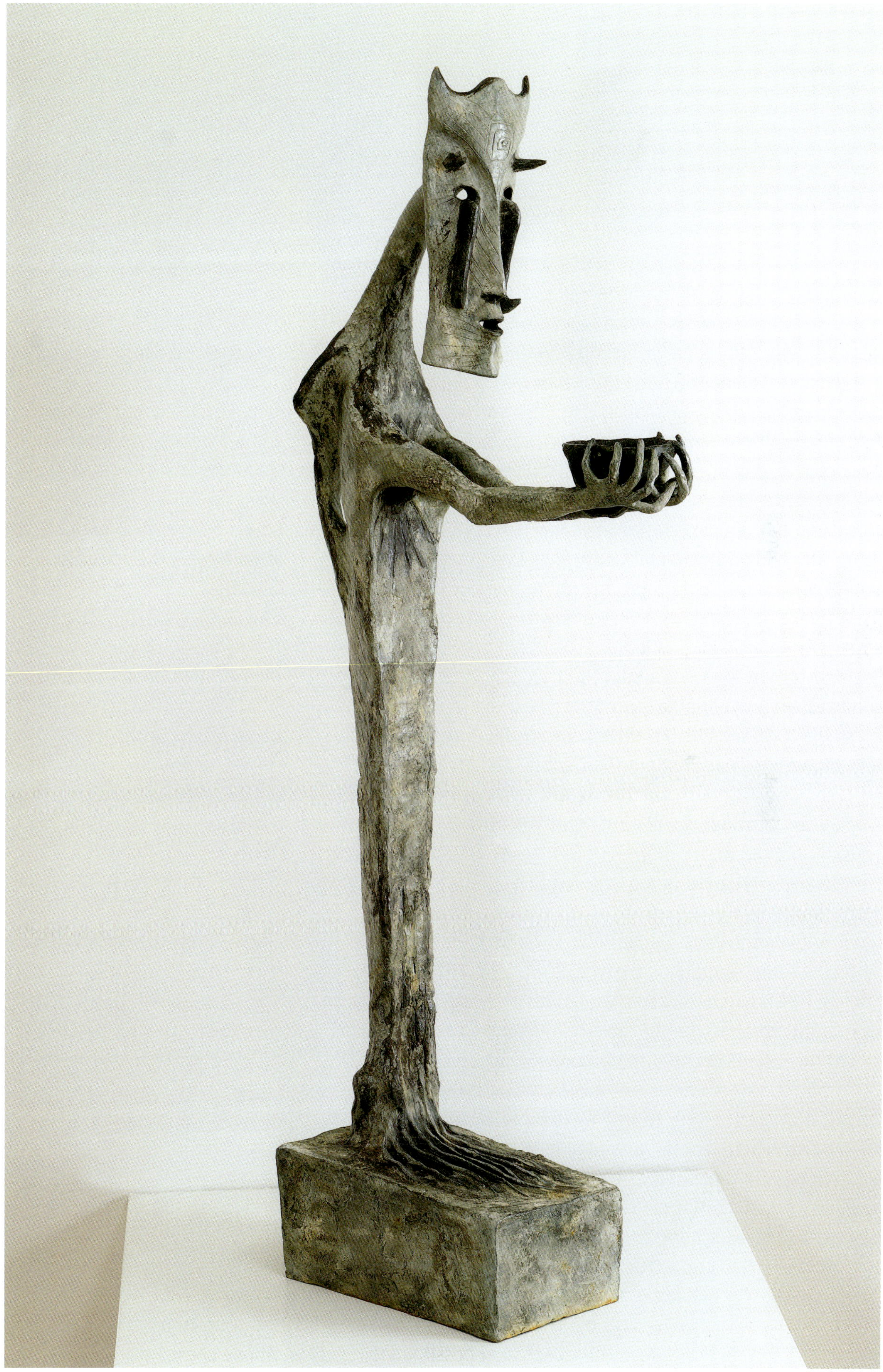

the heart should be. Her bronze pieces became much larger in a series of mysterious entities executed from 1994–5 with titles like *Ing*, *Esfinge*, *Nigrum* or *La Virgen de la Cueva* (Fig.101). Most recently Carrington's bronze sculpture *How doth the Little Crocodile* (1998) (Fig.115), whose title is taken from a poem from Lewis Carroll's *Alice's Adventures in Wonderland*, has been enlarged and placed in front of the Children's Museum in Mexico City's Chapultapec Park. For an artist who has cherished the subversively witty Carroll her entire life, and who can still quote him extensively, word for word, there could be no more fitting monument erected in her honour.

The first half of the 1990s saw the production of three major publications on Leonora Carrington: the exhibition catalogue for *Leonora Carrington: Paintings, Drawings and Sculptures 1940–1990* held at London's Serpentine Gallery in 1991 (Andrea Schilieker, ed.); the exhibition catalogue for *Leonora Carrington: Una retrospectiva* held at the Museo de Arte Contemporáneo de Monterrey in Monterrey in 1994 and at the Museo de Arte Moderno, Mexico City in 1995 (Luis Carlos Emerich and Lourdes Andrade); and Whitney Chadwick's *Leonora Carrington: La realidad de la imaginación* published by the Consejo Nacional para la Cultura y las Artes, Mexico City, in 1994. Numerous studies, essays and articles written in languages from all around the world, as the tokens of her prodigious talent become more known, further supplement these publications. Many aspects of Carrington's artistic legacy, however, remain to be investigated by future scholars, for the real work has only just begun. When I asked Leonora if she had any final comments to impart to her admirers, she recalled perfectly an anonymous sign she saw posted in a theatre visited with her mother at age 15:

The codfish lays a million eggs
The little hen but one
The codfish never cackles when her little task is done
So we praise the little hen
The codfish we despise
Which proves my friends and countrymen
It pays to advertise.

I leave it to you to extrapolate the wisdom hidden within these lines, for undoubtedly, it is both pithy and entirely relevant.

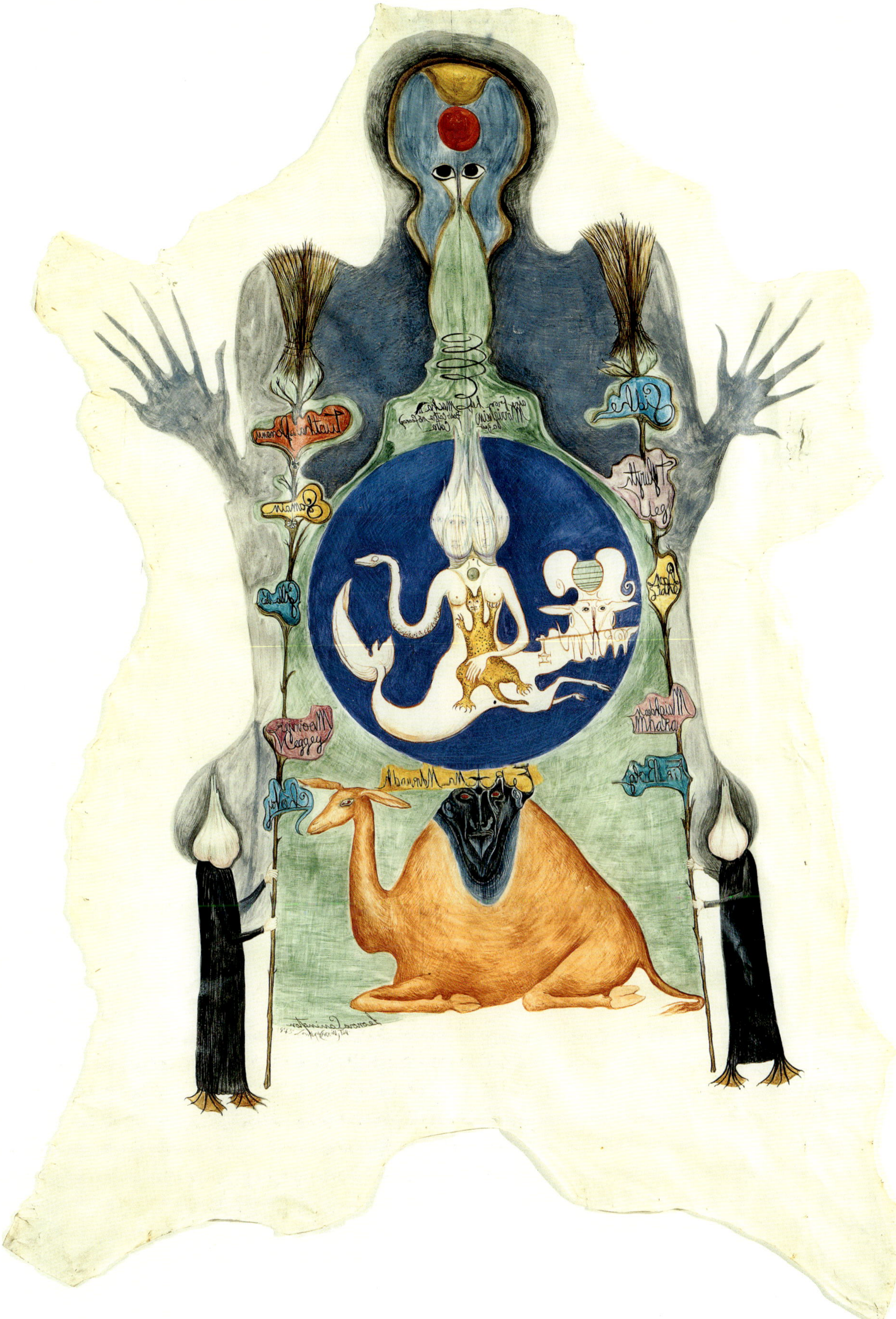

102
Samhain Skin
1975
Gouache on vellum
122 x 82.5 cm/48 x 32½ in
National Museum of Women
in the Arts, Washington, D.C.
Gift of Wallace and Whihelmina
Holladay

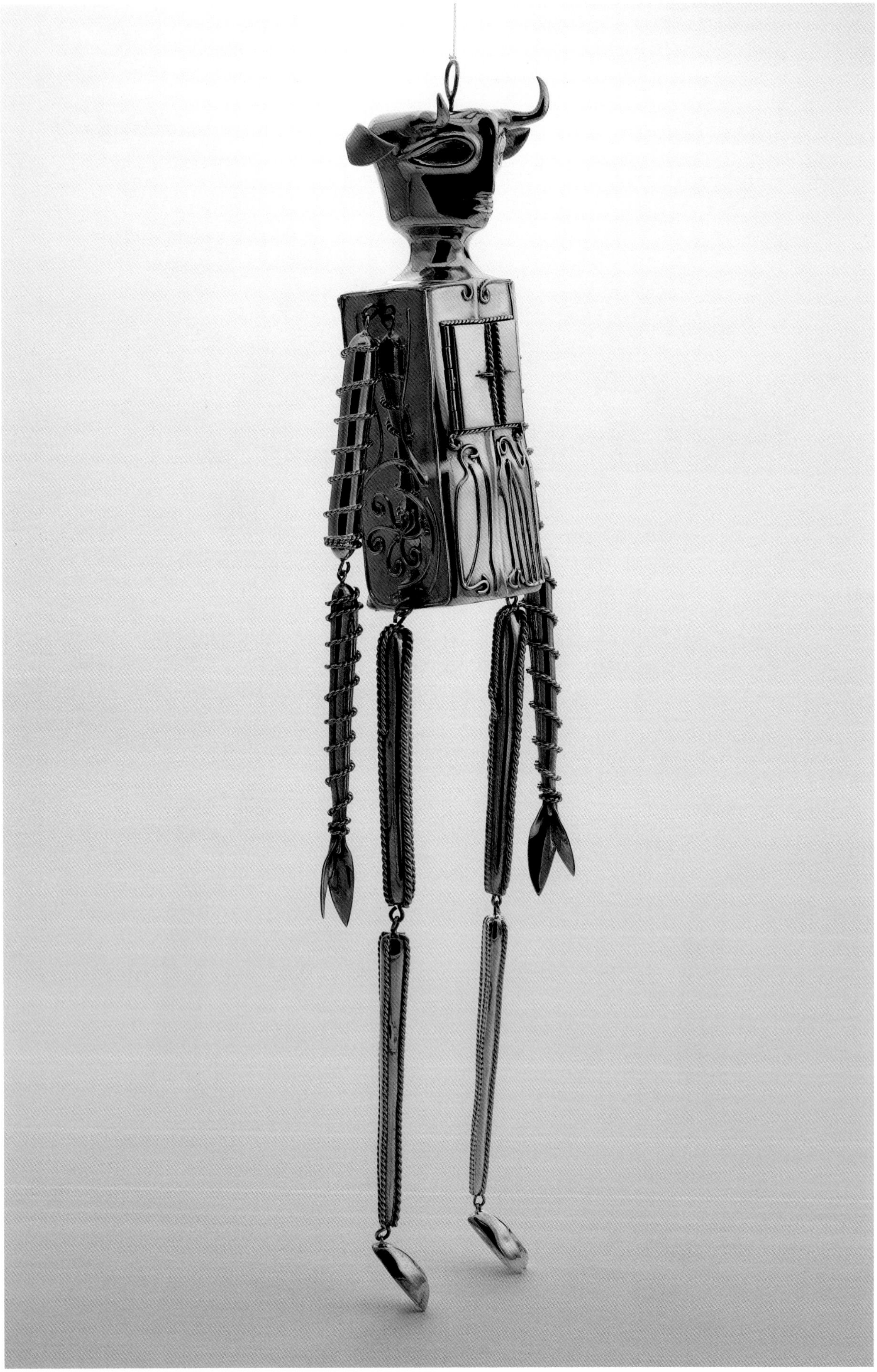

103
La Vaca
1975
Silver .925
H: 47 cm/18½ in
Edition of 10
Tane's Collection
Photo credit: courtesy of the collector

104
Tribeckoning
1983
Oil on canvas
61 x 91cm/24 x 36 in
Private collection

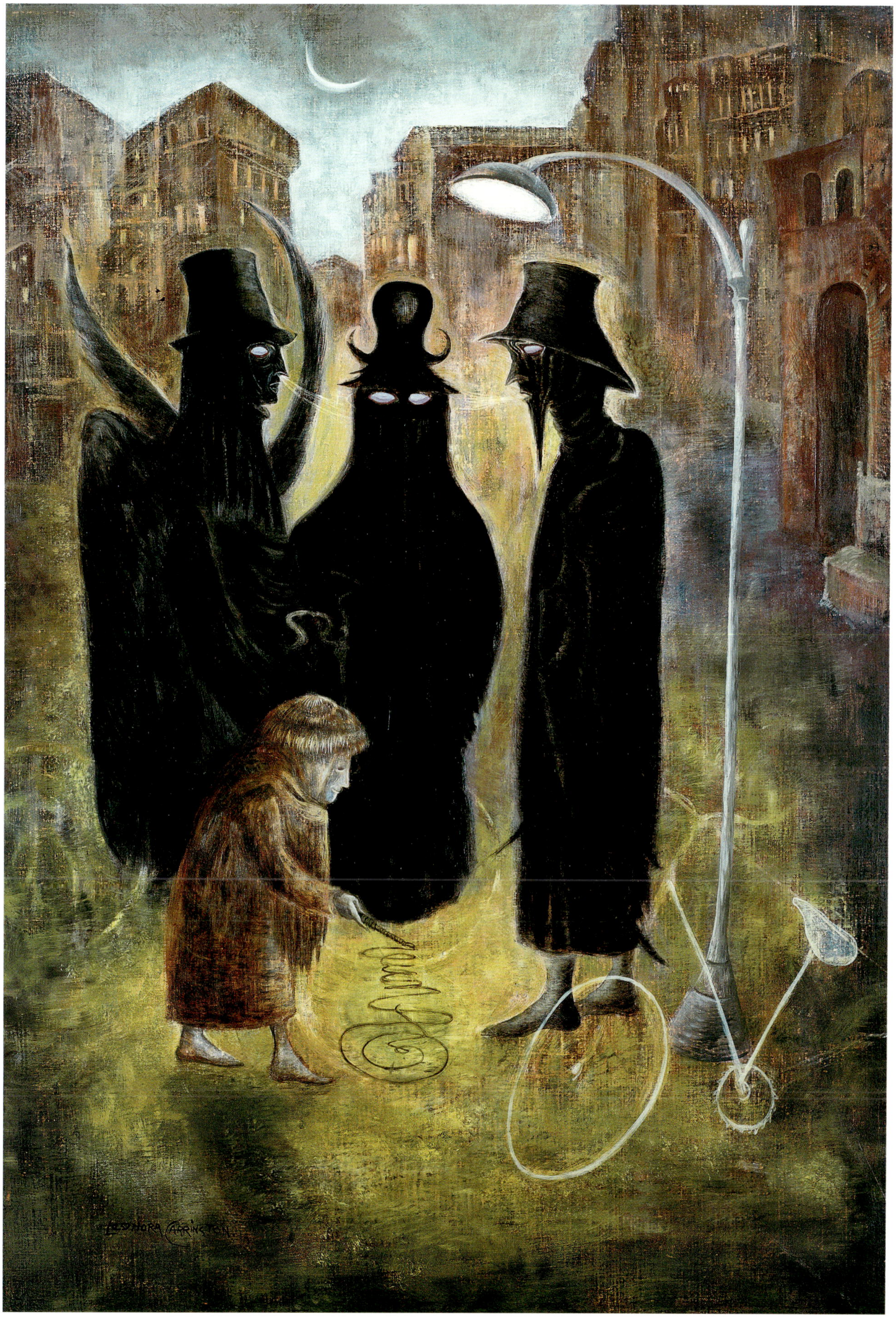

105
The Labyrinth
1991
Oil on wood
77 x 91 cm/30 x 36 in
Private Collection

106
Tell the Bees
1986
Tempera on masonite
61 x 76 cm/24 x 30 in
Private collection

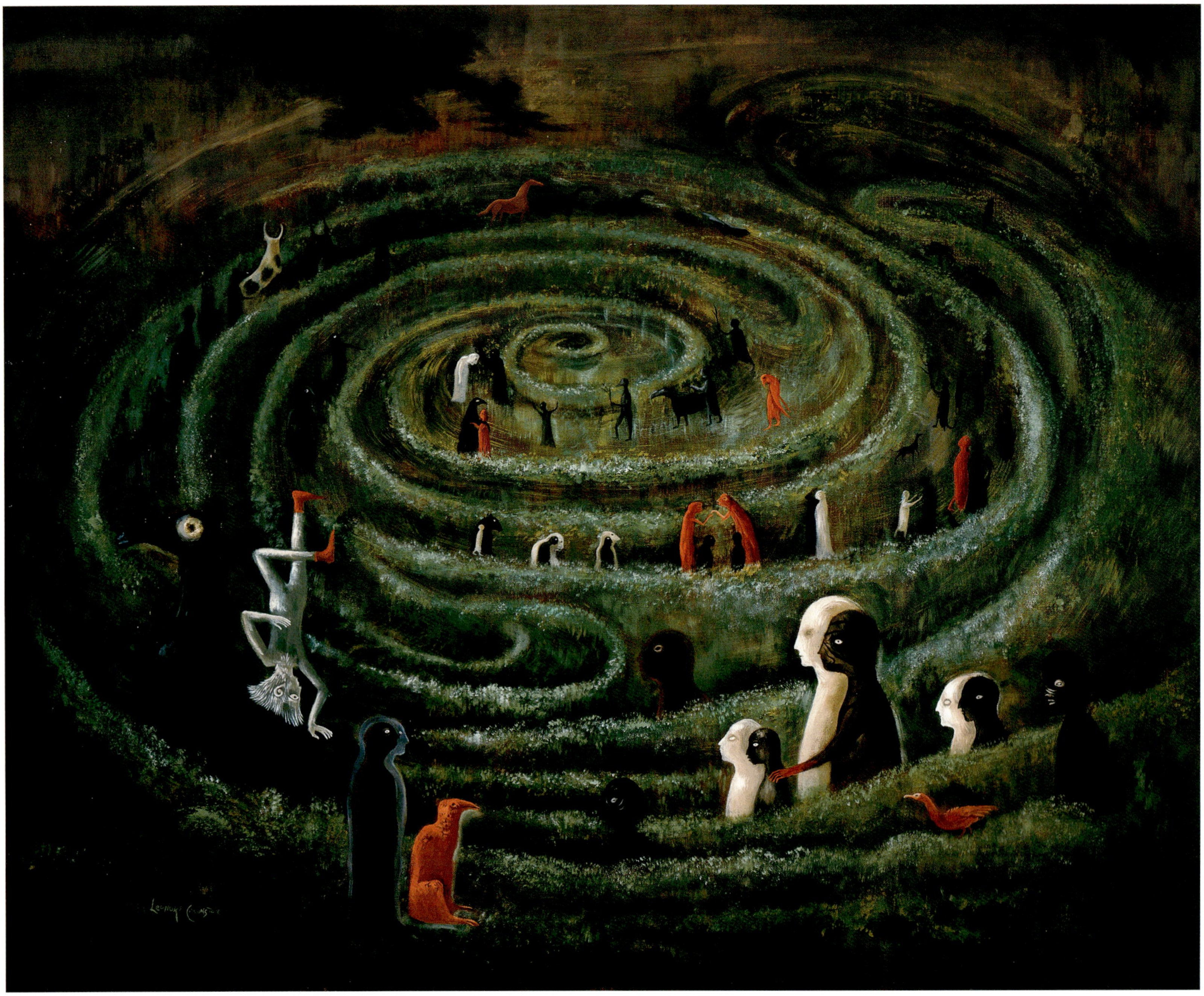

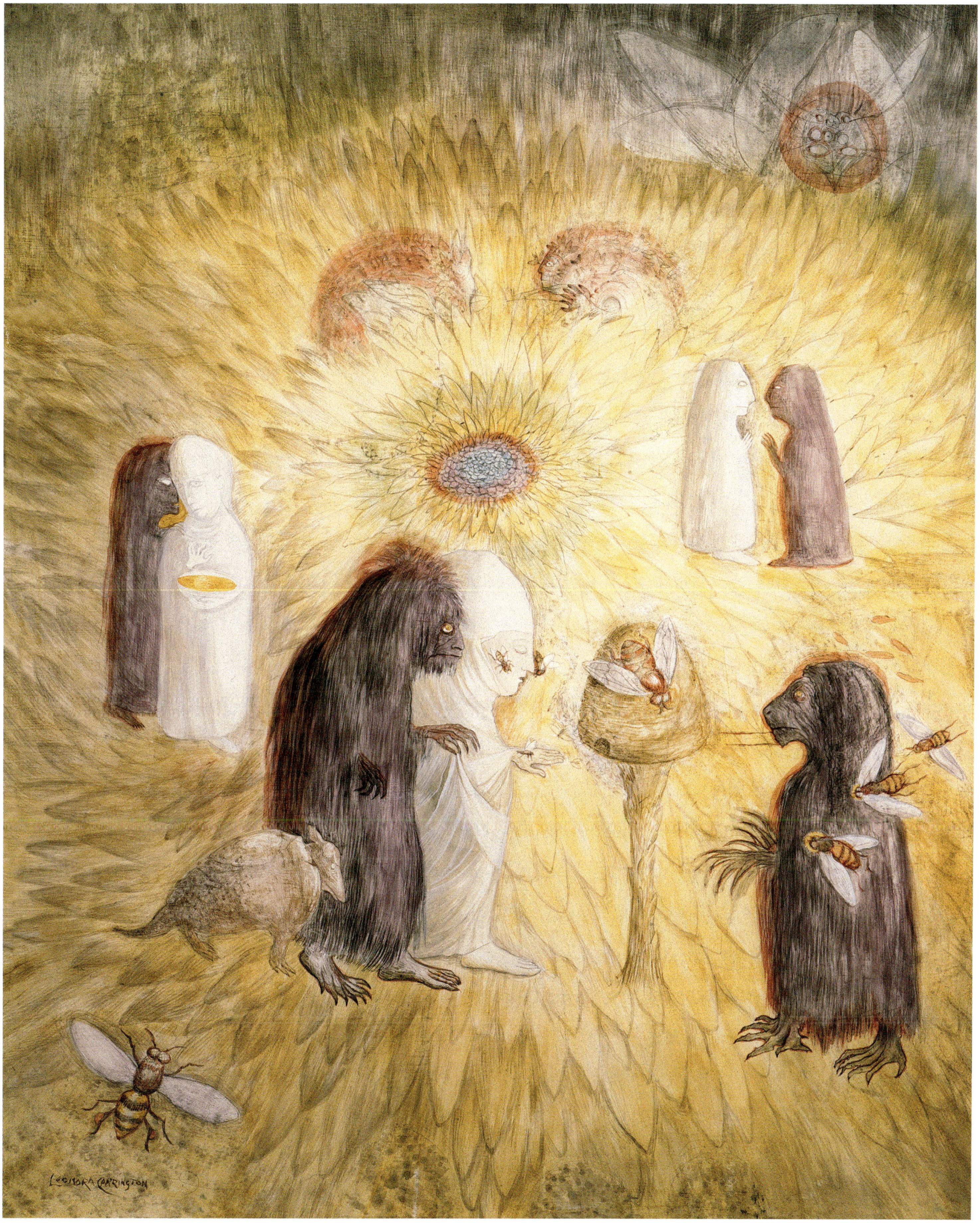

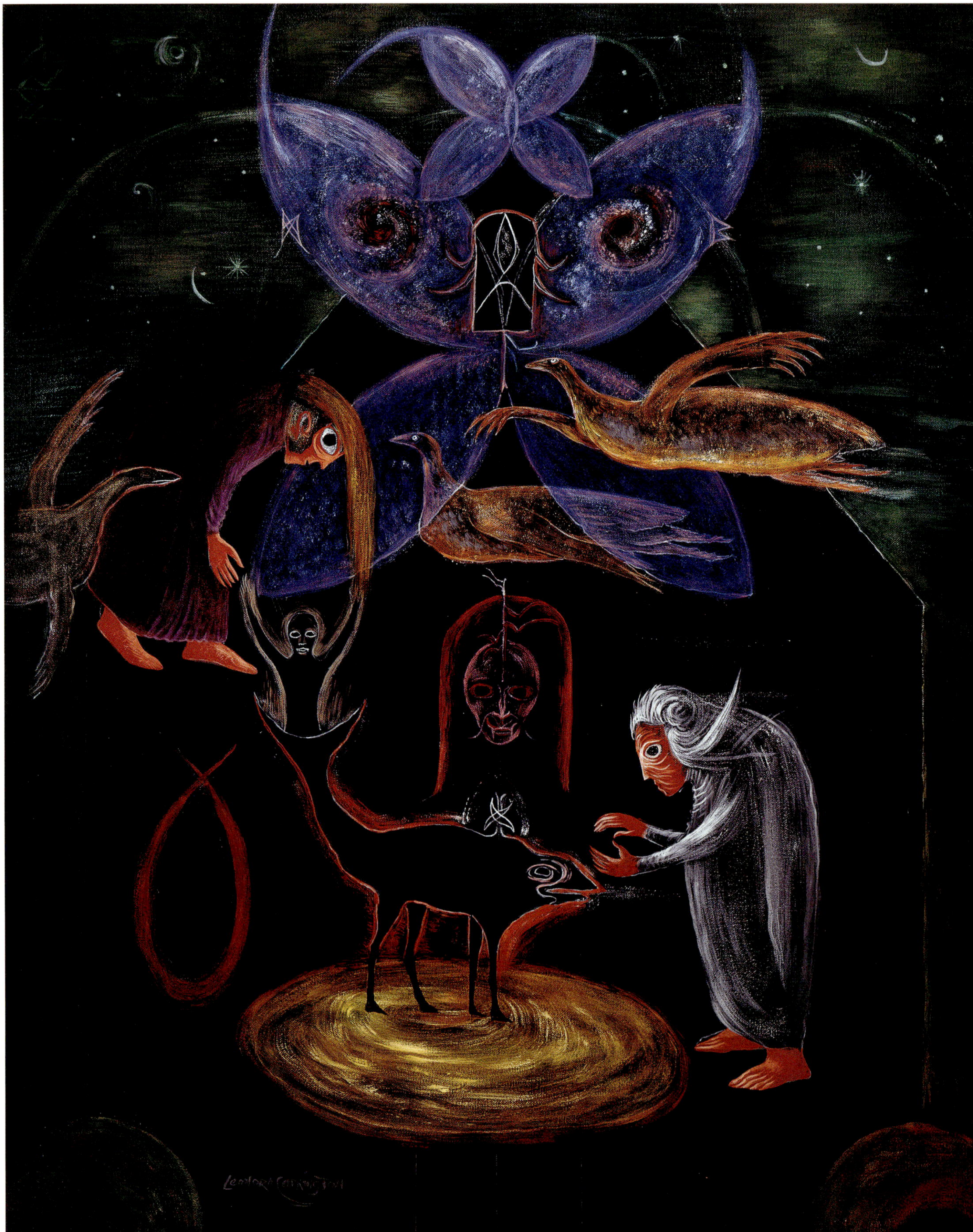

107
Night of the 8th
1987
Oil on canvas
74.5 x 58 cm/
29½ x 23 in
Private collection

108
Cabbage
1987
Acrylic on canvas
91.5 x 61 cm/36 x 24 in
Private collection

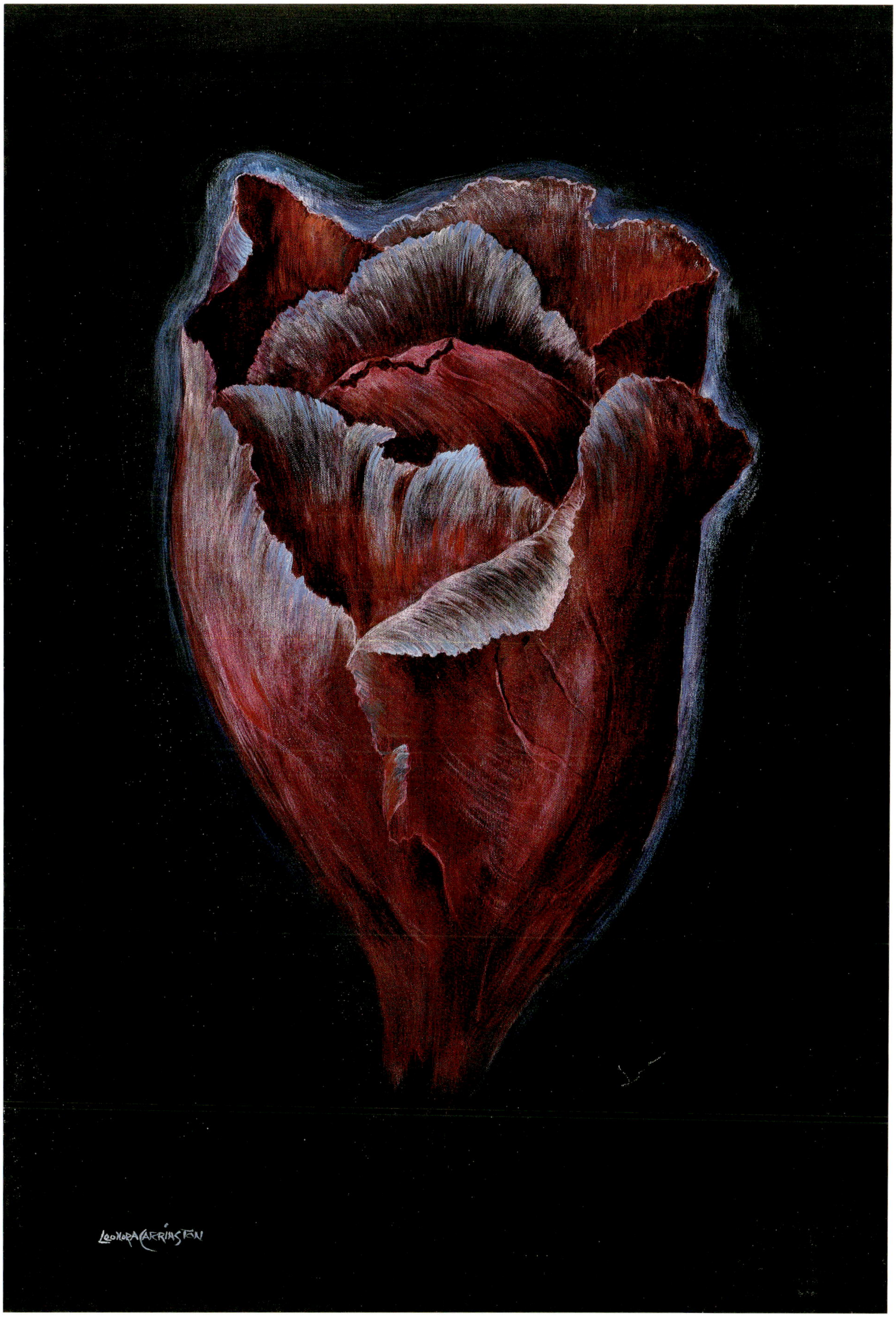

109
Kron Flower
1987
Tempera on panel
61 x 101 cm/24 x 40 in
Private collection

110
Ikon
1988
Egg tempera on three panels
77 x 58 cm/$30\frac{1}{2}$ x 23 in
Private collection

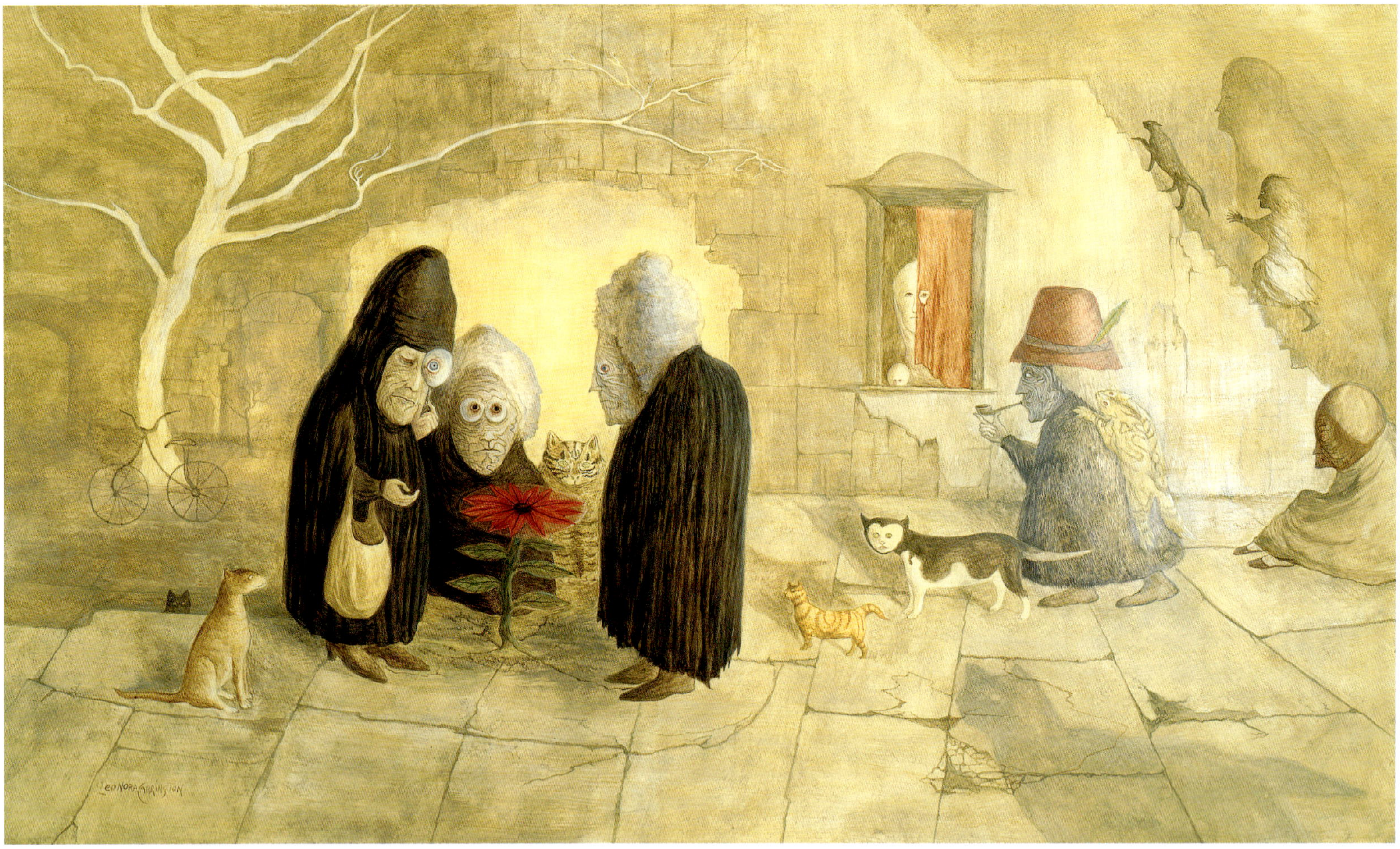

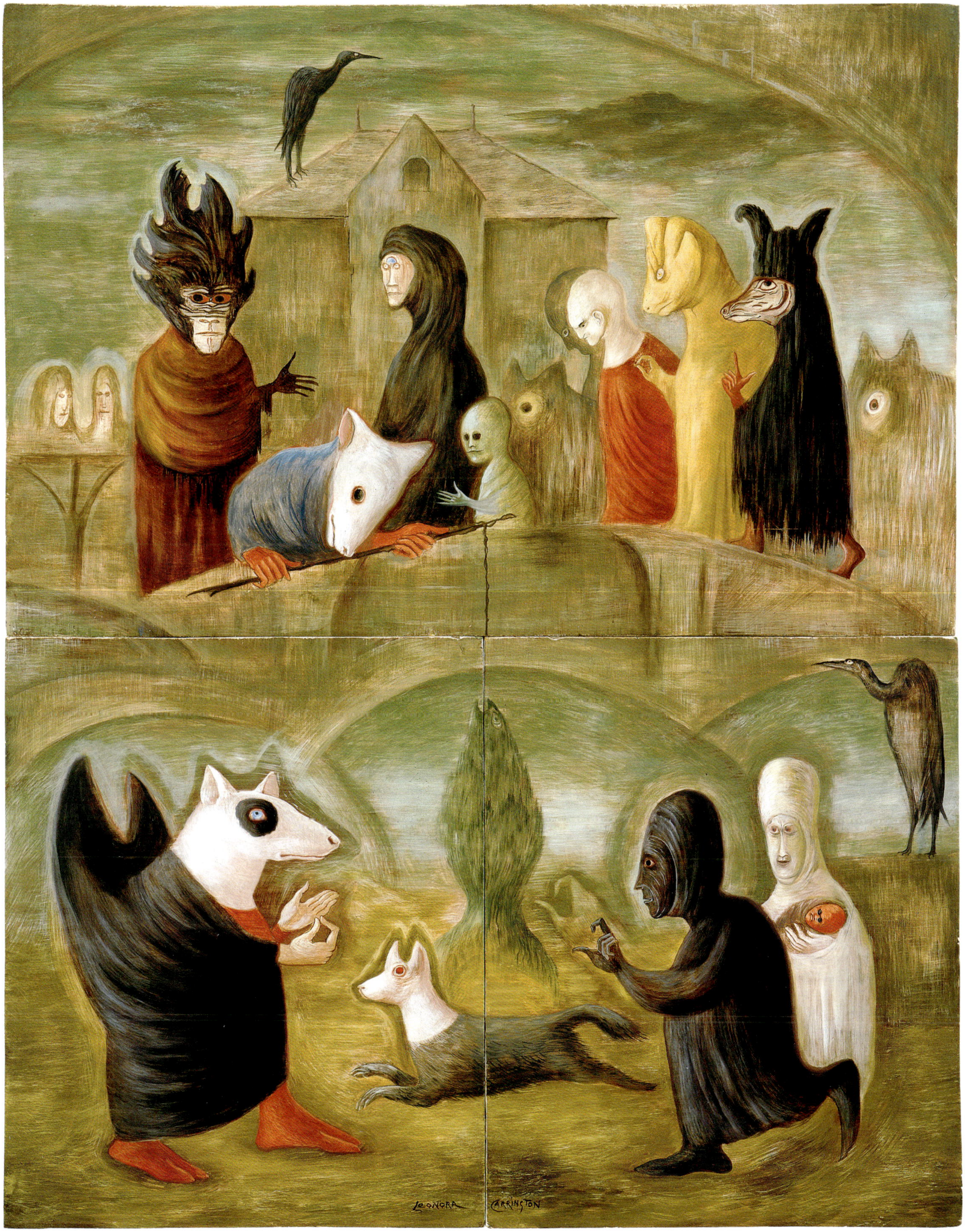
LEONORA CARRINGTON

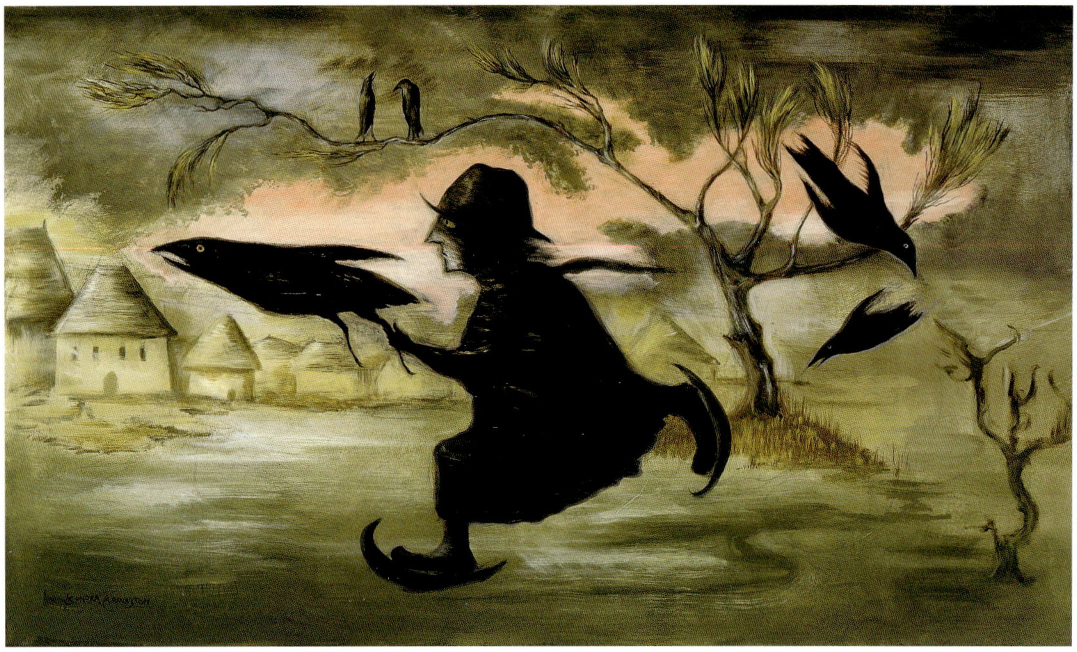

111
Crow Catcher
1990
Oil on canvas
45.5 x 76 cm/18 x 30 in
Private collection

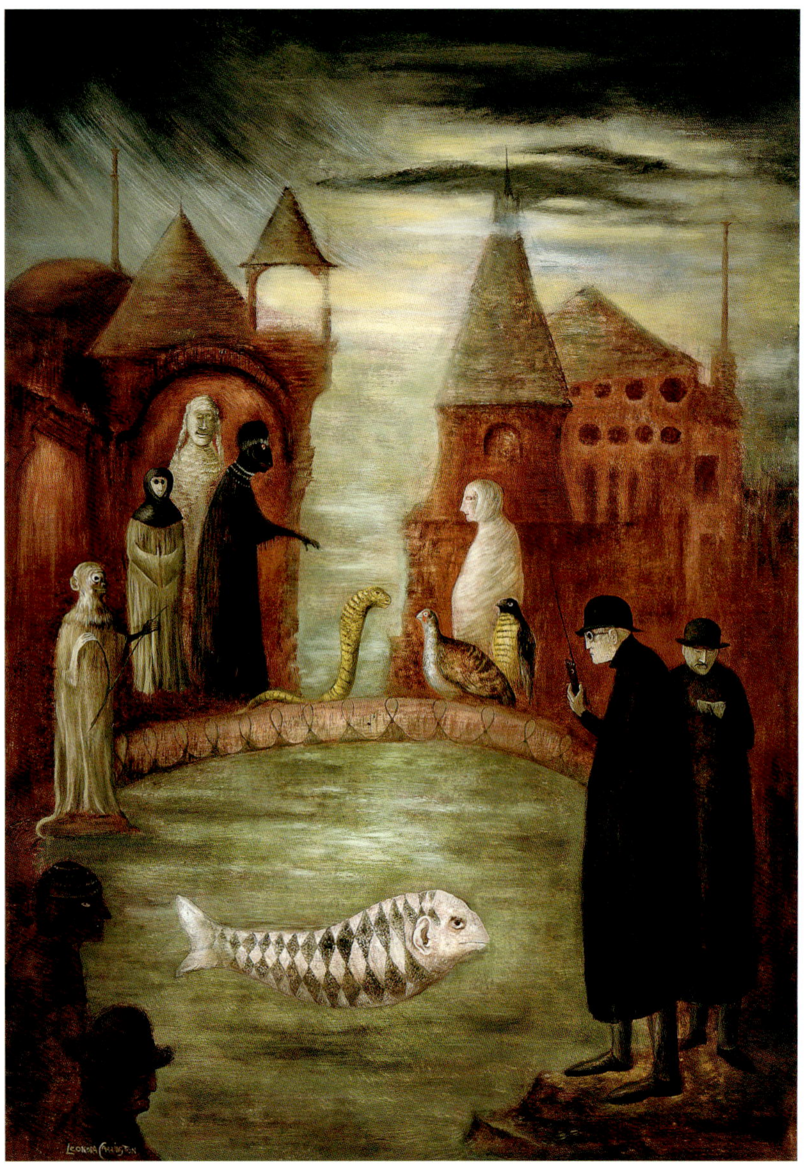

112
March Sunday
1990
Oil on canvas
91.5 x 61 cm/36 x 24 in
Private collection

113
Dog, come here into the dark house. Come here black dog
1995
From a portfolio of five etchings on white paper
Image: 22 x 9 cm/$8\frac{1}{2}$ x $3\frac{1}{2}$ in/ sheet: 36 x 28 cm/14 x 11 in
Edition of 30
Printed by Tiempo Extra Editores, Mexico

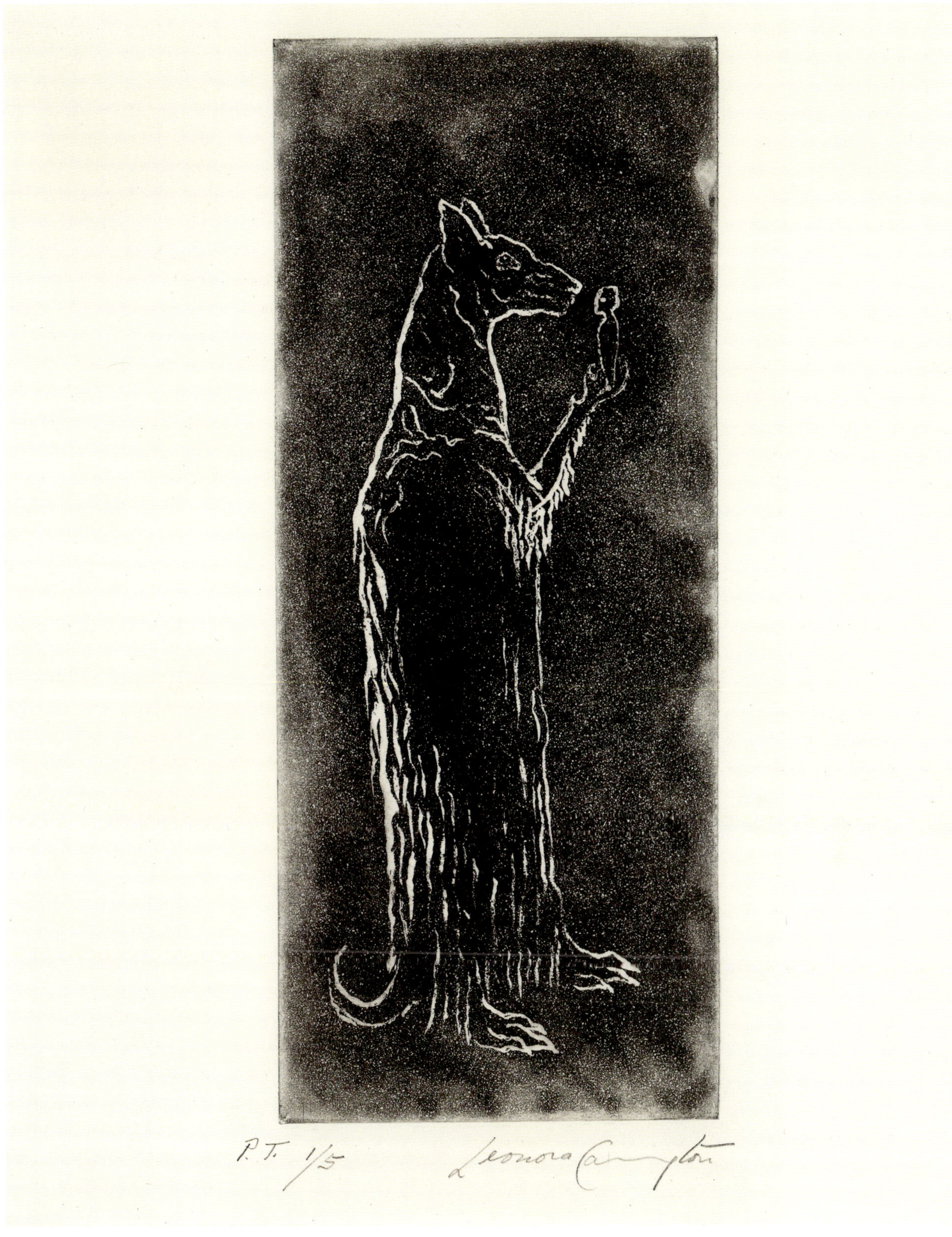

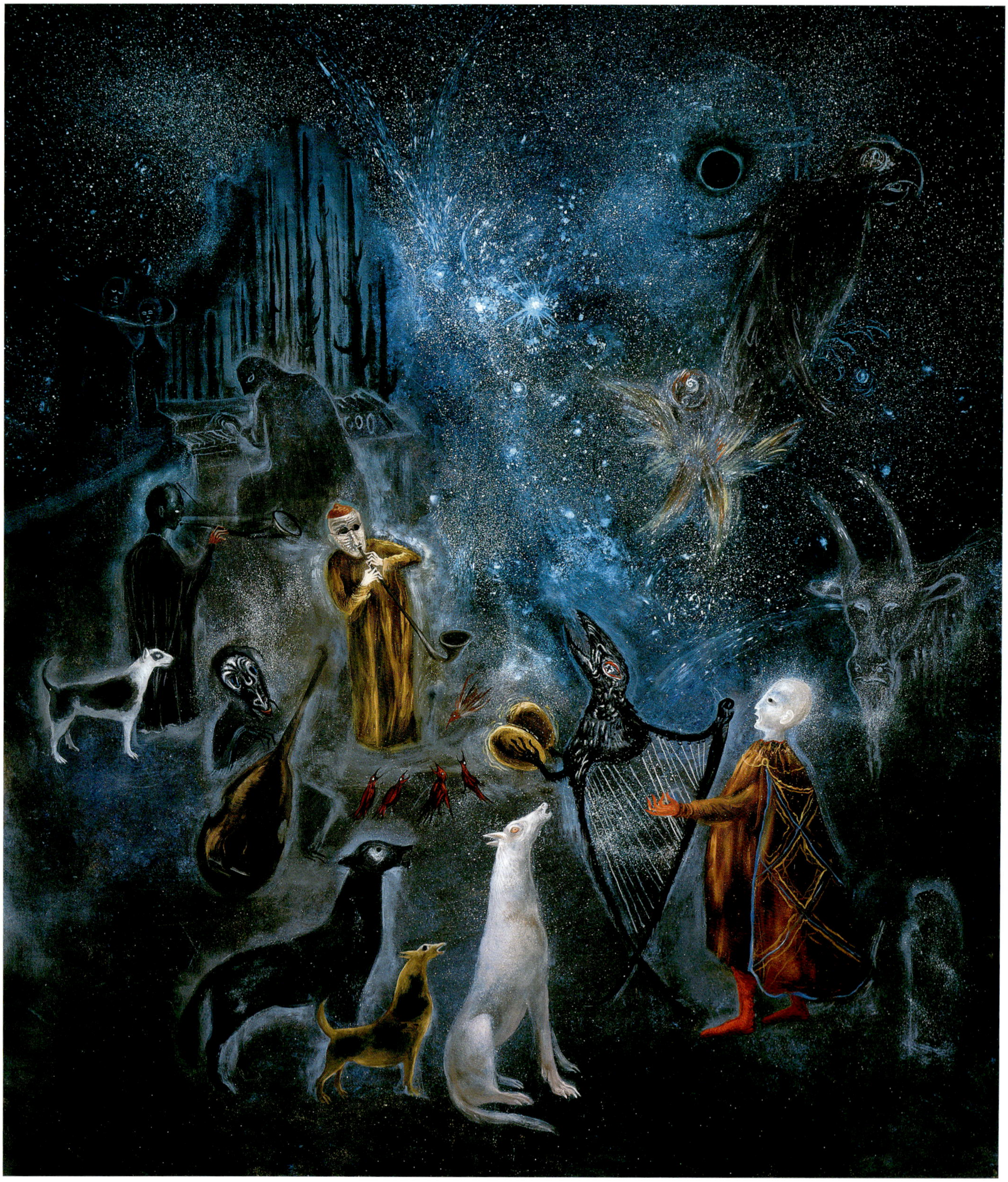

114
The Q Symphony
2002
Acrylic on board
92 x 76 cm/
36 x 30 in
Private collection

115

How Doth the Little Crocodile

2003

Public sculpture in Chapultepec Park, Mexico City

Bronze

8.5 x 4.8 x 1.15 m/28 x 16 x 4 ft

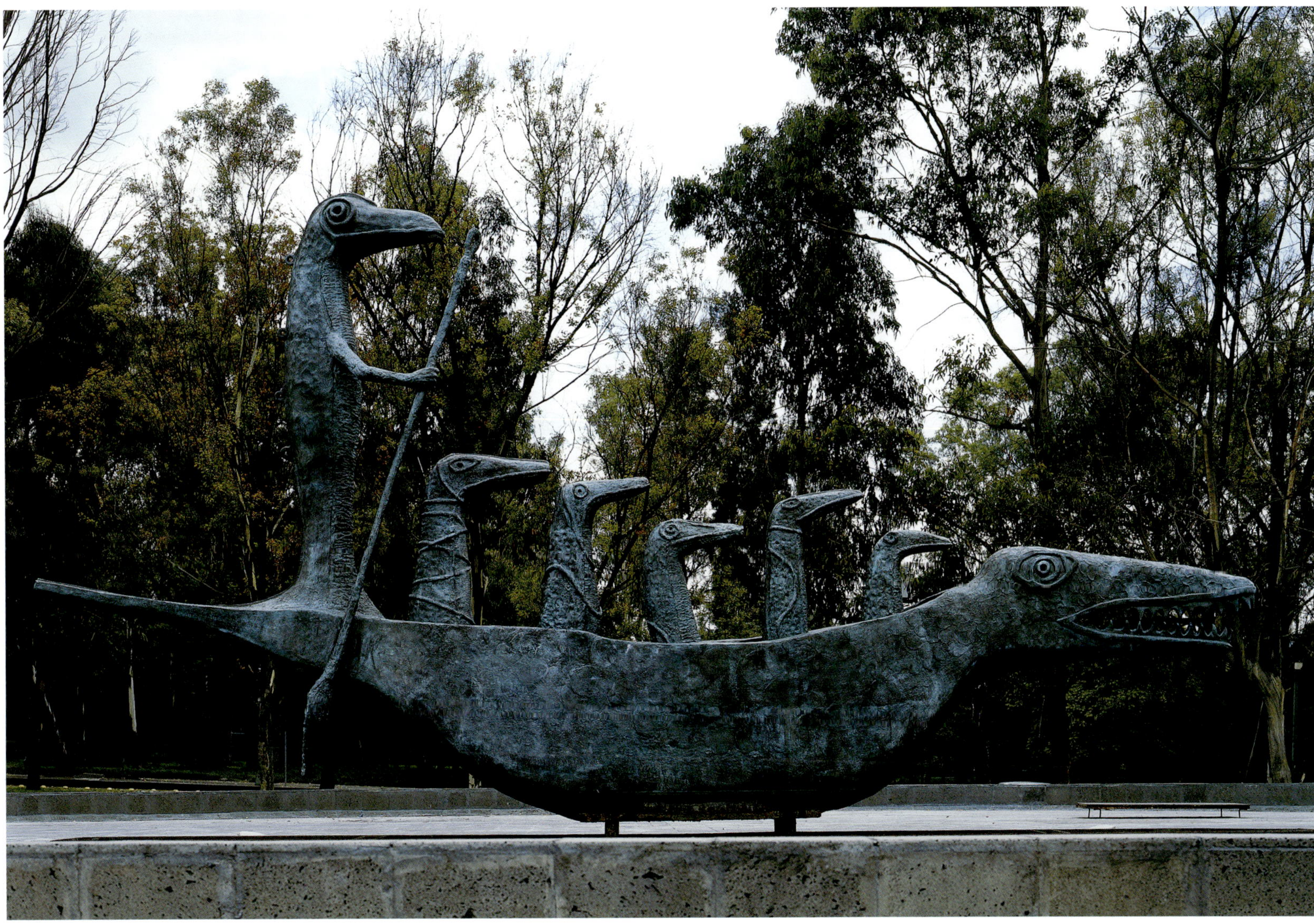

NOTES

Introduction

1 To date Carrington's writings have also been published in Dutch, German, Italian, Japanese, Polish and Portuguese.

2 A portion of *Down Below* was first published as an 'autobiographical fragment' in the February 1944 issue of *VVV* (New York:,no. 4). It was next published in its entirety in 1945 in Paris (*En bas*, Editions de la Revue Fontaine, no. 18) as part of the Surrealist *Collection l'Age d'Or* series.

3 'Well, my *Bedtime Story* video was completely inspired by all the female Surrealist painters like Leonora Carrington and Remedios Varo.' Vince Aletti, 'Madonna with Vince Aletti', *Aperture* (USA), 156, summer 1999 p.44.

Chapter 1

4 Moorhead was a common name in that region, often associated with gypsies, and upon her mother's death relatives confirmed that the Moorheads were in fact gypsies and tinkers. Paul De Angelis, 'Interview with Leonora Carrington', in *Leonora Carrington: The Mexican Years 1943–1985*, San Francisco: The Mexican Museum, 1991, p.33.

5 Marina Warner, Introduction to *House of Fear* by Leonora Carrington, New York: E. P. Dutton, 1988, pp 3–4.

6 Although mentioned in a number of publications on Carrington, this has never been corroborated. Continuing in this literary vein, Pablo Weisz Carrington told me that Leonora's father, Harold Wilde Carrington, was reputedly related to the writer Oscar Wilde.

7 'Leonora Carrington and the House of Fear', produced and directed by Kim Evans. Sixty-minute video documentary. *Omnibus*, BBC, 1992.

8 ibid

9 ibid

10 As told in an interview to the Mexican journalist Manuel Avila Camacho López in 'Max Ernst me enseño nueva forma de vivir', *Excélsior* (Mexico City), 10 February 1974.

11 De Angelis interview in *Leonora Carrington: The Mexican Years*, p.33.

12 Warner, Introduction to *House of Fear* by Leonora Carrington, p.1.

13 In an interview with the artist in February of 1999 in Mexico City, I heard her burst into a spontaneous recitation of 'The Walrus and the Carpenter' from *Alice in Wonderland*, while climbing the stairs of her home, the rhythm of each line punctuated by the ascent of one step. Carrington possesses the remarkable capability of being able to recite countless poems and nursery rhymes accurately.

14 Warner, Introduction to *House of Fear* by Leonora Carrington, p.4. I believe that *The Crock of Gold*, an extraordinary tale of the mythical ancient races of Ireland, exerted a profound influence on the artist in a multitude of ways, not the least of which was a visionary view of the magical powers of women.

15 The case was sensational at the time for a variety of reasons: the number of individuals involved, the fact that the confessions were freely made with no torture incentives, and, finally, that one of those found guilty, Alice Nutter, was a member of the gentry. Anne Llewellyn Barstow gives an in-depth account of the incident in her *Witchcraze: A New History of the European Witch Hunts*, New York: Harper Collins, 1994, pp 41–8. In the nineteenth century the event was further popularised by the publication of William Harrison Ainsworth's novel, *The Lancashire Witches: A Romance of Pendle Forest*, Leipzig, 1849, with its rather lurid and melodramatic descriptions of the region, witches, sabbaths, and so on.

16 According to Leonora, she badgered the nuns by continually asking them annoying questions, such as 'Who said that two and two is four?' From Salomón Grimberg's chronology in *Leonora Carrington: The Mexican Years 1943–1985*, San Francisco: The Mexican Museum, 1991, p.43.

17 Whitney Chadwick, *Leonora Carrington: La realidad de la Imaginación* Mexico City: Consejo Nacional para la Cultura y las Artes, 1994, p.7.

18 De Angelis interview in *Leonora Carrington: The Mexican Years*, p.33.

19 'Leonora Carrington and the House of Fear', produced and directed by Kim Evans.

20 Leonora would later exploit the common perception of backwards writing being associated with witchcraft and would include it in many of her drawings and paintings. The most spectacular and effective example being *Grandmother Moorhead's Aromatic Kitchen* (1975) in which she uses mirror writing for casting the runes (incantations) on a magic circle used to summon the goddess.

21 Alli Acker, *The Flowering of the Crone: A Portrait of Leonora Carrington*, produced and directed by Alli Acker. New York: Reel Woman Trust Foundation, *c.*1987. Ten-minute promotional videocassette for unfinished film project.

22 'Leonora Carrington and the House of Fear', produced and directed by Kim Evans. That her family invented Viyella, literally the very cloth of school uniforms and conformity, make her poor school evaluations more ironic.

23 Manuel Avila Camacho López, 'Max Ernst me enseño nueva forma de vivir'.

24 ibid

25 De Angelis interview in *Leonora Carrington: The Mexican Years*, p.34. Also, according to Orenstein, the taste of freedom and creativity she experienced as a boarder in their house that year changed the course of her life. 'Leonora Carrington: Another Reality', *Ms.*, August 1974, p.27.

26 Her coming-out dance inspired one of her most brilliant and subversive stories, 'The Débutante', first published as part of *La dame ovale*, a collection of six stories, published in 1939 by Editions G. L. M. in Paris and accompanied with collages by Max Ernst.

27 Photographs of Leonora in evening dress, accompanied by her mother, were published in a number of London newspapers at the time, as was the custom for débutantes. It was these very photographs that would later be mockingly reproduced in a variety of Surrealist publications as representative of the stultifying life the artist escaped from.

28 Reproduced in Manuel Avila Camacho López, 'Max Ernst me enseño nueva forma de vivir'.

29 The choice of reading material is an interesting one. At the time, a young woman of 18 found reading this modernist novel would be shocking enough since it dealt with adultery, drug addiction, prejudices against homosexuality, and had graphic depictions of sex. However, doing so publicly in the royal enclosure at Ascot would take her rebellion to a new level. It was most certainly an act that would not attract potential suitors from good families! The novel also deals with the use of meditation and spirituality as alternative healing techniques, subjects she would be interested in later. When she moved to Mexico in the 1940s she became a friend of Huxley, an author she admired throughout her life.

30 De Angelis interview in *Leonora Carrington: The Mexican Years*, p.34.

31 Manuel Avila Camacho López, 'Max Ernst me enseño nueva forma de vivir'.

32 Gloria Orenstein, 'Leonora Carrington: Another Reality', *Ms.*, August 1974, p.27.

33 'Jezzamathatics or Introduction to the Wonderful Process of Painting' first appeared in *Leonora Carrington: Exposición de óleos, gouaches, dibujos y tapices*, Mexico City: Instituto Anglo-Mexicano de Cultura, 1965. It was reprinted again in *Leonora Carrington* Brasil: IX Bienal de São Paulo, Instituto Nacional de Bellas Artes, 1967 and in Juan García Ponce, *Leonora Carrington*, Mexico City: Ediciones ERA, 1974.

34 From Marina Warner's introduction to Leonora Carrington, *House of Fear*, New York: E. P. Dutton, 1988, p.5. A variation on the quote comes from a Mexican newspaper interview where her father says, '... la pintura es para homosexuales y drogadictos'. Manuel Avila Camacho López, 'Max Ernst me enseño nueva forma de vivir'. Such an absurd and hurtful statement stayed with Leonora for a long time and she often quoted it in interviews.

35 Lourdes Andrade, 'Leonora Carrington: Magic, Mist and Surrealism', in *Leonora Carrington: Una retrospectiva*, Monterrey, N.L.: Museo de Arte Contemporáneo de Monterrey, 1994, pp 21–2.

36 There is no reason to doubt that there were other sketchbooks, but I was able to examine these in facsimile at Brewster Arts Limited, Carrington's dealer in New York City. Brewster had facsimiles of a series of watercolours dated 1932–3 that also depicted scenes reminiscent of fairy-tale book illustrations. Perhaps Carrington was familiar with the work of Arthur Rackham and Edmund Dulac, whose illustrations for children's books were popular during the early part of the twentieth century. I strongly believe that Leonora Carrington was profoundly influenced by such illustrations, which undoubtedly filled her childhood library, and also by the fabulous stories that accompanied them.

37 Founded in 1891, it has subsequently changed its name to Chelsea College of Art and Design.

38 As told to Manuel Avila Camacho López in 'Max Ernst me enseño nueva forma de vivir'.

39 De Angelis interview in *Leonora Carrington: The Mexican Years*, p.34.

40 As told to Avila Camacho López in 'Max Ernst me enseño nueva forma de vivir'. This is the only time Carrington mentions an instructor from the Chelsea School of Art. Little is known about Jean de Botton (1895–1978) except that he was French and later emigrated to the United States (working primarily in California), where he had a modest career as a painter, specialising in cityscapes and marine scenes.

41 ibid

Serge Chermayeff was a Russian student in London when his parents lost their fortune in the Russian Revolution. He later established himself as one of London's leading interior designers and architects. In the 1930s, at the time of his contact with Carrington, he was at the centre of the Modern Movement in England along with his friend, the German émigré Eric Mendelson. He emigrated to the United States in 1940 where he held academic positions at Harvard and Yale. The choice of so illustrious an overseer, on the part of her father, does indicate some sensitivity to her ambitions.

42 ibid

43 ibid

44 In a 1933 brochure entitled 'The European Mediterranean Academy' Ozenfant states: 'Tuition begins with the practical study of the technique of drawing and painting, including the laws of combination of colours and of chemistry; leads to a knowledge of the characteristics and values of the various techniques, and the structure of objects of natural and artificial origin.'

45 As told to Manuel Avila Camacho López in 'Max Ernst me enseño nueva forma de vivir'.

46 Warner, Introduction to *House of Fear* by Leonora Carrington, p.6.

47 De Angelis interview in *Leonora Carrington: The Mexican Years*, p.34.

48 Stella was seven years older than Leonora; the two women had much in common. Stella became a Surrealist painter, and later a photographer, living and working for many years in India. Her most recent retrospective exhibition *Rediscovery* was held at CFM Gallery in New York, April–May 1999.

49 De Angelis, 'Interview with Leonora Carrington', *El Paseante* (Madrid), 17, 1997, unpag.

50 In an interview with Whitney Chadwick, Ursula Goldfinger also told of how Carrington and a friend enjoyed shocking the hotel guests in the lobby by conducting loud conversations about their imaginary syphilitic symptoms. Whitney Chadwick, *Women Artists and the Surrealist Movement*, Boston: Little, Brown and Company, 1985, p.67.

51 Interview by the author with Stella Snead on 6, 7 and 14 February 2001, New York.

52 As told to Marina Warner, Introduction to *House of Fear* by Leonora Carrington, p.6. This is confirmed by Ursula Goldfinger who told Chadwick that she remembers Leonora at times painting things that were not in keeping with the 'strict formal geometry' taught by Ozenfant. Chadwick, *Women Artists the Surrealist Movement*, p.67.

53 Chadwick goes on to state that the bohemian beret, the saucy cigarette dangling from her mouth, and her claw-like hands, among other things, lend the figure a 'demonic quality'. Chadwick, *Women Artists and the Surrealist Movement*, p.68.

54 As late as 29 July 2003, Carrington could remember her friend Joan with great admiration, and excitedly tried to explain to me (at her home in Mexico City) how truly daring and unconventional she was.

55 Chadwick, *Women Artists and the Surrealist Movement*, p.78. Later, Chadwick also mentions that at this time Carrington purchased other books on esoterica and Sir James Frazier's *The Golden Bough: The Roots of Religion and Folklore*, 1890. Of particular interest, in light of her future involvement with Tibetan Buddhism, is that she also read Alexandra David Neel's *With Mystics and Magicians in Tibet*, London: John Lane, 1931, and *Initiations and Initiates in Tibet*, London: Rider & Co., 1931, which Chadwick describes as 'an account from 1931 that describes the trials of an independent woman during a trip of enlightenment in the Himalayas'. In *Leonora Carrington: La realidad de la imaginación*, Mexico City, 1994, p.8.

56 Read, Herbert (ed.), *Surrealism*, London: Faber & Faber Ltd, 1936. With essays by André Breton, Hugh Sykes Davies, Paul Eluard and Georges Hugnet. There is some discrepancy in Carrington's view that her parents were overwhelmingly against her art career. If this were true, then why would her mother give her an art book to encourage her interests?

57 Snead stayed with Ozenfant for five years and followed him to New York where in 1939 he opened the 'Ozenfant School of Fine Arts' at 208 East 20th Street. He also lectured at the New School for Social Research and taught, for short periods of time, at Yale, Harvard, Cooper Union and elsewhere. Since Leonora would renew her friendship with Snead while living in New York from 1941–2, we may assume she kept in some contact with him. Interview by the author with Stella Snead on 6, 7 and 14 February 2001, New York.

58 For example, Marcel Jean states: 'Leonora Carrington had made paintings and drawings without any formal training until she was nineteen when she started attending Ozenfant's studio (this artist was giving lessons in London at the time) but her compositions owed nothing to the 'purist' preoccupations of the former director of *L'Esprit Nouveau*.' Marcel Jean, *The History of Surrealist Painting*, New York: Grove Press, 1959, p.289. Nevertheless, the fact that she studied with Ozenfant seemed to impress the art world and it is mentioned as early as 1942 in Peggy Guggenheim (ed.), *Art of this Century 1910–1942*, New York: Art Aid Corp., 1942.

Chapter 2

59 Breton would later include Carrington as the only woman in his *Anthologie de l'humour noir,* Paris: Editions du Sagittaire, 1945, expanded edition that included Carrington, 1950, seeing her as part of a long line of British humourists.

60 Warner, Introduction to *House of Fear* by Leonora Carrington, p.5.

61 De Angelis, interview in *Leonora Carrington: The Mexican Years*, p.34.

62 Fourteen years her senior, Ernst met and married Aurenche when she was 22 years old and he was 36. Similar to the later situation with Carrington, Marie-Berthe's wealthy parents did everything they could to prevent their marriage.

63 Ernst married Lou Straus, an art historian, in 1917 and their son Jimmy was born in 1920. In 1922 he began an affair with Gala Eluard and lived with her and her husband Paul in an awkward threesome arrangement. By 1926 their relationship began to cool and he also received a divorce from his wife. In 1927 he met Marie-Berthe Aurenche, who worked as a secretary in an art gallery, and they were married later that year. From 1936 through 1940 he was involved with Leonora Carrington and became divorced from his second wife in 1939. He met the wealthy American collector Peggy Guggenheim in 1940 and they were married in 1941, and in 1942 he met another American, the painter Dorothea Tanning, 21 years his junior. Ernst and Guggenheim were soon divorced and

in 1946 he married Tanning. Among his many other romantic relationships were the artists Meret Oppenheim and Leonor Fini.

64 De Angelis, interview in *Leonora Carrington: The Mexican Years*, p.36.

65 As told to Manuel Avila Camacho López in 'Max Ernst me enseño nueva forma de vivir'.

66 Acker, *The Flowering of the Crone*, 1987.

67 ibid

68 Roland Penrose, *Scrap Book 1900–1981*, London: Thames and Hudson, 1981, p.107.

69 One cannot help thinking of Carrington's beloved Lewis Carroll and the Mad Hatter's tea party scene from his *Alice in Wonderland*.

70 The liberation and relief she must have experienced being with Ernst, a famous artist who took her ideas and work seriously, cannot be overstated. For example, in an interview with Susan Rubin Suleiman, Carrington talked about the 'huge putdowns' she received as an art student in London, such as 'Forget it, you're no good, and anyway there are no good women artists.' Suleiman concludes: 'Literally he brought her into a new life – a new city, a new language ... a world where art was respected and women artists were not automatically dismissed.' From 'The Bird Superior meets the Bride of the Wind: Leonora Carrington & Max Ernst', in Whitney Chadwick and Isabelle De Courtivron (eds), *Significant Others: Creativity & Intimate Partnership*, London: Thames and Hudson, 1993, p.106.

71 Acker, *The Flowering of the Crone*, 1987.

72 De Angelis, interview in *Leonora Carrington: The Mexican Years*, p.36.

73 Sheena Wagstaff, 'Surrealist in the Mid West', *Interview*, August 1990.

74 As told to Manuel Avila Camacho López in 'Max Ernst me enseño nueva forma de vivir'. Her 'guardian' reacted with equal intensity, as Carrington tells it 'Serge Chermayeff, the man whom my parents put in charge of my honor, called me a whore', F. Orgambides, 'Leonora Carrington: "No me arrepiento de mi vida"'. *El País, La Cultura* (Madrid), 18 April 1993, p.30.

75 De Angelis, interview in *Leonora Carrington: The Mexican Years*, p.36.

76 Manuel Avila Camacho López in 'Max Ernst me enseño nueva forma de vivir'.

77 Gloria Orenstein, 'Leonora Carrington: Another Reality', *Ms.*, August 1974, p.28.

78 Manuel Avila Camacho López in 'Max Ernst me enseño nueva forma de vivir'.

79 Jane Perlez, 'Woman in the News: Leonora Carrington, Surrealism Lives', *New York Post*, weekend magazine, section 3, 6 December 1975, p.1.

80 Jimmy Ernst, *A Not-so-still Life: A Memoir*, New York: St Martin's/Marek, 1984, p.87. The Freudian implications of this make the story bear repeating: Jimmy describes his first meeting with Carrington in 1937 when he arrived at his father's home unannounced one afternoon: 'One of the most beautiful women I had ever seen told me in English-accented French that she expected him to be back in about an hour. She made me tea, and in the course of conversation told me that she loved Max and that they were living together. Her name was Leonora Carrington and her dark, glowing beauty so affected me that I found it difficult to talk to her coherently. My unexpected visit must also have been awkward for her, and she broke into one of our mutual silences suddenly. "Look here, it must be strange for you to find me here instead of Max. All of this just happened so recently that you perhaps didn't even know I existed. Max has told me a great deal about you, and he was a bit apprehensive of your reaction. He loves you very much, and I hope that you and I can become very good friends." She got up, kissed me on both cheeks and graciously left the room. That allowed my hammering heart to return to normal.'

81 ibid p.91.

82 ibid pp 113–14.

83 ibid p.109.

84 Chadwick sums up the artist's position at this time thus:

> Surrealism offered many women their first glimpse of a world in which creative activity and liberation from family-imposed social expectations might coexist, one in which rebellion was viewed as a virtue, imagination as the passport to a more liberated life. Leonora Carrington's background and life typify in many ways those of other women associated with the Surrealists and her personal rebellion began long before she met the group in 1937. She was, in effect, a kind of embodiment of all that the movement held dear in its women: young, beautiful, vivacious, uninhibited, and in possession of an imagination that knew no limits. From the beginning, her revolution was an individual one, having nothing to do with either Marx or Freud, a direct frontal assault not on the family as an institution, but on one particular family, hers.

Chadwick, *Women Artists and the Surrealist Movement*, p.67.

85 It is a safe assumption that within the context of Surrealist painting, it was the women artists who were most drawn to self-portraiture, such as Leonor Fini, Frida Kahlo, Dorothea Tanning, Eileen Agar and Valentine Hugo. It is an interesting phenomenon although Carrington, with the exception of this spectacular example, painted them only on rare occasions.

86 Acker, *The Flowering of the Crone*, 1987.

87 Interview with the artist at her home in Colonia Roma, Mexico City, February 1999.

88 Warner, Introduction to *House of Fear* by Leonora Carrington, p.1.

89 I have chosen Leonardo da Vinci over many other artists in the Uffizi because I found a certain correspondence between him and Carrington, such as writing backwards, drawing horses, and diagramming inventive machines.

90 This gesture is particularly popular in Italy and she may have learned it while living there. It has a variety of uses and when used in an encounter with another person can either repel evil or extend a curse. Georgiana M. M. Colvile also notes that the hyena approaches Carrington from the left, the direction of *sinistra* (evil). 'Beauty and/is the Beast: Animal Symbology in the Work of Leonora Carrington, Remedios Varo and Leonor Fini' in *Surrealism and Women*, Cambridge, MA. and London: The MIT Press, 1991, p.163.

91 For a more thorough understanding of Victor Witter Turner's (1920–82) theories on liminality see 'Liminal to Liminoid, in Play, Flow, and Ritual: An Essay in Comparative Symbology' in his book *From Ritual to Theater: The Human Seriousness of Play*, New York: PAJ Publications, 1982.

92 Whitney Chadwick, *Leonora Carrington: Recent Works*, New York: Brewster Gallery, 1988, p.2.

93 Victor Turner, 'Frame, Flow and Reflection: Ritual and Drama as Public Liminality' in Michel Benamou and Charles Caramello (eds), *Performance in Postmodern Culture*, Milwaukee: University of Wisconsin Press, 1977, p.41.

94 I pair 'bestial' and sexuality here to intimate that Carrington, now sexually experienced, perhaps equated her sexuality as belonging to the natural, and hence animal realm. She was also well aware of the fact that her mother would be highly disapproving of a sexual relationship enjoyed out of marriage and might consider her daughter's liaison with Ernst as bestial in a pejorative sense.

95 Warner, *House of Fear*, p.2.

96 ibid

97 In an interview with Sheena Wagstaff, Carrington explained how the two art forms were interrelated:

> Writing and painting are alike in that both come out of fingers and go into some receptive artifact. The result is read or seen through the organs and those who receive the art. It's not a question of people making the *wrong* interpretation. Most people aren't able to form *any* opinion. Once a dog barked at a mask I made; that was the most honorable comment I ever received.

From 'Surrealist in the Mid West', *Interview Magazine*, August 1990, p.20.

98 Henri Parisot, a French publisher, was her lifelong literary adviser.

99 Leonora Carrington, 'The Débutante' in *The House of Fear*, New York: E. P. Dutton, 1988, p.44.

100 For a thorough analysis of 'The Débutante', in terms of psychological and esoteric content, see Bettina L. Knapp, 'Leonora Carrington's Whimsical Dreamworld: Animals Talk, Children are Gods, a Black Swan Lays an Orphic Egg', *World Literature Today*, 51 (6), autumn 1977, pp 525–30.

101 Annette Shandler Levitt, 'The Horses, Birds, and Crones of Leonora Carrington', in *The Genres and Genders of Surrealism*, New York: St Martin's Press, 1999, p.71.

102 Julia Kristeva, *Powers of Horror: An Essay on Abjection*, trans. Leon S. Roudiez, New York: Columbia University Press, 1982, p.4.

103 Chadwick, *Women Artists and the Surrealist Movement*, p.79.

Chapter 3

104 Salomón Grimberg, 'Leonora Carrington', *Art Nexus*, 26, October–December 1997, p.62.

105 Peggy Guggenheim, *Out of this Century: Confessions of an Art Addict*, New York: Universe Books, 1979, p.216.

106 Whitney Chadwick, *Women Artists and the Surrealist Movement*, p.12.

107 Chadwick notes that the majority of the women artists she contacted who were associated with Surrealism positively recalled the support and encouragement they received from Breton and other Surrealists:

> Many of them were learning to be artists in the face of strenuous family disapproval, others had found their training in art school rigid and mechanical, almost all of them were in revolt against the conventional female roles assigned to them by family, class, and society. Surrealism provided a sympathetic milieu and served as an important milestone on their journeys towards artistic and personal maturity. Beyond this there is little consensus.

ibid p.11.

108 Acker, *The Flowering of the Crone*,1987.

109 Chadwick again offers the most thorough history of the term and its application in her *Women Artists and the Surrealist Movement,* see pp 33–4.

110 Warner, Introduction to *House of Fear* by Leonora Carrington, p.6.

111 Orgambides, F. 'Leonora Carrington: "No me arrepiento de mi vida"', *El País*, *La Cultura*, 18 April 1993, p.30.

112 Jane Perlez, 'Woman in the News: Leonora Carrington, Surrealism Lives', *New York Post*, Weekend Magazine, Section 3, 6 December 1975, p.1.

113 ibid p.19.

114 'My father was in the midst of making a very important change in his life. He was turning his back on Paris and had finally completely broken with the Surrealists. He was tired, he told me, that minor squabbles within the group were constantly being blown into major confrontations with their "conscience" André Breton.' Ernst, *A Not-so-still Life: A Memoir*, New York: St Martins/Marek, 1984, p.106.

115 ibid p.109.

116 Manuel Avila Camacho López in 'Max Ernst me enseño nueva forma de vivir'.

117 Warner, Introduction to *House of Fear* by Leonora Carrington, p.15.

118 Jimmy Ernst repeatedly tried to warn his father of the dangers of staying in France but he was so captivated with his new home and Carrington that he turned a deaf ear on what he must have known were legitimate concerns. 'Here [Saint-Martin-d'Ardèche] he hoped to establish for himself and his great love, in his own words, "a little bit of peace." And indeed one of his most powerful works of that period is a large canvas appropriately titled *Un Peu de Calme*. In light of this, my suggestions to him concerning his personal safety in Europe evoked nothing more than a slightly quizzical annoyance.' Ernst, *A Not-so-still Life*, p.106.

119 Roland Penrose, *Scrap Book 1900–1981*, p.122.

120 This painting evinces the 'black humor' of many of Carrington's short stories written between 1938–42. In 'The Bestial Fictions of Leonora Carrington' Annette Shandler Levitt provides an insightful analysis of some of their recurrent themes, one of which is the consumption of bones, rotting flesh and other unsavoury and 'unholy' substances. Of particular relevance to this painting is her discussion of *White Rabbits*, written by Carrington in New York in 1941. The story concerns a diseased couple who live in a disintegrating house with one hundred rabbits to which they feed carrion, occasionally eating a rabbit as well. Levitt notes that the story echoes the gross banquet scene in *The Meal of Lord Candlestick* and Levitt makes an observation that has resonance for this painting: 'Eating rabbit stew is not barbaric, but in this context it becomes so, as nurture and murder, elegance and decay seem inextricably entwined.' *Journal of Modern Literature*, 20 (1), summer 1996, p.70. In another story by Carrington, 'As They Rode Along the Edge', written sometime between 1937 and 1940 while in St. Martin d'Ardèche, the protagonist Virginia Fur commands her friends, the forest animals, to turn against a group of humans about to eat a wild boar. In the apocalyptic chaos that ensues the tables are turned and the prey eats the predators.

121 Warner, An Introduction to *House of Fear* by Leonora Carrington, p.15.

122 Chadwick, *Women Artists and the Surrealist Movement*, p.66.

123 Fiona Bradley, *Movements in Modern Art: Surrealism*, (exh.cat.), London: Tate Gallery Publishing, 1997, p.53.

124 ibid pp 164–5.

125 Mara R. Witzling (ed.), *Voicing Our Visions: Writings by Women Artists*, New York: Universe, 1991, p.311.

126 Leonora Carrington, 'Fly, Pigeon' from *The Seventh Horse and Other Tales*, New York: E. P. Dutton, 1988, p.28.

127 Rubin Suleiman, 'The Bird Superior Meets the Bride of the Wind: Leonora Carrington & Max Ernst' in Whitney Chadwick and Isabelle De Courtivron (eds), *Significant Others: Creativity & Intimate Partnership*, London: Thames and Hudson, 1993, p.115.

128 Nor, of course, could Ernst have been safe in Germany since his painting *La belle jardinière* had toured Germany in Hitler's 1937 exhibition of degenerate art.

129 Ernst, *A Not-so-still Life*, p.106.

130 ibid p.156.

131 Marcel Jean, *The History of Surrealist Painting*, New York: Grove Press, 1959, p.300.

132 Decalcomania was a Surrealist technique supposedly invented by Oscar Dominguez. Rich, unpredictable patterns were obtained by either taking an impression from, or sponging, layers of liquid paint: figurative motifs were then developed by overpainting. The idea behind the technique, using chance textures to suggest forms and images, had the goal of evading conventional expression of authorial intention, equating the practice with the concept of 'Automatism'.

133 Many of Ernst's decalcomania paintings (1940–42) dealt directly or indirectly with Carrington: of particular interest are two works from 1940 *J'ai bu du tabouio* and *The Painter's Daughters*, which feature human/horse hybrids. In each work a standing figure stretches out an arm, terminating in a cryptic hand gesture reminiscent of Carrington's in *The Inn of the Dawn Horse*, although different in form there is a similar iconic solemnity. Paintings from the series that also feature Carrington are *The Stolen Mirror* (1941), *Alice in 1941* (1941), *Napoleon in the Wilderness* (1941), *Europe After the Rain* (1940–42) and *The Anti-Pope* (1941–2).

134 In her autobiography, Peggy Guggenheim explained the details of this transaction: 'It seems that Leonora Carrington had gone mad and made over their house to a Frenchman in order to save it from the Germans, not knowing that he would take advantage of the situation and seize the property.' *Out of this Century: Confessions of an Art Addict*, New York: Universe Books, 1979, p.228. Dorothea Tanning gives a chilling account told her by Ernst of returning home to find a group of men sitting in his kitchen, each with a finger missing (a precaution against conscription)

and, feeling sorry for him, letting him stay as an overnight guest in his own house. *Birthday*, San Francisco: Lapis Press, 1986, p.52.

135 Guggenheim, *Out of this Century*, p.228.

136 ibid p.229.

137 Tanning, *Birthday*, p.52.

138 Carrington had been threatening to murder Hitler and calling for the metaphysical liberation of mankind. Chadwick, *Women Artists and the Surrealist Movement*, p.84.

139 According to Katherine Conley, Carrington's institutionalisation was the result of the intervention of three men: Van Ghent, whom Carrington found quite sinister and whose son worked for her father's company; the British consul, who had her locked up in a hotel room at the Ritz Hotel; and finally Gilliland, the head of Imperial Chemicals (ICI) in Spain, who had her taken first to "an operating clinic full of nuns" and eventually to the clinic in Santander on the north-western coast of Spain, by tricking her into thinking she was going to the beach.
'Beyond the Border: Leonora Carrington's Terrible Journey', in *Automatic Woman: The Representation of Woman in Surrealism*, Lincoln, NE: University of Nebraska Press, 1996, p.61. Conley gives a thorough and excellent analysis of both the writing of *Down Below* and the text itself.

140 Morales, Luis, 'La enfermedad de Leonora', *El País*, *La Cultura* (Madrid), 18 April 1993, p.31.

141 'Leonora Carrington in the House of Fear', produced and directed by Kim Evans, *Omnibus*, BBC, 1992.

142 André Breton, 'Manifesto of Surrealism (1924)', *Manifestoes of Surrealism*, Ann Arbor: The University of Michigan Press, 1972, p.5.

143 Chadwick, *Women Artists and the Surrealist Movemen*t, p.35.

144 Orgambides, F., 'Leonora Carrington: "No me arrepiento de mi vida"', p.30.

145 Pierre Mabille, 'Acerca de Abajo', *La Cultura en México*, Supplemento de Siempre!, Mexico City, DF, 9 January 1974, p.6. (*Abajo* translated by Cesar Moro, a special edition supplement of the review 'Siempre' no. 622.)

146 ibid, p.6.

147 Warner, Introduction to *The House of Fear* by Leonora Carrington, p.18.

148 Written in 1459 by Johann Valentin Andreaes and first published in 1616, this text was translated by the British occultist A. E. Waite, the designer of the Waite tarot deck.

149 Carrington, 'Down Below' from *The House of Fear*, New York: E. P. Dutton, 1988, p.195.

150 ibid p.186.

151 ibid p.192.

152 Conley, Kathleen, 'Beyond the Border: Leonora Carrington's Terrible Journey', in *Automatic Woman: The Representation of Woman in Surrealism*.

153 Breton, André, *Anthology of Black Humor*, San Francisco: City Lights Books, 1997, p.335. Breton's *Anthologie de l'humour noir*, Paris: Sagittaire, 1945, written and compiled in 1940, was censored by the French government and not published until 1945, at which time Carrington was included. It received very little attention in 1945 and was reissued in 1950 and again, before Breton's death, in 1966. It was not translated into English until 1997 by Mark Polizzotti, San Francisco: City Lights Books, 1997. The only other woman included in this book was the Surrealist poet Gisèle Prassinos, Carrington's very inclusion places her on equal footing with the other authors in the anthology such as Franz Kafka, Arthur Rimbaud, Edgar Allan Poe, and so on.

154 Edward James, Introduction in *Leonora Carrington*, (exh.cat.), New York: Pierre Matisse Gallery, 24 February–13 March 1948.

155 The Carrington family did actually send Leonora's nanny, Mary Kavanaugh to Lisbon to see what was going on. Nanny was very frightened of being in a foreign country and was not helpful in carrying out the family's plans. Carrington was fond of saying that Nanny was sent by submarine, although later she mused, 'I might have invented that, I'm not sure.' 'Leonora Carrington in the House of Fear', *Omnibus*, BBC, 1992.

156 She had met him by chance at a dance hall in Madrid the previous week. Leduc, a friend of Picasso's from her Paris days, recognised her and signalled her to meet him in Lisbon.

157 Guggenheim, *Out of this Century*, p.239.

158 Paul De Angelis, 'Interview with Leonora Carrington', *El Paseante* (Madrid), 17, 1997.

159 ibid

160 Guggenheim, *Out of this Century*, p.266.

161 Ernst, *A Not-so-still Life*, pp 213–14.

162 The idea for a show devoted exclusively to women came from Marcel Duchamp, who first suggested it when they were still in Europe. When he revived the idea after her gallery opened in the fall of 1942, Guggenheim was receptive, in part because of its daring. 'The bohemian world of art had room for women as mistresses or models but not as serious artists in their own right. Some women painters toiled in the shadow of well-known husbands or lovers and sacrificed their own opportunities to the careers of the men. Others simply could not get their work shown.' Jacqueline B. Weld, *Peggy: The Wayward Guggenheim*, New York: Dutton, 1986, p.235.

163 Leonora Carrington, 'Waiting', *VVV*, June 1942, pp 49–50.

164 This title was meant to suggest an immigrant's first naturalisation papers. Jean, *The History of Surrealist Painting*, p.312. For more information on this exhibition see Lewis Kachur, *Displaying the Marvelous: Marcel Duchamp, Salvador Dali, and Surrealist Exhibition Installations*, Cambridge, MA: MIT Press, 2001.

165 This riddle, which starts 'Brothers and sisters have I none, but this man is my son' runs for eight refrains and is usually found in children's books where it is used as a logic puzzle.

166 These pairings were called 'Mise en scène d'André Breton' and some of his other couplings were the Holy Grail with Picasso, and 'La Communication interplanetaire' with Ernst.

167 Rosicrucians are an esoteric, secret, worldwide society using, supposedly, magical knowledge drawn from alchemy. The name comes from pamphlets written by Christian Rosenkreutz whose tract *The Chymical Wedding of Christian Rosenkreutz* has been discussed previously.

168 I believe that Breton viewed Carrington with a greater respect after her madness; at least he seemed to pay greater attention to her work and seemed to be more interested in her visual output, looking at it in a different light. This is apparent in his introduction to the artist from his *Anthology of Black Humor*:

> From one of those journeys that offer little hope of return, and that she related with devastating precision in *Down Below*, Leonora Carrington has retained a nostalgia for the shores that she once approached and that she has not despaired of reaching anew, this time without brooking any resistance, as if granted a permit to travel in either direction at will. There is proof enough of this in the admirable canvases she has painted since 1940, no doubt the most laden with the modern 'marvelous,' which are penetrated by an occult light and which can teach us much about her vision, both physical ('The duty of the right eye is to plunge into the telescope, whereas the left eye interrogates the microscope') and mental ('Reason must know the heart's reasons and every other reason').

Breton, *Anthology of Black Humor*, p.336

169 ibid p.335.

170 Luis Buñuel, *My Last Sigh*, trans. Abigail Israel, New York: Alfred A. Knopf, 1983, p.181.

171 Breton, *Anthology of Black Humor*, p.335.

172 This issue, along with an insert, acted as a catalogue for the show. Included in this issue was Breton's 'The Legendary Life of M. E., Preceded by a Brief Discussion on the Need for a New Myth', Joseph Cornell paid homage with a collage of engravings called 'Story without a Name for M. E.', a photograph of Ernst in a feathery jacket seated cross-legged among his kachinas by James Thrall Soby, and another photo of Ernst taken by Berenice Abbott. According to Warlick, this issue of *View* celebrated Ernst as the alchemist-magician of the Surrealist movement and reveals their continued fascination, during the early 1940s, with hermetic philosophy. To confirm this idea she notes that other texts on hermeticism were featured in issues of both *VVV* and *View*. M. E. Warlick, *Max Ernst and Alchemy: A Magician in Search of Myth*, Foreword by Franklin Rosemont, Austin: University of Texas Press, 2001, p.171.

173 Leonora Carrington, 'The Bird Superior: Max Ernst', *View*, 2, April 1942, p.3.

174 ibid

175 Guggenheim, *Out of this Century*, p.266

Chapter 4

176 With regard to Spanish refugees in particular, part of Mexico's motivation was not only to support the Spanish Republican cause but it was hoped that these mostly professional-class Spaniards would act as a stimulus to economic and cultural development. Janet Kaplan, *Unexpected Journeys: The Art and Life of Remedios Varo*, New York: Abbeville Press, 1988, p.85.

177 Martica Sawin, in her exhaustive survey, *Surrealism in Exile and the Beginning of the New York School*, Cambridge, MA: MIT Press, 1995, presents an invaluable study of the Surrealist exodus from Europe and the spread of their artistic practices. The chapter entitled 'The Mexican Connection', outlines the arrivals, settlings, and departures of artists such as Wolfgang Paalen and Alice Rahon with Eva Sulzer, Esteban Francis, Gordon and Jacqueline Onslow Ford, Matta and others.

178 Commenting on this quote, Jacqueline Barnitz succinctly summarised Breton's position: 'He was of course, projecting a Eurocentric vision on a culture that seemed to fulfill his dreams of the marvelous and exotic.' Jacqueline Barnitz, *Twentieth-century Art of Latin America*, Austin: University of Texas Press, 2001, p.103. Breton told a Mexican interviewer in 1938: 'I find Mexico to be Surrealistic in its landscape, in its vegetation, in the dynamism of its mixed races, and in its highest aspirations.' From Rafael Heliodoro Valle, 'Conversations with André Breton', *Revista Universidad*, Mexico City: National Autonomous University of Mexico, June 1938, 29, pp 5–8.

179 See André Breton, 'Souvenire du Mexique', *Minotaure*, ser. 3, 6th year; 12–13 May 1939, pp 31–47; and *Mexique*, Paris: Renou and Colle, 1939.

180 Ida Rodríguez Prampolini, *El surrealismo y el arte fantástico de Mexico*. Instituto de Investigaciones Estéticas, Universidad Nacional Autónomo de Mexico, 1969, p.96.

181 'Surrealism, Wartime, and New World Imagery: 1928–1964', essay in Jacqueline Barnitz, *Twentieth-century Art of Latin America*, Austin: University of Texas Press, 2001, p.107.

182 Ida Rodríguez Prampolini, *El surrealismo y el arte fantástico de México*, p.96.

183 Hayden Herrera, *Frida: A Biography of Frida Kahlo*, New York: Harper & Row, 1983, p.254.

184 Paul De Angelis, 'Interview with Leonora Carrington', *El Paseante* (Madrid), 17, 1997, unpag.

185 Martica Sawin, *Surrealism in Exile and the Beginning of the New York School*, 1995, p.279. Varo's self-sufficient attitude may have inspired Carrington to find means of support for her own family. Although Chikki worked as a commercial photographer, Carrington was also a substantial contributor to the household income.

186 Whitney Chadwick, 'Leonora Carrington: Evolution of a Feminist Consciousness', *Woman's Art Journal*, spring/summer 1986, p.40.

187 According to Janet Kaplan, there was always some distance between the Mexican artists and the influx of Europeans who socialised mainly with each other. The Riveras' rejection of foreign 'colonising' influences, kept them at a public distance at least. Kahlo had met the Surrealists on the occasion of her 1939 exhibition in Paris and had unpleasant things to say about Breton whom she found overly intellectual and affected. Janet Kaplan, *Unexpected Journeys*, pp 87–8.

188 ibid p.93.

189 Leonora Carrington, *The Hearing Trumpet*, New York: St Martin's Press, 1976. Carrington told me that she wrote the entire book while seated in the Café Garibaldi in the Plaza de los Mariachis in the midst of cacophonous noise. My interview with the artist in February of 1999 in Mexico City.

190 Although the subject of their friendship and artistic collaboration would be a fascinating study, so far Carrington has kept her reminiscences private. A retrospective exhibition of their close friends, Kati and José Horna, at the Museo Nacional de Arte in Mexico City, *Los sentidos de las cosas: el mundo de Kati y José Horna* (July 2003–April 2004) provides a tantalising glimpse into the closeness of the four friends and the extent to which they shared ideas.

191 Janet Kaplan, *Unexpected Journeys*, p.95.

192 ibid p.96.

193 ibid Carrington is referring to the Aztec practice of eating human flesh, often of sacrificial victims. This account of the sale of live youths in the marketplace is rather fanciful.

194 'Leonora Carrington in the House of Fear', produced and directed by Kim Evans, *Omnibus*, BBC, 1992.

195 Sawin, *Surrealism in Exile*, p.250.

196 'Leonora Carrington in the House of Fear', *Omnibus*, BBC.

197 Victor Serge, 'Letter from Mexico', *Horizon*, January 1947, p.69.

198 'There is Leonora Carrington, of British descent, on her way back to the fairy-tales of her childhood ... There is no respect either for the boundaries that separate organic and inorganic life ... I asked her about her attitude towards surrealism. "It's the most healthy exercise; it's excellent," she said.' Gustav Regler, 'Four European Painters in Mexico', *Horizon*, 16 (91), August 1947, p.96.

199 The film director Albert Lewin was a friend of Carrington's who tried to get her novel, *The Hearing Trumpet*, published in New York, but according to her no one was interested in the theme of the novel – a 92-year-old English feminist held captive in a medieval Spanish castle turned into a nursing home. De Angelis, (Madrid), 17, 1997, unpag.

200 *The Temptation of St Anthony, Bel Ami International Art Competition*, (exh.cat.), Washington, DC: The American Federation of Arts, 1947.

201 Sawin, *Surrealism in Exile*, pp 280–81.

202 'Unhappy Demons', *Time*, 22 March 1948 and 'Leonora Carrington at Matisse's', *Art News*, 46, February 1948, p.58.

203 Held 18 May–5 June 1948.

204 Whitney Chadwick, *Women Artists and the Surrealist Movement*, p.194.

205 De Angelis, 'Interview with Leonora Carrington', *El Paseante* (Madrid), 17, 1997, unpag.

206 Some of the reviews in the Mexican press included: Ceferino Palencia, 'El arte de ensueño de Leonora Carrington', *Mexico en la Cultura*, 19 February 1950; Jorge J. Crespo de la Serna, 'Las ideas y las formas', *Excélsior*, 5 March 1950; Luis Islas García, 'Triunfos imaginativos', *Excélsior*, 26 March 1950; Margarita Nelken, 'El arte al dia', *Novedades*, 1 March 1950; 'En la exposición de Leonora Carrington', *Excélsior*, 25 February 1950; 'Dos lienzos de la pintora Leonora Carrington', *El Universal*, 22 February 1950; and Fred and Frances Trezevant, 'Exciting Show at Clardecor', *Mexico City*, 3 March 1950.

207 ' ... la impresión de esta exposición de Leonora Carrington, que la Galería Clardecor nos presenta, y que constituye uno de los acontecimientos señalados de nuestra vida artística', Margarita Nelken, 'El arte al dia', *Novedades*, 1 March 1950.

208 'Esta finisima pintora inglesa vive y pinta en México hace ya algunos año. Pero su temperamento no es de los que se circunscriben y limitan por un media ambiente geográfico cualquiera. El mundo en que ella respira es de una amplitud extraordinaria.' Jorge J. Crespo de la Serna, 'Las Ideas y las Formas: Fantasia y realidad', *Excélsior*, 5 March 1950.

209 Donald Cordry, 'Mexico Weaves', *Craft Horizons*, 15, July–August 1955, pp 17–21.

210 Nan Mulder, 'Leonora Carrington in Mexico', *Alba*, 1 (6), December 1991–January 1992, p.6.

211 In Andrea Schilieker (ed.), *Leonora Carrington: Paintings, Drawings and Sculptures 1940–1990*, (exh.cat.), London: Serpentine Gallery, 1991, p.9.

212 Colle, Marie-Pierre, *Latin American Artists in their Studios*, with an Introduction by Carlos Fuentes, New York: Vendome Press, 1994. Published in Spanish as *Artistas Latino americanos en su estudio*, INBA, Noriega editores libro, 1994, p.84.

213 Günther Gerszo as cited in Whitney Chadwick, 'Leonora Carrington: Evolution of a Feminist Consciousness', p.41.

214 De Angelis, interview in *Leonora Carrington: The Mexican Years*, p.42.

215 Close to home, Frida Kahlo was an example of an artist who borrowed the compositional strengths of Mexican Catholic art of all types, to create secular work that possessed great dramatic and psychological power.

216 According to Paul De Angelis, Carrington was influenced by the Renaissance trecento and Quattrocento paintings she saw at the Uffizi in Florence while in boarding school. Of special interest to her were the cassoni painted with moral fables and fairy tales, as well as predella panels. Marina Warner, 'Leonora Carrington's Spirit Bestiary; or the Art of Playing Make-Believe', in Andrea Schilieker (ed.), *Leonora Carrington: Paintings, Drawings and Sculptures 1940–1990*, p.16.

217 ibid

218 Whitney Chadwick, 'Leonora Carrington: Evolution of a Feminist Consciousness', p.41.

219 Leonora Carrington, 'Commentary' in *Leonora Carrington: A Retrospective Exhibition*, (exh.cat.), New York: Center for Inter-American Relations, 26 November 1975–4 January 1976, p.23.

220 Edward James in Introduction to *Leonora Carrington*, (exh.cat.), New York: Pierre Matisse Gallery, 1948.

221 *The Temptation of St Anthony, Bel Ami International Art Competition*, pp 16–17.

222 *Leonora Carrington: A Retrospective Exhibition*, (exh.cat.), New York: Center for Inter-American Relations, p.14.

223 'As above, so below' is the abbreviated and popularised version of a line from the much-quoted alchemical text, the *Emerald Tablet*, attributed to Hermes Trismegistus. The earliest-known version was by Jabir ibn Hayyan in an eighth-century Arabic text that was discovered by E. J. Holmyard and translated into Latin around the thirteenth century. The first law of the table reads: 'True it is, without falsehood, certain and most true. That which is above is like to that which is below, and that which is below is like to that which is above, to accomplish the miracles or one thing.' Lyndy Abraham, *A Dictionary of Alchemical Imagery*, Cambridge (UK): Cambridge University Press, 1998, p.70.

224 Helland likens Graves's focus on a universal feminine archetype as a source of creativity and inspiration to the writings of Carl Jung, with whom Carrington would be familiar by 1960. Janice Helland, 'Surrealism and Esoteric Feminism in the Paintings of Leonora Carrington', *RACAR*, 16 (1), 1989, p.56.

225 Chadwick, *Women Artists and the Surrealist Movement*, p.186.

226 ibid p.24.

227 Leonora Carrington, *Down Below*, Chicago: Black Swan Press, 1983, p.18.

228 In older catalogues this painting is called *Edwardian Hunt Breakfast*.

229 This is another example of Carrington using different cultural sources when referring to goddess figures. She was interested in both ancient Mesopotamian and ancient Egyptian religions and many of her paintings subtly depict mummies, temples; one from 1955, *Adieu Amenothep*, eerily depicts a levitating mummy who is being unwrapped by an odd assembly of onlookers. The cow goddess, Hathor, was of particular interest to Carrington.

230 Leonora Carrington, 'Commentary' in *Leonora Carrington: A Retrospective Exhibition*, (exh.cat.), pp 23–4. I believe she is alluding to Carlos Casteneda's *The Teachings of Don Juan: A Yaqui Way of Knowledge*, Berkeley: University of California Press, which was published in 1972 and received much attention since it dealt with peyote and hallucinogenic drug experiences.

231 Carlos Fuentes, 'Leonora Carrington, or Ironical Sorcery', in *Leonora Carrington: Exposición de óleos, gouaches, dibujos y tapices*, Mexico City: Instituto Anglo-Mexicano de Cultura, June 1965.

Chapter 5

232 'Leonora Carrington in the House of Fear', produced and directed by Kim Evans, *Omnibus*, BBC, 1992.

233 To examine these drawings and many close-ups of the mural please see Andrés Medina and Laurette Sojourné, *El mundo mágico de los Mayas*, Mexico City: Instituto Nacional de Antropología e Historia, 1964.

234 Carlos Fuentes, 'Ironical Sorcery', in *Leonora Carrington: Exposición de óleos, gouaches, dibujos y tapices*, (exh.cat.), Mexico City: Instituto Anglo-Mexicano de Cultura, June 1965.

235 Carrington never made a systematic study of Jung's writings but she was interested in his theories regarding archetypes.

236 Gloria Orenstein, 'Leonora Carrington: Another Reality', *Ms.*, August 1974, pp 27–31.

237 They are similar to her 1968 painting *The Ancestor* (Fig.92), which shows a similarly clad entity holding a cabbage and located within a magic circle.

238 Leonora Carrington in Marie-Pierre Colle, *Latin American Artists in their Studios*, Introduction by Carlos Fuentes, New York: Vendome Press, 1994, p.84.

239 A Mexican term for either a skull or a skeleton character used for Day of the Dead celebrations. These can be folk-art toys, puppets, masks, or even the broadsheet characters created by José Guadalupe Posada.

241 Whitney Chadwick, *Leonora Carrington – Recent Works*, (exh.cat.), New York: Brewster Gallery, 1988, p.4.

LEONORA CARRINGTON: JEZZAMATHATICS OR INTRODUCTION TO THE WONDERFUL PROCESS OF PAINTING

In the early part of the latter nineties I was born under curious circumstances, in a Eneahexagram, Mathematically. The only person present at my birth was our dear and faithful old fox-terrier, Boozy, and an x-ray apparatus for sterilizing cows. My mother was away at the time snaring crayfish which then plagued the upper Andes and wrought misery and devastation among the natives.

My father, a practising golf professional, invented the famous perforated bunker which swallowed Lord Baden Powell's initiates locked in closed combat in the Netherlands.

My early childhood was spent in exhaustive studies of geological conditions of sub-maritimous playgrounds for displaced persons. This, of course, took me far abroad from my native land yet widened and stretched my field of consciousness to such a degree that I had to resort to a jibaro head shrinker to undergo normal mentation in the metropoli of the world.

Undaunted by the wonderful flexibility of the cranial reflex I was able to make a donation of accurate calculi to the Lord Mayor of Chorley who went down to posterity riding the first mechanical Yoghurt eater.

Irrelevant though it may appear I must add that the invention of the painting machine which later became the father mother of modern aesthetics and the great mobile stability for future artistic endeavour was flashed (comet-wise) out of the delicate sensibility of the first computer to the donated to the Bolton cricket team in order to Score where scoring was an obsolete art. The fact that the apparatus became fertile enough to give birth to the painting machine can only emphasise the wonderful nature of Mechanical Chance. Again, if the Centre forward gave it a banana instead of the formula for averages from one to five runs per season perhaps the Computer activity would have been otherwise. These savage Miscalculations gave forth the glorious future of Art, Culture and new and better railwayline girders all over the world.

Due to this Fortuitous Accident, The Painting Machine, new Mediums blossomed like fruitful barnacles on the gnarled bottom of human invention.

'Ergot EN EX HUMIDUS IN CREATUM UNT.'

The Funghi which bellowed the glorious profusion of Late Socromorphic Reason addled necrocritically like a Chinese egg. Quote: 'We are, therefore we are not what we might have been if were otherwise than that which we would have been if we were.' (Professor A. J. Ayer has abundantly demonstrated the empirical logic of this austere Argument.)

Therefore because of the marvellous capacity of the Painting Machine that I entered the Mysteries of Creative Art when, in fact, I was born a Jezzamathician.

Ergot.

I was decubing the root of a Hyporbollick Symposium in order to calculate the outer Denominator of a fig tree into equal Xextopodic chloriomorfacious sections when the latent metamorphosis blurted the great unexpected shriek into something between a squeak and a smile. IT GAVE, so to speak, in order to return.

Magnificat.

IT PAINTED. It painted organic Subterranean Entities, it painted Chthonic faunae in jubilant contrast to the class calculus in exhaustive despeculation on the so-called reductive recapitulation of summarized sentential reason. This miracle was sufficient, of course, to launch a new era in

Neo-proletariat politics based on the ever-inflating ethics of anarcho-organised government, a system of circular dissentation to promote the growth of rice mutations within the artic circle.
A question of well planned drainage from Gleneagles golf course to south Chile only to enter the hole of the poles with Stratoproads from recent outerspacial artefacts.

We feel confident that the general public are now adequately informed on the simple but arduous projection of the Artist from the humid warmth of genealogical gestation to the dizzy freezing point of oil paint on canvas in well established Morphology going from one vicissitude to numberless combinations of zoological colour gnodes to ambivalent orquestration of strangely timed psyclograms deftly intershot with sparrowhawks pressed into tablets of concentrated malice only to explode here and there with the soundless perversity of zero sirns in an incalculable gesture of suspended astonishment.

Note:
This mock 'artist's statement' made its first appearance in *Leonora Carrington: Exposición de óleos, gouaches, dibujos y tapices,* (exh.cat.), Mexico City: Instituto Anglo-Mexicano de Cultura, 1965.

BIBLIOGRAPHY

Writings by the artist

La maison de la peur, Preface and illustrations by Max Ernst, Paris: Collection un Divertissement, Henri Parisot, 1938
La dame ovale, trans. Henri Parisot, with seven collages by Max Ernst, Paris: Editions G. L. M., 1939
With Hans Arp, Marcel Duchamp, Paul Eluard, George Hugnet, Gisèle Prassinos and Max Ernst, 'L'Homme qui a perdu son squelette', *Plastique*, 5, 1939, pp 2–9
'White Rabbits', *View*, 1, December 1941–January 1942, p.7
'The Sisters', *View*, 1, February–March 1942, pp 7–8
'The Bird Superior, Max Ernst', *View*, 2, April 1942, p.3
'Waiting', *VVV*, June 1942, pp 49–50
'The Bird Superior: Max Ernst', *New Roads*, 1943, p.194
'The Seventh Horse', *VVV*, 2–3, March 1943, pp 128–30
'Down Below', trans. Victor Llona, told to Jean Mégnen, *VVV*, 4, February 1944, pp 70–86
'En bas', *Collection l'Age d'Or*, Paris: Editions de la Revue Fontaine, 1945, no. 18
'White Rabbits' and 'The Sisters', in Charles Henri Ford (ed.), *A Night with Jupiter and Other Fantastic Stories*, New York: View Editions, 1945
'Pénélope', *Les quatre vents*, 1, 1946
'Abajo', Parts 1 and 2, *Las Moradas, revista de las artes y las letras*, Lima, Peru, ii, 2 (5), July 1948; (6), October 1948
'Conejos blancos', *Prometeus, revista mexicana de Literatura*, México, Editorial Nuevo Criterio, I (1), February–March, 1949
Une chemise de nuit de flanelle, trans. Ives Bonnefoy, Prologue by Henri Parisot, Paris: Librairie les Pas perdus, 1951
'L'Homme neutre', *Le Surrealisme, même*, 1957
'El príncipe azul Cucú', *Cuadernos de Bellas Artes*, México, Instituto Nacional de Bellas Artes, año II, núm 2, February 1961
'De cómo funde una industria o el sarcófago de hule', *S.N.O.B. Hebdomadario*, Mexico City, 3, 4 July 1962
La dama oval, Mexico City: Col. Ediciones Era, 1965
'La débutante', André Breton (ed.), *Anthologie de l'humour noir*, Editions du Sagittaire, originally published in 1945 but expanded to include Carrington in 1950, Paris: Jean-Jacques Pauvert, 1960
Pénélope, Cahiers Renaud-Barrault (2nd trimester 1969)
Pénélope, Cahiers Renaud-Barrault, 70, Paris: Gallimard, 1971
Down Below, Chicago: Black Swan Press, 1972. Reprint 1983
En bas, Paris: Eric Losfeld, 1973
'Abajo', trans. César Moro, *La Cultura en México*, supplement to *Siempre!*, Mexico City, 9 January 1974
Le cornet acoustique, trans. Henri Parisot, Prologue by André Pieyre de Mandirargues, Paris: Editions Flammarion, 1974
The Oval Lady: Six Surreal Stories, Foreword by Gloria Feman Orenstein, trans. Rochelle Holt, illustrated by Pablo Weisz, Santa Barbara: Capra Press, 1975
'The Débutante', 'A Man in Love' and 'The Neutral Man', in *The Custom House of Desire: A Half-Century of Surrealist Stories*, trans. and Introduction by J. H. Matthews, Berkeley: University of California Press, 1975
La porte Pierre, trans. Henri Parisot, Paris: Editions Flammarion, 1976
The Hearing Trumpet, New York: St Martin's Press, 1976
The Hearing Trumpet, New York: Pocket Books, 1977
'La débutante', trans. Henri Parisot, *Histoires et pièces*, Paris: Ediciones Flammarion, 1977–8
The Stone Door, New York: St Martin's Press, 1977
'The Seventh Horse', *The Autobiography of Surrealism*, New York: The Viking Press, 1980
Down Below, Chicago: Black Swan Press, Surrealist Editions, 1983
The Hearing Trumpet, San Francisco: City Lights, 1985
Pigeon vole: contes retrouvés, trans. Jacqueline Chénieux-Gendron and Didier Vidal, Cognac: Temps qu'il fait, *c.*1986
'El príncipe azul Cucú', *México en el arte*, México, Instituto Nacional de Bellas Artes/Secretaría de Educación Pública, 14, autumn 1986
'Monsieur Cyril de Guindre', *Mexico en el arte*, Instituto Nacional de Bellas Artes, 19, 1987, pp 28–32
The House of Fear, New York: E. P. Dutton, 1988
The Seventh Horse and Other Tales, New York: E. P. Dutton, 1988
'Las vacaciones del esqueleto' y 'La casa del miedo', *El paseante*, 1990, no. 17
Memoria de abajo, Madrid: Col. Libros del tiempo, 1991
The Hearing Trumpet, London: Virago, 1991
La trompeta acústica, trans. Roser Berdagué, with Introduction by Mercè Ibarz, Barcelona: Edicion de l'Eixample, Espai de donnes, 1991
El séptimo caballo, Madrid: Ediciones Siruela, 1992
Memorias de abajo, Prologue by Fernando Savater, Madrid: Siruela, 1992
La casa del miedo. Memorias de abajo, México: Siglo XXI, Cortesía Ediciones, 1992
El séptimo caballo, Mexico City: Siglo XXI, Cortesía Ediciones, 1993
Radeke, Winfried, *Minamina: An Apocalyptic Opera*, *Opus sinistrum*, 1969, play by Leonora Carrington, German translation by Heribert Becker, at Theaterverlag Nyssen & Bansemer, Köln, 19 May 1994
La corneta acústica, Barcelona: Alba Editorial, 1995
The Hearing Trumpet, Boston: Exact Change, 1996

Selected articles about Leonora Carrington

Abelleyra, Angélica, 'Leonora Carrington', *La Jornada*, 27 August 1994, p.25
– , 'La más amplia retrospectiva de la pintora Leonora Carrington', *La Jornada*, 22 July 1994, Cultura section, p.23
–, 'Mi felicidad es no tener miedo a la muerte: Carrington', *La Jornada*, 8 September 1994, Cultura section, p.29

–, 'Leonora Carrington', *La Jornada*, 11 September 1994, Cultura section, p.27
–, 'Leonora Carrington', *La Jornada*, 12 September 1994, Cultura section, p.25
–, 'Leonora Carrington', *La Jornada*, 15 February 1995, Cultura section, p.29
–, 'Leonora Carrington', *La Jornada*, 18 February 1995, Cultura section, p.26
Aberth, Susan, 'Leonora Carrington', Review of *Leonora Carrington: The Mexican Years 1943–1985* at the Mexican Museum, San Francisco, *Art Journal*, fall 1992, pp 83–5
–, 'Leonora Carrington: The Alchemical Kitchen', Ph.D. dissertation, The Graduate Center City University of New York, 2003
Aguilar, María Teresa, 'Leonora: más que anécdota', *El Nacional*, 26 October 1991, p.9
Andrade, Lourdes, 'Tres Mujeres del Surrealismo', *Mexico en el arte*, 11, winter 1985–6, pp 28–31
Annan, Gabriele, 'Male, Grail and Female: A Review of Leonora Carrington's *The Hearing Trumpet*', *Times Literary Supplement*, 27 May 1977
Avila Camacho López, Manuel, '"La Vida hay que Vivirla Como Venga, con Ideales, Temores, Amores y Problemas", Dice Leonora Carrington', *Excélsior*, 11 February 1974, Section B, p.2
–, 'Max Ernst me enseñó nueva forma de vivir', *Excélsior*, 10 February 1974, Section B, pp 1–2
–, Diez entrevistas, 'Leonora Carrington', *Fondo de cultura económica* (Mexico), 1975, pp 43–9
Baker, Kenneth, Review of *The Stone Door*, by Leonora Carrington, *New York Times Book Review*, 1 January 1978
–, 'Surrealist's Work Gets Reality Check', *San Francisco Chronicle Datebook*, 19 January 1992, p.43
Beaumont, Mary Rose, Review of travelling exhibition *Leonora Carrington*, Serpentine Gallery, London, *Arts Review*, 44, April 1992, p.130
Benvenuto, Christine, *Village Voice Literary Supplement*, December 1988, Review of *The House of Fear: Notes from Down Below* and *The Seventh Horse and Other Tales*
Berne, Suzanne, 'Nightmare Tales in a Fairy Tale Land', *San Francisco Chronicle*, 25 December 1988
Butler, J. T., 'Exhibition Review of Leonora Carrington, Center for Inter-American Relations', *Connoisseur*, 191, April 1976, p.307
Cardinal, Roger, 'Preston Harris Museum: Leonora Carrington', *Burlington*, 134 (1068), March 1992, pp 200–201
'The Carrington Revival', *Book World*, *Washington Post*, 24 June 1990, p.15
Castillo, Armando del, 'Es Magnífica la Exposición de la Señora Carrington', Review of Carrington's one-person show at Clar Décor, 26 February 1950 (newspaper unknown)
Chadwick, Whitney, 'Leonora Carrington: Evolution of a Feminist Consciousness', *Woman's Art Journal*, spring/summer 1986, pp 37–42
–, 'Leonora Carrington', *Latin American Art Magazine*, spring 1992, p.42
–, 'Muse Begets Crone', *M/E/A/N/I/N/G*, 14, November 1993, pp 20–23
Cherem, Silvia, 'Leonora Carrington', in *Trazas y revelaciones: Entrevistas a diez artistas mexicanos*, Mexico City: Fundo de Cultura Económica, 2004
Choucha, Nadia, 'Max Ernst and Leonora Carrington: Alchemy, Shamanism and Psychoanalysis', in *Surrealism and the Occult*, Oxford: Mandrake, 1991, pp 105–21
Christensen, Peter G., 'The Flight From Passion in Leonora Carrington's Literary Work', in *Surrealism and Women* (ed. by Mary Ann Caws et al), Cambridge, MA: MIT Press, 1991, pp 148–58
Cohen, Ronny, 'Leonora Carrington at Brewster Gallery', *Artforum*, October 1988, p.150
Colvile, Georgiana M., 'Beauty and/is the Beast: Animal Symbology in the Work of Leonora Carrington, Remedios Varo and Leonor Fini', in *Surrealism and Women* (ed. by Mary Ann Caws et al), Cambridge, MA and London: MIT Press, 1991, pp 159–81
Conley, Kathleen, 'Beyond the Border: Leonora Carrington's Terrible Journey', in *Automatic Woman: The Representation of Woman in Surrealism*, Lincoln, NE: University of Nebraska Press, 1996, pp 49–78
Cottenet-Hage, Madeleine, 'The Body Subversive: Corporeal Imagery in Carrington, Prassinos and Mansour', in *Surrealism and Women* (ed. by Mary Ann Caws et al), Cambridge, MA: MIT Press, 1991, pp 76–95
Crespo de la Serna, Jorge J., 'Las Ideas y las Formas: Fantasía y Realidad', Review of Carrington's one-person show at Clar Décor, *Excélsior* (Mexico City), 5 March 1950
Deffenbach, Nancy, 'Human–Plant Hybrids in the Art of Frida Kahlo and Leonora Carrington', *Curare: Espacio crítico para las artes*, Revisiones de la Historia de Historia del Arte en México, 11, summer 1997, pp 96–129
De Angelis, Paul, 'Interview with Leonora Carrington', *El Paseante* (Madrid), 17, 1997
Diaz, Fernando M., 'Leonora Carrington', *Excélsior* (Mexico City), 16 January 1994, p.5
'Dos lienzos de la pintora Leonora Carrington', Review of Carrington's one-person show at Clar Décor, *El Universal*, 22 February 1950
'En la exposición de Leonora Carrington', *Excélsior*, 25 February 1950
Espinosa de los Monteros, Santiago, 'Leonora Carrington: Like a Messenger', *Art Nexus*, October–December 1995, 18, pp 80–82
Evans, Faith, 'The Reluctant Debutante', *Observer*, 23 July 1989
Freixas, Laura, 'La novia del Viento', *Vogue* (Spain), August 1990, pp 98–103
Gablik, Suzi, 'Leonora Carrington at Iolas and the Center for Inter-American Relations', *Art in America*, 64, March–April 1976, p.111
García Ponce, Juan, 'Leonora Carrington: un lenguaje simbólico que expresa la realidad', *Mexico en la Cultura*, 19 February 1950, p.1
–, 'Leonora Carrington', *Arquitecto*, March–April 1981, pp 2–13
Godrey, Tony, 'Leonora Carrington at the Serpentine', *Art in America*, March 1992, pp 127–8
Grimberg, Salomón, 'Leonora Carrington', *Art Nexus*, 26, October–December 1997, pp 62–5
Hardy, William, 'Carrington Cult', *Tatler*, December, 1991
Helland, Janice Valerie, 'Daughter of the Minotaur: Leonora Carrington and the Surrealistic Image', unpublished Master's thesis, University of Victoria, British Columbia, 1984
–, 'Surrealism and Esoteric Feminism in the Paintings of Leonora Carrington', *RACAR*, 16 (1), 1989, pp 53–61

'Histoire de l'heureux fantôme and Conte de fées mexicain', trans. Jacqueline Chénieux, *Le nouveau commerce,* 30–31, spring 1975

Hubbard, Sue, 'Beasties and Ghosties', *Society Statesman,* 10 January 1992

Hubert, Renée Riese, 'Leonora Carrington and Max Ernst: Artistic Partnership and Feminist Liberation', *New Literary History*, 22 (3), summer 1991, pp 715–45

–, 'Beyond Initiation: Leonora Carrington & Max Ernst', in *Magnifying Mirrors: Women, Surrealism & Partnership,* Lincoln, NE: University of Nebraska, 1994, pp 113-254

Islas Garcia, Luis, 'Triunfos imaginativos', *Excélsior*, 26 March 1950

Jacobs, Barbara, 'Perfil con Lluvia', *La Jornada*, 17 August 1994

Josephson, Nancy, 'The Artful Dodger', *Women's Wear Daily*, 26 November 1975

Knapp, Bettina L., 'Leonora Carrington's Whimsical Dreamworld: Animals Talk, Children are Gods, a Black Swan Lays an Orphic Egg', *World Literature Today*, 51 (6), autumn 1977, pp 525–30

–, Review of *The Stone Door*, *World Literature Today*, 53, winter 1979, p.121

Kunny, Clare, 'Leonora Carrington's Mexican Vision', in *Mary Reynolds and the Spirit of Surrealism*, Chicago: The Art Institute of Chicago, *Museum Studies* 22 (2), 1996, pp 156–79

Landeros, Carlos, 'Con Leonora Carrington', *Excélsior*, March 1966, p.6

'Leonora Carrington', *Geijutsu shincho*, 6, 1990, pp 13–17

'Leonora Carrington at Matisse's', *Art News*, 46, February 1948, p.58

Lima, Robert, 'Leonora Carrington: The Fine Art of Alchemy of the Mysterium Conjunctionis', *Cauda Pavonis: Studies in Hermeticism*, 19 (2), fall 2000, pp 17–25

Mabille, Pierre, 'A propos de *En bas* de Leonora Carrington', in *Traversées de nuit*, Paris: Editions Plasma, 1981, pp 33–41

Massayo Nonaka, 'Leonora Carrington's Mysterious Vision', *Mizue*, winter 1988, pp 141–5

–, 'Leonora Carrington', Review of San Francisco show, *Atelier*, 784, June 1992

Mayers Salkaln, Elaine, 'The Mystery Woman', *Home Design,* supplement of the *New York Times*, 13 October 2002, pp 46–54

Morales, Luis, 'La enfermedad de Leonora', *El País* (Madrid), 8 April 1993, p.31

Mulder, Nan, 'Leonora Carrington in Mexico', *Alba*, 1 (6), December 1991–January 1992, pp 4–7

Nelken, Margarita, 'El arte al dia', Review of Carrington's one-person show at Clar Décor, *Novedades*, 1 March 1950

Neuvillate-Ortiz, Alfonso de, 'Leonora Carrington: Signos mágicos y el nuevo rostro de lo real', *México Arte Moderno*, 2, Ediciones Galería de Arte Misrachi, 1977, pp 29–34

Orenstein, Gloria, 'Leonora Carrington: Another Reality', *Ms.*, August 1974, pp 27–31

–, 'The Occultation of the Goddess: Elena Garro, Joyce Mansour, Leonora Carrington', in *The Theater of the Marvelous: Surrealism and the Contemporary Stage*, New York: New York University Press, 1975

–, 'Manifestations of the Occult in the Art and Literature of Leonora Carrington', in Luanne Frank (ed.), *Literature and the Occult: Essays in Comparative Literature*, Arlington: University of Texas at Arlington, 1977

–, 'Leonora Carrington's Visionary Art for the New Age', *Chrysalis*, 3, 1977, pp 65–77

–, 'La nature animale et divine de la femme dans les œuvres de Leonora Carrington', *Mélusine: Cahiers du centre de recherches sur le Surréalisme*, 2: Occulte-Occultation, Etudes et Documents réunis par Henri Behar, L'Age d'Homme, pp 130–37

–, '"The Chrysopeia of Mary the Jewess": Leonora Carrington's Surrealist Alchemical Tractate', *Cauda Pavonis: Studies in Hermeticism*, 19 (2), fall 2000, pp 1–8

Orgambides, F., 'Leonora Carrington: "No me arrepiento de mi vida"', *El País* (Madrid), 18 April 1993, p.30

Ortega, Julio, 'Ceremonia de Leonora Carrington', *Diario la república* (Lima, Peru), 4 June 1988, p.25

–, 'Ceremonia de Leonora Carrington', *La Jornada* (Mexico), 5 June 1988, p.11

–, 'Belleza enigmática', *Diario 16*, 16 July 1988, VII

–, 'Belleza enigmática', *El Mundo* (Medellin, Colombia), 20 August 1988, p.3

Palencia, Ceferino, 'El Arte de Ensueño de Leonora Carrington', Review of Carrington's one-person show at Clar Décor, *Mexico en la cultura*, 19 February 1950

Perlez, Jane, 'Woman in the News: Leonora Carrington, Surrealism Lives', *New York Post*, *Weekend Magazine*, Section 3, 6 December 1975, pp 1, 19

Pinto, Margarita, 'Leonora Carrington, Memorias', *Unomásuno*, 25 January 1992, p.12

Pohlenz, Ricardo, 'Leonora Carrington, cuentista', *El Economista*, 2 April 1993

Raubold, Susanne, 'Nieder mit der Kleinfamilie', Review of a performance of *Pénélope*, *Berlin-Kultur*, 30 January 1989, p.21

Regler, Gustav, 'Four European Painters in Mexico', *Horizon*, 16 (91), August 1947, pp 96 101

Roco, Augusto, 'Nuestras Exposiciones', Review of Carrington's one-person show at Clar Decor, *c.*1950, publication unknown

Romaní, Marta, 'La pasmosa fantasía narrativa de Leonora Carrington', *Nueva Epoca*, 48, 25 August 1991

Rubin Suleiman, Susan, 'The Bird Superior Meets the Bride of the Wind: Leonora Carrington & Max Ernst', in Whitney Chadwick and Isabelle De Courtivron (eds), *Significant Others: Creativity & Intimate Partnership*, London: Thames and Hudson, 1993

Rüegsegger, Ann, 'Porträt: Leonora Carrington', *Du*, February 1988, pp 68–73, 92–3

Rütz, Jutta, 'Leonora Carrington: Are you Really Syrious?' *Journal of the American Medical Association* (Mexican edn), 3 (2), February 1995

Sáinz, Gustavo, 'Leonora Carrington: Creadora, no musa', pp 18–21 (publication and date unknown, *c.*1976–7)

Schneider Enriquez, Mary, 'Leonora Carrington: Museo de Arte Contemporáneo', *Art News*, March 1995, p.146

Scully, Regina, 'Leonora Carrington: Paintings', *Crescent Magazine*, 2, February 1998, pp 59-60

Shandler Levitt, Annette, 'The Bestial Fictions of Leonora Carrington', *Journal of Modern Literature*, 20 (1), summer 1996, pp 65–74

–, 'The Horses, Birds, and Crones of Leonora Carrington', in *The Genres and Genders of Surrealism*, New York: St Martin's Press, 1999

Spengler, Tilman, *Apropos Leonora Carrington*, Frankfurt am Main: Verlag Neue Kritik, 1995
Szulakowska, Urszula, 'The Alchemical Girl in Leonora Carrington's "The House Opposite"', *Cauda Pavonis: Studies in Hermeticism*, 19 (2), fall 2000
Tanner, Marcia, 'From an Occult Realm', *Artweek*, 23 January 1992, pp 8–9
Tibol, Raquel, 'Leonora Carrington: Excentrica del Surrealismo', *Revista proceso*, 13 February 1995, pp 67–70
Tinoco, Imelda, '"Agresiva" Labor por Difundir la Cultura', *Excélsior*, *c*.1977
Trezevant, Francis and Fred, 'Exciting Show at Clar Décor', *Mexico City*, 3 March 1950
Unterhalter, Sue, 'Leonora's Homecoming', *Yorkshire Post*, 13 June 1990, p.16
Vacio, Minerva, 'Leonora Carrington', *El Financiero*, 18 February 1995, p.42
Velazquez Yebra, Patricia, 'El arte mexicano en vuelo', Review of *El mundo mágico de Leonora Carrington* at la Galería de Arte del Aeropuerto Internacional de la ciudad de Mexico City, *El Universal*, 29 June 1991, p.4
Wagstaff, Sheena, 'Surrealist in the Mid West', *Interview*, August 1990
Warner, Marina, 'Leonora Carrington', *Burlington*, 130 (1027), October 1988, pp 796–7
–, 'Back from Below', *Independent Magazine*, 22 July 1989, pp 42–5
Wooster, Ann Sargent, 'Leonora Carrington at Iolas', *Art News*, 75, March 1976, p.141

Selected exhibition catalogues

Arte e alchimia, XLII (exh.cat.), Exposizione Internazionale D'Arte, La Biennale di Venezia. A cura di Arturo Schwarz, 1986, Edizioni La Biennale, Realizzazione Electa Editrice
Biller, Geraldine P. (Guest Curator), *Latin American Women Artists 1915–1995*, (exh.cat.), Milwaukee Art Museum, Milwaukee, WI, 3 March–28 May 1995; Phoenix Art Museum, Phoenix, AZ, 7 July–1 October 1995; The Denver Art Museum and Museo de las Americas, Denver, CO, 28 October 1995–14 January 1996, and The National Museum of Women in the Arts, Washington, DC, 8 February–29 April 1996. Essays by Bélgica Rodríguez, Edward J. Sullivan, Marina Pérez de Mendiola
Billeter, Erika and José Pierre, *La femme et le Surrealisme*, (exh.cat.), Lausanne, Switzerland: Musée Cantonal des Beaux Arts, 1987
Carrington, Chagall, Dubuffet, Giacometti, Lam, MacIver, Matta, Miro, Tamayo, Tanguy, (exh.cat.), New York: Pierre Matisse Gallery, 1948
Chadwick, Whitney, *Leonora Carrington: Recent Works*, (exh.cat.), New York: Brewster Gallery, 1988
–, *Leonora Carrington*, (exh.cat.), New York: Brewster Arts Ltd. 1997
Cinco mujeres: Leonora Carrington, María Izquierdo, Frida Kahlo, Alice Rahon, Remedios Varo, (exh.cat.), Mexíco City: Galería Arvil (25th anniversary), essay by Lourdes Andrade, 1995
Conaty, Siobhán M. (Guest Curator), *Art of this Century: The Women*, (exh.cat.), East Hampton, New York: Pollock-Krasner House and Study Center, 1997
The Disquieting Muse: Surrealism, (exh.cat.), 9 January–16 February 1958, Houston: Contemporary Art Museum
Emerich, Luis Carlos (curator) and Lourdes Andrade, *Leonora Carrington: Una retrospectiva*, (exh.cat.), Museo de Arte Contemporáneo de Monterrey, Monterrey, N.L., Mexico City, 1994 and Museo de Arte Moderno, Mexico City, 1995
Escultura: Pequeño formato, (exh.cat.), Galería de Arte Mexicano, 28 July–10 September 1994
Exposición retrospectiva de pinturas y tápices de Leonora Carrington, (exh.cat.), Mexico City: Museo de Arte Moderno, July–August 1960
Exposition Internationale du Surréalisme, (exh.cat.), Paris: Galerie Beaux-Arts, 1938
First Papers of Surrealism, (exh.cat.), Foreword by Sydney Janis, New York: Coordinating Council of French Relief Societies, 1942
Frida Kahlo, Diego Rivera, and Twentieth-Century Mexican Art: The Jacques and Natasha Gelman Collection, (exh.cat.), Museum of Contemporary Art, San Diego, 14 May–4 September 2000
García Ponce, Juan, *Leonora Carrington*, (exh.cat.), Monterrey, Mexico: Sala de Exposiciones, 1979
Grimberg, Salomón and Edward J. Sullivan, *Leonora Carrington*, (exh.cat.), New York: Brewster Gallery, 1995
Leonora Carrington, (exh.cat.), Introduction by Edward James, New York: Pierre Matisse Gallery, 24 February–13 March 1948
Leonora Carrington, (exh.cat.), Brasil: IX Bienal de São Paulo, Instituto Nacional de Bellas Artes, 1967
Leonora Carrington, (exh.cat.), Galería de Arte Mexicano, Mexico City, November 1996–January 1997
Leonora Carrington: Exposición de óleos, gouaches, dibujos y tapices, (exh.cat.), Mexico City: Instituto Anglo-Mexicano de Cultura, June 1965. Essay by Carlos Fuentes
Leonora Carrington and Gabriel Weisz-Carrington: Pintura y poemas and The Dark Book, (exh.cat.), 3–23 December 1998, New York: Brewster Arts Limited
Leonora Carrington: The Mexican Years 1943–1985, (exh.cat.), San Francisco: The Mexican Museum, [Albuquerque, NM]: Distributed by the University of New Mexico Press, 1991
Leonora Carrington: Recent Paintings, (exh.cat.), Iolas Gallery, New York, 1974. (Reprint of 1948 Matisse Gallery essay by Edward James)
Leonora Carrington: Recent Paintings, (exh.cat.), New York: Brewster Gallery, 1977
Leonora Carrington: A Retrospective, (exh.cat.), Tokyo Station Gallery, East Japan Railway Culture Foundation, 1997
Leonora Carrington: A Retrospective Exhibition, (exh.cat.), New York: Center for Inter-American Relations, 26 November 1975–4 January 1976 and at the University Art Museum The University of Texas, Austin, 18 January–29 February 1976
Leonora Carrington: La Vocación y sus reflejos, (exh. cat), Mexico City: Museo de la Secretaría de Hacienda y Crédito Público, 13 November 2003–1 February 2004
McCabe, Cynthia Jaffee, *Artistic Collaboration in the Twentieth Century*, (exh.cat.), Washington, DC: Hirshhorn Museum and Sculpture Garden, Smithsonian Institution Press, 1994
Mexique: Peintres contemporains, (exh.cat.), Chateau D'Antibes, Musée Picasso, 15 July–21 August 1980

Mundy, Jennifer (ed.), *Surrealism: Desire Unbound*, (exh.cat.), Princeton: Princeton University Press, 2001. A Tate Exhibition September 2001–January 2002, Metropolitan Museum of Art, New York, 6 February–22 May 2002

The Peggy Guggenheim Collection, (exh.cat.), Art Council of the Tate Gallery, London, 31 December 1964–7 March 1965

La planete affolée: Surréalisme, dispersion et influences 1938–1947 (exh.cat.). Musée de Marseille, 1986

Schilieker, Andrea (ed.), *Leonora Carrington: Paintings, Drawings and Sculptures 1940–1990*, (exh.cat.), London: Serpentine Gallery, 1991

Scott, Sue, *Selections from the Ellen and Jerome Westheimer Collection*, (exh.cat.), Oklahoma Art Center, 15 April–3 July 1988

Los sentidos de las cosas: El mundo de Kati y José Horna, (exh.cat.), essay by Karen Cordero, Museo Nacional de Arte, Mexico City, 2003

Steinbaum, Bernice, *Crossing the Threshold*, (exh.cat.), New York: Steinbaum Krauss Gallery, 6 December 1997–3 January 1998

Sullivan, Edward, *La Mujer en México (Women in Mexico)*, Mexico City: La Fundación Cultural Televisa: Centro Cultural/Arte Contemporáneo, 1990. Exhibition held at the National Academy of Design, New York 27 September–2 December 1990; Centro Cultural/Arte Contemporáneo, Winter 1991; Museo de Monterrey, Spring 1991

Surrealism: From Paris to New York, (exh.cat.), New York: Arnold Herstand Gallery, 1990

Surrealism in Art, (exh.cat.), New York: M. Knoedler & Co, 5 February–6 March 1975

Le Surréalisme, 1922–1942, (exh.cat.), essay by Patrick Waldberg, Musée des Arts Décoratifs, Paris and Haus der Kunst, Munich, 1972

Le Surréalisme et l'amour, (exh.cat.), Paris: Gallimard/Electra, Pavillion des Artes 6 March–18 June 1997, Les musées de la Ville de Paris

Surrealismo y arte fantástico en México, (exh.cat.), essay by Ida Rodriguez Prompolini. Departamento de Artes Plasticas, Galería Universitaria Aristos, Universidad Nacional Autónoma de México, 1967/68, UNAM.

Tane arte/objecto: Exposicion arte objeto veinte esculturas en plata, (exh.cat.), Mexico City: Instituto Nacional de Bellas Artes, Mexico City, 1979

The Surrealist Vision: Europe and the Americas (exh.cat), Greenwich, CT: The Bruce Museum, 1998

Tapices de Leonora Carrington, (exh.cat.), Mexico City: Galeria de Antonio Souza, 1957

The Temptation of St Anthony, Bel Ami International Art Competition, (exh.cat.), Washington, DC: The American Federation of Arts, Barr Building, 1947

Uncovered and Recovered: Women Artists in the Modernist Tradition. Paintings from the Collection of Jeri Louise Waxenburg, (exh.cat.), Ketchum, Idaho: Sun Valley Center for the Arts, 12 February–22 March 1999

Wasserman, Krystyna, *Sketchbooks: The Intimate Journeys*, (exh.cat.), Washington, DC: The National Museum of Women in the Arts, 6 June–9 December 1994

Weisberger, Edward (ed.), *Surrealism, Two Private Eyes: The Nesuhi Ertegun and Daniel Filipacchi Collections*, (exh.cat.), New York: The Guggenheim Museum, 1999, vols 1 and 2, hardcover edn distributed by Harry N. Abrams

Wimer, Javier, *Exposiciones itinerantes portadas de los libros de texto gratuitos*, (exh.cat.), February 1990, Mexico City, Col. Comision Nacional de los Libros de texto gratuitos

Selected bibliography

Ades, Dawn, *Art in Latin America: The Modern Era, 1820–1980*, New Haven: Yale University Press, 1989

–, *Surrealist Art: The Lindy and Edwin Bergman Collection at the Art Institute of Chicago*, London: Thames and Hudson, 1997

Aletti, Vince, 'Madonna with Vince Aletti', *Aperture* (USA), 156, summer 1999, pp 44–51

Alexandrian, Sarane, *Surrealist Art*, New York: Praeger Publishers, 1969

Amor, Inés, 'Una Mujer en el Arte Mexicano – memorias de Inés Amor', with essays by Jorge Alberto Manrique and Teresa del Conde, Mexico City: Ciudad Universitaria, 1987

Andrade, Lourdes, '¿Te acuerdas Rousseau?' *Artes de México*, 63, Enero 2003, pp 12–21

Baciu, Stefan, 'Points of Departure: Towards a History of Latin American Surrealism', *Cahiers Dada Surréalisme*, 2, 1968, pp 133–53

Barnitz, Jacqueline, *Twentieth-century Art of Latin America*, Austin: University of Texas Press, 2001

Baron, Jacques, *Anthologie plastique du Surrealisme*, Paris: Filipacchi, 1980

Benayoun, Robert, *Erotique du Surréalisme*, Paris: Société Nouvelle des Editions Jean-Jacques Pauvert, 1978

Bradley, Fiona, *Movements in Modern Art: Surrealism*, London: Tate Gallery Publishing, 1997

Brandon, Ruth, *Surreal Lives: The Surrealists 1917–1945*, New York: Grove Press, 1999

Breakwell, Ian, 'Stories of the Eye: Part 2', *Artscribe*, 90, February/March 1992, pp 66–8

Breton, André, *Nadja*, 1928. Reprint, New York: Grove Press, 1960

–, *Mexique*, Paris: Renou and Colle, 1939

–, 'Souvenire du Mexique', *Minotaure*, ser. 3, 6th year; 12–13, May 1939, pp 31–47

–, *Anthology of Black Humor*, trans. and Introduction by Mark Polizzotti, San Francisco: City Lights Books, 1997

Buñuel, Luis, *My Last Sigh*, trans. Abigail Israel, New York: Alfred A. Knopf, 1983

Leonora Carrington: Libertad en bronce 2000, Mexico: Impronta editores, 1999

Caws, Mary Ann (ed.), *Surrealist Painters and Poets: An Anthology*, Cambridge, MA: MIT Press, 2001

Chadwick, Whitney, 'Muse as Artist in Surrealism', *Art in America*, July 1985, pp 120–29

–, *Leonora Carrington: La realidad de la imaginación*, Mexico City: Consejo Nacional para la Cultura y las Artes, 1994

–, *Women Artists and the Surrealist Movement*, Boston: Little, Brown and Company, 1985

Chazán, Sara, 'Feminine Sensibility as Viewed in Mexico by some Artists, Art Critics, and Art Historians', in *Artes visuales*, publication of el Museo de Arte Moderno, Chapultepec, Mexico, 1, 25, January–March 1976

Coleby, Nicola (ed.), *A Surreal Life: Edward James 1907–1984*, Brighton & Hove: Royal Pavilion Libraries & Museums, 1998

Colle, Marie-Pierre, *Latin American Artists in their Studios*, Introduction by Carlos Fuentes, New York: Vendome Press, 1994. Published in Spanish

as *Artistas Latino americanos en su estudio*, INBA, Noriega editores libro, 1994
Conde, Teresa del, 'Esculturas intimistas en el metal lunar', *Artes en México*, 52, 2000, pp 58-80
Cordry, Donald, 'Mexico Weaves', *Craft Horizons*, 15, July-August 1955, pp 17-21
Dada and Surrealism Reviewed, text by Dawn Ades, London: Arts Council of Great Britain, 1978
Dortch, Virginia M. (ed.), *Peggy Guggenheim and her Friends*, Milan: Bernice Art Books, 1994
Ernst, Jimmy, *A Not-so-still Life: A Memoir*, New York: St Martin's/Marek, 1984
Fauchereau, Serge, *Les peintres révolutionaires Mexicains*, Messidor, 1985
–, 'Surrealism in Mexico', *Artforum*, September 1986, pp 86-91
García Ponce, Juan, *Leonora Carrington,* Mexico City: Ediciones ERA, 1974
Guggenheim, Peggy (ed.), *Art of this Century, 1910-1942*, Preface by André Breton, Hans Arp and Piet Mondrian, New York: Art Aid Corp., 1942
–, *Confessions of an Art Addict*, New York: The MacMillan Company, 1960
–, *Out of this Century: Confessions of an Art Addict*, New York: Universe Books, 1979
Heller, Nancy G., *Women Artists: An Illustrated History*, New York: Abbeville Press, 1987, p.20
Jean, Marcel, *The History of Surrealist Painting*, New York: Grove Press, 1959
Kaplan, Gilbert (ed.), *Surrealist Prints*, New York: Atlantis, distributed by Harry N. Abrams, 1997
Kaplan, Janet, *Unexpected Journeys: The Art and Life of Remedios Varo*, New York: Abbeville Press, 1988
Kassner, Lily, *Diccionario de escultura mexicana del siglo xx*, Mexico: Universidad Nacional Autónoma de México, 1983
Lauter, Estella, *Women as Mythmakers*, Bloomington: Indiana University Press, 1984
Levy, Julien, *Memoir of an Art Gallery*, New York: G. P. Putnam's Sons, 1977
Lobo, Carlos González, 'Surrealismo en México', *Artes Visuales*, revista trimestral Museo de Arte Moderno, Chapultepec no. 4, October-December 1974 pp 9-13
Lowe, John, *Edward James: A Surrealist Life*, London: William Collins & Co., 1991
Medina, Andres and Laurette Sejourne, *El mundo mágico de los Mayas*, texts by Andrés Medina and Laurette Sejourné, illustrated by Leonora Carrington, Mexico City: Museo de Antropologia e Historia, 1964
Modern Miniatures: The Redefining of the Small, New York: Brewster Fine Arts Ltd, 1996
National Museum of Women in the Arts, New York: Harry N. Abrams, Inc., 1987
Orenstein, Gloria, 'Women of Surrealism', *The Feminist Art Journal*, spring 1973, pp 1, 15-21
–,'Art History and the Case for the Women of Surrealism', *Journal of General Education*, 27 (1), spring 1975, pp 31-54
–, 'The Reemergence of the Archetype of the Great Goddess in Art by Contemporary Women', *Heresies*, 2 (1), issue 5, 1982, pp 74-84
–, 'Women of Surrealism', in Judy Loeb (ed.) *Feminist Collage: Educating Women in the Visual Arts*, New York: Teacher's College, Columbia University, 1979, pp 35-58
–, 'Reclaiming the Great Mother: A Feminist Journey to Madness and Back in Search of a Goddess Heritage', *Symposium*, spring 1982, p.141
–, *The Reflowering of the Goddess*, New York: Pergamon Press, 1990
Peden, Margaret Sayers, with photographs by Carole Patterson, *Out of the Volcano: Portraits of Contemporary Mexican Artists*, Washington, DC: Smithsonian Institution Press, 1991
Penrose, Roland, *Scrap Book, 1900-1981*, London: Thames and Hudson, 1981
Pierre, José, *L'univers Surréaliste*, Paris: Loiris, 1983
Poirer, Maurice, '"Women Surrealists", review of Women Surrealists show at Hoffeld', *Art News*, October 1985, p.133
Rabinovitch, Celia, *Surrealism and the Sacred: Power, Eros, and the Occult in Modern Art*, Cambridge: Icon Editions, 2002
Rasmussen, Waldo (ed.), *Latin American Artists of the Twentieth Century*, New York: Museum of Modern Art, distributed by Harry N. Abrams, 1993
El retrato Mexicano contemporaneo, with essays by Paul Westheim and Justino Fernandez, Mexico City: Museo Nacional de Arte Moderno, 1961
Roche, Julotte, *Max et Leonora: Récit d'investigation*, Cognac: Le temps qu'il tait, 1997
Rodríguez Prampolini, Ida, *El Surrealismo y el arte fantástico de Mexico*, Instituto de Investigaciones Estéticas, Universidad Nacional Autónomo de Mexico, 1969
–, 'Dada & Surrealism in Mexico', *Latin American Art*, 2 (4), fall 1990, pp 55-60
Rosemont, Penelope (ed.), *Surrealist Women: An International Anthology*, Austin: University of Texas Press, 1998
Rouvre, Germain, 'Entretien avec Leonora Carrington', La Femme Surréaliste, *Obliques*, pp 91-2
Rubin Suleiman, Susan, 'A Double Margin: Reflections on Women Writers and the Avant-garde in France', *Yale French Studies*, 75, 1988, pp 148-72
–, *Subversive Intent: Gender, Politics, and the Avant-Garde*, Cambridge: Harvard University Press, 1990
Sawin, Martica, *Surrealism in Exile and the Beginning of the New York School*, Cambridge, MA: MIT Press, 1995
Seggerman, Helen-Louise, 'The Mexican Women's Hour', *Art News*, February 1991, p.27
Serge, Victor, 'Letter from Mexico', *Horizon*, January 1947, pp 63-70
Sills, Leslie, *Visions: Stories about Women Artists*, Morton Grove, IN: Albert Whitman & Co., 1993
Smith, B. C., 'Shakespeare Society Scores with *The Tempest*', *The News* (Mexico City), 9 July 1959, p.8
Somolinos Palencia, Juan, *El Surrealismo en la pintura mexicana*, Arte Ediciones, 1973
Los Surrealistas en México, essays by Octavio Paz, Ida Rodriguez Prompolini, Juan Somolinos Palencia, Mexico City: Instituto Nacional de Bellas Artes, Museo Nacional de Arte, Mexico City, 1986
'Los Surrealistas en México', *México en el arte*, 4, fall 1986, pp 4-48

Tanning, Dorothea, *Birthday*, San Francisco: Lapis Press, 1986

Tashjian, Dickran, *A Boatload of Madmen: Surrealism and the American Avant-Garde, 1920–1950*, New York: Thames and Hudson, 1995

Taylor, Sue, 'Into the Mystic', *Art in America*, 89 (4), April 2001, pp 126–9

Torre, Mario de la (ed.), *Agpa: Artes gráficas Panamericanas*, text by Octavio Paz and Stanton L. Catlin, Edición privada de Cartón de Colombia, S.A., 1979

Traba, Marta, *Art of Latin America, 1900–1980*, Baltimore: John Hopkins University Press, 1994

'Und ich sehe nichts, nichts als die Malerei': autobiographische Texte von Künstlerinnen des 18- 20 Jahrhunderts, Frankfurt am Main: Fischer Taschenbuch, 1987

'Unhappy Demons', *Time*, 22 March 1948

Vidler, Anthony, 'Homes for Cyborgs', in *The Architectural Uncanny: Essays in the Modern Unhomely*, Cambridge, MA: MIT Press, 1992, pp 147–64

Walsh, Maria, 'Becoming Intense, Becoming Animal, Becoming Imperceptible', *Make,* 82, December 1998–February 1999, pp 14–17

Warlick, M. E., *Max Ernst and Alchemy: A Magician in Search of Myth*, Foreword by Franklin Rosemont, Austin: University of Texas Press, 2001

Warner, Marina, *From the Beast to the Blonde: On Fairy Tales and Their Tellers*, London: Chatto & Windus, 1994 and New York: The Noonday Press, Farrar, Straus and Giroux, 1996

Weisz, Gabriel (with illustrations by Leonora Carrington), *The Dark Room*, Mexico City: Tiempo Extra Editores, 1991 (limited edition of 60)

Weld, Jacqueline Bograd, *Peggy: The Wayward Guggenheim*, New York: E. P. Dutton, 1986

Witzling, Mara R. (ed.), *Voicing Our Visions: Writings by Women Artists*, New York: Universe, 1991, pp 306–19

Works from the Peggy Guggenheim Foundation, New York: The Solomon R. Guggenheim Museum, 1969

Films and documentaries

Acker, Alli, *The Flowering of the Crone: A Portrait of Leonora Carrington*, promotional video produced and directed by Alli Acker, New York: Reel Woman Trust Foundation, 1987

The Beloved, directed by Sarita Siegel and produced by Taggart Siegel, 12.25 mins. Based on a short story by Leonora Carrington. An Alchemy Films production, 1997

Danziger, Avery, *Edward James: Builder of Dreams*, a documentary film, Top Drawer Productions, 1995

'Leonora Carrington in the House of Fear', produced and directed by Kim Evans, *Omnibus*, BBC, 1992

INDEX

Note: page numbers in italics indicate illustrations

AB EO QUOD (1956) 82 *92*
Abbott, Berenice *51*, 52
Abstract Expressionism 59
Agar, Eileen 25, 37
Aix-en-Provence 45
The Alchemical Kitchen 9
The Alcove: An Interior with Three Women (Fini, c.1939) *41*, 42
Álvarez Bravo, Manuel 57
Amor, Inés 63–4
Amsterdam 37
The Ancestor (1968) *116*
And Then We Saw The Daughter of the Minotaur (1953) *87*
Animus Macquína (1962) *113*
Annunciation (da Vinci, 1472–5) 32
Anthology of Black Humor (Breton) 51
Aragon, Luis 28
Archimbaldo, Giuseppe 19
Are You Really Syrious? (1953) *88*
Arnum, Archim von 38
Arp, Hans 29, 53
Art of This Century (New York) 53
Ascot (Berkshire) 19
The Attirement of the Bride (Ernst) 46
Aurenche, Marie-Berthe 25, 26, 28, 29, 38

Balzac, Honoré de 54
The Bath of Rabbi Loew (1969) 102, *105*
Baziotes, William 53
Beaton, Cecil 19
Bel Ami International Art Competition 63, 70
Bellmer, Hans 53
Bénédite, Danny *45*
Bern 19
Bernal, Ignacio 62, 97
Bird Pong (1949) *75*
'The Bird Superior: Max Ernst' 42, 55
Birthday (Tanning) 53
Bizarre magazine 64
Blackpool 14
Blom, Gertrude 97
Bosch, Hieronymus 70
Bradley, Fiona 42
Brewster Arts Ltd 103
Breton, André 8, 25, 28, 37, 47, 48, 51, *51*, 52, 53, 54, 57, 59
British Museum (London) 20
Brothers and Sisters Have I None (1942) *52*, 53, 53–4
Bruegel the Elder, Pieter 70
Buñuel, Luis 52, 54

Cárdenas del Rio, President Lázaro 57
Cabbage (1987) *135*
Café Flore (Paris) 28, 29
Cahiers d'Art 45
Calder, Alexander 53
The Candle Game (1966) *114*
Carrington, Arthur 11
Carrington, Chagall, Dubuffet, Giacometti, Lam, MacIver, Matta, Miro etc exhibition (1948) 63
Carrington Cottons 11
Carrington, Gerald 11
Carrington, Harold Wilde 11
Carrington, Leonora *14, 18, 19, 20, 26, 37, 38, 51, 56, 69, 94*
  art schools 21–3
  boarding schools 15, 18
  childhood 11–14
  esoteric interests 97, 102–3, 122, 126, 128
  motherhood 64, 66
  reluctant débutante 19–21
  wartime experiences 38–55
Carrington, Maureen (*née* Moorhead) 11
Carrington, Patrick 11
Carroll, Lewis 14, 34, 128
Casting the Runes (1951) *90*
Cat Woman (La Grande Dame) (1951) *96*, 97
Chadwick, Whitney 22, 33, 35, 47–8, 63, 128
Chagall, Marc 53
The Chair, Daghda Tuatha dé Danaan (1955) 82, *95*
Chelmsford (Essex) 15
Chelsea School of Art (London) 21
The Chymical Wedding of Christian Rosenkreutz (Valentin, 1459) 49
Chermayeff, Serge 21
Chicago 103
Chiki, ton pays (1947) *61*
The Chinese Children (Ernst, 1920) 25
Chirico, Giorgio de 53
Chorley (Lancashire) 11
The Chrysopeia of Mary the Jewess (1964) 102, *104*
Clark, Ann 37
Clayton Green (Lancashire) 11
Clongowes College 11
Co-ordinating Council of French Relief Societies 53
Cockerham (Lancashire) 11
Cocteau, Jean 22
The Conjurer (*c.*1950s) *80*
Conley, Kathleen 50
Contemporary Arts Museum (Houston) 64
Cordry, Donald 64
Cornwall 26
Coronel, Rafael 97
Courtaulds 11
Craft Horizons magazine 64
The Crock of Gold (Stephens) 79
Crookhey Hall (Lancashire) *10*, 11, *12*, *13*, 15
Cross and Blackwell 22
Crow Catcher (1990) *138*
Cubism 21

Davies, Hugh Sykes 25
The Days of Gabino Barreda Street (Gerzso, 1944) *59*, 60
De Angelis, Paul 52
The Dead Queens of Cockerham (*c.*1950s) *80*
'The Débutante' (1939) 34–5
Delvaux, Paul 53
Darvault (*c.*1950) *76*
The Disquieting Muse: Surrealism 64
Dog, come here into the dark house. Come here black dog (1995) *139*
Down Below (1941) *47*, 50
Down Below (book, 1945) 8, 42, 46, 48–51, *51*
Dream by a Young Girl about a Lake (Ernst, 1940–2) 45
Duchamp, Marcel 28, 37, *51*, 52, 53
The Dybbuk (1967) 102

Edgeworth, Maria 11
Editions G.L.M. 34
El mundo mágico de los Mayas (1963) 97, *101*, 102
El Poliedro de Hod (1965) 102
El Rarvarok (1963) *110*
El Retrato Mexicano Contemporaneo exhibition (1961) 97
Eluard, Gala 29
Eluard, Nusch *26*, 27
Eluard, Paul 25, 28, 29, 45
Epona (Celtic goddess) 32–3
Ernst, Jimmy 29, 38, *51*, 52, 53
Ernst, Max 7, 9, 25–7, 37, *37*, 38–46, *38*, *45*, 51–3, *51*, 53, 55, 64
Estoril 51
Estremadura 45
Europe After the Rain (Ernst, 1940–2) 45
Evans, Walker 53
Exhibition by 31 Women (1943) 53
Exposición Retrospectivo de Pinturas Tapices de Leonora Carrington exhibition (1960) 97
Exposition Internationale du Surréalisme (1938) 37

Ferren, John *51*
Ferret Race (1950–1) *84*
Fidelin, Ady (Adrienne) *26*, 27
Figuras Mitica: Ballarin I (1954) *17*
Figuras Mitica: Ballarin II (1954) *17*
Fini, Leonor 25, 42
First Papers in Surrealism (1942) catalogue 53
The First Surrealist Exhibition (1936) 25
The Floor 4706th (1958) *109*
Florence 18–19, 25, 30
'Fly Pigeon' (1937–40) 44
The Flying Ur Jar (1953) *89*

Forbidden Fruit (1969) *118*
Francés, Esteban *59*, 60, 63
Francesco di Giorgio 19
Franz Joseph, Emperor 11
Friday the 13th (1965) *113*
Fry, Varian 45

Galería de Antonio Souza (Mexico City) 64
Galería de Arte Mexicano (Mexico City) 57, 63–4, 97
Galerie Beaux-Arts (Paris) 37
Garden Aeroplane-Trap (Ernst, 1934) 25
The Garden of Paracelsus (1957) *107*
The Gardens (*c.*1950) *78*
Gascoyne, David 25
George V 18, 19
Gerzso, Günther *56*, 58, 66
Giacometti, Alberto 29, 53
The Giantess/Guardian at the Egg 63
Gil, Guillermo 51
Giovanni de Paolo 19
Goldfinger, Erno 22, 25, 26
Goldfinger, Ursula 22, 25, 26
Gomes, André 46
Good Morning Dr Fischer (*c.*1951–2) *86*
Grandmother Moorhead's Aromatic Kitchen (1975) 122, *123*
Graves, Robert 32, 79
Green Tea (La Dame ovale) (1942) *24*
Guggenheim, Peggy 37, 45, 46, 51, *51*, 53, 55

Hampstead (London) 26
Hayter, Stanley William *51*
The Hearing Trumpet (1950, 1976) 59, 60
Hérold, Jacques *45*, 46
Holy Sepulchre convent (Chelmsford, Essex) 15
Horizon periodical 62
Horna, José *56*
Horna, Kati 58
The Horses of Lord Candlestick (1938) *36*, 53
The Hour of the Angelus (1949) *74*
The House Opposite (1945) *65*, 68–9
How doth the Little Crocodile (2003) 128, *141*
Hugnet, Georges 25
Hugo, Valentine 25
Human Figure (Ernst, 1931) 25
Hunt Breakfast (1956) *82*, 93

Ikon (1988) *137*
Imperial Chemicals Industries (ICI) 11, 51
International Surrealism Exhibition (1940) 57
Izquierdo, María 57

Jacobs, W.W. 14
James, Edward 51, 63, 66, 70
Jean, Marcel 45, 64
'Jezzamathatics or introduction to the Wonderful Process of Painting' (1965) 20, 149–50
Jeux d'enfants (Tanning) 53
Joyce, James 11
Julien Levy Gallery (New York) 57

Kahlo, Frida 57, 58
Kaplan, Janet 57
Kavanaugh, Mary 12
Kiesler, Frederick J. *51*, 52, 53
Klee, Paul 53
Kristeva, Julia 35
Kristine Mann Library (New York) 103
Kron Flower (1987) *136*

The Labyrinth (1991) *132*
La Chase (1942) 53
La Dame ovale (Green Tea) (1942) *24*, 53
La Dame ovale (short stories, 1939) 34–5
La Maison de la peur (1938) 34
La Toilette de la mariée (1940) 42
La Vaca (1975) 126, 128, *130*
La Vieja Magdalena (1988) 126
La Virgen de la Cueva (1995) *127*, 128
Lam, Wifredo 53
Lamba, Jacqueline 57
Lancaster 15
Lancaster, Bishop of 15
Largentière 45
Le Corbusier 21
Le Grand adieu (1958) *109*
Le Surrealisme même periodical 64
Leduc, Renato 28, 51–2, 54, 57
Léger, Fernand *51*, 52
Leonardo da Vinci 32
Leonora Carrington: Paintings, Drawings and Sculptures 1940–1990 exhibition (1991) 128
Leonora Carrington: Una retrospectiva exhibition (1994) 128
Leonora in the Morning Light (Ernst, 1940) 44
Lepidopteros (1969) *117*
Les Distractions de Dagobert (1945) *56*
Les Milles camp 45
Letter to Dana (1957) *103*
Levitt, Annette Shandler 35
Lisbon 44, 46, 51, 70
Litany of the Philosophers (1959) *111*
Lizarraga, Gerardo 56, 58
Llona, Victor 48
London 23, 25–8
Lord Candlestick's Horses (1938) 37
Loriol (Drôme) camp 45
Lukas, Michel 46

Mabille, Pierre 48
Madrid 46, 51, 70
The Magdalens (1986) *125*, 126
Magritte, René 53
Malcolm, King of Ireland 11
Manifesto of Surrealism (Breton, 1924) 47
Map of Down Below (*c.*1943) 49–50, *50*, 54
March Sunday (1990) *138*
Marseilles 46
Masson, André 52, 53
Matta 53
Maupassant, Guy de 63
Mayor Gallery (London) 25, 26
The Meal of Lord Candlestick (1938) 37, *38*, 39, 41
Megnen, Jeanne 48
Mérida, Carlos 97
Mexico 7, 8, 30, 48, 57–72, 75–7, 79, 82–3, 93–4, 97, 102–3, 122–6, 128
Miller, Lee *26*, 27, 39
Miró, Joan 53
Mirror of the Marvellous (Péret) 48
Mondrian, Piet *51*, 52
Moore, Henry 53
Morales, Dr Luis 46, 49
Moro, César 57
Motherwell, Robert 53
Ms magazine 28, 103
Mujeres Conciencia (1972) *62*, 63, 103
muralist movement 57
Museo de Arte Moderno (Mexico City) 128
Museo de Arte Contemporáneo de Monterrey 128
Museo Nacional de Arte Moderno (Mexico City) 97
Museo Nacional de Antropologia (Mexico City) 97

Nadja (Breton) 49
Naturaleza Muerta (Still Life) (1960) *106*
Negri, Nina 37
New Burlington Galleries (London) 25
New York 21, 42, 46, 47, 51–5, 57, 63, 103
Night of the 8th (1987) *134*
Nîmes 45
Nine, Nine, Nine (1948) *73*

O'Higgins, Pablo 97
Oppenheim, Meret 25, 37, 53
Opus Magnus: Conjunctio (1628) *93*
Orenstein, Gloria 28, 103
Orozco, José Clemente 58
Ozenfant Academy (London) 21–3, 26, 52
Ozenfant, Amédée 21, 27, *51*, 52

Paalen, Wolfgang 57, 58
Padua 19
Pailthorpe, Grace W. 25
Paris 19, 21, 27, 28–35
Parisot, Henry 34

Pastoral (1950) *77*
Paterson, Patricia 15
Paz, Octavio 58
Pendle Hill (Lancashire) 15
Pénélope (1957) *102*
Penrose, Miss 18
Penrose, Roland 25, 26, 27, 39
Péret, Benjamin 48, *56*, 58, 59, 60, 63
Picasso, Pablo 28, 53, 60
Pierre Matisse Gallery (New York) 51, 52, 63, 66
Pig Rush (1960) 103, *106*
Pisanello (Antonio Pisano) 19
Plain Chant (1947) *73*
Ponce, Juan García 103
Portrait of Dr Morales (*c.*1943) *49*
Portrait of Joan Powell (*c.*1936) *22*, 22–3
Portrait of Leonora Carrington (Fini, 1939) *41*, 42
Portrait of Max Ernst (1939) 42, *43*, 44, 55
Potter, Beatrix 14
The Powers of Madame Phoenicia (1974) *121*
Prado (Madrid) 70
Purism 21

The Q Symphony (2002) *140*
Quattrocento 25

Rahon, Alice 58–9
Ray, Man 29
Read, Herbert 23, 25
Red Mark (*c.*1950s) *80*
Regler, Gustav 62–3
Reid Mansion (New York) 53
Reina de los mandriles (1959) *112*
Renaissance 30, 68
Ritz Hotel (London) 19
Rivera, Diego 57, 58
Robert Gallery (Amsterdam) 37
Rome 19
Ruiz, Antonio 64

Sachiel, the Angel of Thursday (1967) *115*
Sacrament at Minos (1954) *98*
Sage, Kay 45
St. Martin d'Ardèche 38–44, 54
St Mary's convent (Ascot, Berkshire) 15
Samain (1951) *85*
Samhain Skin (1975) *129*
Santander Mental Asylum (Spain) 46, 50, 51, 52, 57
Self-Portrait: Inn of the Dawn Horse (1937–8) 22, 30–5, *31*, 46
Self-Portrait in Orthopaedic Black Tie (1973) *120*
Seligman, Kurt *51*, 52, 66
Seraphita (Balzac, 1834) 54
Serge, Victor 62
Serpentine Gallery (London) 128
'The Seventh Horse' 53
Sidhe, the White People of the Tuatha dé Danaan (1954) 82, *83*
Simon, M. 19
'The Sisters' (1942) 53
The Snakes (1961) *100*
South Africa 51
Spain 8, 45, 46, 70
Stephens, James 14–15, 79
Straus, Lou 29
Surrealism 7–8, 18, 23, 25–35, 37, 42, 51, 52, 53, 57, 59–60
Swift, Jonathan 14
Syssigy (1957) *108*

Taeuber-Arp, Sophie 37
Tamayo, Ruffino 97
Tanguy, Yves 28, 45, 53, 60
Tanning, Dorothea 45, 53, 55
Tell the Bees (1986) *133*
Temple of the Word (1954) *99*
Temptation of St Anthony (1947) *70*, 75–7, 79
Temptation of St Anthony (Bosch) *70*
Tête Double (Ernst, 1936) 25
Thoresen, Elisa 37
Took My Way Down, Like a Messenger, To the Deep (1977) 122, *124*, 126
Town & Country Magazine 63
Toyen 25, 37
Tribeckoning (1983) *131*
Trotsky, Leon 57
Tuesday (1946) *67*
Turner, Victor 33
Two Children Menaced by a Nightingale (Ernst, 1924) 25

Uccello, Paolo 19
Une Chemise de nuit de flanelle (1951) 64
Une semaine de bonté (Ernst, 1934) 34
United States 45
Untitled (*c.*1949–50) *16*
Untitled (1952) *91*
Untitled (1964–5) *119*
Untitled three-panelled folding screen (1954) 81

Vail, Laurence 46
Varo, Remedios 30, 37, *56*, 58, 59–60, 64
Venice 19
View magazine 53, 55
Villa Air Bel (Marseilles) 46

'Waiting' (1941) 53
Warner, Marina 37–8, 48, 68
Weisz, Emerico 'Chiki' *56*, 58
The White Goddess (Graves) 79
'White Rabbits' (1941–2) 53
Who art thou White Face? (1959) *112*
Winkie (horse) *14*
Wolf, Miriam 56
WW magazine 53

Yarrow, Catherine 46